HIGHLANDERS

THE CAUCASUS

KAZAKHSTAN

RUSSIAN FEDERATION

KRASNODAR
PROVINCE

Krasnodar

Stavropol

STAVROPOL
PROVINCE

*Caspian
Sea*

Lazarevskoe

ADYGEYA

Sochi

KARACHAYEVO-
CHERKESSIYA

Nalchik

Kizlyar

KABARDINO-
BALKARIA

CHECHNYA

ABKHAZIA

INGUSHETIA

Khasavyurt

Elbrus
(17,523 ft.)

NORTH
OSSETIA

Grozny

Sukhumi

Makhachkala

C A U C A S U S

Vladikavkaz

Black Sea

SOUTH
OSSETIA

Kazbek
(16,558 ft.)

M O U N T A I N S

DAGHESTAN

Derbent

Batumi

AJARIA

GEORGIA

Tbilisi

Quba

Ganja

TURKEY

ARMENIA

AZERBAIJAN

Baku

Yerevan

NAGORNO-
KARABAKH

Ararat (16,946 ft.)

Stepanakert

NAKHICHEVAN
(AZER.)

Lenkoran

o *Miles*   300

o *Kilometers*   300

IRAN

© 2000 Jeffrey L Ward

HIGHLANDERS

A Journey to the Caucasus

in Quest of Memory

Yo'av Karny

FARRAR, STRAUS AND GIROUX

New York

Farrar, Straus and Giroux
19 Union Square West, New York 10003

Copyright © 2000 by Yo'av Karny
All rights reserved
Distributed in Canada by Douglas & McIntyre Ltd.
Printed in the United States of America
Designed by Debbie Glasserman
Maps designed by Jeffrey Ward
Photographs by Yo'av Karny
First edition, 2000

In memory of my parents,
Esther Szyfman Karny
and
Elimelekh Krasnyansky-Karny,
who kindled my curiosity and
taught me to remember

CONTENTS

The Circassians may have given Europe chivalry, knights, and Arthurian myths. They thought dying of old age in one's bed was an unforgivable disgrace—so they fought to the heroic end. A century and a half later, only a handful stay on in a provincial Russian Riviera by the Black Sea, exacting revenge on a nemesis long-dead, begging the attention of the living (and begetting none). This is also the story of their sworn enemies, the Cossacks, former law-enforcers-turned-victims, who would like so much to have a second shot at the whip.

This is the tale of a land named after its mountains, Daghestan, where dead Muslim saints are endowed with magical powers—but none as magical as the one exercised by terrain. For centuries, high altitude (coupled by human resilience) shielded the tiny nations of Daghestan against a long succession of conquerors. Archaic languages and quaint outlooks survived in the highland, which would have been swept away in the plains. Then came the Russians, then rose an unsmiling imam, and then began a thirty-year war, still casting a long shadow 140 years later. Some would like to start it all over again. Could a peculiar land survive? Indeed, *should* it survive?

PART III: THE GODS OF THE MOUNTAINS • 199

Every Man and His God • "Naught But My Destitution to Plead for Me" • The Bearer of the Genes • "The Stream Was Warm, the Stream Was Red" • Kishiyev Comes Home • Shame On You, Haji Tolstoy • Bringing Rancor to the Arsanov Court • How the *Zikr* Saved Their Islam • The War on the *Zikr* • "Wahhabis Send Sufi Sheikh to Hell" • Abdul Wahhab the Jew (and More) • Romanticizing the "Black Faces" • Abdul Latif Had a Beetle and Two Hundred Tanks • "The Golan Should Be Chechen" (It Nearly Was) • The Last People of the Sabbath • Wrestling with the Spirits • A Hebrew God on the Iranian Border • "My Cossacks? Jews?"

On the road to Baghdad, a North Caucasian goatherd had a revelation. He went home and taught his people a new path to God. Dance, he told them. And they have danced in despair for a century and a half. They are the Chechens, remarkable and incomprehensible, defiant and vengeful, rising from the ashes time and again. But if they owe the shepherd and the dance so much, why are those zealots from the Arabian desert so angry? Then comes the story of fellow seekers of God, the mysterious People of the Sabbath, whose revelation remains unknown.

PART IV: REMEMBER AND FORGET: THE POLITICS OF MEMORY • 349

The Dark Side of Elbrus • The Ghosts of Caucasian Albania

Can a whole nation lose its memory? It sure can, if the memory is stored exclusively in the minds of people who plan to pass it on when they reach old age—but then they never reach old age. This happened to the Balkars, a tiny Turkic nation in the North Caucasus. On the other side of the Caucasus, a mightier Turkic nation, Azerbaijan, seeks a past in the mists of antiquity. A slighted neighbor, Armenia, picks up the gauntlet, and a bitter war of words ensues. Would only sticks and stones break one's bones? Not in the Caucasus.

EPILOGUE: THE CAMOUFLAGED MOUNTAIN • 405

High mountains are a feeling.
LORD BYRON

PROLOGUE

A HIGHLANDER'S MIND

The storyteller was Ali Aliyev. A small man, with a deeply lined face and an ever-present filterless cigarette, he was an exceptional narrator, a flowing fountain of facts and vignettes, whose knowledge of the mountains was unequaled.

It was a late summer day, we were seated in Makhachkala's only outdoor café, and a light breeze was blowing our way from the nearby Caspian Sea. Makhachkala is the capital city of a semi-autonomous state, perhaps the only one in the world defined solely by its terrain. It is called Daghestan, literally "Land of the Mountains," a constituent republic of the Russian Federation whose name had appeared in travel literature seven centuries before the first Russian set foot on its territory.

Aliyev, like the majority of Makhachkala's residents, was a first-generation plains dweller. I came to him to hear the story of his people, the Laks, who for many centuries had inhabited the central highlands of Daghestan. The young Soviet regime, he told me, loathed any kind of preexisting order, including that which attached an ethnic group to its landscape. Beginning in the 1920s, it resolved to transfer Laks from their ancestral highlands to the lowlands. The Laks, masters of endurance—whose military skills had made them desirable warriors in armies all the way to the eastern shores of Africa—began to die in the thousands.

You see, Aliyev told me, the body of a Lak highlander could be transferred to another altitude, but not his spirit.

This is a book about the spirit of mountain dwellers. I have met it in the Caucasus, but it can be found on many other peaks and highlands the world over. It is this spirit, ill defined as it is, which may account for astounding perseverance, explain a dogged sense of pride, and excuse

irrational pursuits of liberty. It is hard to quantify or qualify, and in
determining its origins, one may need to borrow poetic abstractions like
the one from Lord Byron that serves as an epigraph for this book. This
author has run out of rationalizations in the course of his long journey
to the Caucasus. He began with geopolitics, continued with geo*physics*,
and ended up with a lot of *meta*physics. The following pages may serve
as his excuse.

In 1994 a unique international conference was held in southern Russia.
Delegates of mountain dwellers from four continents gathered in
Nalchik, a provincial capital in the North Caucasus region. For a couple
of days, Central Asians, Africans, Middle Easterners, Central Europeans, and South Americans rubbed shoulders, discussing in earnest the
main thing they had in common: altitude.

Theirs was the notion that even if people share few genes, they may
still share a destiny; that perceptions need not be dictated by hereditary
factors or cultural predisposition but could be affected by the temperature outside, or the thinness of the air one breathes, or the height of
trees, or their absence. Theirs was the notion that *altitude* shapes
attitude—a wonderful antidote, I thought, to the accentuated tribalism
and hyped-up nationalism of the day.

Few venues in the world would have been more appropriate for the
mountaineers' conference than the lush green city of Nalchik, leaning
against the slopes of Europe's most mysterious mountainous range, in
close proximity to the continent's tallest summit, the Elbrus. Nalchik
was an apt choice for another reason: it was at the epicenter of an
attempted mountaineer revival. Groups of Caucasian highlanders of
whom the outside world had hardly ever heard were staking claims to
land, culture, and language—artifacts of collective identity that had
been long denied them.

The Nalchik conference was only a folkloristic event. It founded no
international, issued no manifestoes, challenged no existing ideology or
creed. Its deliberations inspired no rich benefactor to endow a chair of
"comparative mountain studies" in any university that I know of. Its
organizers seemed more interested in the curiosity that life close to or
above the clouds may offer. By establishing a topographic affinity with
other alpine peoples, they signaled their hope that their elevation might
one day confer on them the peaceful prosperity of a Switzerland. And
why not? They have the scenery, the imposing peaks, the magnificent
ski trails, the unpolluted air, the exotically outdated traditions—and all
that for a fraction of any Swiss franc–denominated price.

Implicit in the Nalchik conference, however, was a more profound resemblance. The originators of Switzerland's success, after all, were not the clever tour packagers and able hoteliers; nor were they the secretive, unscrupulous bankers. Switzerland's founders were the bearers of an ancient mountaineer spirit, conceived in adversity. Switzerland would be little more than somebody else's backyard if its medieval peasant-rebels had not striven for freedom, defied odds, discarded political realism, ignored geography—and successfully capitalized on landscape. The Swiss started early enough to be spared the need to wave nationalist banners, or produce ancestral licenses to deny their neighbors' rights as they were asserting their own. The framework of their freedom and the resulting prosperity has been their domicile, the mountains, irrespective of language or religious denomination.

It is harder to imagine any group of highlanders more inconsistent with the modern Swiss model than the Chechens of the Northeast Caucasus, about halfway between Nalchik and Makhachkala. They are the proverbial mutineers in Russian imperial history, an unhappy, angry, vindictive lot with few compunctions to their credit. But did the Swiss not start that way? Do they not idolize to this day one angry mountaineer of the fourteenth century named Wilhelm Tell, who picked up his bow and arrows and aimed them at a powerful foreign prince? Where did *he* draw his inspiration from, four centuries before the American and French revolutions turned such acts into a matter of routine?

The fabled Swiss may have found it where the Chechens did: in elevated forests enveloped by cold mist, where the ghosts of long-dead ancestors were haranguing them to reclaim possession of the air they breathed.

I did not go to the Caucasus in the first place in search of the Chechens; nor are the Chechens at the center of this book. At the time, I was barely aware of their existence, never sure who they were or where they lived—and yet I kept encountering them. My first foray to the mountains (in the summer of 1991) predated by only a couple of months the dawn of their rebellion, and my most recent visit (in the fall of 1996) coincided with its triumphant climax. But I cannot deny that their tale, more than any other, inspired me to write this book.

The Chechen uprising against Russia has engendered so much agony and misery as to call into question whether it was worthwhile at all. It has taken so many ugly, bloody, and cruel turns as to exasperate even the most devoted friends of the Chechen cause. Nevertheless, the astonishing courage and audacity that this small nation displayed, and the improbable, unprecedented victory they scored in 1996, have left me in awe time and again, wondering about the origins of Chechen behavior.

As I was watching the war, it dawned on me that even though airplanes and missiles were being used in abundance, and even though neither the Russian army nor the Chechen rebels were lacking in modern weaponry, this was a struggle divorced from modernity, a throwback to an age in which highland clans engaged the mighty in pursuit of a primordial concept of freedom. The highlander may be a Chechen, or he may be an Afghan, or he may be a Kurd, or he may be a Swiss—or he may be what English speakers have long come to mean by the term *highlander*, a Scot.

It was no accident that soon after its release in 1995, one of the most popular foreign films in the North Caucasus was *Braveheart*, a Hollywood depiction of a thirteenth-century rebellion by Scottish highlanders against an encroaching English king, led by one William Wallace. Many hundreds of pirated videocassettes of the film circulated in Caucasian markets, and it won fulsome praise from military heroes and tribal potentates. One of its greatest fans was Shamil Basayev, a daring Chechen rebel field commander who terrorized parts of southern Russia and led invasions of Daghestan in the summer and fall of 1999. By his own words, he was a William Wallace of the Caucasus.

The affinity of twentieth-century Caucasian highlanders with thirteenth-century Scots is striking. Even though the Chechen war and its attempted extensions were eventually draped in the garb of holy Islamic struggle—and this book treats the religious factor very seriously—I think those events were essentially another instance in an ancient saga of highlanders instinctively reaching for their swords in defense of the most basic liberty: not to answer to a foreigner.

The Scots, the Swiss, and the Chechens are not the only highlanders who have acted thus. It is to the highlands, *la montaña*, that various guerrilla movements in Latin America turned for recruits and sympathy. The fierce highlanders of southwestern Arabia managed to preserve the oldest independent Arab state, Yemen, from the summits of their impenetrable mountainous retreats. The highlanders of Afghanistan have probably bloodied the noses of more oppressors, domestic and foreign, than any other group in recent memory. The Kurdish highlanders of Iraq led a long war against long odds under the name *Those Who Are Not Afraid to Die*, and indeed they died in the tens of thousands. The Apache Chiricahua of the American Southwest offered perhaps the most ferocious resistance of all Indian tribes to U.S. and Mexican occupation, and from their ranks rose the legendary chief

Geronimo, who eluded thousands of federal troops with a handful of warriors. Later Americans, the highlanders of Appalachia, though not involved in liberation wars, nonetheless demonstrated a yearning for freedom and, to quote one of their chroniclers, John C. Campbell, had "independence raised to the fourth power,"[*] at times to the detriment of their cause.

What is it about highlanders that makes them such unyielding practitioners of liberty? There is an obvious answer in many of the cases: since the beginning of time, elevation has provided the most efficient line of defense against outside attack. In the words of a distinguished British historian of the Caucasus, W.E.D. Allen, the mountains became "a good haven for remnants in flight from the cursing of the fairer lands, and where, once set, they might hold their peace against the conquerors . . . and scrape a meager life, fall to a great obscurity among the nations, and cause some idle men to wonder on their ancient coming."[†] The region became a Noah's ark of eccentric lives, an undiscriminating reserve of esoteric groups and customs. Many of the newcomers indeed fell "into great obscurity," melted into their environment, and left behind only traces of their original genetic substance. But some pressed on, nurtured their own uniqueness, and survived long enough to be remembered and chronicled.

Safe in their natural fortresses, they grew accustomed to methods of self-governance and to concepts of egalitarianism that were unheard of in the plains. The arts of compromise and deal making were alien to their state of mind. Negotiating one's freedom rarely occurred to them.

Nineteenth-century European romantics, on discovery journeys to the Caucasus, never tired of reminding their readers that Mount Kazbek, whose magnificent snow-capped summit adorns the main passage across the Caucasus range, is where the furious gods of Greek mythology banished the first great rebel of all time, Prometheus. The persistence of the myth among Caucasians, as well as the prevalence of similar myths, and the place of honor accorded individual rebels and outlaws in local cultures, illustrate how natural dissent, defiance, and eccentricity are to the dwellers of the mountains.

The Caucasus has two main claims to fame, outside its awesome topography: it is at the heart of a popular theory on the origin of races, and it

---

[*] John C. Campbell, *The Southern Highlander and His Homeland* (Lexington: University of Kentucky Press, 1969).

[†] W.E.D. Allen, *A History of the Georgian People* (London: Kegan, Paul, Trench, Trubner & Co., 1932), p. 27.

boasts one of the greatest diversities of language anywhere on the planet.

The theory on race interests me only insofar as it makes a bit more difficult the attempt to speak collectively of the inhabitants of the Caucasus. Even those who have never heard of the Caucasus, as well as many who have, freely use *Caucasian* as a synonym for *white*. That, of course, is not how I use it in this book. For *Caucasians*, read "indigenous inhabitants of the Caucasus," some of whom are white or pale, some swarthy, some dark.

It is certainly true that the Caucasus, especially Daghestan, in its northeast, offers an astonishing, indeed confusing variety of languages. That diversity was already noticed by the ancients. Some two thousand years ago, a Roman historian counted "one hundred languages" in a single port city of the Caucasus. A millennium later, an Arab geographer named Daghestan "the mountain of languages."

An Arab legend ascribed it all to the narrowness of mountain passages: God's mule, which was carrying a pouch of languages to be distributed worldwide, stumbled on one of those treacherous paths, the sack opened wide, and the languages were scattered all over and remained there for posterity.

A likelier explanation for the diversity is that the impassable terrain and harsh climate kept small communities free from external influence. Because mighty empires rarely bothered with mountaintops, no centralizing cultural influence forced the fragments together. Elsewhere, archaic languages evolved toward simplicity of use and broad literacy, but in the Caucasus they remained in their pristine state—unwritten, unread, and helpfully uncontested. At times the diversity borders on the farcical and would seem to an outside observer the act of a prankster. What else would one call a little village whose inhabitants speak a language so complex as not to be comprehensible even to their immediate neighbors? Or a semi-autonomous region about half the size of Kentucky that is the officially sanctioned home of six "major" nations (that is, those with more than 70,000 souls to their name) and nearly thirty "minor" ones (the smallest numbering only 600)?

And yet the extraordinary diversity that has earned the Caucasus much attention among fans of cultural curiosities does not necessarily suggest hopeless division; nor is it a sure recipe for a second Bosnia (a gloomy forecast that some observers, most of them Russians, have come to see as self-evident).

Their multiplicity of languages notwithstanding, these highlanders have much in common: the <u>Nart epics,</u> a Caucasian mythology with roots that stretch from the Caspian to the Black Sea; the *lezginka* dance, claimed by almost every single group as its own; the *khinkal*, an essential ingredient of highlander cuisine, also universally claimed as exclusive; as well as common traditions of warfare. Islam is certainly another common feature, but in some cases it is relatively new, just two or three centuries old, and in any event, it is highly idiosyncratic, a far cry from what Westerners name, and sometimes misname, "Islamic fundamentalism."

Another illustration of a mountaineer *identity* is the relative arbitrariness of ethnic designations. Many of the names by which the diverse groups are now known did not emerge until the Russian invasion of the Caucasus began in the late eighteenth century. The names were often forced onto the natives through historical ignorance and a lack of common sense (a phenomenon well known wherever European colonizers encountered indigenous populations).

Collective names in the Caucasus had previously, and for many years after Russia's takeover, amounted to little. Designations such as "Circassians," "Lezgins," and "Tatars"—nowadays used to refer to specific ethnic groups—were used liberally and imprecisely and were applied to all mountaineers. The Russian poet Mikhail Lermontov, a chronicler of Russia's war against the peoples of the Caucasus, used these terms interchangeably, as if they were synonymous.

They *were* synonymous.

As late as 1990, a famous mountaineer intellectual, the late Abdulrahman Avtorkhanov, called on the peoples of the mountains to shed all their superimposed appellations and call themselves *Circassians* (a label that the Soviets had attached to one group of people in the Northwest Caucasus). There was nothing chauvinistic about his call, since he himself was Chechen. He did not care for his own designation, because he viewed the system of ethnic markers as artificial, a deliberate hindrance to unity.

To Avtorkhanov—a controversial figure whose hatred of the Soviet Union drove him into German arms in World War II—only one factor mattered: landscape. In that respect, he must have been the most non-modern nationalist among the collection of dissidents from non-Russian regions of the then–Soviet Union, who shared his Munich exile during the cold war era, hoping against hope that their nations would one day regain their independence. Unlike the overwhelming majority of nationalists who were eager to protect national identities even if they had first to invent them, Avtorkhanov hankered for a well-established nonnational (or supranational) pre-Russian past.

One may encounter remnants of that past only a few miles outside of Nalchik, where a very small people lives. Outsiders now call them

Balkars, but they have for themselves only a territorial designation, *taulu*, meaning "mountain men" in their Turkic language, and for generations, they have referred to their chief as *taulu-bey*, or "chief mountain man."

It was in the Caucasus mountains, toward the end of World War I, that a unique state was founded (which soon thereafter foundered), named simply the Mountainous Republic, which sought to embrace the entire Caucasus, from sea to shining sea. It even managed to send a delegation to the Versailles peace conference, but amid the animosity of both protagonists in the Russian Civil War, Reds and Whites, who agreed on nothing save the desire to keep the Caucasus for Russia, it collapsed very quickly.

The triumphant Communists frowned on the notion of a mountaineer identity. They wanted unity, all right, but membership in their "Soviet nation of toilers" was to be determined by class. Clearly, they needed no competition from a determining factor called *altitude*.

It took Lenin and Stalin, his commissar of nationalities, only a couple of years to begin the dissolution of mountaineer structures. By the time they were finished, the North Caucasus was divided into seven ethnic republics, regions, and districts, all nominally autonomous, giving the area more national borders per square mile than any other part of the world. (Daghestan was something of an exception, in that it did unite different nationalities, with no single dominant group; it was too small and too crowded to be divided, and most of its individual components would not have survived on their own.)

In 1990, as the Soviet era was drawing to a close, delegates of the indigenous peoples held a conference and announced the formation of a Confederation of Mountainous Peoples, but the tentative attempt to reestablish a sense of highland identity went nowhere. Evidently, the people of the Caucasus were not gripped by excitement at the prospect of unification. Years of Soviet indoctrination had convinced many of them that their incorporation into Russia in the preceding centuries had been accomplished voluntarily, through "acts of union," which the local Communist bosses rarely missed an opportunity to celebrate. (In Nalchik I saw signs celebrating the "440th anniversary" of one of those unions.) The old bosses are still very much in power almost everywhere in the North Caucasus. It is therefore no surprise that the Chechens—having more arms and more eager fighters than a state of peace could accommodate—decided to attempt unification by force. In the summer of 1999, many hundreds of them invaded Daghestan and announced their intention to establish an Islamic union between the two neighboring republics, likely to be followed by further expansion. Their evident inspiration was a Daghestani-Chechen theocratic state that had existed for some thirty years in the mid-nineteenth century, that transcended tribal lines, and that had Arabic as an official language.

Bound by a long Caucasian tradition, the Chechen groom forgot to ask his intended Daghestani bride what she thought of the idea, or else he did not think much of her opinion. Apparently only a minority of Daghestanis, perhaps a very small one at that, were willing to go down the path of a total war with Russia. Nonetheless, some form of regional unity may yet be the destiny of the Caucasus.

Russians tend to shudder at the sound of such words. Each time a voice of protest against Russia is raised in the Caucasus, many Russians, particularly those engaged in shaping public opinion—politicians, academics, journalists—see a plot to dismember the country. The Caucasus was—to borrow an American expression—Russia's *last frontier*, and its slow annexation coincided in time with America's westward expansion. To Russians, the Caucasus is at least as Russian as the Dakotas are American.

Other parallels, however, are lacking. The Russian South has never been fully incorporated into the Russian mainstream, mostly because it never attracted enough immigrants to de-nativize it demographically. (Russians are a small minority in the Northeast Caucasus, though they constitute a plurality of the population in the Northwest, where ethnic cleansing under the czar was far more thorough.)

Unfortunately, Russian governments have always believed that in approaching the Caucasus, one had better load one's gun first. A direct chain links the atrocities committed by Russia's famous military commander of the Caucasus, Aleksey Yermolov, in the first quarter of the nineteenth century, and those committed by Boris Yeltsin's army in the 1990s. In between, explicit blueprints were drawn for the extermination or deportation of the indigenous population, and at times those plans came close to fulfillment. Most notorious was the wholesale expulsion of four tiny Caucasian nations in 1943–44, precisely at the time Jews were being herded into death trains in Nazi-occupied Europe. The near-absence of guilt feelings or public expression of remorse in Russia over those events is telling.

Russians used to blame the mistreatment of Caucasians on Russia's nonrepresentative governments, headed by autocratic czars or general secretaries. That is to say, it was not Russia or ordinary Russians who had afflicted so much misery on their colonized neighbors—it was rather some nasty individuals, usurpers. Not only were the Russian masses free of complicity in the crimes, they were victims themselves. One may find this reasoning running all the way from Tolstoy to Solzhenitsyn (both of whom treated Caucasian resistance with respect or even admiration). But the events of 1994–96 in Chechnya, while a democratically elected government was in place in Moscow, suggest that the blame cannot solely be laid at the feet of autocratic regimes. As one Russian liberal politician intimated to me, most of the Russian opposition to the war was generated by its failure; had Russia triumphed "within two hours," as the generals vowed it would, Muscovites would have showered confetti on the returning troops.

Indeed, the opportunity to shower confetti rose again three years later. In September 1999 Russia's war on the Chechens began again, this time to the acclaim of the Russian populace. It bore the hallmarks of revenge: the humiliated Russian generals, the heralds of victory-in-two-hours, were given a chance to redeem themselves. They had had ample time to rehearse, and they were determined not to let any "traitorous politician" (as one of them put it ever so subtly) stand between them and the confetti.

The eagerness to avenge defeat was so evident as to make one suspect that this war was inevitable, regardless of what the Chechens themselves might or might not have done. And yet what the Chechens *had* done made it so much easier for Russia to strike, with the unexpected support of its citizenry (who had been so traumatized by the casualties in the previous round).

I refer particularly to the attempted Chechen invasion of Daghestan, in July and August 1999, accompanied by public vows on the part of Chechen military commanders to overthrow the Russian yoke in the entire North Caucasus. Russia also blamed the Chechens for the concurrent bombings of apartment buildings in Moscow and a couple of provincial cities, which exacted a heavy civilian toll. So self-destructive would the Chechens have been in committing such acts of terror that many suspected the involvement of Russian provocateurs—even though Chechen leaders years earlier had issued explicit, on-the-record warnings that urban warfare in the streets of Moscow was very much an option. No Chechen role in the bombings has been proven, but the events in Daghestan, and the threat to turn Russia's border provinces into a war zone, sufficed to convince reluctant politicians and disillusioned citizenry that the incorrigible Chechens really had it coming this time.

Why would the Chechens want to provide the Russians with an excuse to wage a new war? Logic would have it, after all, that a small nation should not take its chances too often with a mighty neighbor.

The reason, in my view, is that since the 1996 victory, the Chechen national movement has shifted course as a result of political impotence and short-sightedness. The Chechen struggle for independence, launched in 1990, has been hijacked by a hard core of non-Chechen Islamic militants to whom Chechnya is but a metaphor, one term in a much broader equation: revival of Islam's fortunes worldwide. Chechnya has played the same role in their mind that Afghanistan did in the 1980s, Bosnia in the early 1990s, Kosovo in the late 1990s, and the Palestinian territories all the while: handy battlefields in which non-Muslim encroachment was to be resisted, and with it what they perceived as a soft, corrupted, and unfocused form of Islam.

Following classic revolutionary rationale, the militants, mostly Arabs, were not out for a simple victory, if only because victory implies a subsequent attempt at normalization, rapprochement, and, God forbid, coexistence. Nothing is more abhorrent to the outside Islamists than the notion of coexistence, in that it entails political compromise and cultural exchange. Independence for an obscure Lilliput called Chechnya was never *their* cause, even if they pretended otherwise. Evidently, the attainment of de facto independence, in 1996, was a dead end to them. They needed a perpetual conflict as a beacon to the entire body of Islam.

Chechnya, unlike Bosnia and Kosovo, was a good place to pursue such a course for two reasons. First, the outside world would never step in the way it did elsewhere, out of caution (the perceived need not to alienate Russia). And second, Chechen culture already had a built-in bias toward militancy and futile heroics. Excitable Chechen military leaders with little historical perspective were no match for the politically sophisticated preachers of a cosmic Islamic gospel.

Which is how hapless Chechnya began to disappear into a black hole in the fall of 1999.

As this book goes to press, I am reading a letter from a Chechen woman I greatly admire who lives in Amman, Jordan: Na'imah-Polla Daghestani, a proud, dignified, and highly cultured custodian of her people's collective memory. "We are very upset over this second recent war," she wrote me. "We certainly do not support terrorism or extremism from any side. But we believe this latest Russian onslaught on Chechnya has very little to do with fighting terrorism and everything to do with a centuries-old plan to wipe out the Chechens.

"I myself have stopped watching the news because it is too painful to see our people slaughtered and our land burned and destroyed. At the present, Fakhri [her husband, Dr. Fakhruddin Daghestani] is the president of the Friends of Chechnya Society and in that capacity has sent over a hundred letters to heads of state and prominent politicians of the world asking them to intervene to stop this genocide. We . . . only wish some of the governments that have the power to positively influence events in Chechnya would intervene before Russia reduces the Chechen nation again to just a few thousands. After all, even endangered animal species get protection and laws enacted to preserve them.

"That is what we have become, an endangered species in the human kingdom."

But it is not only Russia that has sought to rewrite history. Highlanders have done so, too.

A good highlander was expected to be able to recite his family tree seven generations back, which would take him to the eighteenth century or even earlier, given the legendary longevity of the highlanders. Not only were they able to do so without the help of genealogical Web sites, but for centuries they did it without even the benefit of written language. Recitation was the cornerstone of mountain mnemonics, the equivalent of what the Romans called *loci et res*: a thorough training of the mind to help it retain facts and figures. And retain them they did, not only names of dead men but also an astonishing repertoire of folk stories, myths, and poems. Travelers were struck to find highlanders who could repeat by heart epics "ten thousand lines long" (as reported by Soviet author David Tutaeff in the 1930s). Remembering one's ancestral lineage was a matter of identity, but it was also a practical requirement: this is how marriages between close relatives were prevented.

Memory, however, had a downside. Because the highlanders were required to remember, they often became incapable of forgiving. One result was that blood feuds lingered for centuries. It is said of one tough highlander, Joseph Stalin, that he was in the habit of killing not only his opponents (real or imaginary) but also their offspring, because he assumed they would one day seek revenge. As much as he was a ruthless, professional revolutionary of the industrial age, his concept of memory may have remained a highlander's. (He was Georgian, with possible Ossetian ancestry, the Ossetians being a native North Caucasian people.)

Retaining the forgettable and avenging the forgivable are still defining characteristics of some highlanders, be they individuals or clans or nations. Memory thus often lies at the roots of conflicts whose stubbornness and irrationalism tend to exasperate outsiders.

Anyone steeped in history would admire the long memory of the highlanders, but those interested in progress and civility would frown. Americans often stun foreign observers with their lack of historical memory, but they win universal acclaim for their pragmatism. It seems that the great French philosopher Ernest Renan had a point when he opined, "It is good for everyone to know how to forget."

I traveled to the highlanders of the Caucasus in quest of memory, mostly *theirs* but also *mine*. I owe my reader a few words of explanation about the way in which my own roots have helped shape my impressions of the Caucasus and indeed have induced me to place it at the center of my life for quite some time.

As I have pointed out, the issue of memory is central to this book: actual memory, imagined memory, and contrived memory. Actual memory is, of course, what a person remembers for a fact. Imagined memory is what he erroneously assumes to be a fact. Contrived memory is what he believes to be helpful to his cause regardless of its truthlessness, or perhaps exactly because of it.

I was born and grew up in a land where all three kinds of memory enjoy a tense yet creative coexistence. It is a land far more ambivalent about memory and remembrance than its reputation suggests. Israel, after all, is founded on the premise of great antiquity. Not only does it claim direct lineage to a commonwealth that ceased to exist some two thousand years ago, it often flirts with a past even more distant and hazy, and in doing so it comes very close to committing historical frauds (such as the recent official celebration of Jerusalem's "3,000th anniversary," or the public claim by a former prime minister, the son of a great historian, that a Jewish nation shared this planet with the Chinese and the Indians "4,000 years ago." Both contentions are highly dubious).

Yet much more than most outsiders and insiders assume, forgetfulness is built into the Israeli system of values. The mid-term past is selectively wiped out. I was born at the last moments of the pre-amnesic past and was pulled out of it before I completed my first year. My birth certificate tells me that I was initially Yo'av Krasnyansky, but soon after my arrival, a family conclave conspired against most of the consonants in our Polish-Ukrainian surname and reduced it to Karny, a name purely fabricated and entirely ahistorical—in Hebrew it means, awkwardly, "of horn"—yet that earns me the periodical attention of an Irish-American genealogical society. ("We will tell you when and how the first *Karnys* [or *Kearnys* or *Carneys*] arrived in America," they advise me periodically, enclosing an invoice.) In Israel, *Karny* is a name without fingerprints whose bearer can easily be a Yemenite Jew, or a Polish Jew, or none of the above.

The extent to which I refused certain aspects of the Israeli memory shredder is largely my mother's doing. Not well educated herself, she nonetheless formed around me a line of defense against the onslaught of memory manipulation and made me aware of its dangers. A native of Poland, she sent me down the paths of Eastern European history and literature from a very young age. The heroes of my childhood were Henryk Sienkiewicz's seventeenth-century Polish squires fighting a losing battle to survive in the shadow of grabby empires. Through my mother's lenses, I came to be a grudging admirer of heroic futility. The grudging, I need add, began years later, as the Byronic fervor of my youth receded and was replaced by the sad realization that the proposition "freedom or death" would have lost in almost any referendum throughout history. Most people, however gallant their impulses and however romantic their poets, routinely and dishearteningly prefer life, even if unfree.

But the Caucasus is a place of great gallantry where freedom has been regularly preferred to life and peace. There are theories that trace Europe's own medieval traditions of chivalry back to the Caucasus. Some scholars even believe the King Arthur epic to be a Caucasian myth with a Saxon accent. The Caucasus is a place of enormous heroism, much of it futile. As a result of their gallantry, the Circassians of the Northwest Caucasus lost virtually everything in the nineteenth century, and millions of them are now dispersed throughout the Middle East. Only a tiny fraction of the original population has remained in the mountains, and my book opens with a visit to their remnants, struggling to cling to a fading memory of catastrophe and injustice.

In his book *The Day Lasts More Than a Hundred Years*, Chingiz Aitmatov recounts how ancient tribesmen in Central Asia created of their vanquished enemies a new type of human called *mankurt*, a person without a memory. They would shave a prisoner's head, then wrap it with the warm skin of a camel just slaughtered, and let the skin shrink around the captive's skull as it dried. The enormously painful procedure would have the effect of "squeezing out" the captive's memory. He who survived the torture would then become the most precious of all slaves: devoid of memory, bereft of desires or aspirations, he would obey his master of his own will, which of course was no will at all. The *mankurt's* masters would not have to guard him or guard against him—he would be highly economical and effortlessly manipulable.

One day, Aitmatov writes, a mother ventured out into the vast steppe in quest of her *mankurt* son. When she finally found him, she attempted to awaken his memory, to no avail. She then exclaimed in despair: "They can take your land, your wealth, even your life. But whoever thought, whoever dared to attack a man's memory? Oh God, if you do exist, how did you give such power to people? Isn't there evil enough on earth without this?" When the *mankurt's* masters heard that their slave's mother had arrived to reclaim him, they did not bother chasing her away. "You have no mother!" they told the *mankurt*, and commanded him to kill her. He did.

Aitmatov, whose own father perished in one of Stalin's concentration camps, wrote the book in the heyday of Soviet neo-Stalinism, while Leonid Brezhnev was still in power. There is little doubt that he intended the *mankurt* story as more than a fable of ancient life: Soviet Kirgizia (now independent Kyrgyzstan), where he was born, served as dumping ground for members of small Caucasian nations, deported wholesale to Central Asia in the harsh winter of 1944 with the clear aim of wiping out as many of them as possible and severing for good the ties between the survivors and their past.

The Soviet war on memory was enormously successful; the land was filled with *mankurts* who were seemingly willing to shoot their own mothers, if only figuratively. As a result, one of civilization's most unusual mosaics is in grave danger. Spotted owls may survive deforestation in the American Northwest, rare plants may be saved in the rain forests of Madagascar or Brazil, but the rare human species of the Caucasus may be gone in just a few decades with only scant attention paid to their plight by the outside world. A very small number of those who survived with their memory intact have been trying to rescue the past, but they may be too late. This is a book about them, devoted to their courage and mindful of their near-hopelessness.

The book ends with the tale of a curious war over remembrance, fought between two nations of the South Caucasus, Armenia and Azerbaijan. Seemingly an academic quarrel of little bearing on the present, it helped facilitate a deadly conflict that created, directly or indirectly, 1.5 million refugees. An Azeri scholar in Baku, a veteran of the academic trenches, thought she had accomplished a coup de grâce when she announced to me triumphantly, "Every people in the world has a history based on land. There is the 'history of France,' or 'the history of England,' or the 'history of Italy.' Every people—but for the Armenians. In their case, it is the 'history of the Armenians,' because 'Armenia' as such has never existed."

The Jews, I said. There is also a "history of the Jews," no land attached.

"All right, the Jews as well," she acknowledged reluctantly. "But only those two."

I smiled at her final salvo, but some Armenians to whom I repeated the story did not share my amusement. How dare she! they said, and went on to remind me that an Armenian civilization predated the rise of Christianity by who-knows-how-many-centuries. They were almost as certain of that as the mayor of Jerusalem was of his city's three thousand years to the day. I have the profoundest empathy for them. When I was a high school student in Israel, government-commissioned lecturers used to tell us that for Israelis, conceding anything, even in a debate over an obscure past, would cast a doubt over our very right to be where we are. We are older—we were told—and we have always been the rightful owners of everything.

Luckily, fewer Israelis believe this nowadays, though such notions still prevail in Caucasian minds. I suspect this is a common affliction of ancient peoples who experience rebirth, or at least of young peoples who experience a great yearning to be older.

My objections to the manipulation of memory and the fabrication of the past, as well as my misgivings about heroic futility, are, I think, written all over this book. But at no time do I want my reader to mistake my criticism or misgivings for a lack of empathy. This is a book written with the utmost respect for aspirations and pain. There is not a single group in the Caucasus that does not deserve its place in the sun.

That country is quite covered by darkness,
so that people outside it cannot see anything in it;
and no one dares go in
for fear of the darkness . . .
and they still live in that darkness
and always will. . . .
For God is always ready to help
and succor his loyal servants.

We have found at the other end of Europe
a strange country,
where giant peaks wait for you—
remote, sublime, inaccessible to all
but their most patient lovers.
If you worship the mountains
for their own sake;
if you like to stand face to face with Nature
where she mingles the fantastic and the sublime
with the sylvan and the idyllic
[. . .] in perfect harmony;
where she enhances the effect
of her pictures by the most startling contrasts,
and enlivens their foregrounds with some
of the most varied and picturesque specimens
of the human race—
go to the Caucasus.

THE CIRCASSIANS

KRASNODAR
PROVINCE

N

Krasnodar

• Stavropol

STAVROPOL
PROVINCE

R U S S I A N F E D E R A T I O N

ADYGEIYA

Cherkessk •

• Pyatigorsk

• Lazarevskoe

KARACHAYEVO-
CHERKESSIYA

Prokhladny • Mozdok •

Sochi •

Nalchik •

KABARDINO-
BALKARIA

NORTH
OSSETIA

C A U C A S U S   M O U N T A I N S

ABKHAZIA

Vladikavkaz •

Black Sea

0   *Miles*   200

0   *Kilometers*   200

GEORGIA

SOUTH
OSSETIA

© 2000 Jeffrey L. Ward

Part I

THE LAST SWORD DANCE OF THE SHAPSUG

THE NOSE

This might be a story about a nose, a tempting plot to any connoisseur of classical Russian literature: a nose, mysteriously removed and lost, assumes a life of its own, shows up in unexpected places, creates turmoil, and engenders speculations on the dark nature of the human condition.

The backdrop of my story cannot match Nikolai Gogol's St. Petersburg for imperial opulence and self-importance. This story will take place in a little seaside resort, just a few dozen miles away from where cartographers contend Europe ends and Asia begins.

It is the story of an ancient tribe whose name used to be synonymous with heroism and valor. Members and relatives of this tribe practiced the art of chivalry centuries before medieval Europe saw its first knight. They were numerous, and mighty, and invincible—until Russia started coveting their land.

And now they are almost gone. Those few who remain may have only a couple of decades before they too are swept from the stage of history. Their final farewell gesture carries the echo of a macabre dance performed in a mythical past by a giant-warrior of the highlands. Highlander folk tradition has it that when the giant's time came to leave the earth, he summoned all his fellow giants and engaged them in a crazed dance, during which he cut off their heads and limbs. Satisfying his appetite for bodily parts, he finally dropped his blood-soaked dagger into the sea and vanished. It is with the amputating sword of a highlander and a farewell dance by the Black Sea that my story begins.

·   ·   ·

One night in 1996, when the town of Lazarevskoe was safely asleep and only the murmur of the waves could be heard from a distance, a 150-year-old blood feud was finally reaching its culmination. The ancient admiral was completely unguarded and entirely unsuspecting when the young avengers approached him. They reached for his nose, cut it off in one fell swoop, and disappeared into the night, leaving the helpless Mikhail Petrovich in a state of disgrace and humiliation.

What kind of people would afflict such an indignity upon a man so talented, courageous, and patriotic? Thus pondered Lazarevskoe's residents the following morning, hurrying off to their little train station, as the sun rose on Russia's deep south. "Nothing is sacred anymore," grumbled Russians to Armenians and Armenians to Ukrainians, who all constitute a large majority of the town's population. "Not even statues of the dead are left in peace."

For the nose so ill-treated was chiseled in stone, much like the rest of Admiral Lazarev. The old man had been dead since 1849, and his likeness had just been brought back from a municipal warehouse and installed in the pretty train station of the town that bears his name.

Mikhail Petrovich Lazarev was an unlikely candidate for a nocturnal vendetta. In his day he was an esteemed scholar and a strong believer in a universal Russian mission. The scope of his knowledge and his insatiable intellectual curiosity would place him next to the great figures of the Renaissance.

He carried Russia's imperial insignia as far as Antarctica and named remote islands after Romanov emperors. (In 1820, Lazarev, alongside

He believed in the ultimate imperialist dictum: "The border is not finished."
Admiral Mikhail Lazarev, the conqueror of the Shapsug

Admiral Fabian von Bellinghausen, was the first explorer to sight Antarctic land.) He mapped Russia's most distant shores and demarcated its new frontiers—a Lewis and Clark to the Russian Far East. He was the first naval commander in history to have sailed around the world, not once, not twice, but thrice.

He also served his country in battle with great distinction. He was baptized by fire, as a midshipman in a British warship under the command of Horatio Nelson, in the Battle of Trafalgar (1805). Twenty-two years later, he was rewarded with the rank of admiral for his role in the defeat of the Ottoman fleet in the Battle of Navarino, and his ship won the first St. George decoration in Russia's naval history. Later, as commander in chief of the Black Sea fleet, he was hailed for his active interest in the architectural beautification of Sevastopol, the large Crimean port city and the fleet's home base.

In short, Admiral Lazarev belonged in the gallery of empire builders—those whose military genius was matched by their ability to excite the imperial nation's imagination and whet its appetite for further conquests. He was an ardent follower of Catherine the Great's ultimate imperialist dictum, "The border is not finished." A Briton would recognize in him a Lord Kitchener and a David Livingstone joined together. An American might hear in him the sound of Horace Greeley's tantalizing words, "Go west, young man!"

Only Lazarev's "young man" was sent south, and in heeding the call, he helped launch one of the longest wars that any colonial power ever fought, one of complete disinheritance. Which is how the admiral earned his place on a Caucasian hit list, so long after his bones had turned to dust.

Lazarevskoe may not have turned out to be an embodiment of the admiral's worldly ways. It is a quintessential provincial resort, boasting a splendid beach and a few Soviet-era sanatoria, with a little mountain rising in its midst, covered with lush green vegetation.

It is a place born for sunny days. Come summer, Lazarevskoe awakens, repaints its train station white and red, and opens its arms to Russia's tired masses, exhausted by a year of labor, fleeing the big cities in search of rest and sea and sun. Rarely does Lazarevskoe see a foreign tourist or hear the sounds of a foreign language, even in these post-Soviet days. Foreigners prefer the bigger and better-known city of Sochi, about forty miles to the south, the gem of the Russian Riviera.

Despite its status as a regional administrative center, Lazarevskoe is not known for the volume of dramatic news it generates—which is why

Lazarevskoe is the improbable site of the Shapsugs' last battle, a quintessential provincial resort, with a little green mountain rising in its midst.

the locals were so scandalized by the attempted statuecide. They were wondering if the disease raging to the south had finally caught up with them: the breakup of law and order and the rise of anti-Russian sentiments among non-Russian minorities.

Were the ruffians who so tormented Mikhail Lazarev's stony replica really sending a metaphoric message, and was the nose affair a harbinger of much worse to come? Would those who bust busts one day bust people?

These were the questions on my mind when I got off the train at Lazarevskoe on a late summer day in 1996, hoping to find out what had so agitated Lazarev's assailants.

Russia has always been enamored of iconoclastic acts, and statues have routinely offered a convenient target for holy rage. Since the collapse of Soviet Communism, many pedestals have been orphaned: satellite nations have marked their newly found freedom by throwing Lenins out of their main squares; Muscovites dared not touch Lenin but celebrated the fall of Communism with the overthrow of a stony Feliks Dzherzhinsky, Lenin's secret police chief.

In Grozny, the capital of Chechnya, a statue blown to pieces provided one of the earliest sounds of a national uprising. The pieces belonged to a contemporary of Admiral Lazarev's, Aleksey Yermolov, a fellow general who led the first major Russian expeditionary force against the natives of the Northeast Caucasus in the 1810s. Elsewhere, two centuries might be sufficient to induce an ounce of forgetfulness, hence forgiveness—but not in the Caucasus, where long memories seem to be the most lasting natural resource.

It so happened that 1996 marked the three hundredth anniversary of the founding of Russia's Black Sea fleet—a time for patriotic commemoration, no matter that the present fleet was rotting in Ukrainian Crimea. Lazarevskoe's local authorities had decided to pay homage to the fleet by reintroducing Lazarev, placing him on the train station platform, the town's nerve center, where so many of Lazarevskoe's residents were bound to come across him day in and day out. For most of them, the new Lazarev statue was an inconsequential piece of marble, one of those tokens of reverence for the past of which civilized communities are fond. To a minority, it was a daily reminder of a catastrophe.

"He was the man who destroyed our nation, who committed genocide unprecedented in history." The speaker was Majeed Chechukh, a local teacher turned businessman and nose assailant, who believed that his people were running out of time; that the goal set by Lazarev was about to be accomplished; that the sounds of Shapsug, his people's language, already barely audible along the coast, were about to vanish forever.

In late 1827, a triumphant Mikhail Lazarev returned from the Battle of Navarino, where a combined British-French-Russian fleet had destroyed the Ottoman navy and secured Greece's independence. Russia, obsessed with its self-designated messianic mission to reclaim Constantinople for Christianity, was eager to weaken Ottoman Turkey even further and was

Majeed Chechukh was the delicate nocturnal guerrilla who spearheaded the assault on Admiral Lazarev's nose.

hoping, as a more mundane reward, to win control over the straits linking the Black Sea with the Mediterranean. Lazarev was assigned the task
of building up Russia's naval strength in the Black Sea, to prepare for the
inevitable confrontation. He even drew up a plan for the occupation of
Constantinople, one that remained under consideration for many
decades after his death. Driving Turkey's Muslim allies out of the Black
Sea coast, where present-day Lazarevskoe lies, was a top priority. "We
were like a bone stuck in Russia's throat," explained Chechukh. "They
needed our lands, but they did not need us."

In the 1830s and 1840s, Lazarevskoe was at the center of a savage
war. It served as a launching pad for Russia's expansion into lands
densely populated by a people called Adyghe, better known to the
outside world as Circassians (which is how I will refer to them from
now on).*

In 1839 the war of the Shapsug coast came to the attention of Russians
through a painting by Ivan-Hovhannes Aivazovsky, an Armenian-Russian
painter, the visual chronicler of the Russian navy throughout the nineteenth century. *Landing at Subasha*, as he named his painting, was inspired
by his meeting with Admiral Lazarev and others just outside present-day
Lazarevskoe. This early form of war coverage excited the imperial capital
of St. Petersburg, and the czar of the day, Nicholas I, bought it from the
painter for two thousand silver rubles, a vast amount by contemporary
standards, said to equal a Russian general's annual salary.

Lazarevskoe was bitterly fought over. In 1840 a powerful alliance of
Circassian tribes managed to storm it and level it to the ground. Most of
the victors belonged to the Shapsug, who had lived in and around
Lazarevskoe for centuries.

Few colonized nations anywhere in the world ever put up such a prolonged resistance: for another twenty-four years, the Shapsug and their
chief allies and neighbors to the south, the Ubykh, would fight a losing
battle to check Russia's advance. The final phase of their desperate campaign, in 1864, coincided with the American Civil War, which is perhaps one reason why it never won the Western attention it richly
deserved. Defeat heralded not only occupation and humiliation but the
actual end of national existence.

---

* In Russia and the Middle East they are known as Cherkess, a word that may have historically meant "brigands." *Circassian* is used here in an inclusive sense, to encompass all
the old Adyghe tribes, including those still living nowadays in Russia. The highly confusing Soviet system of ethnic classification, inherited by Russia, recognized three distinct Circassian nationalities: Kabardins, Cherkess, and Adyghe. Other Circassian
groups, unrecorded by the Soviet census, are scattered throughout the Middle East, particularly in Turkey, Syria, and Jordan.

Russia's terms of surrender required the Circassians to come off their mountains, disarm, and resettle in the plains, where they would be under the gazing eye of czarist troops. But hundreds of thousands of them refused the favor, boarded Turkish boats, and headed for exile in the Ottoman Empire, where, they believed, their fellow Muslims would let them pursue their ancient way of life. Their migration, however, turned out to be an unmitigated disaster. Tens of thousands of them perished at sea, remembered in sorrowful elegies still cited and sung in the diaspora. Many others who survived the high seas died of diseases and starvation once they landed. Of the survivors, many were assimilated into Turkish society and are lost forever, such as the Ubykh, now regarded as an extinct nation. Of the mighty Shapsug tribe, only a few thousand still inhabit their ancestral land, struggling to keep the flame. It was a handful of these Shapsug survivors who took aim one night at Admiral Lazarev's statue.

"Under his direct command," said Chechukh of Lazarev, "five major landings took place. Under his watch, dozens of villages were wiped off the earth." One of those villages was Pseshap, which meant "River's End." On Pseshap's ruins, a settlement was built and was christened Fortress Lazarev, Lazarevskoe's precursor. How many of Lazarevskoe's residents and visitors realize that, I do not know. The colored brochures distributed to tourists fail to mention it. It is as though history began with Russia.

"Not many years are left for us before we disappear—unless things change dramatically," said Chechukh, who also headed the local branch of Adyghe Khassa, the Circassian Grand Assembly, a worldwide organization formed to pursue the Circassian cause. Chechukh's goal was to turn the Lazarevskoe region into a semi-autonomous Shapsug "national district," in an attempt to forestall, perhaps reverse, cultural assimilation.

The problem is that in such a district, by Chechukh's own admission, the Shapsug would constitute less than one-seventh of the population. His is an uphill battle. In the aftermath of the Chechen war, the plea for "national rights" does not resonate well in Moscow ears, particularly if it emanates from the unruly Caucasus. The Shapsug activists have little leverage in their arsenal, save for occasional acts of unorthodox defiance, such as grabbing a nose and running.

Admiral Lazarev died fifteen years before the Shapsugs' final defeat. Russia's ultimate blows against them were dealt by other commanders. But even in his lifetime, Lazarev was not the Shapsugs' main nemesis among Russian generals. A long line of czarist officers had shed far more

Circassian blood than he did, and with far greater cruelty. But to judge Shapsug motives against strict factual criteria would be to miss the mark. Chechukh and his friends were not writing a textbook, they were making a point: by establishing a clear culprit, they were reclaiming a pristine, unspoiled past that the likes of Lazarev had obliterated.

It was that past that had captivated the imagination of many Westerners in the nineteenth century. Following the usual maxim of the time (and perhaps our time as well), the less they knew, the more they idealized. The Circassians, indeed all North Caucasians, came to be associated in the European mind with valor and selflessness. From as far away as Boston, Massachusetts, an American, George Leighton Ditson, had to come and see for himself "that people, who, in my own country, bear such a charmed name—about whose history hangs so mysterious a halo—associated with all that is noble and chivalrous in the field, all that is spirited and patriotic."

Wars on stony replicas of the dead are perhaps as old as our civilization. Jewish zealots struggled against likenesses of Greek and Roman kings, and Byzantine monks excommunicated the images of dead saints. Wars against icons—mostly against *somebody else's* icons—are continuing in earnest. Albanian nationalists celebrated their return to Kosovo by toppling the imposing statue of Dusan, a Serb king not seen in town since the fourteenth century. Even in the United States, a young country with a short memory, past icons may inflame emotions, as was the case in 1999 when black leaders in Richmond, Virginia, threatened a civic boycott unless a huge portrait of General Robert E. Lee were removed from a public wall. But while Kosovo's Albanians had NATO, and America's blacks have a powerful civil rights movement, the Shapsug of southern Russia had only iconoclasm left in their armory, and they utilized it to their best ability. The ethnographic institute of the Russian Academy of Science in Moscow furnished them with a letter suggesting that Lazarev's statue belonged more appropriately in his native Vladimir, the ancient city in the Russian heartland, about 150 miles outside of Moscow. True, the old sailor would have much preferred the salty scent of the sea to the staleness of an old landlocked city. But as one Shapsug told me, smiling broadly, "That has been taken care of. Now that he no longer has a nose, he wouldn't mind the odors anyway."

THE NARTS

Peace to Circassian hearts is dear,
Their native land, their home frontier,
But freedom, freedom, heroes' lease,
Is more than fatherland or peace!
"To mock and shame the Russian might,
Depart we now our mountain height"
LERMONTOV, "IZMAIL BEY"

My first encounter with Circassian aspirations was quite accidental. In the early fall of 1992, I was planning to fly from Moscow to Yerevan, as the war news from Karabakh grew grimmer by the day. Armenia-bound flights were highly irregular, as the economies of all parties concerned were sliding down a steep hill. A colleague, Dutch journalist James Dorsey, suggested a modified route with better chances of arrival, via Nalchik, the leading city of the North Caucasus.

With a population of 300,000, Nalchik is an agreeable resort town, renowned for the curative power of its springs. It is shrouded in ancient forests, is blessed by a rich river system, and leans against the slopes of gorgeous, snow-capped summits. Not far from it stands the Caucasus's tallest summit, Mount Elbrus. The city also serves as the capital of Kabardino-Balkaria, a constituent republic of the Russian Federation, a semi-autonomous state with its own parliament and president (the first Circassian president ever elected anywhere in the world).

My knowledge of the Circassians at that time was confined to stereotypes common in Israel, where they fall under the ungenerous and bland category of "minorities." They were Muslims, and they spoke Arabic, but we knew them to be different at least in one respect: Unlike the Arabs, they served in the Israeli military and did so with distinction. Later I was to learn that serving valiantly in somebody else's army was common for the Circassians, and their unconditional devotion was offered not only to Israel but to its Arab enemies as well.

Years later, in New York, I came to befriend a young Circassian from Syria, an articulate and well-informed partner in long debates over Middle East politics, who was struggling to find his place in the United

Scenic Nalchik, where the giant Narts almost woke up

States. One day he told me he had decided to join the U.S. Marines, under a program that offered permanent residence to foreigners who choose to defend America.

But will you qualify? I asked him skeptically.

His normally amiable countenance hardened, and he said very quietly, "I am Circassian."

I recall smiling at his bravado, but the response was perfectly consistent with the image Circassians projected in Israel.

In Nalchik, in September 1992, for the first time I came across Circassians who were employing their military skills in the service of their own national agenda. The city was hearing loud calls to arms: Circassian volunteers were invited from all over the Caucasus to help the Abkhaz in their war against Georgia.

The Abkhaz are not quite Circassian, but they are blood relatives. The great majority of Abkhaz had departed in the same exodus that depopulated the Shapsug coast in 1864. The few left, about 90,000 of them, live along the Black Sea shore, a small minority in an autonomous republic that nonetheless bears their name and has been a part of Georgia for more than sixty years. Being Georgians did not matter all that much, and in any event little could have been done about it, for as long as Georgia itself was a component of the Soviet Union (though some Abkhaz began to clamor for separation from Georgia back in the

1970s). But now that the old empire was disintegrating, Abkhaz nationalism reasserted itself, with the barely disguised help of certain elements in Russia, keen on weakening Georgia. Given the Abkhaz' small numbers, they were in desperate need of outside help, and the Circassian cousins, as well as other North Caucasians, offered the largest pool of volunteers. Nalchik was made operational headquarters for the campaign, and its streets bustled with uniformed Circassians, rebels with a cause—for the war provided them with an opportunity to prove that their celebrated chivalrous spirit had not been entirely vanquished by 130 years of Russian rule.

Proponents of Circassian national revival bemoaned the decline of the national ethos even more than the loss of independence and land. "Circassians had an extreme degree of courage," said Zaur Naloyev, one of the foremost Circassian intellectuals and a resident of Nalchik. "Shame to the Circassian was worse than death. For a Circassian, to die of old age was a disgrace. A true Circassian should die in full bloom, defending his homeland or his compatriots."

Naloyev, a founder of the Circassian national movement Khassa (members of which assailed Admiral Lazarev's statue), then related a story of the Circassian prince Atazhukin. "He had a very long beard. One day he was walking to noon prayer at the Mosque. A peasant girl noticed him and exclaimed: 'It is the first time that I see a white beard on the face of a prince!' In other words, she had never seen an old prince, because real princes die young in battle. Atazhukin was ashamed. After the prayer he mounted his horse, joined the troops, and suffered mortal wounds in battle. With his last gasp he murmured: 'I am so happy that I do not have to die in my bed.'

"In Circassian mythology," Naloyev went on, "the concept of a Garden of Eden does not exist. It is substituted by public esteem and glory. That is the highest place a Circassian can aspire to reach." It is not that Naloyev would like to see Circassians dying in battle in pursuit of public esteem, but he is concerned that one of the greatest fighting nations of all times had been reduced to collective laziness and indifference, no longer inspired by lofty ideas, weakened by docility. Surviving 130 years of Russian and Soviet rule may have required such docility, but for the Circassians to enjoy a post-Soviet renaissance, they had better regain some good old Circassian virtues. The trumpets of war had saved their ancestors from prolonged periods of indulgence. Perhaps Abkhazia would harden the complexion of the present generation as well.

Young volunteers to the war presented themselves daily at headquarters, and a torrent of pilgrims from the Circassian diaspora suggested that the Circassians were regaining some of their old instincts. (I met a

Circassian general from Syria, turned supermarket owner in Florida, who stopped by to offer some tactical advice to the troops.) Even the Circassian flag—three crossed arrows pointing at twelve stars—was making something of a comeback. It was designed around 1830, when the Circassians had made an unsuccessful attempt to interest the European powers in their cause. Their friends in Europe even announced the establishment of a Circassian state, which remained largely on paper. 1830 was now alive in Naloyev's memory, reminding him of the futility of self-esteem and honor without good politics. "Chivalrous conduct at the time was simply a laughing matter," he mused. "Sadly, my ancestors were incapable of reforming themselves. They were too proud. They were blessed with a lot of courage but with little vision. They had no politicians among their leaders, people who might have been able to guide them into survival rather than death or banishment."

Circassian unity was now being revisited, 162 years after its false start. Would 1992 go down in memory as the beginning of a Circassian renaissance? Such were the thoughts racing in the minds of Circassian intellectuals and political activists. With hindsight, I am far less sure that they seriously occupied the minds of ordinary Circassians. But at that time of general excitement, and given the centrifugal tendencies evident throughout the former Soviet Union, it did seem that the Circassians' turn had finally come.

Arriving at Nalchik's tiny airport in the fall of 1992, we came across a tall, bearded, heavy-set young man who kindly agreed to give us a ride to town. He was a doctor at a local hospital, a native of Syria. As such he was one of a handful of diaspora Circassians who decided to come home, to a land their ancestors had abandoned a century and a quarter earlier. Zionists would describe the act as *aliyyah*, or "ascension," as in the case of a Jew "going back" to the land of Israel. Impressed with the remarkable parallel (and being fully aware that my interlocutor, Syrian and Muslim that he was, would not be flattered by the comparison), I bombarded him as discreetly as I could with questions about the political unity of Circassians. He became increasingly uncomfortable—neither of the societies he belonged to, the Middle Eastern nor the Caucasian, was used to open talks about such matters—and he finally offered to drop us in a place where all our questions would be properly addressed. "First," he suggested, "you should check into a hotel."

The hotel we were taken to was a quintessential Soviet building, with little thought for aesthetics—tall and dilapidated but reasonably clean. It overlooked a very large urban park, the pearl of the local leisure industry, indeed one of the most agreeable I have ever visited in any city in the world. Here the many Soviet vacationers seeking the comfort of the famous Caucasian springs would have strolled.

Our hotel was named Nart. To the mind of the Soviet bureaucrat who sanctioned the name, *Nart* was but a harmless folkloristic allusion, a local fairy tale of sorts. The Narts are mythical giants of extraordinary prowess who are at the center of an elaborate set of epic tales that have been related for millennia across the full length of the Caucasian range. Some of the tales resemble so closely the legends of King Arthur and the Knights of the Round Table that several scholars have even suggested that the original Camelot emerged out of Caucasian mists and was carried to British shores by North Caucasian mercenaries, who helped fill the depleted ranks of Roman legions during the late phase of the empire.

I must confess that certain aspects of the Nart epos strike me as closer to Monty Python's parody of the Holy Grail tale than to the original. (The Nart holy grail is actually a cauldron called *amonga*.)

A case in point is the tale of Peterez, the mightiest of all Narts, which may offer the most remarkable parallel to the Arthurian legend, even if Peterez shared few of Arthur's redeeming features, showed little magnanimity toward his fellow Narts, and spent his life in a spree of senseless killing. His tenure on earth came to an end in a befitting crescendo: he summoned the Narts to burn him alive, and they happily obliged. While burning, Peterez performed a crazed sword dance and at the same time kept cutting off the heads and arms of Narts unfortunate enough to come close to the stake. He told them that he would not depart from the world until they grabbed his sword and dropped it into the Black Sea. With enormous difficulty, the giant-knights carried Peterez's dagger to the water and threw it in. Peterez then disappeared in a storm of lightning and gale winds—not the first one in ancient literature to thus ascend to heaven.

To students of myth, Peterez's sword and King Arthur's Excalibur are one and the same. It has even been suggested that there may be a link between Excalibur and Kalibes, the name of a tribe of smiths who dwelled in the Caucasus in antiquity and made a living manufacturing the sharpest-edged swords in the region. There may also be parallels between Peterez and Prometheus of Greek mythology, another giant, or Titan, who passed the divine secret of fire to humans, only to be punished severely by his fellow gods. As we have seen, Prometheus' fabled place of banishment was on the top of the second-highest summit of the Caucasus, Mount Kazbek.

Not all Nart motives were as farcical as Peterez's death, however. Another celebrated Nart was Badynoko, a selfless, brave character who defended his native land against the unscrupulous Chints, a group of savages bent on "exterminating anything that was alive." Had not, after all, the nineteenth-century Russian army scorched the Caucasus, often "exterminating anything that was alive"? Was it not time for Badynoko to come back and lead his people in a war of redemption and liberation?

In the lobby of Nart Hotel, I ran into a young Circassian from Jordan who believed just that. He was in his mid-twenties and introduced himself as Yaqub Yusuf. He had arrived in Nalchik to participate in an international congress of the Circassian nation. He was euphoric. "It is a time of great hopes for us. We believe that the Narts may be waking up," he said. (Later I was to find that *Nart* is a fairly popular name among members of the North Caucasian diaspora in Jordan.) Yaqub Yusuf was Shapsug. From him I first heard of the last remaining Shapsug of Lazarevskoe and their struggle to win autonomy. "Please go and visit my people," he said. "Not many are left, but they crave freedom as much as their forefathers." My notes from that day show that Yaqub Yusuf's words first raised the idea in my mind of writing a book about his long-ignored nation—which is how I found myself on the platform of Lazarevskoe's train station, four years later almost to the day.

TIME FOR WAR

In the mid-nineteenth century, seven major Circassian tribes occupied the Northwest Caucasus, from the Shapsug and the Ubykh of the Black Sea coast to the Kabardins, three hundred miles inland. The Kabardins, whose capital is Nalchik, are the main survivors of the nineteenth-century catastrophe. They are the most numerous of all Circassian nationalities in Russia (upward of half a million)*, and they are the only Circassian group that constitutes a plurality in an autonomous republic that bears its name, Kabardino-Balkaria, which they share with the Turkic-speaking Balkars.†

The major reason for the Kabardins' continuous good fortune is that they offered relatively little resistance to Russian expansion, and among all the Muslim peoples of the North Caucasus, they may have had the longest relationship with Russia. They even provided Ivan the Terrible, the founder of the Russian empire, with a wife, Altynjan, the daughter of a powerful Kabardin prince, who was subsequently christened Maria. According to a modern biographer of Ivan, the Russian-born member of the French Academy Henri Troyat, himself part Circassian, Maria "was wild and cruel by nature . . . depraved, vindictive, a liar, and something of a witch." In sort, a perfect match for a czar who used to torture political prisoners with his own hands just for fun. Few Circassians would

---

* The last Soviet census of 1989 counted 394,651 Kabardins, an astonishing increase of 22.7 percent over the 1979 census, which in itself was an increase of 14.9 percent over 1969. Few Soviet nationalities of this size grew as fast. The growth itself may owe to a greater sense of comfort on the part of small nationalities in the declining days of the Soviet Union hitherto reluctant to divulge their ethnicities.

† The other two are known in Russian as Karachayevo-Cherkessiya and Adygeiya, situated between Kabardino-Balkaria and the Black Sea coast.

concur in this unflattering portrayal of their princess, whom they have elevated in the course of the centuries into a virtuous beauty. Princess Maria gave Ivan a son and heir, who might have founded a dynasty of Circassian czars had he not died in infancy.

Soviet historiography made much of those early ties. 1957 saw a mass celebration in Kabarda of the four hundredth anniversary of the "voluntary union with Russia," a notion at which Circassian nationalists scoff.* They counter that as late as 1739, more than 180 years after the "voluntary union," Russia recognized Kabarda's independence in the Treaty of Belgrade, concluded at the end of a four-year-long war with Ottoman Turkey. Under its terms, Kabarda was to become a buffer state between the two warring parties. The treaty was "guaranteed" by France, and it lasted for about thirty years. It was the last instance in which the independence of any North Caucasian nation was recognized internationally.

It was a common Soviet practice to undermine nationalism in the Caucasus by predating the beginning of Russian presence in the region, presenting it as the result of a voluntary union or natural "drawing together" (*sblizhenie*) between Russians and highlanders. Even the Chechens, Russia's fiercest opponents in the Caucasus, had their share of "volunteering" in Soviet historiography. As for the Kabardins, they seemed not to insist too much on factual accuracy. Even in 1997, well after Moscow had given up its monopoly on historical truths, Kabardino-Balkaria celebrated another anniversary of its "voluntary union." The only Kabardins I spoke to who took a strong exception to these anniversaries were members of the Kabardin People's Congress, a nationalist organization whose influence was waning. For other Kabardins, the crude modification of their history was taken almost as a compliment, evidence of Russian affection. When I asked one Kabardin why his people had not followed the Chechen example in rebelling against Russia, he said, "But why should we? We have become Russians by choice."

The Kabardins have shared few of the Shapsug tribulations. They quit fighting Russian expansion decades before the Shapsug, refused repeated exhortations to rejoin, accepted resettlement in the plains, where the Russians could easily control them, and proved far more pliable than most other Circassians.

Zaur Naloyev, the Kabardin intellectual and a relentless campaigner for the Circassian national cause, acknowledged to me the mutual love

---

* Moscow's assertion was based on a misunderstanding. Maria's father did offer "submission" to the Russians, but he offered the same to Russia's chief enemies in the Caucasus as well. Historian Chantel Lemercier-Quelquejay contends that the submission "was not an act of allegiance but merely a gesture of politeness with no practical meaning." See *The North Caucasus Barrier* (New York: St. Martin's Press, 1992), p. 37.

between his people and the Russians. Even Stalin, a somewhat unlikely lover of small Caucasian nations, smiled on the Kabardins. During World War II, he banished four Caucasian nations to Central Asia, including the Kabardins' partners in the autonomous republic, the Balkars, in retribution for their alleged collaboration with the Nazis. Yet he spared the Kabardins, though many of them welcomed the invading German army. One of their elders even offered Adolf Hitler a white Kabarda horse as a birthday gift.

Naloyev related an intriguing story about the odd whims of the tyrant. "In 1943, when the regime started planning for the deportations, the Kabardins were also on the list, alongside the Chechens, the Ingush, the Karachai, and the Balkars. The list was submitted to Stalin. He took a look and then crossed the Kabardins off with his thick red pen.

"He turned to those around him, leading figures of the Communist Party, and asked: 'Don't you know, comrades, that all over the world the Circassians' name is synonymous with heroism? If they were not effective in the defense of the Soviet Union, who is to blame?'"

According to Naloyev, Stalin had a soft spot for the Kabardins ever since he convalesced in one of Nalchik's spas in 1921. Just before leaving for Moscow, he addressed the local authorities, ending his remarks with the words: "The Kabardins are good and honorable, you had better cultivate this honor."

And so in the fall of 1992, in Nalchik—built by the Russians in the eighteenth century to further their advance into the Caucasus, a city where the Russian language reigned supreme and Circassian etiquette was all but forgotten—the highlanders were attempting a revival of their fortunes.

A city library building had been partly requisitioned to serve the headquarters of the self-esteem boosters. There, on the third floor, in a large room with a colored map of the Caucasus and a small Circassian flag, I met Yuri Magomedovich Shanibov, the president of the Confederation of the Peoples of the North Caucasus. He was a busy man, claiming the distinction of heading the first Circassian army in a century and a quarter. Well, sort of.

Fifty-six years of age at that time, with a full head of hair, wearing thick-rimmed glasses, Shanibov was running a war room. He was drafting volunteers to join the Abkhaz in their war with Georgia and clearly relished his own reincarnation as a military commander. It was time for change, having spent most of his adult life as a Soviet district prosecutor and professor of Marxism-Leninism. I visited him at the time Oliver

Yuri Magomedovich Shanibov was ready to march a North Caucasian army into Tbilisi. "I am Jim Garrison of the Caucasus," he announced.

Stone's *JFK* was making the rounds, even in the Caucasus, and Shanibov introduced himself in the following words: "I was doing exactly what mister Jim Garri*son* was doing," stressing the last syllable in Garrison's name. Jim Garrison was, of course, the New Orleans district attorney who concocted the theory that inspired a generation of JFK conspiracy buffs. I told Shanibov that Garrison was a highly controversial figure, and some people might not like to be compared with him, but he took my interjection for a compliment and laughed heartily. "I am controversial, too, you know, and I also live in the south."

Shanibov's confederation was inspired by two short-lived attempts to federalize the North Caucasus after the collapse of the czarist empire. For a brief period, the highlanders tried to accentuate common features determined by topography rather than submit to divisions based on clan or tribe affiliation. Neither attempt sat well with Soviet interests, and the first one was quashed by arms, the second by Communist Party edicts.

The present-day confederation was founded in 1990 in Sukhumi, the capital of Abkhazia. Of the eight autonomous republics that were to constitute the confederation, only two, Abkhazia and Chechnya, eventually were represented on the government level. The rest, run mostly by Soviet-era Communists, frowned on the attempted infringement on their jurisdiction. These entrenched despots were not about to bow out gracefully—they had to be pushed out.

Chechnya provided the example: it was the only autonomous republic in which the Soviet-installed government was overthrown by a coup, in 1991, followed by the suspiciously overwhelming electoral victory of the coup maker, Jokar Dudayev. Dudayev was immediately elevated to an icon of North Caucasian self-empowerment. His framed, autographed photo adorned Shanibov's office, as well as the offices of other nationalists.

Abkhazia offered the highlanders their first opportunity to put their new agenda to test, and it was a relatively easy one given that highlanders had fought against Georgians for centuries (though they had also enjoyed prolonged periods of coexistence). A desperate Georgian king once begged Russia to come to his country's rescue because the highlanders were abducting "half of Georgia," which was only a slight overstatement, in that kidnapping had been a mainstay of the highland economy. In the long nineteenth-century war to pacify the highlanders, Georgia, by now a czarist province, had been Russia's staunchest ally. At one point, the highlanders' supreme leader, Imam Shamil, planned to march on Tbilisi, Georgia's capital, to teach it a lesson. And though highlanders and Georgians shared many customs, often intermingled, and could hardly be distinguished from each other, the highlander still fancied himself as a great warrior standing up to the decadent ways of the Georgian.

Conveniently for the confederation, Georgia had fallen out of Russian favor. It had turned to a strong nationalist creed and sought to distance itself from the one state that had secured its survival against Muslim enemies since the late eighteenth century. Georgia's new ways threatened Russia's strategic position on the northern fringe of the Middle East and even in the Black Sea. Admiral Mikhail Lazarev's very legacy was at stake—and who better to help Russia reclaim at least part of that legacy than the descendants of Lazarev's vanquished enemies, the highlanders?

Russia tolerated the militarization of the Circassians and their allies, undoubtedly in the hope that, being bled dry in Abkhazia (and elsewhere), the Georgians would come begging for Russian protection as they had in the 1780s and 1790s, when invading Persian armies drained their blood. (A horrific Persian massacre of perhaps one third of Tbilisi's population, in 1796, laid the ground for Georgia's incorporation into the czarist empire five years later.) There were a number of retired Soviet military officers among the highland volunteers to Abkhazia, and it was widely known that local Russian military units offered logistical support to the "army of the confederation," as Shanibov was fond of calling it.

Russian complicity notwithstanding, and whatever one might think of the political justification of the Abkhaz cause and however critical one might be of its tragic human repercussions (the displacement of a quarter million Georgians)—highlanders flocked to the flag, believing they were serving a genuine national and regional cause.

At the time of my first visit to Nalchik, in 1992, Shanibov denied angrily that he was doing Russia's bidding in Abkhazia. He talked at length about Russia's attempts to undermine his war effort, and he insisted that Georgia had the Russians to thank for the fact that its ragtag army had not as yet been beaten soundly on the battlefield.

When I came back to Nalchik in 1996, however, long after the Abkhaz war had been concluded with a decisive Georgian defeat, Shanibov acknowledged, if only reluctantly, that "perhaps what we were doing at the time was not inconsistent with Russia's desires."

That the confederation was not an anti-Russian organization was evident from Shanibov's biography and outlook. This self-styled "Jim Garrison of the mountains" was a proud *Soviet Man*, who complained to me in 1992, and again when I visited him four years later, that America had conspired to destroy the Soviet Union. Perhaps in 1996 he would have given up on his dreams of pan-Caucasianism if only the clock could be turned back and the old Union restored. But in those heady days of 1992, with uniformed and armed young men guarding his headquarters and foreign journalists knocking on his door, Shanibov fancied himself as a great Adyghe general, ready to remold politics and redraw maps.

At some point, I suggested he go to the map at the other end of his long meeting table, and show me his military offensive plans. I did so tongue in cheek, ready to join him in a good laugh. To my astonishment, he jumped off his chair and went straight to the map. His demeanor changed instantly, he became visibly excited, and his nose even started bleeding. Before my eyes, the self-effacing scholar was transformed, making me wonder what he might have done if he had had real power to march armies back and forth, and not just the self-induced illusion that he could do so.

"If Russia stopped interfering," he said, "I would march into Tbilisi within a month." Tbilisi lies about 250 miles to the south and is connected to the North Caucasus by a single bad road across picturesque peaks and valleys.

And why, I asked, would he want to march into Tbilisi?

That was easy. He wanted to get rid of "all those fascists. . . . Everyone in the Georgian government is fascist." He said he would install a new government in Georgia that would immediately pull out of Abkhazia and recognize its independence.

What if the Georgians proved obstinate? Would the war continue indefinitely? I asked.

"Absolutely. One hundred years, two hundred years if necessary."

And then?

Shanibov softened up a bit, smiled, and said, "Eventually a Caucasian confederation will be created all the way from the river Don to Mount Ararat." His border lines were quite impressive. His confederation would have covered most of southern Russia as well as the independent states of Georgia, Azerbaijan, and Armenia, and perhaps have a slice of Turkey for dessert.

In reality, the ideas of pan-Caucasian unity were far less silly than Shanibov's military plans might suggest. As late as the eighteenth century, a "Caucasian" state of sorts, transcending national affiliations, did exist, under the Georgian king Irakli. It included only a minority of the Caucasians, but in its heyday it was described in glowing terms, a truly cosmopolitan place in which genes were exchanged freely, towers of Babel flourished, and a variety of facial features and customs intermingled.* Irakli's accomplishments so impressed Frederick the Great of Prussia, another king in quest of territorial aggrandizement, that he declared only two monarchs in the world worthy of respect: "I, in Europe, and in Asia—the invincible Irakli, King of Georgia." (Both went down to defeat, and Irakli is the one who signed Georgia's independence away to Empress Catherine the Great in 1783, becoming a vassal. Under his grandson even the semblance of nationhood was done away with, and Georgia became an administrative Russian province.)

A few days after our meeting in the fall of 1992, Shanibov was arrested by representatives of the federal government for "endangering the security of the state and spreading war propaganda." He was driven to Krasnodar, the largest provincial center in southern Russia, to face his accusers. There he was let go, and his supporters spread the story that he "escaped."

His detention generated considerable agitation among Kabardin nationalists, and the local government seemed to be teetering on the brink of collapse. An excited Shanibov addressed a rally of many thousands and demanded the "complete withdrawal" of Russian troops from Kabardino-Balkaria. Perhaps, if only briefly, he saw himself as a modern Prince Rededey facing up to a perfidious Prince Mstislav.†

---

* In the words of W.E.D. Allen, the distinguished British historian of the Caucasus, "Thus Irakli, with his Georgian nobles, his Armenian diplomats and agents, and his Cherkessk, Ossetian and Kalmuk mercenaries, held together for over half a century a strange kingdom of his own creation . . . [that] stretched from the Daryal to Nakhichevan, from the mountains of Likhi to the foothills of Daghestan and the sandy plains of Shirvan. Not more than half the people living under the authority of the king in Tiflis were Georgian. . . . [His kingdom] demonstrated the capacity of Georgian, Tatar and Armenian elements to beat out a common political life, so long as they had a breathing period free of foreign intervention." W.E.D. Allen, *A History of the Georgian People.*

† The first major battle pitting Russians against Circassians (1022), was decided by a duel between the commanders of the rival armies, Prince Mstislav of Rus and Prince Rededey of Tmutarakan. It was the Circassian, steeped in centuries of chivalrous warfare, who suggested it. The Russian, not trained in the gallantry of his enemy, stabbed him to death on the spot. The Circassian principality fell to Rus, and the princely family was vanquished.

If Shanibov had been more daring, and the local authorities less confident in dealing with him, Kabardino-Balkaria's name might now be far
less obscure to foreign ears. It could have emerged as a second pole of
instability in southern Russia, alongside Chechnya. That was Dudayev's
hope, and he was bitterly disappointed by Shanibov's lack of resolve.
Years after the event, Shanibov would credit himself with preventing a
"second Chechnya" by showing self-restraint and cooperating with the
local government. (He led government agents to a secret arms cache
that might have been used for a coup.) Be that as it may, the Kabardin
revolution was nipped in the bud, never to be heard of again, and the
largest Circassian group on Russian soil reverted to its characteristic
docility.

The end of the Abkhaz war in late 1993, and the complete defeat of
Georgia, consigned the confederation to the margins. A year later
Shanibov stepped down, claiming to have been debilitated "through a
wound suffered during the Abkhaz war." When Russia attacked Chechnya in December 1994, he tried to reclaim the presidency but was sum-
marily dismissed. The Chechen war showed just how feeble the
confederation's thunder was. It failed miserably not only to help the
Chechens militarily but even to raise public solidarity with them in
other parts of the Caucasus. The easily inflammable Shanibov managed
to exclaim, with great pathos, that "tens of thousands of volunteers from
all the republics of the North Caucasus will go to war with the Russian
aggressors," but that was his last whimper.

When I saw him again in the summer of 1996, he spewed forth the
most remarkable conspiratorial theory about America, one that would
have no doubt endeared him to his role model, Jim Garrison. The
American government, Shanibov told me, has resolved to "clean out the
Caucasus and bring down Russia," and that was the only way the events
of the previous five years could and should be understood.

What made the Americans so interested in the Caucasus?

"Simple," he said. "They have concluded that in the next century, the
planet will be able to sustain only one billion people, and they are determined to make sure that all the survivors will be from the developed
countries. I call them the 'golden billion.' The next global war will be
fought not over oil but over clean air and fresh water. And the Caucasus,
being one of the ecologically cleanest areas in the world, will be a
reserve for the 'golden billion.' But first, they need to rid themselves of
Russia."

At that moment, Shanibov no longer spoke to me as a Circassian
nationalist or even as a highlander. He had been converted to what the
Russian press calls "red-brown," a combination of Communist and fascist.

His hallucinogenic theories about America could have come from an editorial in *Zavtra*, the mouthpiece of extreme Russian chauvinism. I could not help the sensation of creeping sadness. An extraordinary opportunity to help revive the Circassian spirit had been wasted through narcissistic posturing, demagoguery, and irrationalism.

There was, however, one moment when Shanibov's rambling touched me deeply by reminding me of the enormous pain that any dweller of this highland must carry if his historical memory has not been completely obliterated. It came during our 1996 meeting, and Shanibov, already a has-been, was devoting his time to teaching. We were seated in his tiny office at Nalchik University, a cubicle of a room, dimly lit, where there was barely enough space for a second chair. No one was queuing in to seek favors or advice, and the phone was not ringing off the hook. I saw no uniformed guards, no pilgrims from the Circassian diaspora, no operational maps. A late summer breeze blew our way, and we talked about history—his, the confederation's, Russia's, the world's.

Toward the end of a very long conversation, almost as an afterthought, I mentioned the relations between Circassians and their Turkic neighbors, the Balkars and the Karachai. Shanibov stiffened. He launched into a tirade of complaints about how the Turkics were rewriting history. "The Balkars say that we, the Circassians, are invaders," Shanibov said, "and that they—the Balkars and the Karachai—are the indigenous peoples who lived here since time immemorial, and therefore the Caucasus belongs to them."

I looked at him puzzled, more because of the unexpected temperamental turn than because of anything he was actually saying. He apparently interpreted my expression as a display of supportive attentiveness and went on to ask, "Can you believe that? They are dead serious! The Caucasus belongs to them!

"But you don't need to be a historian or a scholar to refute this. Since when is the Caucasus the 'historical motherland' of the Turks?" Shanibov's sarcasm grew pointed as he accompanied his words with resolute hand motions. "Do you know where the Turkic motherland is? Have you ever heard of Lake Karachai in Siberia, the one that is now contaminated with radioactive fallout? That's where they're from. Yet the Russian authorities, even the Soviets before them, gave their blessing to their pretense that they are indigenous Caucasians. They promise the Karachai and the Balkars that they will exterminate the Circassian nations."

But who are "they"? I asked, a bit startled.

"The Russian state," he said. "It is trying to put us against all our neighbors. That is why they have revived the militarized Cossacks."

He was referring to the highlanders' ultimate nemesis, the armed settlers who began to flock to the Caucasus in the sixteenth century and laid the groundwork for Russia's future expansion. They soon became fierce competitors for the Caucasus's scarcest commodity, agricultural land. The Cossacks of the Terek Region (so named after the Terek River, the highlands' main source of water) dominated the Caucasus till the end of the czarist empire. The Bolsheviks disarmed them, and Stalin killed many and destroyed their collective identity. Now, as post-Soviet Russia was seeking a national identity, an attempt was being made to revive the Cossacks as subcontractors in safeguarding Russia's frontier. At the time of my visit, the Cossacks were demanding the right to be rearmed, and Moscow was tilting their way, sending a chill down Circassian spines. The highlanders had played a zero-sum game with the Cossacks for so long that, in their eyes, nothing good could come from the rising fortunes of the Cossacks.

At the height of the first Chechen war, in 1995, Russia summoned the Cossacks from all over the Caucasus and southern Russia to a special conference. The alarm bell went off. Russia's "flirtation" with the Cossacks—warned the highlands' best-known politician on the national level, Ramazan Abdulatipov—would "frighten all the mountain peoples of the Caucasus."

> If it is [official] policy, then in response we must call together the Dzhigits [heroic horsemen of previous Caucasian wars] from all the canyons. If the [Cossack] Don or Kuban Troops are being restored, then we must allow all peoples to restore their military traditions and their military detachments. There is no people in the Caucasus that does not have these traditions.

And so the specter of another highlander-Cossack war was rising again.

"LITTLE COSSACKS MINE"

Not with the plough is our dear, glorious earth furrowed,
Our earth is furrowed with the hoofs of horses;
And our dear, glorious earth
Is sown with the heads of Cossacks
FROM A SEVENTEENTH-CENTURY COSSACK REBEL SONG

On June 11, 1774, a major Circassian force from the principality of Kabarda launched an attack against a small Cossack settlement by the name of Naur. According to the Russian commanding officer, no fewer than 10,000 Kabardins took part in the attack, and they were repulsed by 800 Cossacks, among whom were women armed with pots of hot water. Thus was born a Russian Alamo with a happy end, a myth that was nurtured and inflated as time went on. The Kabardin force was expanded to 14,000, the Cossack force was reduced to 200, and the hot water was transformed into cabbage soup. For decades Cossacks used to openly mock their Kabardin neighbors asking them, "Dear fellow, were you served cabbage soup at Naur?"

The epic tale of Naur illustrates the centrality of the Cossacks to the Russian "frontier" culture, a frontier they had been claiming for the czarist throne for three hundred years before the highland was finally incorporated into Russia. They were not only the defenders of Russia's Alamo but also Russia's Minutemen, its Wild West adventurers, and instruments in its quest for its manifest destiny (to use Aleksandr Herzen's analogy)—as well as the exterminators of its Indians.

The Cossack phenomenon, evocative as it may be of frontier pioneers elsewhere (not only in the United States but in South Africa, Israel, and French North Africa as well), is unparalleled in its length of duration and its breadth of territory. Some trace the "first Cossack" to the twelfth century, but definitely not later than the fifteenth century. The Cossacks' easternmost units briefly colonized the Aleutians, fully expecting to reach for Alaska and perhaps California; their southernmost units braced themselves for the eventual takeover of the Euphrates and the Nile.

The origins of the Cossacks are murky. Many are the descendants of Slavic serfs, who opted out of a society so regimented and static that people faced the death penalty just for deciding to quit the hereditary occupation to which fate had assigned them. But many Cossacks are neither Russian nor Slavic. Their very name suggests Turkic roots and possibly means "free men." Turkic, Tatar, and Mongol blood undoubtedly flows in Cossack veins, together with Russian and Ukrainian. Incredible as it might sound, in the mid-nineteenth century, there were even reports of Jewish Cossacks. They were not necessarily Semitic, but their existence in the Cossack ranks served to affirm how eclectic this collection of people was.*

By the end of the eighteenth century, Russia had emerged as the largest contiguous empire in history, stretching from the Pacific to Central Europe. The debt owed to the Cossacks for that extraordinary accomplishment cannot be overstated. Indeed, without them, much of what is Russia would simply not have come into being.

What made the Cossacks so instrumental in Russia's imperial drive was the fact that they were not merely soldiers on the payroll of an emperor; they were not Russian replicas of Britain's Gurkhas or France's Foreign Legionnaires, although they possessed traits of both. They represented a *caste* rather than an army; they lived off the land they had fought for and occupied, and therefore they had far greater motivation to cling to their possessions than a strictly disciplined professional force would have had.

Through the late eighteenth century, the czars allowed the Cossacks an unusual degree of autonomy, so much so that the Cossack "hosts" are now described by historians as "republics" that enjoyed democratic liberties unthinkable in Russia proper, where unlimited autocracy prevailed. The basin of the river Don, which marked Russia's southern border at that time, was the site of the best-known Cossack host—and an enclave of individual freedoms. The Cossacks had a saying—"From the Don no one is handed over"—and Russian serfs fled there in droves to escape the harshness and arbitrariness of feudalism. This anomaly was potentially dangerous to the survival of Russian autocracy. The Cossacks, being so valuable to Russian military needs, had to be kept firmly under the imperial sway. Otherwise, cataclysmic eruptions were inevitable, with unforeseeable consequences.

---

* The Jewish Cossacks, whose presence was reported as late as the eve of World War I, belonged to an indigenous Russian sect popularly known as Subbotniks, or "People of the Sabbath." They are discussed elsewhere in the book, pp. 302–47.

The volatility of the Cossack temperament and the military nature of their organization, coupled with their growing population and economic needs, and topped by a largely anarchistic outlook, generated the most momentous rebellions anywhere in Europe prior to the French Revolution. The Cossacks were led by chiefs larger than life, boundless in their heroism, fearless and savvy and—for a while—seemingly invincible.

Two Cossack rebels, Stenka Razin in the seventeenth century and Yemelian Pugachev in the late eighteenth, came tantalizingly close to overthrowing the imperial dynasty and establishing in Russia a "popular" government. Razin's attempt coincided with the rise of Oliver Cromwell in England, at a time when the entire continent was going up in flames; and Pugachev's was finally put down just a few months before the American revolution. One can only imagine what our world would look like had an Oliver Cromwell or a George Washington emerged in Russia before the dawn of the modern era.

In July 1774, exactly two years before the American Declaration of Independence, Yemelian Pugachev released a document astonishingly evocative of the one composed two years later in Philadelphia. Given that it was authored by a semiliterate Cossack in the Volga Valley, who had little knowledge of the French Encyclopedists or the writings of John Locke, it is nothing short of inspired.

> By this decree . . . we grant to all hitherto in serfdom and subjection to the landowners the right to be faithful subjects . . . award them the villages, the old cross and prayers, heads and beards, liberty and freedom, always to be Cossacks, without recruiting levies, soul tax or other money taxes, with possession of the land, the woods, the hay meadows, the fishing grounds, the salt lakes, without payment or rent, and we free all those peasants and other folk hitherto oppressed by the malefactor gentry. . . . With the extermination of these enemies, the malefactor gentry, *everyone will be able to enjoy a quiet and peaceful life, which will continue evermore.*

If the last, italicized words required some polishing, they got just that two years later. "Unalienable Rights," scribbled a non-Cossack across the ocean, "are Life, Liberty and the pursuit of Happiness."

From the outset, the target of Cossack expansion was, by and large, Muslim populations. And yet even in the heyday of brutal colonization, Muslim natives found themselves sharing grievances with Cossacks rather than exchanging bullets. Both, in different ways, were victims of the Russian imperial system. In the 1770s Cossacks and Bashkirs (a Turkic people in the Urals) joined forces in what became the most dangerous rebellion that any Russian government faced before the Bolshevik Revolution; that of Pugachev. At the height of the rebellion, it engendered so much fear that the imperial court entertained the thought of fleeing from St. Petersburg to Riga.

The Pugachev rebellion was a watershed in Cossack history. Up to that time, the Cossacks had represented to the huge masses of Russia the only hope of liberation from virtual slavery. In the words of Aleksandr Herzen, the great Russian radical philosopher, the Cossacks were "knights-errant of the Russian common people."

With Pugachev's rebellion, the Cossack spirit peaked. Pugachev's defeat and execution signaled the beginning of a new phase. After lending their might and spirit to popular rebellions for two centuries, the Cossacks, in the words of the historian Paul Avrich, "became a pillar of the autocracy, a Praetorian guard to quell popular disturbances, a symbol of imperial authority rather than of freedom and independence as before."

It was in this capacity that the highlanders met them, during the Great Caucasian War of the mid-nineteenth century and the ensuing decades. It is *those* Cossacks who have lingered in the highlander memory. And it is the descendants of those Cossacks who have done little to assuage the suspicions and soothe the wounds.

I t is said that the first Cossacks appeared in what is now Chechnya, in the Northeast Caucasus, perhaps as early as the late fifteenth century, fleeing a Russian ruler, Ivan III. They lived there on their own, answerable to none, in a sort of peaceful coexistence with the highlanders. Then, as Russia grew stronger, they petitioned Czar Ivan IV ("the Terrible") to forgive their defection and let them back into the fold. Ivan relented but set a condition: the Cossacks should erect a fortress on the river Sunja and name it after him. The deal struck between the Cossacks and the *batiushka*, or "little father" (which is how czars came to be known to their subjects), was described in a contemporary song:

> *"Little father of all, Orthodox Czar,*
> *What will you give and grant unto us?"*

> *"I will give and grant, little Cossacks mine,*
> *The Terek River that runs so free,*
> *From the ridge itself to the wide blue sea,*
> *To the wide blue sea, to the Caspian."*

That was of course very gracious of Ivan the Terrible, who established a tradition of granting as gifts territories that were not his to grant. To imagine the importance of the Terek River, one need only think of the centrality of the Mississippi and the Colorado Rivers in the experience of American pioneers as they were trekking westward. Or the Portuguese settlers moving up the Amazon, or the British colonists along the Nile Valley. It is not that the Terek matches any of those grand rivers in width or length—indeed, it would hardly qualify as a brook in comparison. And yet it is the lifeline and the main tributary of all Northeast Caucasian rivers. It runs from northern Georgia, across Ossetia, Ingushetia, Chechnya, and Daghestan, to the Caspian Sea. The entire history of Caucasian colonization, resistance, and submission took place on its banks, and it witnessed much savagery and heroism, "like a storm it rushes weeping / every tear is foamy spray," in the words of Lermontov, who made the Terek a bearer of gloomy news of cruelty and death as it was flowing into the Caspian, "full of longing, full of grace." Lermontov called that poem "The Terek's Gifts," surely with a sigh of sadness.

The pact with Ivan the Terrible eventually gave rise to the most famous, and infamous, Cossack military structure in the Caucasus: the Cossacks of the Terek. Cossack colonies mushroomed across the length of the region, with their typically light-blue-painted houses and little Orthodox church spires. It was to such a colony, or *stanitsa*, that I traveled on the morning after my interview with the Circassian leader Yuri Shanibov, eager to find out about the people who were, as he proclaimed, so bent on "exterminating the Circassian nation."

It is not only a North Caucasian who would shudder at the sound of the Cossacks' name; so would a Jew of Eastern European ancestry. I remember my maternal grandmother, an octogenarian at that time, switching instinctively to a whisper whenever I asked her to recall an unwelcome visit by the Cossacks to her native village during the Russian Civil War some sixty years earlier. My paternal grandmother's family fled out of Oratov, the small town in Central Ukraine where she was born, as the call "the Cossacks are coming" was echoing in the streets.

For Jews in the western parts of the Russian empire, *Cossack* was not merely an ethnic designation or a group affiliation. It was the most evocative, menacing reminder of their vulnerability, a constant commentary on the fragility of their existence at the mercy of an arbitrary ruler who was ever ready to unleash these proverbial henchmen against them. Before the Holocaust, many Jews used the word *Cossack* in the

same manner that *Nazi* or *SS* would be used later on—that is, as a synonym for *evildoer*. The greatest collective trauma for Jews prior to the
Holocaust was the widespread massacres of Jews at the hands of Cossacks in Ukraine in the seventeenth century, which contemporary rabbinical literature equated with the Roman destruction of the Jewish
commonwealth in Palestine in the first century A.D.

In 1919, as the White armies came close to overthrowing the young
Bolshevik regime in the Russian Civil War, up to 200,000 Jews perished
at the hands of Cossack soldiers, who spearheaded the counterrevolution. Those massacres, writes historian Richard Pipes, "were a prelude to
and rehearsal for the Holocaust." The ablest and most dedicated mur-
ders came from the ranks of the Terek Cossacks. In the town of Fastov,
south of Kiev, they

> tortured and mutilated hundreds of Jews, many of them women and
> young children. Hundreds of corpses were left out in the snow for the
> dogs and pigs to eat. In the midst of this macabre scene the Cossack
> officers held a surreal ball in the town post office, complete with
> evening dress and an orchestra . . . while their soldiers went killing
> Jews for sport, the officers and their *beau monde* drank champagne and
> danced the night away.

It was then, in the early fall of 1919, that my father's great-aunt was
slaughtered by Cossacks. Her name was Malkah (Hebrew for "queen").
My father was born a few months later, on his parents' escape route to
Palestine. He was named Elimelekh, Malkah's partial masculine equivalent, in his aunt's honor.

My own excursion to the Caucasus was very much inspired by my
ethnic identity and my consuming interest in my people's experience.
The suffering and unlikely survival of tiny nations has touched me since
childhood, in no small measure because of my grandparents' tales of
persecution at the hands of a hostile majority. Yet not until well into the
process of conducting research for this book did I come across evidence
of the participation of North Caucasian Cossacks in this century's pre-
Holocaust holocaust, one that had had such a dramatic effect on my
own family. Unbeknownst to me, I had a far closer affinity with the
highlanders than I could have ever guessed.

Soon after the massacres of the counterrevolution, however, the
Terek Cossacks themselves joined the long list of victims of the Bolshevik Revolution, and for the next two decades they were to see their own
young and infirm devoured by an oppressive government. Their distinct
institutions were dissolved, their lands were confiscated, their commu-

nities were banished en masse to Siberia or to Russia's far north, their identity was obliterated, and their traditions were banned.

Through the tricks this century has played on so many small ethnic groups, the Cossacks managed to be, very visibly, on both sides of the divide, both afflicting and suffering injustice within one generation. Since sympathy to those deceived by history was my main motive for being in the Caucasus in the first place, with whom was I going to sympathize? Was it going to be the persecutor-turned-victim or the victim-turned-persecutor?* Or was it perhaps time to act by the principle that the chronicler's best judgment is judgment reserved?

The *elektrichka*, the unassuming suburban train that is a common feature of mass transit in Russia, took me from Nalchik to Prokhladny, the home of the Cossacks I was to see, on an August day in 1996, when the Caucasus was bracing for the worst. The fighting in Chechnya had flared up suddenly, the Chechens were mounting an astonishing campaign to retake Grozny from regular units of the Russian army, and fears of a regional spillover effect were again enveloping the neighboring republics.

My fellow passengers were immersed in their newspapers, devouring with evident incredulity the dispatches from Chechnya. My young Russian companion sobbed quietly as he read a report in a Russian tabloid about the hapless Russian soldiers stuck in a war for which they cared so little and about which they understood even less.

No wonder Prokhladny itself was a bit tense. No sooner had we arrived and begun to move through the station than we noticed a tall young man who was keeping close watch of our movements, without trying too hard to remain invisible. He finally approached us and with gentle assertiveness asked us what exactly we were up to in that touristic nonattraction of the Caucasus.

"Cossacks," I said. "We are looking for the offices of the Cossack union." This voluntary collaboration with the local security organs—whom, no doubt, the young man represented—paid off, because by the time we finally found a Cossack officer, two hours later, our presence had become sufficiently known. No less a person than the commander in chief of all Cossack units in the Caucasus was awaiting our phone call, and the local Cossack leadership of Kabardino-Balkaria was huddling in a tiny office, ready to welcome us.

---

* According to the Cossacks, they suffered mistreatment at the hands of the highlanders beginning in 1922. Much of the Terek Cossack District was divided among the newly formed highlanders' autonomous republics, such as Daghestan, Chechnya, North Ossetia, and Kabardino-Balkaria. See pages 39–40 and 47.

Prokhladny, now the second-largest city in Kabardino-Balkaria, with a population of perhaps 30,000, was founded as a Cossack colony. At the time of my visit, the city hall was still adorned by a sign proclaiming Prokhladny's two hundred and thirtieth anniversary, which had been celebrated the year before. In this respect, the local city government, like virtually everyone else in the Caucasus, was taking great liberties with history. The supreme Cossack leader himself told me that the earliest birthday Prokhladny could claim is 1784, and the town was thus nearly twenty years younger than its celebration suggested. Why was the city claiming unfounded longevity? Oh well, said the Cossack, smiling cryptically, and turned to another subject.

The word *prokhladny* in Russian means "cool," the most modest name of any Cossack colony in the region. Others are named proudly after emperors, generals, and manly professions. Whence the chill in Prokhladny? Local tradition has it that the place was so named by the indignant Empress Catherine who, during a sightseeing tour of her Caucasian domains, met a chilly reception from the local Cossacks. "*Prokhladny*," spewed the empress, and instructed that the unpleasant place should henceforth be called thus.

Catherine was not the last czar to keep an eye on the Cossack population, lest germs of rebelliousness reappear. But all in all, she and her successors had few reasons to complain. Even now, having been deceived by the state they had helped expand, the Cossacks I met protested their unswerving loyalty to Russia. Indeed, they considered themselves Russia's only true patriots.

The old Orthodox church of Prokhladny was bustling with life, a far cry from its former state of disgrace only ten years earlier, at the time of official atheism. Freshly painted, capped with two silver domes, the church had a pleasant grace to it.

In the little garden beside the church, I spotted a memorial tablet commemorating those who had been "persecuted by the Stalinist criminals." The Prokhladny tablet contrasted interestingly with the indifference I met in Nalchik, the provincial capital, almost each time I asked anyone about the region's bloody past. People would either shrug me off or show surprising leniency toward their former oppressors. I heard Balkars, quintessential victims of Stalinism, heap praise on the head of the dead tyrant who had come close to exterminating them. The Cossacks, however, do bear a grudge, even in the otherwise forgiving environment of the Lord's house.

Inside the church, among ancient-looking Russian icons, the flames of dozens of burning candles were arching and stretching, twirling in semicircular motions as if in a communal prayer, long projections of their silhouettes dancing on the walls in unexpected directions. A gaunt Ukrainian lady, dark blue kerchief tied around her head, huge eyeglasses covering about two-thirds of her drawn face, was selling candles to the faithful and earnestly writing down the names of the seekers of blessing. Come Sunday mass, she said, the good priest would include all the names in the religious chanting, beseeching God to forgive their sins.

No need to pay for this service, the lady hastened to explain, and then added gravely, staring at my companion: "Only *Christians* can be included in the prayer." The young man, a resident of Moscow, long-haired and more audacious in his dressing style than any of the locals, nodded, and said, "That's all right, I *am* Christian." He was, at least by birth, though by the time of our pilgrimage, he had switched loyalties and become a devout member of a mystical Indonesian sect. His new creed was sufficiently ecumenical, though, for him to cross himself in front of churches, hold his temples piously in front of mosques, and display impressive knowledge of synagogues as well. The Ukrainian lady seemed unsure of his willingness to be saved in Christ, but she finally relented and wrote down his name. Her gravely questioning gaze then shifted to me, with the same skepticism. "No," I preempted her warning, instantly revealing my theological failings, "I am not Christian, thank you." She nodded with the quiet satisfaction, I imagined, of a guardian of the faith, keeping the heathens at bay.

The church was located in Prokhladny's historical district, where, despite decades of persecution and dislocation, a flavor of Old Russia still prevailed. The houses were reminiscent of those Tolstoy had documented for posterity 150 years ago in a Cossack *stanitsa* about two hundred miles to the east of Prokhladny (in his story *The Cossacks*).

They are carefully thatched with reeds and have large carved gables. If not new they are at least straight and clean, with high porches of different shapes; and they are not built close together but have ample space around them, and are all picturesquely placed along broad streets and lanes. In front of the large bright windows of many of the houses, beyond the kitchen gardens, dark green poplars and acacias with their delicate pale verdure and scented white blossoms overtop the houses, and beside them grow flaunting yellow sunflowers, creepers, and grape vines.

I have nothing to add to the master's depiction.

It was there, a short distance from the church, that I came across the first sign of Cossack revival: a Cossack shop and a tiny suite of offices in an open courtyard, turning to the street. The offices belonged to the Union of Terek Cossacks, and the shop, run by a young blond man, offered a limited variety of Cossack paraphernalia. Most of the items were of a military nature and were locked, Soviet style, behind glass, well beyond the reach of a customer's hand. This might be the New Russia, but old distrust died slowly. The inventory included some uniforms, epaulettes, boots, and whips. What, after all, is a Cossack without the lead-weighted whip, the *nagayka*, that dreadful instrument of authority, applied so harshly to enemies of the throne? An image deeply engraved in the minds of early Russian revolutionaries was that of mounted Cossack troops breaking into a mass of demonstrators or bystanders, lashing mercilessly as they crushed any sign of unrest or disloyalty toward "Little Father." Maksim Gorky recalled how a Cossack horseman broke into a rally in 1905 and assailed one of the participants: "Swooping down from his dancing horse . . . he slashed him across the face, cutting him open from the eyes to the chin. . . . Brandishing his tarnished shaft of steel he let out another shriek and, with a wheeze, spat at the dead man through his teeth."

The offices, across the yard from the shop, consisted of two rooms, modestly furnished. The first room functioned as a reception area, where a large mural was splashed across the full length of one of its walls. The theme was a Cossack wedding, and it featured Cossack men in their traditional garb, daggers stuck in their belts. In the main room an old Cossack man, sporting a bushy white mustache, was leafing through a pile of folders under the watchful gaze of Saint Vladimir, the founder of Russia; Aleksandr Nevsky, Russia's medieval unifier, in full armor; a large John the Baptist overshadowing a smaller Jesus and Mary, all of whose colorful portraits adorned one of the walls. Below them a more mundane poster showed the full spectrum of Cossack military ranks, with their distinct names. They were nowhere to be seen for about seventy years but resurfaced when the government sanctioned the revival of Cossack institutions in 1990. On another wall hung a calendar displaying photos of each of the Cossack atamans of Russia.* The calendar proclaimed in bold Cyrillic letters

KAZACHEMU RODU NYET PEREVODU

---

* *Ataman* is an ancient title akin to *chief*. It may have derived from ancient Gothic or from a Turkic language, in which it would have meant "master of the horses."

"The Cossack bloodline will never perish."

Testifying to that continuity was Vladimir Kryshanovsky, the old Cossack who welcomed us, a proud bearer of a Cossack rank equivalent to sergeant-major. He looked considerably older than the seventy years he claimed. But Kryshanovsky had particularly extenuating circumstances: he was a child of what Russians call "the years of repression." The old Cossack carried in his pocket a laminated card, the size of a driver's license, issued for him by the Russian government, which certified: "The bearer of this document has the right to enjoy benefits in accordance with the legislation on persons recognized as victims of political repression. This document does not expire, and is valid everywhere." I thought the last sentence was a telling addition, unnecessary in most countries where history is, by definition, irrevocable, and status which emanates from historical events therefore could not "expire." But this is Russia, a land not yet at peace with itself, and here the past is still incomplete. Russians over a certain age know that the past could still change many times over, and a rehabilitated "class enemy" could still be sent back to his former disgrace.

Kryshanovsky was but a young child when Stalin targeted the North Caucasus in his infamous de-kulakization campaign, the class war he waged to physically destroy millions of irredeemable "exploiters," the "rich" peasants known as kulaks. Many of them were pitifully poor, and it was their refusal to join collective farms that brought upon them total eradication. The countryside became desolate, a man-made famine engulfed the land, and millions perished. In the Prokhladny area, Kryshanovsky told me, at least one-third of all Cossacks died. "Our recent history in the North Caucasus is one of blood and pain," he sighed. "We became the main target for the Soviet government right from the beginning. In 1922 the authorities told the Chechens and the Ingush that they could have our lands, but first we had to be evicted. And we were evicted all right. Thirty-seven thousand of us were slaughtered. We, the Terek Cossacks—had anyone ever been as loyal as we to the crown, to the motherland? Look at our reward!"

He invited us to sit while he called his superior, the ataman of all Terek Cossacks, Vladimir Shevtsov. "You are lucky," he announced, beaming. "The ataman happens to be in Prokhladny today. He travels so often that it is difficult to track him down. So much to be done to rectify the past!"

What, for example, would he rectify? I asked Kryshanovsky.

"At the time of the czar," he said, "we used to have a large Cossack administrative district that was called the '*oblast* of all Terek Cossacks.' The Communists destroyed it piece by piece. First in the 1930s, they gave Prokhladny and another region, Maisky, to Kabardino-Balkaria. Then they gave another region, Mozdok, to North Ossetia. In 1957 they gave Naursky and Shelkovskoy to the Chechens. The Cossack region of Kizlyar was given to Daghestan. We were divided, wedges were driven between our communities, our common history was brought to an end, and a genocide is being committed against us in each of these republics. We have absolutely no rights. None!"*

As Sergeant-Major Kryshanovsky was briefing me on the horrors of the last eight decades, Ataman Shevtsov walked in briskly. A stocky man, he was wearing a standard military uniform with a short, fading black necktie, which contrasted almost comically with his high, shining boots. Shevtsov's outfit was no charade, though—he was indeed a military man, having risen to the rank of major-general in the Soviet army. At the time of his retirement he served as commander of a military school. At sixty, officially retired, he was not about to slow down. As head of all Terek Cossacks, he had the entire Caucasus for a realm, at least nominally.

Shevtsov was a bit snappy and impatient, projecting a no-nonsense approach that befit a military person but perhaps also illustrated a cultural difference between these agents of Russian expansion and the native peoples whose neighborhood they had joined. A member of an indigenous nation would consider sacred his duty to treat a guest, however unexpected, in the most lavish manner, at times in a fashion that is not only overstated but even self-injurious. Many of these extravagant hosts often hover barely above subsistence levels and can ill-afford feasts in honor of complete strangers. The sanctity of hospitality among Caucasians is such an article of faith that modesty in performing it is no virtue, and failing to deliver it would be considered eccentric, almost uncivilized. I was to find out the importance of this just a few hours later, when divergent Cossack and indigenous traditions collided in front of me.

Driving me in his Soviet-made Zhiguli car to meet with the local

---

* The word *genocide*, I found out, is used quite loosely in the former Soviet Union, in a way not consistent with its definition under international law. It is pity that such a powerful term is so cheapened, particularly in a land where many events in the last few centuries really would have amounted to genocide. At no time did any of my interviewees suggest that Cossacks were exterminated physically by highlanders. They did argue that Cossacks were losing ground, literally and figuratively, in the North Caucasus in a way that posed a threat to their continued existence as a group.

Cossack leadership, Ataman Shevtsov shrugged off my silly attempts to engage him in a conversation about Prokhladny's urban landscape, or the cost of gasoline, or people's clothing. He was restless throughout our interview, often jumping to his feet and pacing the room to and fro, his bootheels clicking on the wooden floor. At one point he grew visibly exasperated at the course of the interview, perhaps feeling that it had become too platitudinous. "Well," he snapped, "if there's nothing else you need to know, I'll be on my way!" Fortunately, he relented, dropped to his chair, and spent another hour with us. His speech was generally slow, and he lost his line of thought time and again. But he was unequivocal in his allegations and denunciations: the most powerful men in Russia have conspired against the Cossacks, he said, and the Chechens were among the Cossacks' deadliest enemies.

Like so many others I had met in the North Caucasus, he was openly nostalgic about the Soviet Union. "I was raised as a member of the multiethnic Soviet people," he declared with such solemnity that one could almost hear "The Internationale" playing in the background. "At my school we had members of many nationalities, but at no time was anyone asked whether he was Russian, or Balkar, or Korean, or Kabardin. No one posed that question. I wonder who is posing the question so bluntly nowadays."

What Shevtsov did not volunteer was that the reason "no one posed questions about nationality" at his school was that the Soviet system made such questions entirely redundant: every single individual was required by law to register his nationality on his identity card. If anything, the system was *obsessed* with people's national origins, not oblivious to them, and once a nationality was established, there was no way out. But even more baffling was that Soviet virtues would win nostalgic approval from a prominent leader of the Cossacks, among the longest suffering of all Soviet groups, to whom the benevolent rules of the "multiethnic Soviet people" had never applied. What would Shevtsov have thought if, as a student in a Soviet military academy, he had come across leaflets distributed in 1920 to Red Army soldiers in Ukraine urging the wholesale liquidation of Cossacks by "fire and sword"?

But consistencies do not abound in the Caucasus. To my great astonishment, I came across many people whose strong nationalism was matched only by their great enthusiasm for the dead Soviet state, the presumed sworn enemy of all nationalisms. Of course, Russian cynics, as well as trained Russia hands in the West, might tell me that this is no contradiction at all, and that much of the nationalism we have witnessed in the Caucasus and elsewhere was inflamed artificially, either by would-be restorers of the Soviet Union bent on undermining the "new Russia," or by opportunists seeking to capitalize on destabilization, by pitting neighbors against each other.

Another possibility is that Soviet Men, to use the stock phrase, opted for nationalism out of frustration, because they saw nationalism as the only alternative to the fallen supranational state.

It is sometimes alleged that Jokar Dudayev, the leader of the Chechen independence movement, "hated Russia but loved the Soviet Union," and his movement was but a part of an all-encompassing plot to revive the old Union. Such was the belief of quite a few of his civilian Chechen opponents, people with whom I met in Grozny and elsewhere. I thought at the time that they were arguing the impossible, that theirs was just a propagandistic attempt to discard Dudayev. I still have no evidence that Dudayev's motives were anything but patriotic, yet having visited other parts of the Caucasus and having spoken with people whose backgrounds resembled Dudayev's, some of whom strongly approved of Dudayev's leadership and methods, I am more inclined to accept that the phenomenon of nationalism in the Caucasus is much murkier and more multilayered than I had previously assumed. Nothing illustrated this better than the nostalgia expressed for the old Soviet system by the Cossack Shevtsov and the Circassian Shanibov, presently on opposite sides of the nationalistic divide. They implied strongly that they would have preferred to see the Soviet Union preserved, even if its preservation had come—as undoubtedly it would have—at the expense of their own nationalistic aspirations. Asserting Kabardin or Cossack rights in the post-Soviet universe was not the grand prize, only a consolation one.

Conspiratorial and psychoanalytical theories aside, I felt a degree of empathy for the Cossack ataman Shevtsov. He had been raised and nurtured by the Soviet system, richly rewarded by it, and when it came to discussing nationalism any way other than negatively, he was still charting unknown waters. After all, the very term *nationalism* was a bad word in Soviet vocabulary, as close to being a political obscenity, as, say, *imperialism, capitalism,* or *Zionism.* Even as he and his colleagues were thundering against Chechens and Kabardins, it was important for the ataman to maintain his impeccable credentials as an "internationalist."

The main Cossack headquarters for the republic of Kabardino-Balkaria were located in an unassuming apartment building next to Prokhladny's city hall. They consisted of a single medium-sized room, adorned with a Russian flag and a Cossack coat of arms. Seated there in silence were the ataman of Kabardino-Balkaria, two of his colleagues, and a fourth unidentified man. I had not called them to announce my arrival, yet miraculously they were all there, awaiting me, confirming that invisible hands were taking care of the relationship of production between journalists and subject matter. There was little doubt in my mind that I was being followed in most of the Caucasian destinations I visited. No one ever tried to interfere directly with my movements, but subtle signals were sent every now and then to remind me not to go too far in indulging my curiosity. Some of the signals sent to me were funny, and I appreciated the humor. Others were clumsy and annoying. In Prokhladny I was thankful for the anonymous grand facilitator who made sure I would be kept busy.

The grand facilitator, whoever he or she was, also made sure that I would not get "only one side of the story." And so another person, the aforementioned "fourth man," was squeezed into the room, much to the Cossacks' chagrin. Not only was he not Cossack, he actually served in the executive of the Kabardin People's Congress, a nationalist organization whose raison d'être was to offer loud resistance to the revival of the Cossacks. The ethnic and political affiliations of that gentleman were not revealed to me until very close to the end of the meeting, and they contributed to an amusing climax, as the patient reader may still find out.

My Cossack interviewees provided me with an alternative version of history. When I asked them about the Cossack role in the Great Caucasian War of the mid-nineteenth century, I was told that no such role had ever been played. The republican ataman, a former police officer by the name of Aleksey Vasilievich Dyerbaba, then added reproachingly, "We don't know where you got this information from," as though my question, dealing with events that predated the birth of my interlocutor's great-grandfather, constituted a seditious act unto itself. "The Cossacks only guarded borders and led convoys," Ataman Dyerbaba added didactically. Cossack landholdings in Kabardino-Balkaria were acquired *legally*, not through the use of force, he asserted. The czarist government approached the Kabardin princes around 1825, a committee was established with equal representation for both parties, the deeds were transferred, and money changed hands, "You may check the archives in Nalchik and Moscow if you so will." Upon the completion of the process, the Russian government handed the lands over to the Cossacks. Members of the Poltava regiment of the Ukrainian Cossacks constituted the majority of the new settlers.

Nearly one hundred years later, in the 1920s and 1930s, the dekulakization took place. Cossack homesteads were replaced by collective farms, the Cossack settlers were suppressed, many were imprisoned, others were banished. Yet the community has survived. In Prokhladny, 70 percent of the population is Cossack, "attested to by the traditional Cossack names they bear," Dyerbaba said.

Yet only a minority of Cossacks in the region have bothered to register with the reinstated Union of Terek Cossacks—no more than 4,500 individuals in all. The great enthusiasm of 1990, when Cossacks were allowed again to stand up and be counted, has subsided. Why? "Initially, the state met us halfway. But the promises embodied in the laws and decrees never materialized," explained Dyerbaba.

His boss, Ataman Shevtsov, interjected: "The presidential decree on rehabilitation of the Cossacks as a nation, and subsequent decrees to that effect, have been ignored not only here but throughout the entire Terek region. It is bad faith that has frustrated their implementation. It is not our own indifference. For four hundred years, we have demonstrated our effectiveness as a group."

Why then has it not worked out for the Cossacks at a time when so many other ethnic groups have found their voice and reasserted their identity?

"Nowadays," answered Shevtsov, "the president and the government are surrounded by forces that are simply not interested in the revival of the Cossacks."

Who are they? I pressed on.

"You will have to find out for yourself," Shevtsov replied unsmilingly. He then proceeded to a favorite theme of the post-Soviet world. "The main opposition to our revival comes from the mafia—and it is well known that such people have a lot of clout around the president. They claim that their objection to the restoration of our special status is that such a status would be 'irreconcilable with the constitution of the Russian Federation.' But this is only a subterfuge."

Shevtsov referred to an objection raised in Russia to the wholesale arming of the Cossacks, which is what a restoration of their pre-1917 status would entail. Critics warn that the rearmed, self-governed Cossacks, outside normal state structures such as the military or police, could pose a grave danger to the future stability and democracy of Russia. The potential for abuse of power by such a rogue army would be enormous, and the temptation for a high-handed president to employ the Cossacks against political rivals might prove irresistible.

Indeed, if we are to believe the highest estimates of Cossack population in Russia, at over ten million, is it entirely impossible that one day a rearmed Cossack nation could seek dictatorial powers for itself? Remember Pugachev? He was roaming the Russian heartland only 225 years ago, and we already know that many in the Caucasus seek to pick up where their ancestors left off in the eighteenth century. A future well-organized Cossack nation, driven by a messianic urge to save Russia in spite of herself, could conceivably engage in a massive attempt to remold history.

On the other hand, if a Cossack is not armed and is not used for military purposes, then what is he? Could the survival of Cossackdom be limited solely to the artistic power of dancing troupes whose costume-clad members would entertain a Sunday audience in a far-flung fairground, tapping their heels on a hastily assembled platform, raising the tip of their knees to waist level and whirling in circles to the sound of a two-hundred-year-old tune? That is to say, could the Cossack survive solely as a museum relic?

YERMOLOV COMES (OH, NO!)

> *No matter what the future power in Russia is like, Cossack troops will exist. The state needs such a sound and cheerful population accustomed to order. Cossacks will obey any new power which spells order and an opportunity to work in peace.*
> GENERAL BOGAYEVSKY, EXILED ATAMAN OF THE DON COSSACKS, 1928

In 1997 the Cossack cause found an unlikely ally in the top echelons of Russia's government: the Jewish billionaire Boris Berezovsky, then deputy national security adviser to President Yeltsin. He openly acknowledged Moscow's inability to establish law and order in southern Russia. "If the lives of hundreds and thousands of people are threatened," he told a Cossack gathering, "they should be given a chance to protect themselves, their homes, their families."*

The idea was popular among Russian nationalists and communists, and Yeltsin finally put his signature to a decree conferring official status on the Terek Cossacks, placing them "in state service" and ordering a handover of arms to their members. A decree signed is not necessarily a decree implemented (the last fifteen years of Soviet and Russian life have certainly proven that), but the sound of Yeltsin's pen scratching on the Kremlin stationery was the sound of history coming full circle. No longer were the Cossacks prime candidates for extermination "by fire and sword."

But what would the Cossacks do with the arms they sought and began to obtain? Worth noting are the ominous words spoken in early 1997 by Vladimir Ponomaryov, Cossack ataman in the city of Pyatigorsk, just across the border from Kabardino-Balkaria.

---

* Absurdly, in 1999 Berezovsky was elected the sole parliamentary deputy of Karachaevo-Cherkess, the semi-autonomous republic, the nominal national territory of two mountainous peoples who feel threatened by the Cossacks. (He resigned after a few months for unrelated reasons.) But the election of Berezovsky, a carpetbagger if there has ever been one, serves to illustrate the hollowness of the system: Slavs constitute an overwhelming majority of the population in this "ethnic" republic.

Grozny has never been Chechen, and it won't be. We saved them from the Turks, who would have slaughtered them all if it had not been for Christian Russia. Chechens have always just been bandits.

If we had been called on to do the job, then we would have annihilated them all, left nothing behind but ashes. Next time the Chechens won't be so lucky.

We have weapons, and we have people who can fight in the best Cossack traditions. If those Chechen bandits can have grenades and rockets, why can't we defend ourselves?

A telling monologue in which the silly and the wicked are joined together.

Ataman Shevtsov, my host in Prokhladny, made similar remarks about the Ingush, very close ethnic relatives of the Chechens. They are locked in a bitter ethnic conflict with their Ossetian neighbors, and Shevtsov promised to come to the Ossetians' aid. Why? Not because any Cossack interests are involved. The reason, by his own admission, was sheer vindictiveness. The Ingush hurt the Cossacks seventy-five years ago, and, "we Cossacks have a genetic memory, too." Little wonder, in face of this rhetoric, that the highlanders question Cossack motives.

One of Shevtsov's colleagues in the all-Russia leadership of the Cossacks went further. Speaking of the Chechens, Vladimir Naumov, "war minister" in the Moscow-based Union of Russian Cossacks, told the newspaper *Obshchaya Gazeta*:

Even at the end of the twentieth century, the use of military force is necessary with regard to some people who for a decade now have been living under laws which reject the national laws. . . . For years these people robbed, stole cattle, killed, and looted. And all this has been regarded as the highest level of work available in that territory. We must teach them peaceful, creative jobs.

At forty-five, Naumov was a relatively young man. Born and raised in Moscow, he had little experience in the ways of the Caucasus and, apparently, little knowledge of the region's history. Otherwise, I presume, he would not have used words that so chillingly evoke those spoken by General Aleksey Yermolov 170 years earlier. Yermolov was Russia's warlord in the Caucasus, who, in an advisory note to his sovereign, Emperor Alexander I, described how he proposed to deal with the Chechens:

When the fortresses are ready, I shall offer the scoundrels . . . rules of life, and certain obligations, that will make clear to them that they are subjects of your Majesty. . . . If they [do not] submit . . . I shall propose to them to retire and join the other robbers from whom they differ only in name, and in this case the whole of the land will be at our disposal.

Yermolov still inspires many of the Cossacks. In the spring of 1996, the Cossacks named a battalion of volunteers after the old man and sent it to fight against the Chechen "bandits." In doing so, they followed to the letter Yermolov's own hope when he was appointed commander in chief in the Caucasus in 1816.

I desire that the terror of my name should guard our frontiers more potently than chains or fortresses, that my word should be for the natives a law more inevitable than death. Moderation in the eyes of the Asiatics is a sign of weakness, and out of pure humanity I am inexorably severe.

Yermolov, a genuine war hero who helped defeat Napoleon and marched into Paris in 1815, fancied himself a great expert on the "Eastern mentality." He claimed to know how to speak to easterners from a position of strength, never conceding anything, always condescending and terrorizing. Tales of Yermolov's habits are many, including a famous one about feigned rage during a trip to Persia in which he acquired, quite deliberately, the reputation of a bloodthirsty lunatic.

Yermolov, or Yarmoul, as he was known to the natives in an Arabized form of his name, did not deliver the Caucasus to his emperor but laid the groundwork for the prolonged and costly Caucasian war that bogged Russia down from 1830 to 1859. But he did accomplish one thing that he set out to do: his name did terrorize generations of highlanders and foster hatred and fear. A hundred and seventy years later, Chechen nationalists finally blew up his imposing statue in downtown Grozny, the city he founded. The savagery he unleashed forever marred relations between the North Caucasus and Russia.

I must confess that I was stunned when I learned that the Cossacks had chosen Yermolov's name for their battalion. What kind of message did they think they were sending? Was it that, should the Chechens not lay down their arms right away, a Yermolov-like solution was awaiting them? It is not as though the Cossacks were in a position to deliver, but the slight to Chechen honor could best be compared with, say, Mexico's military fighting Chiapas Indian rebels under Hernán Cortés's banner.

Ataman Vladimir Shevtsov was the proud founder of the Yermolov Battalion. "No one was willing to volunteer to go there but the Cossacks," he told me, moving around the room, with—as I could hardly fail to notice—an inflated chest. I am not sure I had ever seen a general with an inflated chest before and always assumed the words to be a worn literary cliché. Now, however, as the general walked me through the list of glories he had earned, I saw before me a veritable inflated chest. I kept scribbling in my notebook the word "peacock," as I was following his gestures and body language.

"The general staff of the army and the commander of the Caucasus military district appealed to me personally, as ataman of the Terek Cossacks, and asked that we form a battalion," Shevtsov told me. "And we, the Cossacks, being the best organized part of the population, managed to attract enough volunteers and dispatch them to Chechnya.

"We fared so much better than the regular army. Do you know why? Because unlike the army, we sent no eighteen-year-old kids who had no idea how to fight. We sent fathers and grandfathers who had been hardened in battle, people who could stand up to the Dudayevites [loyalists of Jokar Dudayev]. I believe that this battalion saved the lives of dozens or hundreds of Russian soldiers."

According to Shevtsov, the battalion had, at its peak, 800 enlisted men, of whom 24 were killed and 256 wounded, a fairly large proportion. "They fought in Grozny, in Vedeno, in Shali." Shevtsov proceeded to name some of the best-known sites of the Chechen war, then added proudly, stressing every syllable, "This battalion, all by itself, occupied seven towns and major villages. It arrived in Chechnya on March 2, 1996. Six days later it engaged the bandits, and for the ensuing three months, it did not cease."

Chechens and Daghestanis to whom I later quoted Ataman Shevtsov's boastings responded dismissively, and some laughed derisively. "If the Cossacks did so well," one retorted, "how come one-third of them were hit?" Some suggested the actual casualties were even higher.

But why did you name the battalion after Yermolov? I asked Shevtsov.

"Why not?" retorted the ataman.

Well, his name was intertwined with extermination and depopulation, I suggested.

Shevtsov waved his hand dismissively. "This is a manipulation of national ideas," he said. "You can use many names in many ways. We did not choose Yermolov's name because the native peoples have antipathy toward him, but because Yermolov respected Cossack rights."

"Besides," he continued, "Stavropol is populated by members of all Caucasian nationalities. It is a multiethnic city. And yet a monument for Yermolov is being erected there." (Stavropol is a provincial capital in southern Russia, just over 150 miles north of Prokhladny.)

I reminded the ataman that the Chechens considered Yermolov's statue an affront and removed it. Are you not in fact sending a signal to the Chechens or others—I asked—that you do not care in the least about their grievances?

Shevtsov stared at me mischievously, paused for a moment, clearly wondering if the guest from Washington should be offered the following analogy, and then said: "In America you have a very good book. It is called *Gone With the Wind*—I assume you know it. The book described very well the war between the North and the South, all that the warring generals inflicted on each other's sides, and how awful the war was. And yet the war did not prevent Americans from erecting monuments to the generals of both sides, did it?"

Well, general, this is a good point indeed, I answered, a bit taken aback by his unexpected foray into American history. And yet I can assure you that no Southerner, however forgiving and tolerant, would appreciate an attempt by a Northerner to build a monument in downtown Atlanta in honor of General Sherman.

The Cossack chief shook his head and laughed heartily.

None of the highlanders I spoke to betrayed any particular fear in face of a Cossack army-to-be, and yet all expressed outrage.

"This is a very simple matter," said Zaur Naloyev, the Kabardin intellectual and founder of the Circassian national movement Adyghe Khassa. "The Cossacks have always been an antinational force, an instrument for the repression of all non-Russian nations. The Cossacks are consumed by hatred of all non-Russians. We have always suffered discrimination in areas populated by Cossacks."

"I am not opposed to the revival of the Cossacks," said Haji-Murat Ibragimbeili, a retired Soviet colonel and military historian. A native of Daghestan, Avar by nationality, Ibragimbeili had warned against "profound ignorance of the Caucasus among Yeltsin's advisers" well before the Chechen war. I spoke to him in Moscow in 1994, about five months before Russia launched its attack against Chechnya. "Let the Cossacks revive!" he exclaimed. "They were repressed in the 1920s, they experienced tragedies, they lost their elites, their best and ablest were banished or forced out of the country, they suffered physical extermination. But all that notwithstanding, I am completely opposed to their military revival."

Ibragimbeili, a colorful man who used to teach history in a major Soviet military academy, was married to a Chechen woman and claimed close friendship with Jokar Dudayev. I went to see him under the impression of a full-page article he wrote in the liberal Moscow daily

Nezavisimaya Gazeta, in the summer of 1994, arguing that the core of future conflicts in the Caucasus would be competition over agricultural lands between Cossacks and highlanders. Should that not be resolved quickly, he prognosticated, it would spell disaster and end up in a bloody conflict.

"Let them revive spiritually, culturally," he said of the Cossacks. "Let them go back to their former lifestyle, to cultivation of the land, to self-government. But should they ever be reincorporated into a military structure, the results would be tragic." He paused, looked at me gravely, and reiterated, "Tragic! Why? Because the highlanders are born fighters. Faced by armed Cossacks, they would fight, and *this* would lead to a second all-Caucasian war. The present Russian leadership simply does not understand what kind of genies it is letting out of the bottle by encouraging the rebirth of the Cossack military spirit."

Since the outbreak of the conflict in Chechnya, warnings of an all-Caucasian war have been heard frequently in Russia—but they have proved wrong. At the end of the day, irrespective of their natural solidarity with the Chechens, most highlanders may not possess the "military spirit" Ibragimbeili was talking about, or else they simply refused to summon it back from the past for a cause in which most did not really believe or in any event were unwilling to shed blood for. Unlike the Chechens, the overwhelming majority of highlanders I have spoken to, including nationalists, accepted that they were destined to live under Russian control and sought a better deal within that context. General Dudayev's attempts to expand the war beyond Chechnya's borders failed completely. Elites all over the North Caucasus, old Soviet apparatchiks and rich New Russians, seemed to join hands in preventing any spillover effect. The Chechen war remained, at times almost incomprehensibly, a one-province war.

On the other hand, a future conflict with the Cossacks might assume an entirely different form. It could not only transcend the borders of the ethnic minirepublics in the Caucasus but also spill over into the Russian provinces to the north, where a large Cossack population lives. Even if most highlanders do not harbor strong anti-Russian sentiments, the anti-Cossack sentiment is widespread, if dormant. Distant history helped foster it, and Soviet education helped augment it.

Take, for example, the absolute contempt for Cossacks shown by Abu Movsyaev, the head of Chechnya's secret services, shortly after the end of hostilities with Russia in 1996. In a newspaper interview he went so far as to deny the existence of the Cossacks. Clearly, people who do not exist require no recognition, let alone special attention. He said of Cossack opposition to the settlement in Chechnya:

The dog is barking, but the caravan is moving on. We were fighting for two years against enormous Russia. No Cossacks as such exist today. Real Cossacks would eschew a conflict with the mountain people. Those who stage rallies are Communist drunkards. The genuine Cossacks were always worthy of their name.

This back-handed compliment, accorded the dead and denied to the living, does little to allay Cossack fears. Little can be expected of a dialogue in which both parties strive to dehumanize each other. I quoted the Cossack "war minister" earlier as reducing the Chechens to "lawless cattle thieves." The Chechen secret police chief retorts that the Cossacks are alcoholics in the pay of Communists. Cossacks are bringing back the demons of the Yermolov era. Highlanders accuse them of being assassins of nations. Is the rhetorical hyperbole a harbinger of worse things to come?

At the time of its establishment in 1990, the Confederation of Caucasian Peoples was first named Confederation of the Mountainous Peoples. The subtle difference should not escape us. *Mountainous* is an exclusionist term and applies only to the indigenous population whose presence in the Caucasus predates that of Cossacks and Russians.

Sincerely or otherwise, the Confederation's founders then decided to reach out to the non-mountaineer elements as well and dropped the topographic requirement for membership. The rationale was there for any one to recognize. Large ethnic Russian populations reside in all eight autonomous provinces in the Caucasus, constitute an overwhelming majority in one, and are on par with the largest indigenous group in two. Excluding the Russians automatically from the confederation would have sent an ominous signal, with the potential of upsetting interethnic relations in the Caucasus the way they were upset elsewhere in the former Soviet Union, for example in the Baltic states. Unlike the Baltic region, the Caucasus, at least outside of Chechnya, has seen little serious Russophobia. I have never come across any local nationalist in the Caucasus who openly and seriously agitated for Russians to leave because they were "newcomers," as Baltic nationalists argued in the case of the hundreds of thousands of Russians who had settled in their states since Soviet occupation in 1940. In the Caucasus, the sense of neighborliness and even affinity between locals and Russians is real and pronounced. This is one major reason why sympathy for the Chechens never evolved into an open clamor to join in a regional war against Russia, and why the atrocities committed by government troops against the

Handwritten margin note: But my Russian friends + acquaintances are generally suspicious + fearful

Chechens did not generate animosity toward Russian individuals, in any event not on a significant scale. Highlanders, outraged and embittered as they were about Russia's heavy hand in Chechnya, did not associate "the evil emanating from the Kremlin" with their own Russian neighbors.

By dropping the "mountaineer" designation, the confederates seemed to send a signal that theirs was no longer an ethnic club thriving on polarization but a regional association whose members' interests were defined pragmatically rather than genetically.

The attempt to join Cossacks and highlanders under the umbrella of the confederation may have been inspired to some extent by the first instance in regional history in which both parties found themselves fighting the same war, on the same side, completely voluntarily, and not through the coercion of an omnipotent Russian government. That occurred at the time of the Abkhaz war, when both Cossacks and highlanders came to the aid of rebellious Abkhazia, in its controversial war against Georgia. But that was no more than a marriage of convenience. The highlanders were there to help the Abkhaz gain freedom; the Cossacks were there to destabilize Georgia, with the hope that Georgia's collapse would precipitate the restoration of Russia's historical borders, of which the Cossacks had been the traditional custodians. In Abkhazia, no sense of shared destiny was born in blood, and no regional partnership replaced that which had been forged by genes.

"We have given up on working within the confederation," Ataman Dyerbaba, the former police officer, now leader of the Cossack community in Kabardino-Balkaria, told me. "We cannot accept the confederation's programs and ideas."

What is the problem? Are they too nationalistic? I inquired.

"Yes, they are. Look at *us*—our rights have been infringed upon for years. But *they* raise their voices only about the infringement of *their* rights."

The fourth man in the room, who up to that point had kept silent, finally interjected. His name, he said, was Sufaddin Shaoyev, which did not strike me as particularly Cossack. "Right"—he chuckled—"I am Kabardin." Shaoyev, wearing a worn beige suit with a narrow, red-striped black tie, was in his early fifties, a former Communist apparatchik ("secretary of the party organization in a commercial cooperative," he said) who had made the switch to nationalist politics almost overnight. Now he was an activist in the Kabardin People's Congress. A resident of Prokhladny since 1965, he still felt ill at ease among his Cossack neighbors.

He was there, at the Cossack headquarters, self-invited, apparently with the aim of contradicting the two atamans as subtly as the circumstances would allow. Consequently he would scold the Cossack in one sentence and then pretend that he had spoken only of the past and that none of the Cossacks present had been remotely involved. Gradually I understood that he was talking to me tongue-in-cheek. "There were many scoundrels, if you'll excuse the expression, among the Cossacks at the time their communities were restored," Shaoyev recalled. "But fortunately, the situation has improved, thanks to the previous ataman and particularly thanks to Shevtsov. You see, in 1992 I attended the Cossack *krug* [assembly], and I came across a man there whom I once had barred from membership in the Communist Party because I knew him to be a thief. There were many of his kind there, troublemakers."

What kind of trouble? I wondered.

"You know about the problems that arose last century, don't you? It was in that assembly that I heard for the first time talk about the creation of a Cossack state."

But why would a "Cossack state" have been a threat to you?

"Everything that I told you should be understood in context," Shaoyev replied. "You know that the Kabardins fought for Russia as valiantly as the Cossacks, if not more so. As early as 1904, we had a Kabardin battalion fighting as part of the czarist army against Japan, and they proved themselves to be heroes. Just count the medals they were awarded, and compare them with decorations of other groups— you'll see that we are inferior to none, not even the Cossacks. And the same goes for World War I. So when I hear a Cossack talk about independence and secession from Russia, I feel slighted and embittered as a Russian patriot."

The exchange grew surrealistic, as the Cossacks were squirming in their chairs. One did not need much imagination to guess what kind of thoughts were running through their minds while the impertinent native was questioning their Russian patriotism in the presence of a foreigner.

Their patriotism! Only half an hour earlier, Ataman Dyerbaba had quoted to me Tolstoy's words, "The Cossacks made Russia." Made it for what? So their descendants would have to tolerate this insolence, in their own community, coming from a highlander? In other parts of the world, allegations lighter than the ones Shaoyev had just made would have met with bitter recrimination. But the Cossacks just gritted their teeth and kept silent, at least for the moment.

I asked Shaoyev how he felt about Cossack revival. "That depends what you mean by revival," he snapped back. "It is clear that there is no need to go back to the last century, to the time of the Caucasian War. But if by 'revival' you mean that Cossacks should be free to wear their national dress, then yes, by all means. Or if they want to revive the Cossack language, then . . ." Shaoyev paused, his eyes shining with delight as if he were about to score a valuable point in this argument in which the metaphoric and facetious took precedence over the rational and straightforward. "Come to think of it," he said as if the thought had just occurred to him, "I do not know that a Cossack language even exists."

The causticity of Shaoyev's sarcasm became increasingly apparent. He knew only too well that a "Cossack language" did not exist. Ex-Communist that he was, and at least somewhat familiar with Leninist teachings, the gibe about language was his way to dismiss the entire notion of a "Cossack nation." The Bolshevik "scientific" approach to the national question, commissioned by Lenin and authored by Stalin as early as 1913, stipulated that "a nation is a historically evolved community of language, territory, economic life, and psychological makeup manifested in a community of culture." If only one of the components were missing, the Bolshevik doctrine would conclude that a group did not deserve to be recognized as a nation and would not be entitled to self-determination. By pretending to forget for a brief moment that the Cossacks had no language of their own and then regaining his memory, Shaoyev was leading me to the inevitable conclusion: the Cossacks are fine as a cultural curiosity, but anything beyond that is unacceptable.

"I am not concerned about the revival of traditions or the restoration of land," he insisted, "so long as they are not granted police functions. They may mean well, but it is possible that among them are bad people, cheats, who might kindle a fire should they ever have the whip in their hands."

And so ended the peaceful phase of my visit to the Cossack headquarters, because Ataman Dyerbaba could take it no longer. Avoiding Shaoyev's eyes, he pronounced slowly and angrily: "I would dare disagree with the esteemed member of the Kabardin People's Congress. Cossacks never mentioned the word 'autonomy' until the Kabardins and the Balkars began to talk about splitting the republic."

My interview came to an unexpected end as Dyerbaba and Shaoyev turned suddenly on each other, nearly oblivious to my presence, and launched into bitter recriminations over "who started it all." The spectacle was so pathetic that, my voyeuristic instincts notwithstanding, I felt great discomfort and sadness at this minor illustration of unhappy neighborliness in the Caucasus. The sun had already begun to set on

Prokhladny, and it was time to catch the last bus to Nalchik. Intercity public transportation normally ceases as darkness descends on the ever-tense Caucasus. My Russian companion and I bade a hasty good-bye and, once out the door, embarked on a fast sprint to the terminal. We did not relish the prospect of spending a night in Prokhladny.

We were about to board the bus when a hand was laid on my shoulder and a familiar voice greeted us. "I am sorry I could not have offered you a ride to the terminal," said the voice. "You left in such a haste." Sufaddin Shaoyev was standing there, smiling. "It is too bad your Cossack hosts offered you no real hospitality," he went on. "This is not our way in the Caucasus. May I take you to dinner now? I cannot let you leave on an empty stomach."

What a final grand gesture of derision toward the Cossacks, I thought, too stunned to resist. It was as though the Kabardin had written the entire day's script for us, topping it with this theatrical climax at the dusty, crowded bus terminal, where the hungry and tired visitors would be filled with gratitude for the generosity displayed by this adherent to ancient highland etiquette. If a script it was, then the Cossack atamans had been cast perfectly, or perhaps deliberately imperfectly, to make sure that they stepped into the trap at the very end of the day, sufficiently annoyed so as to fail in their duties as hosts. I imagined the Kabardin licking his lips with great satisfaction as the cranky Cossacks opened the way for him to further my education on matters of right and wrong in the Caucasus.

Or perhaps there was nothing at all to that little incident but the sincere expression of a highlander's tradition.

For the duration of the long meal that ensued, as bowls of fresh Caucasian vegetables were served and Russian vodka was poured in abundance (being constantly cajoled to "drink, drink!" in the course of a meal became my most enduring nightmare in the Caucasus), Sufaddin Shaoyev presented to us his credentials as a Circassian nationalist.

"I'll tell you why the Cossacks are here," he said, chewing on a chicken wing. "Do you remember what Hitler promised his SS fighters, once the battle was won in the East? That he would grant them land to settle on. This is exactly what the czar promised the Cossacks—'Win the Caucasus for me, and I will settle you on the land you grab.' He did!

"You must realize that we are not like Indians in America, who were totally outside of the system at the time of their great loss. Our case is different. We were closely involved with the growth of the Russian state for centuries. Kabardins were counted among the first *boyars* [aristocrats] in Moscow. Circassians reached Khiva [the ancient Central Asian principality occupied by Russia in the late nineteenth century, now part of Uzbekistan]. They were the first ones who explored the Caspian Sea. Kabardins were Russia's first governors in the first cities Russia founded in Siberia [in the sixteenth and seventeenth centuries], Irkutsk, Tobolsk, and others.

"When, in 1714, Peter the Great introduced his military table of ranks, his first general was a Kabardin, Kulihulo Cherkassky. You can see him in Repin's famous painting, the one showing Peter the Great in the company of his *boyars*. Look at it carefully—you'll see that they are all clean-shaven save for one who is bearded. That is the Kabardin prince, the only one Peter allowed the privilege of facial hair.*

"So we do not consider ourselves, nor should we be considered, the vanquished party, the one which should be condescended to. We are equal partners in the Russian state and ought to be treated accordingly.

"Before the [Bolshevik] Revolution, we, the Kabardins, dominated the entire North Caucasus. General Yermolov wrote to the czar, 'If we bring the Kabardins under our rule, the rest will follow suit.' And they did. They shed our blood as though it was water."

And yet, I remarked, your bad memories do not seem to shape your attitude toward Russia, nothing like the angry Chechens.

"Yes, that is quite true. One reason is that they suffered much more recently, at the time of their deportation, in 1944."

Clearly, I suggested, other Caucasian nations do not share in the militancy of the Chechens.

"That is true," he said. "It doesn't mean we would never fight. If a general Caucasian war were waged against all the mountaineers, we would surely fight. But it is true that we and the rest of the mountaineers are different from the Chechens. Let me illustrate. Suppose there are two Kabardins in Central Asia, or Siberia, and they are surrounded by twenty hostile Russians. They will surrender. But if the two were Chechens, they would fight—you bet they would.

---

* In 1698, upon returning from his study tour in West Europe, Peter the Great forcibly shaved with his own hands his leading courtiers, including princes, generals, and priests. He spared only three, among them Prince Mikhail Cherkassky, whose princely family hailed from Kabarda. The first of the Cherkassky line was Khorosay, a nephew of a great prince of Kabarda, a father-in-law of Czar Ivan the Terrible. Khorosay moved to Moscow in 1578 and was immediately baptized as Boris. The fully Russified and Christianized Cherkasskys served various czars with distinction as governors, military commanders, and court officials. One was cruelly beheaded by a Central Asian ruler when he tried to carry the Russian imperial torch to the heart of an old Muslim civilization. The success, as it were, of the Cherkasskys reflected an important trait of Russian colonialism, unthinkable in British colonialism: the willingness to fully integrate the colonized peoples, so long as they were willing to completely shed their former identities. Many Caucasian aristocrats found their way to the upper echelons of Russian nobility. Russianness was defined never as a state of genes but as a state of mind.

"But please remember, and please remind Americans, that we had our share of suffering. Few nations suffered as much as we did during Soviet rule. Although we were never deported, our gene pool was destroyed. We had so many princes, some called us 'a nation of princes,' and the entire princely class was decimated, the entire leadership of the nation! Now that Russia has become free, people claim to be descendants of the princes. But this is nonsense."

Shaoyev raised his voice. "The descendants of slaves now claim to be princes!" He uttered the words with so much contempt that they came out almost in a whistle. He rose up, a glass of local cognac in his hand, and exclaimed solemnly, "Our past is dark and heroic. It is our sacred duty to restore our historical memory and the memory of our forefathers. And we thank you, from the bottom of our heart, for traveling such a distance to listen to us."

"THE BRAVEST TROOPS
IN THE UNIVERSE"

Circassians have not been listened to very often this century. Theirs may be the least told story of any major nation under Soviet and Russian rule. They do not have large diasporas in the West to present their case. They offered no strategic temptation to cold war strategists. And they ranked very low on a Western table of "captive nations," not much more than folkloristic curiosities.

That is a far cry from the great romantic halo that surrounded their name in the nineteenth century, when tales of their heroism intrigued Westerners—and even gave rise to a local version of Lawrence of Arabia, a young Scot by the name of David Urquhart, who was an early player of the famous Great Game to check Russia's advance into Asia and the Middle East. Urquhart, a quintessential adventurer and trailblazer of the imperialist age, came close to kindling a war between Britain and Russia, when the Russian navy under Admiral Lazarev intercepted a British ship in the Black Sea whose cargo consisted of arms and ammunition to the Circassians.

Lord Palmerston, then British foreign secretary and one of the greatest statesmen of the imperial era, figured that the freedom of Circassia was not worth dying for. He incurred the wrath of a close Urquhart collaborator and fellow imperial romantic, one Edmund Spencer, who exclaimed in a tone befitting European arguments over appeasement of dictators in the 1930s: "It would appear, indeed as if the whole of Europe at the present moment were governed by statesmen either supine, negligent, or incompetent; or as if they were afraid, by raising the voice of censure, they would draw down upon themselves a frown from the despot of the north."

The West, Spencer said, should be ready "to organize and equip two hundred thousands of *the bravest troops in the universe* [the Circassian, that is], capable of carrying fire and sword . . . to the very gates of Moscow . . . and the result would probably be, the retreat of Russia to her own snowy steppes, and the establishment of European peace on a foundation at once solid and durable."

Palmerston may well have come to regret his earlier diffidence. Twenty years later, as prime minister, he dispatched a British expeditionary force to Crimea, to check Russia's expansion to the south. At that time, he wrote his own foreign secretary, "The best and most effectual security for the future peace of Europe would be the severance from Russia of some of the frontier territories acquired by her in later times, Georgia, *Circassia*, the Crimea, Bessarabia, Poland and Finland." He was too late, in that such a grand design would have required either the total defeat of Russia or an implosion of the Russian state. Such an implosion occurred twice in the twentieth century, in 1917 and 1991, following which Russia lost all the acquisitions named by Palmerston, save for one: the Circassian lands. Apparently, for the Circassians it was either the 1830s—or never.

A few years after the Urquhart experiment had foundered, an equally romantic German made his way to the Northwest Caucasus, ever ready to idealize the noble savage. At the time of his visit, in the 1840s, the Caucasian War had another twenty years to go, and the German scholar, Dr. Moritz Wagner, was clearly looking heroism in the eye.

His first stop was the city of Yekaterinodar, on the Kuban River, quite literally the last outpost of Russian civilization. The opposite bank of the Kuban was Circassian land (now part of the semi-autonomous republic known in Russian as Adygeiya). Yekaterinodar, founded in 1793, was named in honor of Empress Catherine the Great. Its sole goal at that time was to serve as a launching pad for the war against the various Circassian tribes, particularly the Shapsug.

For sixty-four years, Yekaterinodar was a "military town," in a state of perpetual combat readiness, populated mostly by Cossacks. In the city's main marketplace, Dr. Wagner chanced upon a Shapsug tribal chief. The German was left breathless, as he later reported:

I stood some time rooted to the ground before the Shapsug, so powerful was the impression he made upon me. . . . The Shapsug chief appeared quite conscious of his splendid appearance. . . . His uncommonly spare figure, his beautiful foot, the spirit, and chivalrous character of all his movements, the richness of his dress and the splendour of his arms contrasted very favorably with the muscular, but somewhat uncouth make, and the ugly wooly winter clothing of the [Cossacks]. Nor was the contrast less striking between the noble profile of his face, and his magnificent eyes, and the beautiful, well fed, but entirely vacant and unmeaning countenances of his opponents on the right bank of the Kuban.

By the assistance of the Cossacks, who knew the Adyghe language, I succeeded in making the acquaintance of the Caucasian knight, and in entering into a conversation with him. . . . He readily allowed me to examine his beautiful arms, and I showed him my double-barrelled fowling piece. . . . How well he looked, the chivalrous mountaineer! How his eagle eyes flashed!

Dr. Wagner, an avid traveler to the East, was known for his keen eye for male beauty in the distant lands he reached and for his frankness in discussing his observations—which was uncommon in a Europe far less tolerant of such indiscretions than it might be today.

Wagner was not the only traveler in the last millennium who took a note of Circassian good looks. The Genovese traveler Interiano, in the fourteenth century, praised Circassian men as "generally well-shaped and handsome, among whom are to be found figures of uncommon symmetry." His enthusiasm for women was confined to their excellence in "all the duties of hospitality with the most scrupulous attention." Even earlier, the Arab geographer Mas'udi was boundless in adulation of Circassian physique: "There is no nation of purer complexion, of fairer colouring, of more handsome men and more beautiful women, more stately, with narrower waists, with shapelier buttocks, more elegant and . . . comelier than this nation."

Yekaterinodar, where Dr. Wagner fell for Shapsug beauty, is now the capital city of one of Russia's largest and potentially richest provinces, indeed one of the world's leading breadbaskets. The city, still boasting a large Cossack community, has long shed its imperial title and is now called Krasnodar. Accordingly, the province is Krasnodar Krai. Lazarevskoe belongs to the *krai*, but if one were to follow in the footsteps of Dr. Wagner, one would no longer chance upon handsome Shapsug chiefs in Krasnodar's marketplace, or anywhere else, for that matter. Their nation now consists of a handful of villages and is not even recognized as an ethnic entity by the Russian census bureau.

I was waiting for the Shapsug leaders to show up at the Shapsug cultural center in Lazarevskoe's Palace of Culture. The Soviet era generated a large pool of comically overstated terms, and "palace" was a distinct favorite. Hence almost every Soviet town could boast a host of "palaces," one for youth, another for sports, and a third for culture. Lazarevskoe's was no more palatial than any I had seen elsewhere. While I was waiting, the office began to fill with young members of the dancing ensemble, men and women in their late teens and early twenties. They were the residents of six Shapsug villages in the Lazarevskoe district. They all spoke Shapsug as their first language. "Yes, we think primarily in Shapsug,"said one of them, a black-haired man of nineteen who seemed less timid than his friends. By thinking in Shapsug, they did not represent the majority of their peers.

What happened to your nation? I asked him.

"After they were expelled, half of them drowned in the sea," he said in a monotonous voice, which, I had noticed, is how people speak in the Caucasus, even when they discuss the gravest tragedies.

The office served not only as a meeting place but also as a dressing room, so there they changed into their national costumes. Aslan, the impresario, then led them to the Palace of Culture stage, where his accordion set the tone and they started whirling. Their repertoire was quite common: variations of the *lezginka*, the Caucasus's most typical dance, performed (and claimed as an exclusive part of their national heritage) by Georgians, Daghestanis, Chechens, Circassians, and even Cossacks.

And so the descendants of the Shapsug chief have been reduced to a harmless cultural minority, performing exotic dances on public holidays. The Shapsug leader Majeed Chechukh showed me an official brochure, distributed among vacationers, to introduce them to Lazarevskoe's history. "It is a very pretty *buklet*," he said, using a Russified form of the English word *booklet*. "It tells its readers that for many hundreds of years, this region has been populated by Greeks, Armenians, Turks—yet not one word about Adyghe or Shapsug. Moreover, it includes a photo of an Adyghe in his national costume, and the caption reads: 'These are images of the people who once lived here.' That's it! These people are not even named!"

The unnamed could claim the distinction of being the first "ethnically cleansed" nation of the modern era. Adolf Hitler is said to have invoked the genocidal deportation of the Armenians by way of impressing upon his skeptical generals, on the eve of World War II, the shortness of the world's memory of mass atrocities. He might as well have spoken of the Adyghe/Circassians, who only seventy-five years earlier were hurried into waiting Turkish boats, as Russia was quickly ridding itself of up to 1.5 million of them.

Dr. Paul Henze, for many years almost the only American scholar who paid any attention to the plight of the small Caucasian nations, called this episode "one of the greatest mass movements of population in modern history." Yet it is virtually unknown to the outside world and little known even to Russians. Admiral Lazarev's name, currently adorning a mighty battleship in the Baltic Sea, is rarely if ever associated with the ending of nations. Kitchener and Livingstone he might have been, but the admiral also earned the right to be compared with mass exterminators of indigenous peoples, from the Spanish Cortés and Pizarro to America's Custer. Indeed, so close is the resemblance between the treatment of native peoples by Russia and by the United States that in the course of the nineteenth century, Russians regularly compared Circassians with American Indians. George Leighton Ditson, an American traveler, no friend of the Circassians, arrived in the Caucasus in the 1840s, when the Great Caucasian War was in full swing. He later reported a conversation he had with a Russian prince, who told him:

> The Circassians are just like your American Indians—as untamable and uncivilized—and . . . owing to their natural energy and character, extermination only would keep them quiet, or . . . if they came under Russian rule, the only safe policy would be to employ their wild and warlike tastes against others.

Dr. Wagner, the German traveler, heard similar views a few years later and quoted a Russian interlocutor as saying:

> It is a prevalent opinion among the Russians and Cossacks, that a war of extermination should be waged against the Circassians, because these people are perfectly incapable of appreciating gentleness, friendship and benefits conferred, are unsusceptible of any generous emotion, and because it is impossible to civilize them.

This view was not shared by their contemporary, the British traveler Edmund Spencer, who wrote a few years earlier that the Shapsug "as well as the other Circassian tribes among whom I mingled, are lively, communicative, polite, and officious, cleanly in their houses and persons."

The notion that extermination is a deserving punishment for graceless and ill-mannered natives, to be meted out by graceful and well-mannered colonizers, would not have sounded all that improbable even to a well-educated person of the nineteenth century. By the end of a century otherwise perceived as an epoch of progress and enlightenment, the view recorded by Wagner had become rather common among apologists of colonialism.

Peter Gay, the astute historian of nineteenth-century European culture, describes this process as the invention of "alibis for aggression." In
The Cultivation of Hatred, Gay argues that the "history of nineteenth-
century aggression is partly a history of pathology, and the share of
pathology among enthusiastic racist colonizers was impressive. Interestingly enough, what made some of the freebooters angriest at the
indigenous tribes in their path was 'insolence.'"

The evolution of Russian attitudes toward indigenous peoples is discussed elsewhere in this book. Suffice it to say that nowhere have Russian policies scored a bigger success than with the western Circassian
tribes. The eastern tribes—the Kabardins, for example—were luckier
and probably more politically adept, which is why there are quite a few
of them left. Their good fortune also placed them safely distant from
the sea. The littoral tribes, however, had to go because their presence
was an invitation for enemies to use them for subversive purposes, or so
Russia's generals reasoned.

Of all the littoral tribes, the saddest fate befell the Ubykh, relatives of
the Shapsug, whose record of military resistance to the Russians was
one of the most impressive. The entire Ubykh people have left their
ancestral lands without a trace, but about ninety years were necessary to
remove them completely from the face of the earth. Forty years ago, a
Norwegian scholar found only sixteen people in Turkey who still spoke
Ubykh. If genocide is to be measured not only by the perpetrators'
stated goals but by the results as well, then there is little doubt that the
Ubykh deserve a place of honor in any Holocaust museum.

There are still about one million people in Russia who could fall
under the historical definition of "Circassians," and the system inherited
from the Soviet Union subdivides them into three different groups,
each of which has its own national language. The divergence among the
languages is significant but probably less so than that which divides the
various dialects of Italy and Germany. Modern Italian and German are
new creations, the result of the imposition of one dialect over the others. Neither country could have been amalgamated into a unitary state
without the emergence of a common written language. The perpetua-
tion of linguistic divergence among the Circassians has clearly under-
mined any attempt to create a unified Circassian nation.

If the million Circassians wrote only one language, they might now
be closer to forming a "major nation." Absent that, their national languages have become marginalized. Collectively they amount to very
little, their population is spread thin among three autonomous

republics, and in each republic they are classified as a different nationality. Russian is their main instrument of communication, their only
means of progress and enlightenment.

Zaur Naloyev, the prominent Kabardin intellectual, has been one of
the loudest champions of Circassian revival. He was a founder of
Adyghe Khassa, the organization whose Shapsug branch chairman I
went to see in Lazarevskoe. Khassa strove to bring under its wings the
Circassian population of the entire world. As the Soviet sun was setting
in the late 1980s, a magnitude of hopes inspired the Circassian intelligentsia. They thought they might be able to rise from the ashes of the
empire and resume a collective national identity. Naloyev is equally a
testimony to their hopes and to the scope of disillusionment. He told
me the following story about the linguistic evolution of his grandson:

"When a child was born to my son, I forbade anyone from speaking
to him in Russian or Ossetian or any other language but Kabardin.
When I first enrolled him at the kindergarten, he spoke only Kabardin.
By the time he finished kindergarten, he spoke a perfect Russian. Now
he speaks both. This boy attempts to write novels. When he brought
me his first manuscript, I had to bite my tongue. It was a catastrophe for
me. The manuscript was written in Russian, in its entirety. In other
words, Nalchik has become a factory in which our children are turned
into Russians.

"Russian is a marvelous language. We love it. But when it drives away
our own language, it becomes our mortal enemy. This is a paradox, but
we cannot help it. And this is a tragedy, not only for the Kabardins but
for the entire human race. All languages, not only the major ones, are
universal treasures. I am delighted that humans have come to recognize
the importance of protecting endangered species among the plants and
the insects and the animals. I had a dream that one day humanity would
be wise enough to defend endangered species among languages as well.
And I am profoundly disappointed."

"GRANDPA, KHASSA WILL KILL US ALL!"

There are threshold years in history in which whole continents seem to be in flux: no foundation seems unshakable, and no climax unlikely. Such was 1789 in Western Europe, and such were 1848 and 1918 in Central Europe. Such was 1991 all over the landmass that once constituted the Russian and Soviet empires.

Many ethnic groups, from China's border to the Baltic Sea, managed to rise from virtual oblivion, reassert their identities, and pursue their destinies—which had hitherto seemed so inexorably tied with Russia's. Yet the Circassians did not share in this post-Soviet Springtime of Nations. What was the reason? Was it a failure of collective will on their part? Was it the thoroughness of their assimilation into Russia? Was it the inability to articulate a credible common cause, one that would not be too ambitious yet not too modest to inspire?

Zaur Naloyev, the prominent Kabardin nationalist, tried very hard to awaken his people's consciousness. Adyghe Khassa convoked rallies, organized processions, published newspapers—and kept running into the repressive Soviet-era political machine, which after the fall of the Soviet Union was only cosmetically changed and never loosened its grip on the levers of power. Post-Soviet Kabardino-Balkaria is the same backwater satrapy that its Soviet predecessor was, with almost as little democracy.

Naloyev recalled for me at great length the methods and the "tricks" employed by the Kabardin-Balkar authorities against Khassa. One rally against the war in Chechnya, he said, was violently suppressed by the local security forces.

"It was a routine rally we used to call every Sunday. It was mid-winter, February 1996. All of a sudden, three columns of *militsionery* [policemen] stormed the gathering. All of them were heavily armed with submachine guns, truncheons, and shields. They beat people up indiscriminately—elderly men, women, and youth.

"I presided over the rally. A policeman punched his fist against my chest. I blacked out and fell down on the asphalt. At that very moment the same policeman stepped over me." Naloyev, in his late sixties, pointed to his lower abdomen and shoulders to show me the spread of the policeman's legs. "Then they pulled me by the hands and threw me into a waiting police van. There I met my Khassa colleagues, about thirty of them. We were driven to a detention center, and each of us was locked up in an isolated cell. We spent only a few hours there, but that was the essence of official intimidation. The authorities did their utmost to instill fear. Activists were fired from their jobs, while others were refused various commodities such as building material for their homes.

"You see, this republic is democratic only in form. Otherwise, a despotic regime is in charge, entirely opposed to our national revival, even though the president is Kabardin. In terms of the governing system, little has changed here. If anything, the change has been for the worse, because now all power resides in the hands of a single individual, the republican president. And his own power emanates from the president of Russia. There is no one below and no one in the middle. Just two despots, the big one in Moscow, and the small one in Nalchik. Under such circumstances, who can accomplish anything for the nation?"

In all fairness to President Valery Kokov, who is indeed a former Communist boss with little patience for democratic niceties, quite a few of his subjects believe that his iron grip saved the republic from a fate similar to that of Chechnya. With the majority of the people deeply skeptical about the virtues of individual freedoms and political participation, "law and order" are the magic words, and law and order have been delivered, at least compared with their complete collapse in nearby Chechnya. A flood of Chechen refugees served to remind Nalchik's residents that they were relatively fortunate to escape the post-Soviet turmoil with only a few bruises—the few that were inflicted upon the demonized Khassa.

"So demonized were we"—Naloyev sighed—"that in 1990, when we were at the zenith of our influence, the authorities spread rumors that we were planning a pogrom against Russians and Balkars." Naloyev gestured with his hands, mimicking a knife's cutting motion. "People were warned to stay home, not risk going outside lest Khassa thugs would knife them. My own grandson came home from school, breathless and excited, and told me, 'Dyedushka, don't leave home tomorrow, Khassa is going to kill all of us.' But how do you know that? I asked him. 'The teacher told us that, in class,' the little boy replied."

The guilt of politicians aside, Naloyev pins most of the blame for the Circassian failure on the loss of national characteristics. "Let me tell you," he sighed, "the Circassians used to be the most militant of all Caucasians. But they lost their old mentality after the Caucasian War, and after so many of them had been resettled in Turkey. Then came the Bolshevik Revolution, the civil war, Stalin's repression. . . . That is why it is so difficult to raise the masses to any public cause."

In the Shapsug case, one need not look much farther for an explanation. While there are, after all, about 450,000 Kabardins, there are only 9,000 Shapsug. The remnants of this formerly mighty tribe cannot match the ferocity of the Chechens, or the political clout of the Armenians, or the sheer numbers of the Azeris. In the early 1990s, when the Shapsug raised their voices in a demand for autonomy, their would-be thunder resembled a whimper.

"We held a congress of the Shapsug people here," the teacher-turned-leader Majeed Chechukh told me in Lazarevskoe, "and we argued that our right for rehabilitation was as good as anyone's. Opponents told us, 'But how can you demand an autonomy, when you make up a bare one-tenth of the population in the region you want to make autonomous?' We responded that there are 'national regions' within Russia, where the benefiting nations make up less than five percent of the population. Of Russia's nineteen autonomous republics, only in one [Chechnya] does an indigenous nation form an absolute majority.

"You see, the way critics approach our demand for autonomy is entirely erroneous. We do not seek to impose a dictatorship of a minority. We do not even seek a majority in any of the autonomous region's institutions. We just seek representation. We want to make sure that our language is taught at school and our culture does not perish. Only a Shapsug representative would ever bother to pose a question about it. We are virtually disenfranchised.

"When the law on elections was being drafted, we implored the Duma [Russia's federal parliament] and the *krai* [provincial authorities] to reserve at least one seat for the Shapsug, so we would have our voice. They refused us. We only desire what our Shapsug brothers have obtained for themselves in Israel.*

* Chechukh was referring to the tiny Circassian community in Israel, about 3,000 strong, that enjoys relative prosperity and is allowed to run its own school—the only one anywhere in which Shapsug is the main instrument of education.

"And do you know what the response was? A slanderous campaign was unleashed against us. A federal deputy from Sochi [the bigger coastal city south of Lazarevskoe] accused us of plotting to secede from Russia. The head of the *krai* administration [equivalent to a state governor] told the official newspaper that we aspired to join hands with Chechnya, leave Russia, and unite with Turkey."* Chechukh smiled. "Just imagine the absurdity of this!" (The governor at that time was Nikolai Yegorov, a self-styled expert on Caucasian affairs, Russia's former minister of nationalities, and an architect of the disastrous war in Chechnya.)

My conversation with Chechukh took place in a dimly lit office in Lazarevskoe's Palace of Culture. The Palace was gray, uninspiring and dilapidated, yet it offered the six ethnic communities living in Lazarevskoe space in which to exercise their right to national cultural expression, under the watchful eye of a young Armenian who introduced himself to me with pronounced pomposity as "Lazarevskoe's minister of education," no less. He insisted on showing me around, making sure that I would not be "too narrowly focused on a single group." Thus I was led into the Russian national center, where I was acquainted with a balalaika-like musical instrument called *gusli*, which, I was told, was "the oldest in the entire Caucasus."

Having a center for Russian national culture in Lazarevskoe was of course farcical, analogous to having a center for the promotion of the English language in, say, Charleston, South Carolina. Yet by pretending that the survival of Russian culture and that of the Shapsug required exactly the same degree of attention and the same allocation of funds, the local government was dodging the issue, which was whether an indigenous nation, though reduced to a tiny minority, deserved *special* rights. Paradoxically, the Soviet Union had been more inclined than the new Russia to recognize, if only nominally, the concept of special rights.

In the Shapsug case, "special rights" consisted not of raising an army or receiving foreign ambassadors, but primarily of cultivating the Shapsug language in school curricula. "Nowadays local schools give three hours a week to the study of English, and three hours to the study of Shapsug, as though they were on equal footing, the foreign language and the native language," said Aslanbi Khusht, the editor of *Shapsugia*, possibly the only Shapsug newspaper in the world, written mostly in Russian. "On top of that, English is mandatory and Shapsug is voluntary. Russian

---

* Turkey often plays a bogeyman role in Russian ethnic politics, a lasting legacy of the czarist era, when Russia fought numerous wars with the Ottoman Empire over control of the Black Sea region.

is taught twelve hours a week. We accept that. We are citizens of Russia, Russian is the language of the land, we have never refused to study it. But please give us a fair chance to survive as a nation. Today 40 percent of our children cannot speak Shapsug!" Not even his own son, the editor added with a sad smile, and then went on:

"People who oppose our autonomy warn that we are the likes of Chechnya's 'bandits,' just because we refuse to concede complete defeat, recognize our worthlessness within the broad context of Russia's life, and get off the stage once and for all. But look what we are asking for—nothing more than a token of goodwill.

"Now, I'll tell you what else our critics say, the ones who pretend that our autonomy would endanger the well-being of the non-Shapsug majority. They say, 'If you want autonomy, you should propose a referendum in the districts for which you want the autonomy. This is the law of the land, the Duma has passed legislation to that effect. You have the legal route—by all means pursue it, and if you win the referendum, you get your autonomy.

"But they are not serious. They know exactly what will happen in the referendum—our opponents will agitate the non-Shapsug voters, they will use scare-mongering tactics, will tell people that we are dangerous separatists who wish to destroy Russia, and the results can be taken for granted. We will lose.

"The question is why a non-Shapsug should ever be given the right to decide whether the Shapsug nation deserves to survive. This is a matter for us to decide, not for people who settled here after we had been vanquished and uprooted."

Chechukh seconded him. "Remember," he said very quietly, almost inaudibly, "we did not invite the Russians to come here and dispossess us in the first place. But we do not ask anyone to leave. We do not wish to establish a Shapsug state. We just want to make sure that whatever has been left of us will not perish, that the aspirations of Admiral Lazarev will not finally carry the day."

He paused, then added as in an afterthought, "Do you think that what happened here with Lazarev's statue would have ever happened if we had a Shapsug region? I need to explain it to you again—it is enough that such a region be established. The act of establishment will already constitute recognition. We only want the fact to be acknowledged that this land had not been empty prior to Lazarev's arrival, as many Russians believe. Just imagine how many of us would be living here today if our ancestors had not been forced into exile. There were at least half a million of us 135 years ago. There would be millions, many millions, nowadays. There is no doubt about that. Instead, a handful of us are struggling to breathe—and are told that we should first seek somebody else's consent before we are provided the oxygen.

"The question of our survival is not a local question, it is a universal question. Ours is not the only indigenous nation that wars and persecution have reduced to a minority in its own land.

"You see, the bells toll not only for us, but for every single small nation in the world."

As my train was leaving the Lazarevskoe terminal, heading southward to Sochi, I spotted a newspaper announcing the cessation of hostilities in the Chechen war, at the other end of the Caucasus. A triumphant Chechen nation had finally emerged independent, at an enormous cost in human life, with its major cities and towns in ruins. (Or so one would have believed in late 1996, before a cycle of follies undid the Chechen victory, three years later.) Compared with the Chechen act of heroic defiance, the Shapsug attempt on Admiral Lazarev's nose had a comic flavor to it. While present-day Chechens can proudly claim to be on a par with their fearless ancestors, the Shapsug I met had little to do with the startlingly powerful Shapsug chief whom Moritz Wagner had met in Yekaterinodar's marketplace more than 150 years ago. And yet with their valor of yore gone, perhaps the Shapsug have found a great new asset: a sense of humor. Maybe their last battle will be won not by a crazed giant, dancing with swords, but by a good soldier named Schweik, the great antihero of Czech literature who did not think much of dying in full bloom. And even if not, I hope a future chronicler will remember the final sad smile of the Shapsug.

THE PEOPLES OF DAGHESTAN

KALMYKIA

RUSSIAN FEDERATION

NOGAY

• Kizlyar

CHECHENS

• Khasavyurt

CHECHNYA

KUMYKS

Makhachkala

Tarki

DARGINS

AVARS

DAGHESTAN

LAKS

• Ghazi-Ghumuq

AZERIS

Derbent

AGUL

TABASARANS

CAUCASUS MOUNTAINS

GEORGIA

RUTUL

LEZGINS

Quba

• Kryz

Khynalug •

Caspian Sea

N

o Miles 50
o Kilometers 50

AZERBAIJAN

© 2000 Jeffrey L. Ward

Part II

THEIR
SQUARE INCH
IN THE SUN

"So tell me, old man, where is this Daghestan of yours?"
"It is above and below an eagle's wing."
DAGHESTANI TALE

THE TALE OF TWO REDEEMERS

Salau Aliyev would be king. He is a curly-haired man with a prominent square chin, a slightly ironic smile, and a nose so huge and curled that it seems more a proboscis as it nearly touches his upper lip.

Aliyev flirts passionately with the past. There are many layers to this past. His professorial demeanor compels him to peel them off carefully, and a hint of naughtiness makes his otherwise pompous discourse a bit more agreeable. And yet there are moments in which he reaches for such historical heights that his eyes turn misty and the listener's mind, a bit dizzy.

If he had his way, he might bring back to life a mighty empire that dominated the Caspian Sea over a millennium ago, or at least a diluted version of it—a military principality that stood up to foreign invaders for centuries until its incorporation into Russia in the nineteenth century. But

Salau Aliyev would be a king.

this erstwhile professor of linguistics has a more immediate goal, menacing enough to make his critics refer to him as "that madman": he would like to carve out a territory for his small nation of about 300,000 people and establish a rump state. For now he would call it "autonomous *okrug*" (Russian for "district"), but he strongly implies that that would be only the beginning. Still, it would be an essential beginning, because short of autonomy, his people, the Kumyks, co-dwellers with many others in a small province of the Russian Federation named Daghestan, might suffer an irreversible catastrophe, he fears. He turns somber, waves his index finger at me, and pronounces the words slowly: "We will cease to exist."

Similar are the words, if not the gestures, of Gadzhi Abduragimov, a soft-spoken electrophysicist who has spent a lifetime teaching science to Daghestani students. He has a broad smile, reinforced by a long and bushy mustache that, with the shining hairless pate of his scalp, gives him an almost mischievous aura. But a stranger had better not mistake this outward gentility for mellowness. At sixty, Professor Abduragimov is a man with a mission, who, like Salau Aliyev, yearns constantly for a murky past. There was a time, he says, in which his people, the Lezgins, lorded over half of the Caucasus and the Caspian Sea—and yet at present, dispossessed and underprivileged, they are no longer sure of survival.

The Lezgins are one of the many nations of Daghestan, which has the official status of an "autonomous republic" of the Russian Federation.* It is unlike any other part of Russia—indeed, few parallels could be produced anywhere. Thirty-odd nations, speaking some of the world's most exotic languages and heirs to some of the planet's oldest surviving traditions, are all bundled together in one province about half the size of Virginia—possibly the highest density of nationalities per square mile of any territory in the world.

Can such a political entity continue to exist in an era of general disintegration? *Should* it exist, when the clamor of peoples, regardless of size, to dissolve partnerships and make it on their own has engulfed states across the full length of the Eurasian landmass? How could a Daghestan succeed where the Soviet Union, Yugoslavia, and Czechoslovakia have all failed?

Yet tiny, obscure Daghestan, known to few Westerners, might well offer the outside world a useful lesson in harmony and mutual tol-

---

* There are twenty-one "autonomous republics" in Russia, alongside fifty-one *oblasts* (regions), one "autonomous region," ten "autonomous districts" (*okrug*), and six territories (*krai*), all of which are considered equal constituents of the federation. The difference between an "autonomous republic" and the other forms is that republican status is conferred on ethnic groups, whereas "regions" and "districts" are, in most cases, only territorial divisions more akin to American states or German *Länder*.

Gadzhi Abduragimov, a reclaimer of the Lezgin past

erance. Perhaps here, where Europe ends and Asia begins, we will see the dawn of a new era. It would be a welcome challenge to our pessimistic perception of human nature.

In its declining days, the old Soviet Union was metaphorically transformed into a huge terminal, which nations big and small were struggling to leave, either in pursuit of complete independence, or at least in the hope of redefining their status within the new Russian state. At that time, neither Aliyev's Kumyks nor Abduragimov's Lezgins managed to come aboard. The hub, where tickets used to be available in every conceivable direction, is practically closed, the passengers having all but reached their destinations. Yet the two professors are still waiting on the platform.

These two custodians of their nations' cause have one major grievance in common: their peoples were cheated out of their patrimony, their ancestral land has been taken away from them, and they have been left helpless minorities in their own homes. They are told that it is too late now, that one cannot turn back the wheel of history, that it is time to grow up. But they are determined to reclaim their square inch in the sun, even if in doing so they shake the prevailing order and call into question the existence of Daghestan, the validity of international borders, and perhaps the entire delicate equilibrium of the Russian Federation.

With little stake in the status quo, they illustrate the inflammable potential of Daghestan's tinderbox. Is Daghestan too obscure and too distant to get the attention of the overloaded Western mind as a fresh conflagration point? Well, it is no more obscure than Bosnia and Rwanda were before calamity struck. In any event, experience tells us that "obscurity" is a bad reason for turning our eyes away.

Mixed signals are coming from Daghestan. The republic is experiencing minitremors, which may well be only aftershocks to the main seismic event—the war in neighboring Chechnya, where Russia has attempted, twice in five years, to reassert control. If so, the tremors are likely to diminish both in force and in frequency. And yet they may also indicate how acutely fragile the land surface is, how volcanically active, and how unlikely it is to stay dormant for long.

My mission here is not to play the Cassandra, but rather to relate the stories of these small nations that are hanging by a thread, unsure whether a generation hence they will still have a discernible identity, a collective will, a historical memory, and a viable language. In face of the onslaught of modernity, will they still be deserving of the title "nation"?

For many centuries, this land, to fascinated outsiders, has been synonymous with the improbable survival of some of the tiniest nations on earth. It will be a sad twist of fate if it one day becomes those nations' burial ground. All of us will be so much the poorer, our civilization closer to a dull uniformity, our imagination less elaborate, and our minds a bit more inclined toward the simplistic.

I was wondering about the modern mind, the one that owes so much to the simplification of language, as I listened to an eighty-six-year-old man in a remote mountain village called Khynalug, where about two thousand people speak a unique language spoken nowhere else.* "We never realized how complicated our language is," the astonishingly erect and lucid elder said, chuckling, "until some professor came by and told us." With nineteen alleged grammatical cases, Khynalug may hold a world record in complexity. Major languages arose long ago from archaic antecedents, and their simplification was no doubt a prerequisite for the spread of literacy and the emergence of art and science. And yet might we have not lost something in the process? Are we not slightly less subtle for that, our eyes slightly less penetrating?

If it had not been for its impassable terrain and the uninterrupted solitude provided by its mountains, the tribes of Daghestan would have dissolved long ago under the bayonets of conquerors and assimilators. In Daghestan, however, as the invaders were inundating the plains, people merely had to take to the summits and wait for the tide to subside. It always did—until the mid-nineteenth century, when the Russians, abetted by modern military technology, resisted the laws that had governed this land for so long.

No one, not even my two acquaintances, Aliyev and Abduragimov, would prescribe going back to the ostensibly idyllic pre-Russian time. Both men move in the Russian cultural orbit, and their scientific studies would have been unthinkable if it had not been for Russian education

---

* Khynalug is now part of Azerbaijan, but in terms of both its topography and its ethnography, it is inseparable from the North Caucasus. It is discussed further on pages 123–24 and 371–73.

and language. And yet they are consumed by the urgent need to save for posterity that which was bequeathed to them.

At the time of our meeting, Salau Aliyev was preparing for the annual convention of Tenglik ("Equality"), the organization he had founded in 1989 to advance the Kumyk cause. I called on him on a Sunday afternoon in his modest headquarters in downtown Makhachkala, the capital of Daghestan and the North Caucasus's largest metropolis. The place was bustling with activity, mostly of volunteers, who were issuing invitations and making sure that delegates arrived on time and found proper accommodation.

As for Gadzhi Abduragimov, at the time of our meeting, he had already left public life, vacated the leadership of Sadval ("Unity"), the Lezgin national movement, and shifted his energies to a quest for his people's antiquity. He had just published a massive, six-hundred-page tome, a solidly bound and well-printed volume that purported to take a thorough look at Lezgin history. But the book earned harsh reviews from professional historians, who thought that Abduragimov should have limited his academic explorations to physics and left the past to historians and archaeologists. They may have missed the point. His book was intended less to teach than to awaken the memory, and thus the identity, of up to 1.5 million Lezgins. (The estimate is his; official figures are about one-quarter that number.)

Abduragimov's point was best illustrated in the title of an article he wrote for a local newspaper (included in the book): "I, Gadzhi Abduragimov, Lezgin." That title could simply be construed as a factual statement, drawn from Abduragimov's birth certificate and "internal passport," but the portly professor intended it as an act of defiance. He was saying, in effect, that he is *still* Lezgin and *will be* Lezgin, despite the relentless attempts of three governments to assimilate his people. "We Lezgins," he wrote, "have become outcasts in our own homeland."

In mid-nineteenth century Europe, the resistance of small nations to foreign occupation and their clamor for a place in the sun induced not only fervent political activity but also an enthusiastic study of the past, real and imaginary. Eric Hobsbawm and Jacob Talmon, two of the greatest historians of European nationalism, have shown how the intellectual elites of small nations often conspired not merely to embellish the past but actually to invent it from whole cloth, resorting not only to manipulation and half-truths but to outright forgery. Small nations, struggling to survive in the shadow of mighty empires with their far richer cultures, found the notion of past glory, however poorly documented, a constant source of reassurance. It is as though the prophets of nationalism were proclaiming to the world, "We *are* because we *were*," and in so doing implying, "We would not be today if we had not been as great as we were."

My first week in Daghestan, I traveled to a little village by the Chechen border, where I was invited to break bread with the only Kumyk ever decorated as a Hero of Russia, for his role in the seizure of the Nazi Reichstag in Berlin in 1945. I visited peasants vying for scarce lands in what used to be their ancestral domain but that were now claimed by strangers. I sought religious enlightenment from a Sufi scholar in what was described to me as Russia's largest mosque. But nowhere did I get a better understanding of the urgency that Salau Aliyev felt about stemming the course of history than on top of a hill overlooking the city of Makhachkala.

The hill was the capital of the last Kumyk state and is still known by its old name, Tarki, though now it has been reduced to a suburb of the much larger Makhachkala. On the surrounding plains, as late as the 1930s, the Kumyks constituted a clear majority (60 percent, according to Aliyev). Then came Soviet ethnic engineering, which turned demography upside down. By inviting the dwellers of the mountains to come down and hop into the melting pot of the plains, the Soviets quickly rendered the Kumyks a minority, barely one-quarter of the region's population. One does not have to hate cities—I do not—to see how the sprawling metropolis below Tarki's hills became the Kumyk nation's nemesis.

AND SAD FLOWS THE SAMUR

The Lezgin nation's undoing is a river called Samur. In years gone by, it ran through Lezgin land. Now it is an international border, dividing the Lezgins of Daghestan from those of Azerbaijan: such was the trick played on the Lezgin people by modern cartography, and by the dissolution of an empire.

One Sunday morning, Professor Gadzhi Abduragimov drove me in his aging Soviet car to the Samur front line, about five hours south of Makhachkala. There, he said, I would understand his people's tragedy. The spectacle we encountered was astonishing: a fully fortified frontier lay in front of us, one befitting nations at war, which Russia and Azerbaijan are not.

Lezgins, accustomed for centuries to moving back and forth at ease, are now coping with a Berlin Wall of sorts, erected in their midst, driving families and communities apart. What used to be but a few minutes' shuttle to the nearest town has now become a bureaucratic nightmare. I saw many hundreds of people and vehicles being held at bay on the Azeri side of the border, forming a line that, I was told, could at times require a wait of several days.

However accustomed the citizens of the former Soviet Union may be to long lines, however admirable their patience, this is no regular passage.

When the Soviet Union was dissolved at the end of 1991, the Samur, an administrative demarcation line of no particular historical importance or political validity, was accorded the status of an international border. Hitherto it had been a dotted line drawn on a map, at most an excuse for GAI, the unpleasant all-Soviet traffic police, to set up roadblocks and extort money from drivers. In practice, that border was no more relevant than that between two U.S. states.

Lezgins had lived on both sides of the river ages before anyone thought it might become a border. They still do, 55 percent in Russian Daghestan and 45 percent in Azerbaijan—or, if we accept Abduragimov's alternative statistics, 20 percent in Daghestan and 80 percent in Azerbaijan. (The huge discrepancy, according to Abduragimov, is a result of systematic Azeri intimidation, which has led hundreds of thousands of Lezgins to pretend to census takers that they were Azeris.)

It was Russia that pulled the curtain over the Samur, despite early promises to bear the Lezgins in mind. The Russians suspected that Azerbaijan was turning into a major transit point for smuggling arms to the Chechen rebels, as well as for Muslim militants who volunteered to help the Chechens. The suspicion was not unfounded. I myself have met a few individuals who clandestinely crossed Azerbaijan en route to Chechnya, bribing officials along the way. Whether they actually joined in battle or just "visited relatives," as they insisted to me, I could not tell with any degree of certainty. The Russian government, however, had no doubt at all. It disseminated reports of something akin to an international "Islamic legion" fighting alongside the Chechens and accused the Azeris of turning a blind eye. The Kremlin responded by virtually sealing off the border with Azerbaijan.

Standing a few yards away from the Russian-Azeri border under the bright afternoon sun, I was studying the multitude on the Azeri side, about half a mile away. Many of them must have awakened that morning before sunrise, had a quick cup of tea or a bowl of porridge, kissed family members good-bye, and left in a hurry, not knowing how the day would end up or what amount of humiliation was awaiting them at the hands of a suspicious border guard with standing orders not to believe a single word he was told.

No doubt, some of these people would try to cut corners, cheat, or attempt an illegal crossing on foot. Russian soldiers are instructed to shoot them on sight, and shoot them they do, and kill and maim them they do. More fortunate would-be infiltrators may end up in tiny prison cells, made of plywood, in the heart of the Russian border garrison, exactly where Professor Abduragimov and I nearly suffered a similar fate on account of my thoughtless indiscretion.

Upon arrival at the border, I asked a local policeman for permission to shoot video. The policeman, an evidently ill-briefed local, nodded casually at me. But as soon as I aimed my camera, two heavily armed Russian soldiers showed up and solemnly marched me into the barracks, where I was held in detention for about five hours. A severe Russian officer advised me that I had endangered Russia's national security, that I would have to answer for it in a court of law, and that for now I would have to await my uncertain future in incarceration. The dark solitude of a windowless plywood cubicle would have been an anticlimactic end to my Caucasian journey, though Abduragimov kindly attempted to raise my spirits by reminding me how useful an insight I was gaining into the daily plight of his compatriots.

Indeed, as we were standing there in a preincarceration state, while our fate was being debated over secure military phone lines to some remote command post, a desperate male voice emanated from one of the cubicles, relating a grim story about an unsuccessful border crossing, one of many that had landed the bearer of the voice in this jail, where he was being held incommunicado. Could we pass on a message to his family on the Azeri side of the border? he implored us. "What is your nationality?" we asked. "I am Lezgin," came the answer.

I was finally brought before another officer, a young man with raven-black hair, a pleasant countenance, and a greater willingness to condone my indiscretions than was displayed by his colleague. It turned out he was himself Lezgin and at that more empathetic (though by no means less strict) toward culprits and felons. He would let us go, he said, but if I wanted my videocassette back, I would have to call on his superiors in Makhachkala. Eventually he relented and released the tape as well, reminding me that next time he, or any of his comrades in arms, would be considerably less lenient.

"You were lucky," said Professor Abduragimov later, when we assembled around the dining table at a Lezgin family house in a neighboring town. "Few Lezgins get away as easily as you did." Our host, a man of considerable weight and a few-days-old stubble, laughed heartily as he poured Lezgin cognac into my glass. "You might say that you have become an Azeri Lezgin, if only for a few hours," he said.

THE CITY OF
THE GREAT *SHAMKHAL*

Sheyit Hanum Alisheva, a poetess of the Kumyk nation, a gracious lady with contagious laughter, invited me to join her for a Sunday picnic at her family's tiny retreat in Tarki, the ancient town overlooking Makhachkala.

The air was heavy with late-summer aromas, a concoction of sea scents blown ashore by an occasional breeze from the nearby Caspian, and the all-too-familiar smell of leaded gasoline, a lingering feature of many former Soviet cities. Joining in this seasonal blend was dust, a lot of it. Dust is the one commodity that is available in abundance to residents of the Northeast Caucasus, a result of potholed roads and unfinished buildings as well as eastern desert winds and arid terrain. A quick dip in the Caspian would have been an appropriate antidote had it not been for the fact that the sea is almost as polluted as the air above it, at least in the immediate environs of Makhachkala, where nature has fought a losing battle against the acidic leftovers of a now-crumbling industry.

Sheyit Hanum's escape route from the overbearing city to her ancestral hill is very short, only a couple of miles up The Commissars of Baku Street (so named after early martyrs of the Bolshevik Revolution, whom the old regime rendered patron saints of the Caucasus. The commissars have been repudiated elsewhere in the region, especially in Baku itself, but not here).

Sheyit Hanum hails a taxi, which is not really a taxi but a private car whose driver picks up an extra buck on his day off or perhaps even while

I catch a bird's-eye view of the entire Makhachkala plain and the vast Caspian beyond it.

on duty. It takes us but a few minutes' drive to reach the slope of a mountain. There we get off and begin our walk up steep narrow alleys, where heavy rains have disfigured the roads, undone the asphalt cover, and left in their wake nothing but dirt.

About 15,000 people may be living here, and yet no one is accorded the right to remain anonymous. The implicit expectation is that the passerby, even one of evident foreignness, will asknowledge each and every one of the people he comes across. Age determines who approaches whom with an extended hand and the traditional Islamic greeting of *salam aleikum* ("peace be upon you"), the Arabic expression that has survived Soviet rule.

A few more minutes of struggle finally place us in the unassuming center of Tarki, where I catch a bird's-eye view of the entire Makhach-kala plain and the vast Caspian beyond it, shrouded in a summer haze. In between the newly constructed mosque and the ostentatious resi-dence of a local nouveau riche, Sheyit Hanum stops, wipes the sweat off her brow, and proclaims solemnly, "This is our capital."

Little about the place suggests such a distinction, and the visitor must draw heavily on his historical imagination. "Over there"—Sheyit

Hanum points to the hilltop—"there lay the palace." When she recognizes a tinge of incredulity in my eyes, she adds, "There lived the *shamkhal** of Tarki."

Tarki has declined so much since its heyday that a recent Russian guidebook of cities and towns is insultingly oblivious to its existence. To the extent that Tarki is known to Russians, it is almost entirely thanks to its remarkable artist-son, the late film director Andrei Tarkovsky, whom Ingmar Bergman once credited for inventing a whole new language in cinema, "life as a reflection," and of whom he said, "He is for me the greatest." How much of Tarkovsky's genius he owes to his ancestry, one can only surmise. Perhaps an opening to a different past helped reconstruct the Middle Ages in *Andrei Rublyov*, the story of a medieval Russian icon painter, arguably the best film ever made on the era.

Tarkovsky, whose very name obviously derives from Tarki, was no ordinary person. He descended from the Kumyk royal lineage, even if he himself was born in Moscow and was immersed in Russian culture and language, in which his father composed well-regarded poetry. I asked the mayor of Tarki, Habibulla Zalibekov, whether the Kumyks would have installed Tarkovsky on the *shamkhal's* vacant throne. Zalibekov laughed heartily and said, "If he were alive and reclaimed the throne, we would give it to him, why not."

In days gone by, the fame of Tarkovsky's royal ancestors transcended international borders, and their name was pronounced with awe. Of all the indigenous states of the North Caucasus, none was as long-lasting and influential as this Kumyk principality, which for centuries was the leading power of the northern Caspian.

Westerners encountered the Kumyk state only at the time of its decline, when the decadence of its ruler and the good looks of its women were more noticeable features than its former military and political prowess. In 1722 Peter the Great headed the first military expedition of any czar to the Caucasus. He stopped over in Tarki, where he found much sympathy, being perceived as an ally against conniving Persia to the south, which was seeking to bring the Caucasus under its spell. The *shamkhal* showed up in the emperor's camp with a retinue of wives and concubines. Their comeliness so surprised Peter's wife Catherine that she summoned her husband's officers to look at them. A British military observer, attached to the czar's court, later related how

---

* The royal, or dukal, title of Tarki's hereditary rulers.

all Russian men gasped at the sight of "these incomparably beautiful, most lovely creatures."

So widespread was Kumyk influence that their language, closely related to Turkish, had become the nearest thing the region ever had to a native lingua franca (as opposed to the non-native Russian that eventually became the main medium of interethnic communication). So powerful was the *shamkhal* that in 1586 the neighboring Christian kingdom of Georgia implored Moscow to come to its rescue, because the Kumyk and his allies were "abducting half of Georgia." The Russian czar of the day, Fyodor, took eight years to respond by dispatching seven thousand men to rein in the *shamkhal*. Very few members of the expeditionary force ever saw Moscow again. A similar fate awaited two more forces sent against the *shamkhal* ten years later by the fabled Boris Godunov.

The *shamkhal's* correspondence of that era reveals an erudite ruler well versed in world affairs, with a surprising grasp of diplomacy and a keen eye for the international scene. The last *shamkhal*, already a Russian vassal, was removed from his throne in 1867.

Little is left of Tarki's past grandeur. The royal palace lies in ruins, and much of the ancient cemetery is in a state of disrepair. Residents allege that gravestones, notable for their ancient Arabic calligraphy, were used by the Russians—czarist and Soviet alike—in the construction of Makhachkala. Indeed, one Kumyk pointed out to me a spot not far from the parliament building, where, he contended, headstones had been laid to make the city's main boulevard—an outrage, no doubt, but one that would have been entirely thinkable in the heyday of Soviet atheism, when cathedrals were blown up, synagogues turned into gymnasiums, and mosques converted into pigsties.

Now we proceed to the site of our picnic. Our first stopover is the house of one of Sheyit Hanum's six sisters. Unannounced on a Sunday morning, we encounter no sign of life. Sheyit Hanum picks up from the ground a few pebbles and hurls them ever so gently at her sister's windows, and soon the sister emerges, tailed by two little girls. The sister complains of an excruciating headache and goes back inside. Her girls, Elnara and Janet (the latter, I am told, means "paradise" in Kumyk, and its resemblance to the English name is purely coincidental), will join us later and will demonstrate great eagerness to learn a few words of English. Elnara will whirl joyously across town, pronouncing her new vocabulary almost flawlessly.

At the very top of the Tarki hill stands the house of Sheyit Hanum's parents, a simple concrete structure with a garden, featuring a couple of apple trees and grapevines. Sheyit Hanum's father, virtually deaf, has to be yelled at, and the voices respectfully raised in his direction, as well as those respectfully lowered in all other directions, merge into a reassuring cacophony of friendship and hospitality. The mother, a smiling, jovial old lady, joins us, and we finally embark on the final leg of our march to little paradise.

Awaiting us there are Sheyit Hanum's husband, the Avar painter Ibragim Supianov, and his son from a previous marriage, Kamil. Kamil is eighteen and is back at home for the summer from his business studies at Ankara University. He is sustained in the Turkish capital by a scholarship he has obtained through the good Salau Aliyev's Tenglik movement. Kamil is Avar, which means he is of no known Turkic ancestry—normally a prerequisite for Tenglik sponsorship. An exception was made for him, helped perhaps by the fact that his father, who speaks not a word of Kumyk, is nonetheless the one whom Tenglik commissioned to design the flag of the Kumyk national movement.

I hear about Kamil's experience in Turkey as I ensconce myself among the trees in the heavenly plot that Sheyit Hanum and Ibragim so ingeniously carved out. Little streams flow through the garden, man-made terraces make its vegetation look bushier, and narrow paths leading nowhere give it the appearance of spaciousness. Though it is closely surrounded by neighbors, it has a secluded charm, as if you walk in and shut the world out. In the old Soviet Union, little retreats in a remote countryside, by a forest or a river or a hill, helped millions escape a dispiriting conformity. "Going to the dacha," from Moscow to Makhachkala, signified a departure from the imposed mainstream, if only for a brief weekend or an extended Sunday morning.

Painter Ibragim-Khalil Supianov (seen in his Makhachkala studio) may be an embodiment of the Daghestani condition: Avar by nationality, he is nonetheless the maker of the Kumyk flag. What of the Kumyks' grievances against his fellow Avars? Oh, nothing that could not be settled at the family dining table.

I first arrived in Tarki on the eve of a congress of Tenglik, held in a concert hall in the center of Makhachkala, just a few steps away from the republican parliament. Hundreds of deputies attended, many of them in traditional garb, some wearing Muslim skullcaps.

Signs in the Kumyk language, written in the Cyrillic script, adorned the hall. At the sound of a scratchy recording of the Kumyk national anthem, the deputies rose to their feet, but not one person in the hall, not even Salau Aliyev, the leader, joined in the singing. The anthem was still a novelty, and the nation was struggling to acquire a taste for its newly minted symbols.

A large Kumyk flag, designed—or overdesigned—by Hanum's husband, was hanging on the wall behind the stage, an awkward banner of little historical or emotional significance. It is an unusual flag, with a hint of the occult about it. A triangle of ocean blue at the hoist gives way to two broad horizontal stripes of green and red. The vertex of the triangle provides a linchpin for a *triskelion*, three legs or rotors, which appear to form the spokes of a wheel. Inside the wheel are the proverbially Turkic crescent and star (the likes of which appear on many Turkic flags, including that of Turkey). Anatomically dubious as it may be, each of the legs ends with a head: a woman's, a horse's, and a wolf's. This triheaded mythological serpent seems ready to spin off the flag's surface, as if to announce the Kumyks' reemergence on the stage of history.

Salau Aliyev had interpreted it for me when we first met at his office a few days earlier. The blue stands for "our Khazar ancestors" (the Khazars formed a mighty state by the Caspian Sea, perhaps in the sixth century A.D.); the green stands for "our peaceful intention, love of life, and

Salau Aliyev waving the flag, Sheyit Hanum Alisheva (whose husband created the flag) applauding.

attachment to the land" (he then paused and added, as if in an after-thought, "and of course for our Islamic faith"); and the red stands for "our decisiveness, readiness to take brave steps to accomplish our goals." As for the *triskelion*, each of its three legs-rotors represents an ancient stage in the cultural development of the Kumyk nation all the way from the time of the "matriarchate," a semimythical epoch in which women dominated society, for which the female head in the *triskelion* stands. The wolf is a ubiquitous Turkic symbol that has experienced a renaissance since the decline of Soviet Communism. The horse head stands for "the agricultural phase" in Kumyk history.

Previous congresses had been held under the banner of Kumyk autonomy. Tarki would be the capital of the a future autonomous district, and Aliyev would be its president, if not quite a *shamkhal*. In raising, however implicitly, the specter of Kumyk statehood, he was in effect announcing to the world his intention to drive the first nail into Daghestan's coffin, introducing the republic to the disintegrating forces of modern, secular, unapologetic nationalism. "Daghestan was a bad idea to begin with," Aliyev told me.

It is not that the Kumyk nationalists hated the Soviet system as such. After all, the new Kumyk flag features red among its three colors, "to show that we belong to a generation that helped shape the world in Revolution," as Aliyev said. He then went on to invoke Soviet shibboleth that I thought I would never hear again outside of an old Stalinist club: "We have done more than any other nation to strengthen Soviet power, to sustain the Socialist October Revolution."

Salau Aliyev has got a flag with layers of meaning.
All he needs now is a state, but no one will give it to him.

Aliyev's grievance against the system was not that it was conceived in sin or meant to perpetrate evil. It was rather that the system deviated from its founding principles, was hijacked by opportunists. Few of the nationalists I met in the Caucasus invoked the Reaganesque "evil empire" to describe the ancien régime. They preferred to talk about its ineptitude in its declining years, or its ingratitude toward its most loyal subjects, rather than dwell on the original sin of its foundation or its moral irredeemability. They reiterated that if only the old system had undertaken reform more seriously and had been guided in that expedition by more astute leaders, it might well have survived.

"Let me tell you what the regime did here. They mixed us all up, just like this." Aliyev was stirring his tea with pronounced vigor. "The way they picked a nation here, or dropped a nation there, showed their complete disregard for history and geography. But is it not the right of every nation to exercise self-determination on its own soil? Is it not in fact enshrined in the United Nations' founding charter? So why not the Kumyks? Why can't we have our rights respected? How come we have been reduced within half a century from 60 percent in our native regions to a mere 24 percent? And it is not only the Kumyks who have been so treated."

Indigenous peoples have been evicted elsewhere in Daghestan. Aliyev went on to name the Noghai, a fellow Turkic people with an impressive history. (The "Noghai Horde" was one of the successor states to the Mongol Empire, and its alliance with the Duchy of Muscovy, in the fifteenth century, made it a cofounder of the Russian empire.)

He also spoke, to my surprise, of the injustices inflicted upon the Cossacks of the river Terek, in northern Daghestan. Surprise, because the Cossacks, despite their long presence, hardly qualify as "indigenous." They were, after all, the vanguard of Russian colonization of the Caucasus; and elsewhere in the region, they are treated as archenemies of the native peoples and an obstacle to the restitution of local rights. That Aliyev would align himself with the Cossack cause, and would even have Cossacks, sporting their military regalia, as guests of honor at his congress, suggested his nationalism was not only not anti-Russian but actively pro-Russian, at least for now.

Rather, the targets of Aliyev's fury are the neighboring Daghestani nations who moved from their mountainous domiciles and claimed Kumyk lands. Aliyev spoke to me about an anti-Turkic "conspiracy of highlanders," primarily made up of Avars, the dominant ethnic group in Daghestan (about 600,000), who, he said, had orchestrated the massive demographic manipulation and were its main beneficiaries.

"They kept on mixing and mixing and mixing," Aliyev continued, "and the percentage of people living on somebody else's soil kept on growing."

The price the Kumyks paid for Soviet ethnic engineering is evident not only in land ownership. Soviet practices unleashed a far more danger-ous, possibly irreversible process: loss of identity. "The regime started building non-Kumyk villages and towns next to those of the Kumyks," Aliyev said. "And out of that cohabitation grew joint schools and kindergartens, where the Kumyk language no longer had the upper hand because other Daghestanis could not speak it. The republican government then introduced Russian as the sole medium of teaching, beginning in the first grade. In the 1950s we still had ethnic schools in Makhachkala, Khasavyurt, and Buinaksk [the main urban centers of the historical Kumyk areas]. By the 1960s, they had all been shut down. The rationale was very simple: the sooner we forgot our own languages and switched to Russian, the sooner we would become an integral part of 'socialist society.'"

Such mixture could not have been an accident of nature, not in a land where the regime exercised the firmest control over the movements of people, both individuals and groups. To its last breath, the Soviet sys-tem treated requests for a change of residence, however trivial, as though they involved crossing international borders. In a society so rigidly organized, it is hard to see how the flow of highlanders to the plains could have taken place without official fingerprints all over it.

The purpose of resettlement was not all that sinister, in that the living conditions up in the mountains were close to subsistence level, and bringing people down was more practical and less expensive than fund-ing an extensive development of the highland. But an underlying motive was also traceable in Soviet policy on nationalities virtually everywhere: blur distinctions, and force disparate communities to gravi-tate toward the Russian language as the sole medium of communication.

The methods applied during the course of resettlement, particularly in the 1920s and 1930s, were not only cynical but sometimes had deadly results. Take the case of the Lak people, highlanders who were trans-ported wholesale to flatlands that they had never lived in or seen in their entire life. Unable to adjust, they died in droves. Unofficial figures provided to me by Lak activists speak of up to one-quarter of the entire tiny nation perishing in the process.

Sadly, it is the descendants of those forced migrants with whom Salau Aliyev has the sharpest ax to grind. They occupy much of the arable land that Aliyev considers as rightly belonging to his people.

For a few months, between the fall of 1991 and the spring of 1992, Kumyk-Lak hostility reached such a level that the security forces had to intervene between two opposing camps of well-armed men in northwestern Daghestan, in a place called Karaman-Tyube, an outstanding monument to the folly of Soviet ethnic engineering. Prior to 1944, it had been populated mostly by ethnic Chechens. Then at Stalin's order, all the Chechens of the North Caucasus (the ones living both in Chechnya and in Daghestan) were deported to Central Asia for allegedly having collaborated with Nazi Germany. Laks were then transported from their mountainous districts in central Daghestan to the newly vacated Chechen district in western Daghestan and were settled there. In conformity with Stalinist practices, the Chechen district was then renamed Novaya Lakia ("New Lakia").

Forty-six years later, in 1991, the Chechens were permitted to reclaim their old homes. Two generations of Laks, who had known no other home, were told they would be "compensated." But in small Daghestan, land granted to one is land taken from another. In this case the Kumyks, to their mind, were expected to bear the brunt of restoring justice to the Chechens. Based on grim past experience, they expected that more of their land would be handed over to the Laks.

In one stroke, the Soviet genius had managed to pit against each other three small nations, all of which consider themselves victims of the system. Such is the case not only in Daghestan but throughout the Caucasus and across the full breadth of the former Soviet Union. In only a few instances have ethnic clashes arisen as a result of one-sided abuse and discrimination. What makes the injustices virtually unrectifiable is precisely their multisided nature.

It is as though the totalitarian system issued for itself the best insurance policy available: when it pushed people out of their homes and into somebody else's, it locked the door behind them and threw away the keys. The shift of populations has therefore become irreversible, and the dispossessed have nowhere to return to—a story reminiscent of the Jews in Israel, Afrikaners in South Africa, and ethnic Russians in the Baltic states. Each of these groups has a history and ancestral roots hundreds or thousands of miles away from their present home, but they no longer have a home to reclaim in the "old country." Any radical prescription—either wholesale acceptance or wholesale rejection—would entail injustice. Let them stay as they are, and you embrace the original displacement; send them packing, and you cause an equally horrible displacement.

Salau Aliyev's unkempt office was soon filled to capacity. The audience consisted by and large of Kumyk activists who could have recited his lines by heart. Nonetheless they were there to offer moral support. Not only did they nod approvingly as their leader built his case, but they also offered friendly heckling and interjected anecdotes to illustrate the leader's somewhat abstract points.

Stacks of photos were piled up next to me, and I was encouraged to take a look and see for myself the extent of national reawakening among the Kumyks, "after a conscious attempt was made to stall our national development for fifty to one hundred years" (Aliyev's theme). The pictures featured a host of rallies and processions that the Kumyks held in the early 1990s throughout Daghestan, in the heyday of Tenglik, when the Kumyk masses were still thrilled by the freedom to yell at the top of their lungs political slogans that had neither been dictated nor screened by the regional secretary of a Communist Party committee. Sheyit Hanum, the poetess-turned-activist, recalled a huge rally in late 1991 in which "seventy thousand Kumyk women took part."

But were they all Kumyk? I inquired.

"Ninety-five percent were," Sheyit Hanum said.

If so, nearly two out of three Kumyk women in Daghestan must have been there, I said incredulously, noting that the overall number of Kumyks in the 1989 census fell short of 230,000.

"Exactly," Sheyit Hanum confirmed passionately, unperturbed by the improbability of her numbers. Disagreement over statistics notwithstanding, Kumyk women did play an exceptional role in the birth of Tenglik. In 1991 dozens of them held a week-long hunger strike in Makhachkala's main square, demanding to be heard. Many of them spent months organizing, raising funds, and raising hell.

One day, in a Kumyk village by the Chechen border, I was invited to watch the preparation of _khinkal_, the famous Caucasian dumplings that are the staple diet of the Kumyks as well as other nations of the Caucasus. There is a long-simmering argument over whose khinkal is best. This argument is normally conducted in good humor; that afternoon, though, the two Kumyk women kneading the dough refused to fall for my diplomatic impartiality. "Kumyk is the best," the older woman, in her late fifties, informed me with a smile. The younger woman finally relented and acknowledged with a chuckle, "Everyone says that their _khinkal_ is best."

The younger woman was busy flattening the dough with a long, narrow rolling pin and spoke to me without ever raising her eyes from the low wooden table. Her motions were long and measured; she would first knead the dough with her naked fingers, then press it with the rolling pin, then cut it into dozens of symmetrical, square pieces, each of which was to be filled with ground meat and become a fresh and tasty *khinkal*.

I wanted to know why *khinkal* was so central to Kumyk national cuisine, and my folkloristic curiosity launched us into an unexpected exchange on the status of women at home and their role in nationalist politics.

"Our men are very proud," the younger woman said. Her name was Raisa Gambatova, she was thirty-nine, and her wrinkle-free facial skin would have made her look younger had it not been for the common mark of Soviet dentistry in her mouth: five golden teeth the front row alone. "When our men want to brag," Raisa said, "they tell each other, 'Come over to my place, and my wife will serve you the best *khinkal* you have ever tasted.' It's a matter of pride. A man is entitled to ask his wife to prepare *khinkal* even in the middle of the night."

Is it not a shame for the husband to bother his wife so late at night? I asked.

Raisa Gambatova (right) would rise up in arms in pursuit of justice, regardless of the men. But she would be ready with warm khinkal in the middle of the night, if so ordered by her husband. She is seen here with her comrade-in-arms, Sheyit Hanum Alisheva, the Kumyk poetess and activist.

"This is *his* role, and that is *her* role" came the answer. "If she respects her husband, she has to wake up even in the middle of the night and prepare *khinkal*. . . . It's a matter of tradition. If a wife disobeys, the husband loses face. His friends tell him, 'You are not a real man if your wife refuses to serve *khinkal*.'"

If the husband is wrong, shouldn't his wife refuse him? I continued.

"But how could he be wrong if I married him?" Raisa was now using the first person. She was medium height, pale. She was wearing a scarf around her head, a sign of modesty, though some of her hair was still visible, still perfectly black.

Is the husband *always* right?

"Of course he is. He is supposed to tell his wife what to do. His word is the law."

Do you think this may change in the future? Perhaps in the next generation, people will rethink the roles of husband and wife?

"Absolutely not. It will be the case forever. . . . This is our tradition. Russian women may be more liberated, but our situation is different."

Of course, a woman in a rural community in a traditional society is unlikely to champion a feminist agenda. What was so intriguing about Raisa's views is how reconcilable they were in her mind with her role in the Tenglik movement. If Raisa of the *khinkal* is traditional and submissive, Raisa of Tenglik is revolutionary and defiant.

"I'm no politician," she said reluctantly. "I have only tried to benefit my people. I fasted for seven days in Makhachkala." She paused and then added words she was to repeat time and again throughout our conversation: "You know, I am Kumyk. I am proud to be one. I am filled with pride at the very sound of the word."

What precisely have you tried to accomplish? I asked.

"I wanted my people to live in peace, to live well. Somebody should suffer for the common good." She poured flour and worked it into the dough. "We stayed in the main square of Makhachkala for two months, to raise our voices against the MVD and KGB people."*

Were the Kumyks targeted more than others in Daghestan? I asked.

"I cannot answer this. Let older people answer, they know," Raisa responded, uncomfortable about the increasingly political nature of her *khinkal* making. Nonetheless she continued answering, gaining confidence in the process and sharpening her tone.

"Is it so easy to find a job when all businesses are in Avar hands?" she asked, alluding to members of the largest ethnic group in Daghestan,

---

* Abbreviations by which the Soviet Interior Ministry police force and the secret police were known, respectively.

whom Salau Aliyev accused of "taking over" the republic and marginalizing the Kumyks. "They now occupy our land. Most of Daghestan belonged to the Kumyks. The Avars used to live in the mountains."

But that was a long time ago.

"Why a long time?" She instantly dropped the rolling pin and for the first time looked me straight at the eye. "I am thirty-nine years old," she said, enunciating every word with striking intensity. "When I was still a young girl, my parents inculcated discipline in me by saying, 'You had better come home now, otherwise an Avar man will stop by and take you along with him to the mountains.' That is where they were, the Avars, up in the mountains. Now they have come down, they have taken the land, they have assumed all the top jobs. They must think that Kumyk men are not manly enough, and that we are not a nation."

Tiny beads of sweat appeared on her brow, and she wiped them off gently. "If our men could not do anything, then we had to strike on our own. We wanted to help the Kumyks rise to the same high positions taken by the Avars."

Raisa now lifted the rolling pin and waved it in the air. I instinctively stepped back, unsure whether smiling, soft Raisa was going to lose her composure. She was not. But as she related the tale of her political crusade, something happened to her body language. She became more assertive, more articulate—and also more modern. In the proud moments of 1991, she and other Kumyk women gained a voice for the first time. They were no longer mere objects of carnal or aesthetic desire for condescending foreigners as at the time of Peter the Great. They were now the shield of their nation, and as importantly the shield of their husbands.

"We wanted to help our men, to defend them," Raisa said. "The men did not approve. But we were insistent, against their will. They objected to our hunger strike. They told us, 'What are you doing? Stay home!' But we refused to listen."

Was it not a precedent? I asked. If one day you refuse to obey outside the house, is it not possible that the next day you would refuse to obey inside?

"No, no. A husband's word is the law. Within the home, that is. But in society at large, whenever it affects the entire nation, how could one sit at home with her arms crossed?"

Could a woman lead the nation? I inquired.

"Of course. If she is intelligent, she could."

At this point the scarf slid off Raisa's head and landed on her shoulders, exposing her entire wave of hair. She hastened to pull the scarf back. "If a woman were to lead the nation," she went on, "we'd have some order. A woman knows how to work. And a man? What does *he* do?" She almost sneered. "He is seated in a comfortable armchair, eats, drinks, and goes to bed."

Raisa then shifted her attention back to the *khinkal*, singing in the process a Kumyk folk song. Its opening lines were:

> *One day I will become a blue dove*
> *And I will then sit in the blue grass.*
> *Do not rush me, oh stranger, do not rush me now.*

And so the Kumyk national movement had at least one unexpected, lasting result: the politicization of women. That is an extraordinarily rare event in Soviet and Russian history. Almost everywhere else, women have taken a back seat, or come to the fore only at time of war, to protect their soldier-sons (as in the case of Russian women during the Chechen war). Nowhere else have women taken such a prominent leading role, in defiance of the entire male population.

Tradition has it that the Amazons, the mythical tribe of warrior-women, originated in the Caucasus. A report submitted to the Russian czar almost two hundred years ago claims that in the sixteenth century an army of heroic women went to battle in the North Caucasus. (It ended in a draw, and the Amazon general married the chief of the rival army.) The mythical Medea, matron saint of all feminists, was the daughter of the king of Colchis, now part of the modern republic of Georgia—hence a Caucasian princess.

Salau Aliyev rose to his feet and approached a large map of Daghestan that one of his lieutenants had nailed to the door opposite his desk, in order to make it easier for the foreign guest to follow the intricacies of local geography. I asked him to draw the intended borders of his future Kumyk autonomous district. His thick fingers ran all the way from the city of Kizlyar in the north (founded by Cossacks in the mid-nineteenth century to aid the Russian push into the Caucasus) to the southern city of Derbent (site of the oldest continuous urban settlement in the entire Caucasus). He thus claimed for the Kumyks almost the entire plain of Daghestan, as well as most of the Caspian shore. These two regions— the lowlands and the sea—represent the bulk of Daghestan's agriculture, from fisheries to vineyards to corn. In an area so poor in natural resources, where Soviet-style industry has virtually collapsed, Aliyev was seeking for the Kumyks most of the jewels.

Mr. Aliyev—I asked him—if you were the leader not of the Kumyk national movement but, say, that of the Avars, and you were shown this map, do you think you would like that man Salau Aliyev?

"If I were not Kumyk," Salau Aliyev shot back instantly, "I might not like Salau Aliyev. But then I *am* Kumyk, I have the national conscience of a Kumyk, and it is the Kumyks that I have to concern myself with."

And what of the non-Kumyks under your future Kumyk autonomy? After all, they are going to be an overwhelming majority of the population, unless of course you intend to cleanse them.

"Nothing of the sort. No ethnic cleansing is intended."

But how do you propose to have Kumyks in a position of dominance when they are only one-quarter of the population? Does it not contradict the very principle of self-determination that you claim to uphold?

"Not at all. You see, other Daghestani nations already have their own compact areas in which they are in the majority, and thus they could exercise their national rights there. We intend our autonomous district to be multiethnic, but it will belong to the main nation in the area."

In other words, it will belong to the Kumyks?

"Yes, it will. That does not preclude harmony and mutual respect."

But how in a democratic era can a district belong to a minority of its residents?

"Well, it can. Look at Kazakhstan. Aren't the Kazakhs a minority in their own republic? And yet it is theirs, they are in control."*

I can think of another example, I retorted. In Abkhazia, decades ago, the indigenous Abkhaz, a minority of the population (17 percent at the time of the 1989 census), were given control over ethnic Georgians, by far the largest group. The result was a civil war that raged for four years. It was won by the Abkhaz and turned about 250,000 Georgians into refugees. Would not a Kumyk homeland generate the same outcome?

"No, it would not," Aliyev responded. "We will not repeat the mistakes committed in Abkhazia. We will nurture good neighborliness."

Institutionalized minority rule—a notion inconsistent with the Western understanding of what national self-determination is all about—is not unusual in the former Soviet Union. Often nations have been given

---

* 1991 official data give the share of ethnic Kazakhs in Kazakhstan's overall population as 41 percent, a plurality but not a majority. Since then, by some estimates, the Kazakhs have come very close to a majority because of the considerable emigration of ethnic Russians.

autonomy or its semblance, based on a principle other than demographic reality. The logic seemed to be that an ethnic group deserved to be recognized as "titular" in a republic if other ethnic groups in that republic could exercise their own rights elsewhere. Hence, Russians do not need self-determination, say, in Adyghea, where they are in the majority, because they have Russia; Georgians do not deserve the rights that are due a majority in Abkhazia, because they already exercise them in Georgia proper; and so on.

When Aliyev first raised his idea to federalize Daghestan into mini self-governing units, some sneered at him: "Why don't you return to Lake Baikal [in distant Siberia] where your ancestors came from and make your federation right there?" Rudeness and ridicule aside, the advice need not be taken too literally. No one intended for the Kumyks to pack up and leave. The words only reflected the mixture of impatience and disdain with which Aliyev is treated by his critics.

"Aliyev is a brave man," said Daghestan's young minister of nationalities, Magomedsalikh Gusayev, himself a member of a "minor" nationality, the Agul, who number about 25,000 people. "At the time of the Communist regime, Aliyev dared speak out on issues that were considered taboo. But then he started demolishing the most important principle of Daghestani life: that the problems of one nationality, however severe, must never be solved at the expense of another nationality. It is really a political tragedy, perhaps personal as well, that he pursues only Kumyk interests. I have asked him whether his Kumyk state would be democratic or totalitarian. He answered, 'Why, democratic of course.' But then I told him, if it is to be truly democratic, a Kumyk would never be able to lead it." Gusayev paused, and then added, "I think Aliyev is gradually coming back to his senses, but it may be too late for him."

AND HOW HIGH WOULD THE
SHEIKH FLY?

On top of the mountain, overlooking the town of Tarki and visible as far as the shore of the Caspian, a green Islamic banner flies from a pole, marking the grave of a man who preached defiance. This is the resting place of Ghazi Muhammad, the First Imam of Daghestan, the first champion of indigenous rights in the Caucasus, and an early proponent of anticolonialism anywhere along the front line between Europe and the rest of the world.

Below, in the heart of Tarki, is entombed another Muslim sage, a man whose succor and solace have helped the living for many centuries after his own death. His name was Muhammad Ali, and he was a holy sheikh of the Sufi order, a performer of a great many miracles. His memory survived eight decades of Soviet atheism and is now making a spiritual comeback. He is Tarki's patron saint of sorts.

The coexistence between the spirits of the two holy men is uneasy, even if both represent the same faith, which is older in Daghestan than anywhere else in the Caucasus, indeed as old as Christianity is in Russia.

The imam on the mountain was a zealot who sought to transform the land by restoring purified Islam where priests lead and the faithful obey. The sheikh, or what the sheikh stood for in the eyes of his adherents, was the facilitator of harmony, a man whose mystical presence became an acceptable substitute for earthly justice and good government. A Marxist might say he was "opium of the people"; an Islamic puritan would probably say he was at the center of a dangerous heresy that took Islam too far from its origins.

Ghazi Muhammad and Muhammad Ali still epitomize the choice the Caucasus must make. Will its evolution be peaceful, forgiving human frailties rather than sneering at them and punishing them? Or will it be a rupture, like the one across the border in Chechnya? Will its faith be the radical Islam unleashed in the first half of the nineteenth century? Or will it be the less rigid version that has been practiced much longer?

Ghazi Muhammad was laid to rest on the mountaintop in 1832. He inspired the great rebellion against Russia that swept most of the Caucasus for some thirty years in the mid-nineteenth century under the stewardship of his better-known successor, the Third Imam, Shamil. Shamil, however, ended his life in complete submission to Russian rule, and his treatment at the hands of his captors became a token of czarist magnanimity toward a vanquished enemy. In striking contrast, the First Imam died in battle, leading a handful of fighters against a vastly superior Russian army.

Ghazi Muhammad was neither a Kumyk nor a Tarkiite; he belonged to the Avars of the tall mountains. In 1827 he was handed an invitation from the *shamkhal* of Tarki "to come and teach me and my people the *shari'a*," or Islamic law. The Kumyk prince had not bargained for the more belligerent aspects of the imam's gospel. Ghazi Muhammad and his successors had little time for traditional rulers. Local despots were no more acceptable to them than foreign ones—both were considered deserving targets of their holy fury.

Among the nations of Daghestan, the Kumyks ranked fairly low in their support for the Islamic revolution that the nineteenth-century imams unleashed. Some Kumyks joined the rebels' ranks, but their overall enthusiasm never matched that of the Chechens and the Avars, their highland neighbors, who constituted the bulk of the insurgent army. Even in 1840, when Shamil's rebels were roaming freely in the highlands, having reduced Russia's presence to its lowest level in half a century, a Russian commander wrote to his higher-ups that in Daghestan, "only the Kumyks . . . remained in submission to us."

The reasons were both topographic and cultural. It is much easier for mountaineers to wage a guerrilla war. The Chechens could hide in their thick forests (much of which the Russians eventually destroyed), and the Avars could mount their steep cliffs. The Kumyks were dwellers of the plains, where few hiding places existed. Culturally, the Kumyks frowned upon the mountaineers. To them they were riffraff, uncultured and unsettled.

Through the end of the czarist era, the Kumyks were represented disproportionately in local elites, both administrative and cultural. Then they were among the first Communist revolutionaries in Daghestan. Portraits of those revolutionaries are on display at Salau Aliyev's office. He believes, as do others, that if it had not been for the "Avar takeover," Kumyks would have led Daghestan for the past eight decades. Presumably a Kumyk leadership would have spared its people the ensuing troubles. This was the only time I heard a Daghestani nationalist politician railing explicitly against another Daghestani nation.

Clearly the seeds of discontent between highlanders and lowlanders were sown much earlier than Aliyev himself would care to admit. The collision was hardly surprising. Mountain against plain, goatherd against farmer, are but alternatives titles to the tale of the human race.

I noted with interest that Salau Aliyev's office, in contrast to the offices of other nationalist leaders I visited in Daghestan, did not feature the all-too-familiar portrait of Imam Shamil, with his penetrating eyes and handsome beard, his turban-wrapped *burka*, and two double rows of silver bullets across his *cherkesska*. (*Burka* is a headcover made of goat hair, and *cherkesska* is a long Caucasian coat.) Shamil, the great rebel leader who for three decades led North Caucasian armies in an Islamic "holy war" against Russia, is an all-Daghestani icon, so his conspicuous absence from the Kumyk national headquarters helped illustrate to me the path Aliyev had chosen.

Had the venerable imam, known for his authoritarian ways, been alive today, he would undoubtedly be contemptuous of modern, essentially secular nationalism. In raising one of the most successful rebel armies of the colonial age, Shamil was bent on unifying all Caucasian Muslims irrespective of ethnos and tribe, whereas Aliyev, just like any nationalist leader, dwells on the differences.

Nationalism is a new phenomenon in the Caucasus, where resistance to outside coercion had never been ethnically based but was inspired by regional and religious commonalities (probably in that order). In cultivating the notion of separate development, Aliyev is introducing a new uncertainty.

If he had lived and engaged in politics a century earlier, he would have easily blended into the landscape of relatively liberal European nationalism. Late twentieth-century Europeans (seeking unity and drawing closer toward an eventual dissolution of the nation-state) and definitely Americans (who have never believed in one) might perceive Aliyev as a throwback to a darker age.

Muhammad Ali, Tarki's indigenous holy man, lived about a thousand years ago, or so I heard from the mayor of Tarki. His resting place became a shrine, walls were erected around it, and a roof was laid on top. Tombs of holy men, almost indistinguishable from Tarki's either in structure or in concept, can be found across the Muslim world, from North Africa to Central Asia. The worship of dead saints has helped decentralize Islam and has given its adherents local content and symbols. Though their tombs have never taken precedence over Mecca and no sheikh has ever been elevated above the Prophet, native holy men have helped make Islam much more diverse and pluralistic than modern-day puritans would have us believe.

The sheikhs helped keep their disciples and followers close to God. Indeed, they made God more accessible by tolerating departures from the harsh dogma—a system not unlike that of saints in the Catholic church, or *tzaddikim* ("righteous ones") in the Jewish Hasidic movement. After all, a God who is willing to reveal himself to so many mortals and shed his holiness on them must be more tolerant of human frailties, less perfectionist in his expectations of them than the scriptures suggest.

No wonder Islamic purists frown upon the sheikhs and consider their quasi-deification a form of heresy. It is not hard to imagine what they would think of Sheikh Muhammad Ali of Tarki, if they were to hear Tarkiites extol his supernatural powers. It was said of him that after the Friday prayer he would excuse himself and go upstairs, ostensibly to get a loaf of bread. In reality, while away, the sheikh would fly to holy Mecca, some fifteen hundred miles away, and be back in time for the afternoon prayer.

Suffering decades of neglect under Soviet rule, Muhammad Ali's tomb is coming back to life. At the time of my visit, most of the structure had been freshly painted white; new decorations were added, such as a bright color photo of the Ka'aba in Mecca; and coloring was

How high will the sheikh fly, or how low will he lie? The burial site of Muhammad Ali, Tarki's patron saint

restored to fading inscriptions from the holy Qur'an. Most important, a
radical face-lift was given to the square niche in the middle of the tomb,
where the sheikh, his wife, and their daughter were interred. Each of the
family members was installed in a sarcophagus so small as to be mistaken for that of a child.

In days long gone the niche used to be a place of untold miracles performed by the sheikh posthumously. An old woman, the grave's unofficial attendant, told me that believers used to place empty water
dispensers down there just before the tomb was locked for the night.
The next morning they would find the dispensers full to capacity. The
blessed water was then used by the pious to cleanse themselves prior to
the first prayer of the day.

The array of shining colors and fresh odors in the tomb were
financed not by the government—cash-starved, it could not afford to
provide even basic services—but by the Karachayev brothers, whose
sudden wealth has made them quite possibly the richest Kumyks of
Daghestan. So sudden was their enrichment that only a sheikh-induced
miracle could account for it, or so one should hope. All fortunes in
post-Soviet Russia have been sudden, but in Daghestan, the poorest of
Russia's provinces, they may be even more disconcerting than elsewhere.

The woman who introduced me to the tale of Sheikh Muhammad
Ali's miracles was the Karachayev family matron, a dignified lady in her
late seventies whose paleness was underscored by the dark garb wrap-
ping her frail body. The scene could have taken place almost anywhere
in the Islamic world: a pious woman, wearing her modesty on her
sleeves, stands in the sheikh's tomb, seeking daily refinement from holy
spirits, and awaits an affirmation-by-miracle. At least there, a step away
from the ancient dust that used to be Sheikh Muhammad Ali, Soviet
rule seems almost a footnote. That deadliest enemy of all matters
godly had been vanquished, faith endured, and the spirits of medieval
men whom the Soviets intended to exorcise for good are alive once
again.

Nuraddin Karachayev, whose money beautified the flying sheikh's
tomb, is a deputy in the Daghestani parliament and has emerged as the
power behind the throne in Salau Aliyev's Tenglik movement, of which
he is probably the main underwriter. He was said to exercise a moderat-
ing influence on Aliyev. Past experience suggests that Karachayev
might eventually take over the leadership and, in the process, make sure
that it has little bite or bark. The congress I attended was already less

*The custodian of the grave, the lady Karachayev. It is her son
Nuraddin's money that beautified the flying sheikh's tomb.*

exclamatory than its predecessors, and brother Karachayev, seated at
the dais, was elected Aliyev's deputy.

Similar things have happened to other national movements in
Daghestan. In the declining days of the Soviet Union, fiery intellectuals and orators launched them, then had to bow out. Their place was
taken by new power brokers, all young, all of proven deftness in accumulating vast personal fortunes in the shortest periods of time. Quite a
few of them are accomplished in the martial arts. In a land where spiritual mystics used to inspire loyalty and confidence, swollen biceps
now seem to be at least as helpful. (The duality of power has been
there for a long time, sages and outlaws having coexisted for generations, providing the highlanders with two complementary formulae for
survival.)

Daghestan's republican government is a carefully assembled team
that strikes a delicate balance among the nationalities. It recognizes
fourteen ethnic groups for the purpose of representation in a bloated
collective presidency (State Council). It is the only Russian republic
without an "executive president," a clear message that in a land of
minorities, no one could force his will. In reality, the largest ethnic
groups set the pace.

The traditional politicians, who all had graduated with honors from
the Soviet Communist Party, decided to co-opt the young, muscular,
and wealthy nationalists. They offered the well-shaped and well-off a
stake in the system. One became boss of the state oil company, another
was put in charge of fisheries, and a third grabbed the ministry of
finance. Consequently, national movements that might have become
breeding grounds for a dangerous opposition have been transformed
into bulwarks against extremism and *for* the status quo.

The Kumyk Tenglik was the only exception to the rule.* Making a Karachayev the leader would change that and help Daghestan escape a cataclysm, even if in the process the Kumyk people would have to forgo their manifest destiny.

At the time of my visit, one of the most prominent new politicians was assassinated and another had a hand grenade hurled into his fortified mansion in the middle of the night. Little wonder the Karachayevs were accompanied by bodyguards each time they were whisked back and forth in their shining Mercedes-Benz limousines. They were in the construction business—I was told one of them had a brick factory—and were responsible for much of the building activity in Tarki, including their own grand residences, one of them by the side of the renovated mosque, another overlooking the city of Makhachkala.

The one by the mosque, at which I peeked from the top of the minaret, was a little pyramid, stony and bald. The other residence, leaning on the edge of the Tarki hill, with only air between it and Makhachkala, was less assuming on the outside but sumptuous on the inside. One evening I stumbled into it uninvited and unaware of the identity of the owner. I had been told that Aliyev and his lieutenants were gathering there to celebrate the successful completion of the Tenglik congress, and that I would find my friend Sheyit Hanum there.

As I entered, unsure, Karachayev approached me with a broad smile and proclaimed loudly, or at least loud enough for all the legitimate guests to hear, "In my house you are welcome, even if you are not invited." I blushed and murmured an apology, but I was immediately waved to a seat at one head of the long table, across from Aliyev at the other head, and was pressed upon to offer a toast, one of many, to the Kumyk nation.

"Now that our dear guest from Washington has seen our life and talked to our people," said Aliyev, "I am sure he knows how proud we are of our history and how much deserving of a future." He then added mischievously: "I think our esteemed guest has some Khazar blood in his veins. That is why he is so interested in us."

The assembled guests welcomed the words with approving laughter. All gazes turned on me. Caucasian etiquette required me to reciprocate. My glass was refilled (well, not quite, because not even the Caucasus could make a drinker of me, but a drop or two of vodka was symbolically added to make for a full goblet), and I was invited to toast.

"To our common genes," I said.

"To our genes," exclaimed the leadership of the Kumyk people.

---

* In 1998, the Lak national movement also seemed to veer out of control and was involved in ugly riots in central Makhachkala. For more on the Laks, see pages 139–65.

GENERALS IN SEARCH
OF ARMIES

"Salau Aliyev's doings have little to do with the Kumyk nation. It is not Kumyk problems that he is attempting to solve, it is *his*. He only projects his personal problems on his nation. He has the psychological traits of a marginal personality, stuck between two cultures. He is no longer a traditional Kumyk, but he does not feel an integral part of the Russian intelligentsia either."

The speaker was a Daghestani intellectual, a young, bright, and iconoclastic sociologist named Enver Kisriev. He said the same was true of other converts to nationalism in Daghestan. "Think of a general who retires from the Russian army with honors and great experience and comes back to our little Daghestan. His skills do not earn the recognition they deserve. Soon he comes to equate his own personal agony with that of his suffering nation. He then resolves to dedicate his life to the liberation of his people, forgetting only one minor thing: to ask the people whether they want to be liberated, or if they want *him* to be the liberator."

Kisriev is Lezgin, and it was no abstract general that he had in mind, but a fellow Lezgin, Mukhuddin Kakhrimanov, a sixty-year-old veteran of the Afghan war. He was also a former "chief military and political adviser" to the Soviet military delegation in Angola in the 1980s, when that West African country, torn by a bloody civil war, served as an important battlefield of the cold war. Having helped export revolution to the third world, Kakhrimanov headed back home to Daghestan after the collapse of the Soviet Union. There, like many Soviet veterans, he found that what he had stood for was no longer an object of admiration. His advice and expertise were no longer of any use, and in the new times, entirely different skills were required to survive and to thrive. And so the ultimate paradox resulted: the Communist general, the proponent of what the Soviets called "proletarian internationalism," became a nationalist agitator.

There were three more generals like him in the North Caucasus, decorated heroes of the Afghan campaign who sought dramatic mid-life career shifts after the collapse of the country they had served so loyally. The best-known general was Jokar Dudayev, who took Chechnya out of Russia and then led the resistance to Moscow's attempt to quell the rebellion until his own death. Another general was Ruslan Aushev, perhaps the youngest officer of his rank in the entire Soviet army, who became the first president of Ingushetia, the smallest autonomous republic in the North Caucasus.

Dudayev and Aushev are different from Kakhrimanov in that they successfully transformed themselves into nationalist leaders. A case that resembles Kakhrimanov's more closely is that of Sufyan Beppayev, who was deputy commander of the Caucasus military district in the final days of the Soviet Union. Himself a Caucasian, a member of the tiny Balkar nation, Beppayev went home and became the leader of a short-lived and pathetic attempt to create a Balkar republic.

The Balkar Beppayev, just like the Lezgin Kakhrimanov, became a "marginal personality," in sociologist Kisriev's words. Knowingly or otherwise, he merged his own quest for redemption with that of his nation. His rebellion was put down easily, not one shot was fired in anger, and the retired general was then co-opted into the government whose yoke he had sought to overthrow only a few days earlier.*

His was a silly story, yet sad and disturbing. In its wake, the question could have been posed: how much of the national reawakening in the Caucasus and elsewhere is genuine, and how much is a second wind for "marginal personalities"?

My meeting with General Kakhrimanov was set by an unlikely go-between, a senior Daghestani government official who wanted me to see for myself that the nationalities question in Daghestan was not all that complicated or menacing, and that the republic was not headed toward a Bosnian inferno. He thought Kakhrimanov would give me a cool-headed perspective on the plight of the Lezgins, so as to disabuse me of the notion that each nationality has its own hot-headed Salau Aliyev. He was wrong.

* For more on Beppayev's nationalistic career, see pages 363–64.

Kakhrimanov, now a special adviser to the government of Daghestan "on military affairs"—something of a misnomer in the absence of a Daghestani military—welcomed me in virtual battle fatigues. Throughout our long talk, just across the hall from the prime minister's bureau, he kept on blowing the trumpets of war (and incessantly working the gap between his front teeth with a *miswak*, or chewing stick). So incredulous was I at one point, when the general stated the Lezgin determination "to solve our problems with all the means at our disposal," that I openly gasped. "What could you possibly mean by that, general?"

"How is it possible that you, a journalist, would not understand what 'all the means' means?" the general sneered.

"Well, general," I said, "I would much rather you interpreted your own words."

"I hoped," he said pointedly, "that you, as an educated person, would understand. But if you do not, let me help you: if necessary, we will raise arms." He was speaking casually, without raising his voice or gesturing, while his fingers continued to busily work his teeth with the overused chewing stick. "Are we worse than the people of Karabakh?" He was referring to the uprising of the Armenians in Nagorno-Karabakh, which had brought Azerbaijan to the verge of collapse.

Kakhrimanov continued, "I will tell you what *we* can do. If *we* go to war, *we* will need three days to win it. Three days—and we will be in the right place, and hoist our flag. He did not care to explain what "the right place" was, but we were talking about the Lezgin minority across the border in northern Azerbaijan, and there was no doubt that he was describing to me a future military campaign to win control of what he called "eleven administrative regions of Azerbaijan where there is compact Lezgin population." According to his demographic projection, 1.2 million Lezgins lived in Azerbaijan, more than one-seventh of the entire population, and *seven times* the figure recorded by the last official census, of 1989.* The discrepancy, he said, was a result of constant Azeri attempts "to Turkify" the Lezgins, and more than one million of them simply found it more prudent to register as Azeris.

"Why? I will tell you why. Lezgins are not admitted to universities, are barred from professions, and are not allowed to work in the mass media. Besides, the official policy in Azerbaijan is to underestimate the number of Lezgins as much as possible. It started long ago, in Soviet

---

* The last 1989 all-Soviet census recorded 204,400 Lezgins in Daghestan and 171,395 Lezgins in Azerbaijan. Both figures reflected a relative, almost identical decline (5 percent) in Lezgin numbers in both "homelands." Roughly 65,000 Lezgins were counted in other parts of the Soviet Union, mostly Russia, Kazakhstan, and Turkmenistan.

times. You know how easy it was—the party committee had only to issue an order, and that was it, no questions asked. Azerbaijan's official policy was to deny the presence of ethnic groups other than Azeris. The truth, however, is entirely different. Azerbaijan is really a multiethnic state, in which the Turks are only a minority, and it should have become a federation long ago." (His usage of the word *Turks* to denote the Azeris was a throwback to czarist times, when all Turkic speakers of the empire were bundled together and referred to as Turks, or Tatars, or Turco-Tatars. *Azerbaijan* is a modern name that appeared only at the end of World War I.)

Kakhrimanov said that out of Azerbaijan's seven million strong population, two million were Talysh, an ethnic Persian group. The 1989 census put the number of the Talysh at just over 20,000. To believe Kakhrimanov's alternative demography, one has to accept that a tremendous deception took place in Azerbaijan, in which about three million people were misregistered.

Kakhrimanov then went into a long harangue about history and rights, reciting the history of the Lezgins from ancient times. "We were the original Caucasians," he said, complaining that the Lezgins have been victims of envy and superpower machination. "We were renowned for our courage. We had pale skin, we were famous for our good looks, we were hailed as valiant warriors—and because of all those tributes, many of us were sold as slaves across the Middle East. We had an alphabet since before Christ, we had a civilization and culture when the Slavs still roamed the northern forests and gathered mushrooms." (I thought the latter a curious if unintended paraphrase of a line by Benjamin Disraeli, who once mocked an anti-Semitic critic by reminding him that the Jews created "a brilliant civilization . . . more than two thousand years ago, when the ancestors of the manufacturers of Manchester, who now clothe the world, were themselves covered with skins and tattoos like the red men of the wilderness.")

Recognizing my surprise at his historical contentions, the general waved a book at me, which turned out to be by Gadzhi Abduragimov, the physics professor who introduced me to some of the Lezgin people's pain. The book, which became a manifesto for Lezgin nationalists, angered members of other nationalities because of the sweeping nature of its suppositions.

General Kakhrimanov spent the next few minutes arguing that the most important events in Caucasian history involved either the ascendance of the Lezgins or the continuous attempts by a succession of empires, from that of Alexander the Great to Soviet Russia, to divide and humiliate them. Even local toponomy owes much to the Lezgins, he said, in that the name *Caucasus* is but a derivative of ancient Lezgin words meaning "tall mountain," and the Caspian Sea is named after an ancient Lezgin tribe, the Scaspi.*

In the summer of 1995, while in Azerbaijan's capital Baku, I received an invitation to go to an ancient mosque in the old city, a few steps away from the Maiden's Tower, Baku's claim to architectural fame. There I was to meet Ali Musayev, the head of a Lezgin cultural center called Samur, which, unlike the Daghestani Sadval, was sanctioned by the Azeri authorities and could act legally and freely. By choosing the mosque as the venue for our meeting, Musayev was sending a message that was gentler in tone than that of Sadval, yet it was powerfully loaded with symbolism. It had to do with antiquity, that popular theme among Caucasian nationalists.

Twin plaques—one in Cyrillic script, the other in the recently adopted but not yet common Latin script—announced to the visitor "Lezgin Mosque 1161," the year of its foundation. They carried no polemics, no exclamation marks, only a casual statement of fact to remind the visitor that the Lezgins had been here at least eight centuries before a state called Azerbaijan came into being. Not only that, this is a *Sunni* mosque, another aspect of uniqueness in a land that conforms to Shi'i Islam. (To be sure, Azerbaijani Shi'ism is a pale shadow of the one practiced in the only other Shi'i state in the world, Iran, but it nonetheless is an integral part of its identity.) Even before I stepped into the bunkerlike edifice, partly submerged underground, Musayev's message already resonated: *We, the Lezgins, are an ancient people, and we are different.* Musayev did not strike me as a deeply religious person, and my impression was that to him the mosque's significance was primarily cultural.

In this intricate world of symbols, the name of Musayev's organization, Samur, carries significance. "It is named after the river that divides our nation. It is our Berlin Wall," he told me. Only two weeks earlier, a delegation of the organization had been invited to attend a Lezgin national conference in Derbent, Daghestan's second-largest city. As soon as the Samur delegation reached the Samur River, the Russian border guards turned it back.

"Remember how Ronald Reagan stood in Berlin [in 1987] and exclaimed, 'Mr. Gorbachev, tear down this wall'?" Musayev asked me. "I

---

* The existence of a tribe by this name seems to be a historical fact, and it might have been a precursor of the Lezgins, but stating its Lezginness as a fact is one of those liberties taken with history that I came across very often in the Caucasus.

did it here, too, when Vladimir Shumeiko [then speaker of Russia's upper house of parliament] paid a visit. 'When will you tear down this wall?' I asked him in a public meeting. He nodded, promised to examine the problem, and left. The wall still stands." As it did five years later.

To Azerbaijan, Musayev offered the agreeable face of Lezgin nationalism. He helped shift the blame for Lezgin unhappiness to the Russians, who turned the Samur into a fortified border and blocked the free movement of people. A mild man, Musayev was however no match to the fiery Lezgin orators of Daghestan. A year later, when I was in Makhachkala, Abduragimov, the physics professor and nationalist author, responded disapprovingly when I mentioned that I had met with Musayev. "Oh, him," he said. "He has sold out to the Azeris." Of course, political leaders often speak that way of each other, and differences of opinion are made to look as acts of supreme treachery. But there was no mistaking the gap between the Lezgin professor in Baku and the Lezgin professor in Makhachkala, or between the Baku Lezgin and the sword-brandishing General Kakhrimanov. The Azeris would have nodded approvingly at Musayev's urging "the need to be realistic. Every nationality has dreams. The Azeris themselves have a dream of unification with their brothers in Iran. These dreams cannot be realized."

Musayev would settle gladly for "cultural rights," anything that might help prevent the complete loss of the Lezgin language. It is now taught only an hour or two in high schools. The young speak the language only in villages where Lezgins live in large numbers.

"A man such as myself," he continued, "courteous as I am, democrat as I am, cannot possibly seek complete satisfaction of all demands and aspirations. Perhaps one day younger Lezgins, less polite and more impatient, might say of people like me that *we* cannot solve the Lezgin problem, that the time has come for a different approach." He paused, then added, perhaps as a nod of caution in the direction of an unknown listener, "Of course I do not believe it will happen."

The next day I visited Itdayat Urudjev, adviser on nationalities to the president of Azerbaijan. He treated Lezgin complaints dismissively. "In order to protect cultural and linguistic rights, we publish papers, at our expense, in all minority languages," he said. "I would like to pose a question to you: Where in the world can you see a government behaving so generously toward its minorities?"

I thought I must have seen a few.

THE TORAH SCROLL OF KRYZ

On a hill in northern Azerbaijan, outside of the ancient city of Quba, I went one day looking for old Jewish graves. It was the main cemetery of Quba's Mountain Jews, a community so distinct as to have earned an ethnic classification unto itself (*gorskii yevrei*) under the Soviet system, separate from the rest of the Jews (*yevrei*). To their Muslim neighbors, they were but another Caucasian tribe, distinguishable from their environment only by ritual, but otherwise fully blended in. Traditions and legends about the Jews circulate all over the mountains, and echoes, however faint, of their presence endure almost everywhere, even in such places where no Jews are known to live nowadays.

That morning in Quba, I was willing to entertain the most outlandish leads and climb the tallest mountains in quest of Jewish roots. The gardener at Quba's cemetery was more than happy to accommodate me. He lived in a little house within the cemetery perimeter, and it was out of that house that he stepped to greet me and my companions. The gardener was a short man, his head covered with a gray hat, broadbrimmed and spiked. He supported himself with an improvised walking cane, but the evident ease with which he moved and his upright posture suggested the cane's role was primarily ornamental. As he came closer, I could see his aquiline nose and well-trimmed white beard and thought he cut, almost to perfection, a medieval Jewish figure, one that I could recognize anywhere in the world from a mile's distance—but for the fact that he turned out to be not Jewish at all. He was Lezgin, and his name was Nejmettin Aydemirov. His grandfather, he said, had

As he was getting closer, I could see his aquiline nose and well-trimmed beard and thought he cut almost to perfection a medieval Jewish figure, one that I could recognize anywhere in the world from a mile's distance—but for the fact that the old man in Quba turned out not to be Jewish at all. He was Lezgin.

come to Quba from Daghestan. And yet "everybody knows that among the Muslims there are many who are descended from the *juhuti,*" he said, using the highlander designation for Jews.

Are there "Jews" among the Lezgins as well? I asked, wondering if he might not be one of them.

"Among the Lezgins as well," he confirmed, and went on to name five Lezgin villages in which Jews were known to have settled some 275 years earlier, seeking the benevolent protection of Fathali, the khan of the Quba principality. "At the time of their arrival, they were still Jews," the old man mused, sucking on an ancient cigarette holder with a used butt stuck in it. "But later they converted to Islam and began to speak the language of their Lezgin neighbors. From that point on, they were considered as much Lezgin as anyone else, and no one can tell any longer who the 'former Jews' are."

The Lezgin gardener was walking his guests down the hill, introducing us in the process to the Jewish dead of two centuries ago. Lying at our feet was the valley of Quba, where I could easily spot the silver-domed synagogue but not a single mosque minaret. At the other end of the cemetery, as a funeral procession was reaching its climax, mourners were reciting Hebrew prayers. Meanwhile the Lezgin was telling me how Jews arrived here in the first place. It had all happened at the beginning of time, after the death of "the great prophet Suleiman," whose wise governance made Israel mighty and prosperous. Unfortunately, he had two sons, who were jealous of each other and ever bickering. They engaged in a bitter fight over their patrimony and ended up weakening their country so much—the gardener was unsure what to call that country and used "kingdom" and "republic" interchangeably—that the Jews had to leave, dispersed all over the world, "and that is why you would find a small Jewish community anyplace you go."

Aydemirov was of course talking about King Solomon. The partition of Solomon's kingdom was a precursor to the Assyrian and Babylonian exiles of the eighth and seventh centuries B.C. This is an important subtlety because Caucasian Jews, unlike most European and North African Jews, trace their roots back to the destruction of the *First* Temple. Ashkenazi and most Sephardic Jews tend to view themselves as *Second* Temple exiles. Six centuries apart, the Caucasian Jews, rightly or wrongly, claim the distinction of being the oldest Jewish diaspora anywhere. If King Juan Carlos of Spain can argue that "fifteen percent of Spanish blood is Jewish," then Caucasians can undoubtedly claim a portion even larger than that.

"Some of the Jews went to Iran," the gardener continued his historical *tour d'horizon*, "but they did not like it there and eventually moved to the north. They finally settled up there." Illustrating "there," he pointed his cane at the misty summits beyond the horizon. "There, in the mountains, a village exists by the name of Kryz, which they chose for home. But later the people among whom they settled insisted that the Jews convert to Islam. Some did, but those who declined came off the mountain and were welcomed by the khan. Never again has a Jew been persecuted in the mountains."

It is perhaps no accident that in this land, surrounded by impassable mountains, harboring so many imponderables and shielding unresolved mysteries, people are tempted to seek the earliest beginnings. Perhaps the urge to know the exact time at which their ancestors started walking erect on this soil is for them an act of affirmation. These people, who are duty-bound by tradition to recite the names of their male line going back seven generations, may perhaps be compared with icebergs wandering the ocean: the tip catches the eye, representing the self-evident—but the tip tells the observer little about the actual size, strength, and longevity of the iceberg. Most important is the body submerged in the water, or for that matter in the human mind: layer upon layer of active, live memory. The visible is entirely dependent on the invisible, and one need never be deluded by that which the naked eye observes.

If this speculation on the origins of historical memory is a bit too profound, here is an easier alternative. Think of hypothetical dwellers of a hypothetical village in the remote mountains. They wake up one morning, realize how distant they are from the nearest human settlement, and ask each other, "For crying out loud, how did we ever get to this godforsaken place?" Finding an answer may help give a solemn sense to their miserable predicament, may make the harshness of their life feel a bit less arbitrary or haphazard, may turn the ongoing battle against nature into something more worthy. By preserving the memory of their earliest ancestors, they provide themselves with a reason for continuity.

The gardener's story was repeated to me with minor variations by four Mountain Jews who had just taken part in the funeral procession I had observed from a distance. In a mixture of Russian, Azeri, and Hebrew, they first claimed for themselves a few proverbial Khazar genes—a must along the Caspian shore—coupled with those of Persian Jews. Then they confirmed to me "most authoritatively" that "many of the Muslims in this region used to be Jews."

Particularly prolific and voluble on the subject was a heavyset man with a single tooth in his mouth and a traditional Jewish skullcap attached by a pin to his thinning hair. "Thirty years ago," he said, "an old Muslim man came to see us. He was from the village of Uchgyun, the inhabitants of which descended from Kryz. The man was carrying *sefer torah*," a sacred parchment describing the genesis of the world and the rise of the Israelites that is at the center of synagogue ritual.

Why would anyone in Uchgyun have a Torah scroll? I asked.

That is obvious, the man said. "His ancestors in the village of Kryz must have been Jewish." Moreover, he continued, until fairly recently, some Muslims used to light ritual candles come Sabbath.

Kryz is one of those extraordinary North Caucasian phenomena, a nation consisting of only a couple of villages, speaking a Lezgin dialect so distinct as to be considered by some a separate language. The first census of the Soviet era, in 1926, counted barely 607 Kryz, clearly a fragment of a larger tribe that had shrunk during the ages to the point of extinction, possibly one of the twenty-six tribes of Caucasian Albania that Strabo, the Greek geographer, counted two thousand years ago. The Soviet regime may deserve some credit for arresting and reversing the decline of the Kryz. By 1967, the last year for which I have found an official Soviet estimate, the ranks of the Kryz had swelled to 6,000.

Despite their well-established identity, despite their unique language, the Kryz are all identified as belonging to the Azeri nationality, to which they have little relation. Their complicated language is unrelated to the Turkic Azeri. Though not mutually intelligible with most Lezgin dialects, philologists place it within the Lezgin group of languages, which belongs in turn to what is known as the family of "Ibero-Caucasian languages." The latter family has a very broad definition—not broad enough, however, to include Azeri.

How then do the small tribes of the mountains end up being registered as Azeri? The answer, it seems, is the voracious appetite of Azerbaijan (shared by other nations in the region) to remove any impediment, however small, to the formation of a monoethnic state.

Mustafa Kemal Atatürk attempted the same in Turkey, with some success, after World War I. He said, "Turkish is he who says, 'I am Turkish.'" Under his iron grip, the option to say "Hey, I am *not* Turkish" was denied to all non-Turkic Muslims. To this day, no Muslim minority group in Turkey is allowed to nurture its cultural heritage openly or teach its language at school.

Azerbaijan had been cut off from the outside world for too long to be directly affected by Atatürk's formulae, but growing Azeri nationalism was evident even under Soviet rule. Audrey L. Altstadt (whose history of Azerbaijan is not unsympathetic to the Azeris) writes of the "re-Turkization" of the republic in the 1960s and 1970s, during which the "indigenous population" grew from 67 percent to 78 percent of the overall population. She implies that only the Turkic Azeris are "indigenous," and few Azeris would go out of their way to correct her.*

In the year after Soviet collapse, secular nationalists in Azerbaijan gained ascendancy, inspired by their counterparts in Turkey. The nationalist leader Abulfez Elchibey, whose short-lived presidency (1992–93) was an example of good intentions coupled with stunning incompetence, used to wear on his lapel a button displaying Atatürk's image. When I asked him about it, in an interview in the fall of 1992, he smiled and said, "Atatürk has a bad rap, but in fact he was a democrat."

Atatürk may deserve many compliments, but "democrat" is the least probable of them. Similarly, Azeri nationalists, particularly Elchibey, may deserve many compliments, not least for their personal courage and selflessness, but few compliments for their tolerance toward ethnic minorities in their midst.

The results of the campaign to "Turkicize" Muslim minorities was all too apparent to me in the Quba area, as I was looking for villages of the Kryz, the mysterious mountaineers whose ancestors may or may not have been Jewish.

---

* Azerbaijan's Soviet-era boss, now president, Heydar Aliyev, spoke of his attempts in his former incarnation to reinforce Azeri identity. "Azerbaijan adopted a new Constitution in 1978. There's an important article about the Azerbaijani language—that Azerbaijani is the national official language of Azerbaijan. I was responsible for getting the Constitution written. . . . [I]t wasn't easy to write such an article but I succeeded in getting it done" (*Azerbaijan International*, Spring 1994). Aliyev was surely self-serving in portraying his former self as a lifelong champion of the Azeri national cause, but the major fact—the legally established dominance of Azeri—is indisputable.

We stopped in a village about ten miles outside of Quba and knocked on doors at random, until a gate swiveled open and revealed a pleasant courtyard and two young women running for cover. A friendly man in his late fifties, his face shadowed by a few-days-old stubble, invited us in and immediately had tea and sweets served in his garden shed.

"We are Azeri," he said when asked about his ethnicity. He spoke Azeri to the women of the house. At no time did he mention the word *Lezgin*, nor did I raise the issue too explicitly, knowing the discomfort, perhaps even alienation such a question might generate.

"Perhaps you are an Armenian spy," he remarked smilingly while I was taking shots of the village with my video camera. "You give some-body a loaf of bread," he said of the Armenians, "and then they stab you at the back." Perhaps with the anti-Armenian jabs he was trying to establish his bona-fide credentials as an Azeri patriot and nip in the bud any notion that his non-Turkic ancestry could place him in alliance with Azerbaijan's mortal enemies (something quite a few Armenians were banking on). Nonetheless the man made oblique references to "Kryz people" and to the time when "only Kryz" lived in their ancestral village. When asked about Jewish blood, he shrugged and said, "I do not know anything about that, but I know that we are descendants of the Albans," the little-known people who occupied much of the Southeast Caucasus well into the Middle Ages.

The Kryz had to leave their mountainous domicile, he told me, "because they could not take it any longer. It was so difficult to get the basic necessities of life." They settled in the Quba region and estab-lished "thirty villages," recognizable by the common ending of their names, -*oba*. Little "Kryzness" has survived the move to the plains. Here as elsewhere, the isolation of the mountains has been the only way to preserve tongue and customs. Once they were off the mountains, the melting pot awaited the Kryz of Azerbaijan much the same way it awaited the Laks of Daghestan.

A few days later, I inadvertently crossed Kryz on my way to another mysterious village. It was barely twenty-five miles away from Quba, but our little entourage took five hours to reach it, as it was situated close to the end of a nonexistent road that only heavy trucks could cross at great peril. Our truck lost its hydraulic breaks as it was struggling up a hill, and for a couple of minutes of seemingly unstoppable sliding, we came un-comfortably close to joining the spirits of some ancient Lezgins.

The truck was skidding toward the abyss gaping to our right, nothing could have slowed our descent into a narrow stream flowing about two

The nonroad to Khynalug rose up to the huge cliffs, along the edges of many a precipice.

thousand feet below. For reasons our driver later described as "divine," the truck changed course and bumped into the rocks on our left. I was told that an alternative road was being carved out through the mountains for six years and should be ready soon, but that was far from certain and in any event provided us with little consolation.

Meanwhile, in the absence of bridges, our vehicle of no choice, now bruised and beaten, had to serve as an amphibious troop carrier. It was a solid Soviet model that must have been something of a novelty in the 1960s. We owed its availability to the kind hospitality of Quba's provincial governor, whom the president's office in Baku had tipped off in advance of our pending foray in quest of ancient genes. Our vehicle was blessed with the elegance of a racing rhinoceros and the smoothness of a Mercedes car just stripped of its seats and shock absorbers.

The nonroad rose up to huge cliffs, along the edges of many a precipice, until it bade farewell to the last trees and began its ascent into a low-bush-and-bare-hills country. There the village of Kryz suddenly appeared—and almost instantly disappeared—a hamlet of about two

At the very end of the road, almost seven thousand feet above sea level, in majestic isolation, lies Khynalug, the other one-village nation.

dozen rubble houses, more reminiscent of an archaeological site than an actual human habitat, betraying the poverty of its residents. On our way back, we stopped for hitchhikers, an obligatory courtesy in the mountains in the absence of any reliable public transportation. All of our fellow travelers classified themselves as Azeri. When I asked if they could speak Kryz, some nodded, and some did not respond, either because they found it more politic to ignore the question or because the engine's noise drowned my voice.

The odds that the Kryz language will survive are not getting shorter. Its astounding endurance has hitherto been a result of isolation, but now that most Kryz no longer live in the mountains, they are no more likely to preserve their vernacular than any endangered species is likely to survive outside of its original habitat.

A few miles away from Kryz, at the very end of the road, almost seven thousand feet above sea level, in majestic isolation, lies Khynalug, another one-village nation. Here the flat-roofed houses are built as terraces, leaning against each other all the way to the mountaintop, creating in the process an assortment of contiguous promenades, where villagers walk at leisure, reaching out to a sky almost so big as to challenge Montana's supremacy. One night, Alia, a young lady from Baku who traveled with us, looked up with childlike amazement and exclaimed, "I have never realized there are so many stars in the sky!" It was as though we were gazing at the vault of heaven: each star and each constellation looked ever brighter, almost at hand.

In Khynalug an heroic attempt has been made, in the last few years, to transform the local language—like Kryz, identified as "a member of the Lezgin subgroup"—into a medium of writing. A schoolteacher by the name of Rahim Alkhas has devised an alphabet for Khynalug—a spectacular task, given that the language requires fifty-nine consonants and eighteen vowels—and immersed himself in providing a few ounces of written culture. In 1991 he published a translation into Khynalug of the famous medieval poet Nezami, who is known as Persian but is claimed by Azeri nationalists as their own. Alkhas has also published his own book of poems and a historical essay about Khynalug.

Unfortunately the work of this diligent teacher, who deserves admiration and gratitude—a Nobel prize for conservation, if one were added to the list—is likely to have but few readers. No more than a handful of people, perhaps fewer than ten, have mastered the intricate alphabet, I was told, and all the rest are illiterate in their own language. Four hundred Khynalug children attend the local school, where teaching is conducted entirely in Azeri. Alkhas—who has composed and published poetry in five Turkic languages—is fighting a rearguard battle. Khynalug, Kryz, Budukh, and all the exotically named tongues of the treeless mountains are doomed by the advent of modernity.

By the end of the twenty-first century, linguists expect about half of the world's six thousand or so languages to disappear. Even wealthy nations fail to save indigenous languages from extinction. In the richest of them all, the United States, fewer than one-tenth of the Amerindian languages that predated Columbus are still spoken by mothers to their children, and one-sixth are spoken by fewer than ten tribal elders.

If America has failed so miserably, can Azerbaijan be expected to fare better? Should a poor country, where resources are scarce to nonexistent (at least prior to the flow of oil revenues), go out of its way to sustain minilanguages, which would require the compiling of textbooks and the training of teachers? Indeed, would children be well served by gaining full literacy in a language that even in the best of circumstances is bound to remain highly marginal? Is it fair to expect people to so embalm themselves, preventing them from joining the mainstream of society and reaping the benefits of modernity?

Moreover, is linguistic assimilation always driven by political motives? In Azerbaijan, has it really been all along an Azeri plot against minorities, particularly against the Lezgins, or is it but the natural flow of life?

The Daghestani Lezgin leaders have little doubt that the "re-Turkization" was premeditated. "Everything in Azerbaijan belongs to the Turks," General Kakhrimanov said, using again the pre-1917 term to describe the Azeris. "Lezgins are not recognized as a nation, are not represented in the organs of power. Their language is eliminated systematically. Turks are settled on traditional Lezgin lands."*

One reason Azerbaijan responds so angrily to any question about the Lezgins is the lingering suspicion that the questioner has an anti-Azeri agenda. By dwelling on the plight of the Lezgins, or the Talysh of Lenkoran (Länkäran) in southern Azerbaijan, or the Armenians in Nagorno-Karabakh, Azerbaijan's enemies may be trying to prove the country's "artificiality," to show it to be a miniempire in need of decolonization and so to justify an attempt to dissolve it.

The following evaluation of Azerbaijan, for example, appeared a few years ago in *Azg*, a Yerevan newspaper associated with a moderate opposition party:

Azerbaijan, which was artificially created by Russian Communists [and is] composed of various peoples—specifically Armenians, Lezgins and Talysh—has been since the 1920s a center of racial extremism and discrimination, ethnic cleansing, interethnic conflict, and crude human rights violations and, according to observers, presents a real threat to the development of democracy in all the countries in the region.

Overseas supporters of Armenia have included the Lezgins in their wholesale denunciations of Azerbaijan. Such was the case of Baroness Caroline Cox, a member of the British House of Lords and an

---

* In this context "Turks" was a reference not only to Azeris but to Meskhetian Turks as well. Theirs is one of the most tragic tales of the Caucasus. Having been deported from their homes in Georgia, in 1944, by Stalin, they were dispersed in Central Asia. Unlike most other deportees, they were not repatriated after Stalin's death. The declining years of the Soviet Union saw their ejection from their places of exile, and they became an underclass of vagabonds and beggars in many parts of the Caucasus, often detested and harassed by locals. Some are now being resettled in northern Azerbaijan, where I met a few of their numbers. Many Lezgins contended that the Meskhetians were taking over historical Lezgin lands.

indefatigable champion of the Armenian cause on the international scene. She wrote in the *International Herald Tribune* in November 1994:

> Tens of thousands of poor youth—many from Azerbaijan's oppressed Lezgi, Kurdish and Talysh minorities—have been press-ganged and dispatched to their deaths on the Karabakh front.

The Karabakh war (begun in 1988) was indeed highly unpopular in Azerbaijan, and there were instances of public discontent, particularly as military defeat was looming and the human toll was rising. In March 1993, as the Armenians were mounting their final offensive, Lezgins demonstrated in the northern Azerbaijani city of Gusar against the draft. Leaders of Sadval, the Daghestan-based Lezgin national movement, which organized the rally, claimed 70,000 participants, a somewhat unlikely figure.

The played-up coverage of the event in the Russian media so incensed the Azeris that President Abulfez Elchibey, known for throwing tantrums, called on the Russian government to prosecute its own media for "spreading misinformation" and "forged reports." So deeply entrenched is the suspicion that ethnic grievances in Azerbaijan are concocted by foreign meddlers that not one Azeri official or public figure was willing to entertain seriously any of my questions about the Lezgins. One opposition leader, Etibar Mamedov, a former presidential candidate and a historian, interrupted me when I posed the question to him in the summer of 1995. "These are not natural problems," he said. "The goal of those who talk about a 'Lezgin problem' or a 'Talysh problem' is not to solve problems but to create them." The unanimous view that ethnic problems are nonexistent echoes the virtual unanimity in Turkey for many decades on the Kurdish problem.

Disconcertingly, the U.S. State Department seems to have embraced the Azeri view completely, no questions asked. In its 1997 Human Rights Report, the Azerbaijan chapter stated simply: "Indigenous ethnic minorities such as the Talysh, Lezgins, Avars, and Georgians do not suffer discrimination." Clearly some in Azerbaijan believe otherwise, and they deserve to be heard by the United States government. Oddly, the same report points out, only a few paragraphs earlier, that "explicitly ethnically or religiously based parties were prohibited from participating in past elections." By any criteria known to me, restricting the ability of a minority to organize and win representation *is* a form of discrimination.

And yet, legitimate rights of minorities aside, Turkish and Azeri leaders have good reason to suspect the motives of those who bring up the plight of their minorities. Each time Russia deems Azerbaijan unfriendly, the Lezgin issue moves to the forefront. In 1993, at the height of Azeri-Russian tensions, then-President Elchibey was inching closer toward signing a treaty that would allow Western companies to begin developing the oil fields off the Azeri Caspian Sea shore. Russia opposed it for political and economic reasons. On March 25, ten thousand Daghestani Lezgins were allowed to demonstrate for "reunification" and even attempted a crossing of the Samur River into Azerbaijan.

Almost at the same time, the Armenians handed the Azeris a disastrous military defeat in the Battle of Kelbajar, starting a succession of setbacks and humiliations that set the stage for the near-collapse of the Azeri state and for President Elchibey's overthrow the following June. His successor was the veteran Communist Heydar Aliyev, a former KGB general and member of the Soviet Politburo who was immeasurably preferable to Moscow.

Just as Azerbaijan was struggling to survive at the mercy of Armenian troops, another blow was struck almost out of nowhere, also wrapped in ethnic colors. A former Azeri deputy minister of defense installed himself as "president" of a breakaway "Talysh-Mugan Autonomous Republic" in the southern city of Lenkoran. The Talysh are a Persian-speaking minority, officially numbered at just over 20,000, but Armenians often refer to them as a "constituent nation" of Azerbaijan, suffering ethnic discrimination.

The Azeris began to suspect a joint Russian-Armenian hand was attempting to break up their fragile state. Within days of a bomb attack against a Baku metro station which killed fourteen people in March 1996, the Azeri authorities announced that "the explosion was perpetrated by members of the Daghestan-based Lezgin separatist organization Sadval, at the instigation of the Armenian security service, who provided them with the necessary training at a base in Armenia in 1992."

In April 1996 Azerbaijan's minister of national security went even further in alleging that Sadval had bombed the metro "in cooperation with the Armenian and Russian secret services." He made the accusation in a public conference, under the watchful gaze of President Heydar Aliyev, who knows a thing or two about secret services.

A year later seven alleged members of Sadval went on trial for "treason, premeditated murder, and the violation of national equality." They were sentenced to prison terms of two to fifteen years.

As for General Kakhrimanov, the frustrated Daghestani Lezgin, he has never marshaled the army of liberation he so coveted. His dual career as a nationalist agitator and a military adviser to the government came to a bizarre end. On October 4, 1997, the Moscow newspaper *Nezavisimaya Gazeta* carried the following brief report:

> General Mukhuddin Kakhrimanov, a leader of the Lezgin National Council, has been arrested in Makhachkala (Republic of Daghestan) in connection with the September 18 murder of his wife. Police officials claim that Kakhrimanov killed his wife because she had discovered he was having an affair with a younger woman. Lezgin activists have suggested that the murder, which happened two days before the scheduled opening of a congress of the Lezgin National Council, was intended to prevent the planned fusion of that organization with another Lezgin movement, Sadval. Russian officials recently accused Sadval of forming military units. Sadval spokesmen deny those allegations.

LOOKING FOR KHAZARIA

Few phenomena in the Caucasus are more intriguing than the manipulation of the past. Politicians' and academics' efforts to reshape history in the image of contemporary needs are a lasting legacy not only of Soviet times but of the czarist era as well. I must confess an occasional fondness for those who attempt to re-create the past—not because of their often ingenious methods; rather for their sincere belief that the past matters. But the Caucasians—groups as well as individuals—judge it far less benignly, for they feel themselves victims of the rewriting of history.

In Makhachkala I called on Rassul Magomedov, the octogenarian dean of Daghestani historians, who in 1939 wrote the first book ever published in the Soviet Union (or so he claimed) about Imam Shamil, the leader of the nineteenth-century rebellion against Russia. His favorable portrayal of Shamil cost him dearly a few years later, when Stalin decided to do to the dead imam what he was doing to his live comrades: transform him overnight from a popular hero into "an English and Turkish agent."

"They were so good at forging history," Professor Magomedov told me in his comfortable apartment in central Makhachkala. "I was fired from my academic job, I was stripped of my doctorate, I lost my professorship, I became a complete outcast," he said. "There is little doubt that they came close to arresting me and charging me with the crime of belonging to 'the national bourgeoisie,' a class enemy. Then Stalin died and I lived."*

---

* Magomedov was much luckier than Geidar Gusseinov, an Azeri historian whose writings on Shamil angered the Communist bosses in Baku. Gusseinov could take the persecution and humiliation no more and committed suicide.

Elsewhere in the Caucasus, state-sponsored historians have launched campaigns to discredit past resistance to Russian rule. Max Bliyev, a prominent historian at Vladikavkaz University, in the republic of North Ossetia, developed an intricate theory that presented Imam Shamil as a highway robber bent on accumulating booty for himself and his cohorts. Bliyev's writing, toward the end of the Soviet period, still triggers enormous anger among Muslim intellectuals. The Ossetians are Christians and pride themselves on having been Russia's closest allies in the Caucasus for centuries.

At Grozny University, in what was the republic of Checheno-Ingushetia (which split up in 1991, with Grozny remaining capital of the Chechen part), historians were compelled for two decades to teach that Chechnya joined the Russian empire *voluntarily*—a horrendous affront to the Chechens and simply an astonishing distortion of history.

One day in 1996, in the town of Nazran, now capital of Ingushetia, I met a man who had taught at Grozny University when this dogma prevailed. Timurlan Mutaliyev was now head of the Ingush national archives. When we spoke at length about Ingush history, he was articulate and composed. Almost as an afterthought, I touched upon the subject of his Grozny professorship and his life in the shadow of "the dogma." Suddenly his posture changed dramatically—he shrunk in his chair, his head dropped—and he fell silent for a while. He finally raised his eyes, looked at me, and said, "That was the most tragic period of my entire life, something no academic in any society should ever endure. I was faced with an ultimatum—toe the line or lose your job. What could I have done? I objected with everything in me, but I had to make a living, and I didn't want to sacrifice my career. That was the time of the Vinogradov dictatorship"—V. B. Vinogradov was the head of the history department at Grozny University, the author of "the dogma," and its ruthless enforcer.

Later I asked to see Mutaliyev again, but the Ingush scholar was most reluctant. We were seated in his little car in front of the Ingush government headquarters, and I pleaded with him to tell me the story. He finally relented, and we set an appointment for the following evening. I was to leave Ingushetia the next morning. Mutaliyev never showed up. I was convinced that the specter of Vinogradov was still haunting him.*

---

* The National Congress of the Chechen People, a counterparliament of sorts—which in November 1990 lay the foundations for the rebellion against Russia by proclaiming Chechnya's "sovereignty"—deprived Vinogradov not only of his academic status but also of his citizenship and denounced all who supported his "pseudoscientific concepts." Valery Tishkov, a Russian ethnographer and a minister of nationalities in President Yeltsin's administration, described the measures against Vinogradov as indicating "mil-

When I met Professor Bliyev in Vladikavkaz in late 1994, he was preparing for the publication of his alternative history of the nineteenth-century Caucasian War, which faculty members treated as something akin to a sacred text. Many of Bliyev's Daghestani colleagues with whom I spoke trashed his life work as far-fetched and motivated by ignorance and hatred. Of greater interest to me is the state of mind that generated and fostered this ongoing relationship between past and present, one that makes academic works sound like commentaries of current affairs.

If the *nineteenth* century seems a bit distant, what of the *ninth* century? It was straight to the ninth century that Salau Aliyev and Gadzhi Abduragimov took me.

The Kumyks, Aliyev asserted, are direct descendants of the Khazars, a mighty Turkic people who dominated large chunks of what would now be southern Russia: the lower Volga area, the Caucasus, even Crimea and southern Ukraine, "all the way to Bulgaria."

The Lezgins, Abduragimov contended, are direct descendants of the Gutians, a Mesopotamian people from whom we heard for the last time about 4,300 years ago.

Precious little is known about the Khazars, and the mindful reader need not be misled by encyclopedia entries about them, even when accompanied by maps and replete with names and dates. None of this abundant printed material is based on eyewitness accounts or conclusive archaeological findings. We do not know for sure where the Khazars came from, though they are assumed to have been Turkic migrants from the Central Asian steppes. We do not know what language they spoke, where the actual borders of their state were drawn, or what happened to them after their final defeat in the eleventh century.

Nothing sums up the state of our knowledge of the Khazars better than the Serb author Milorad Pavić's vignette about a diplomatic delegation that the Khazar king sent to Byzantium in the ninth century. The

---

itant intolerance toward any deviations from a compatible version of national history." I do not know whether Tishkov was familiar with the allegations that Vinogradov had not merely deviated from "a nationalist version" of history but in fact sought for many years to punish any deviant from his own version of history, sanctioned by the Communist Party of the Soviet Union. Tishkov's involvement in the Caucasus has gone far beyond academic pursuits, and few have escaped his scathing, contemptuous criticism, which bore the hallmark of Soviet-era public discourse.

entire history of his people was tattooed on one of his envoy's skin. Known as the "great parchment," that priceless source, the missing part in the puzzle, gradually peeled off through the various forms of corporal punishment that the hapless bearer suffered. So was destroyed our only firsthand account.

The Khazars' greatest claim to fame may be the tale that in the middle of the eighth century, their royalty and aristocracy converted to Judaism. No lasting testimony exists; nevertheless for centuries the episode has excited the imagination of Jews and non-Jews alike, philo-Semites as well as anti-Semites. In a Jewish history of continuous perse-cution and shrinkage, the voluntary Khazar act of coming aboard has been treated as a ray of light, almost an act of validation and vindica-tion. Israeli high school students are required to study at great length a fictitious medieval composition called *HaKoozari* (*The Khazar*, tellingly subtitled *In Defense of the Despised Faith*), which purports to reenact the entire process of deliberation and theological disputation that led the Khazar king to decide to convert to Judaism. At no time that I recall were my schoolmates and I ever told that we were dealing with pure fic-tion, or that the Jewishness of the Khazars was at best very selective and at worst highly questionable.

The "mass conversion" of the Khazars generated a host of outlandish theories about the Khazar ancestry of the majority of Ashkenazi Jews, providing anti-Zionists with the silliest arguments in their arsenal. ("The Jews do not deserve Israel because they are of Khazar, not Davidic descent" paraphrases some of them.)

Probably the best-known proponent of the theory was the late Hungarian-born Jewish—or should I say Khazar—author Arthur Koestler. Writing in the 1970s, he described the Khazar king's conver-sion to Judaism as a "coup d'état" that was intended to equip his state with an ideology to rival Byzantium's Christianity and the Arab caliphate's Islam—the two empires having been the main protagonists in a struggle for world hegemony. Khazaria, Koestler wrote in apparent seriousness, represented "the Third World" of the early Middle Ages, striving for nonalignment, treading carefully between empires. Koestler's ruminations led him to state that the entire notion of anti-Semitism was "devoid of meaning" because the ancestors of modern Jews

> came not from the Jordan but from the Volga, not from Canaan but from the Caucasus, once believed to be the cradle of the Aryan race; and that ethnically they are more closely related to the Hun,

Uigur and Magyar tribes than to the seed of Abraham, Isaac and Jacob.*

Curiously, Koestler's theory had a precursor during the brief Nazi occupation of the Northwest Caucasus in 1942–43. While the Wehrmacht, mounting its last major offensive of the war, was driving through the mountains en route to the oil fields of the Caspian, the SS was bracing itself to extend the Final Solution. A debate flared up within the German administration over how to determine who was a Jew. No one had any problem identifying Ashkenazi Jews (1,800 of them were slaughtered on a single day outside the North Caucasian city of Kislovodsk); but some German experts suggested that those known as Mountain Jews, who numbered in the tens of thousands, mostly in the Northeast Caucasus, should be spared on the ground of their non-Semitic Aryan-Persian descent. (They spoke a Persian dialect, had Persian features, and were almost indistinguishable from their Muslim neighbors save for religious practices.) But the Germans never reached Daghestan or Azerbaijan, where the bulk of Mountain Jews lived.

Given the thickness of the plot, it is perhaps not entirely surprising that I was so interested in Salau Aliyev's embrace of the Khazars. Not only does he claim that the Khazars are the Kumyks' ancestors, he holds the view that Tarki was the precise site of the earlier Khazar capital, Samandar. (After the loss of the Caucasus, the Khazars moved their capital to Itil, presumably in the lower Volga region.) Of Samandar, an Arab historian, Ibn Hawkal, wrote: "[It has] so many orchards and gardens that from Derbent [in southern Daghestan] to Serir the whole country is covered with gardens and plantations belonging to this city. It is said that there are about 40,000 of them." That is all very impressive, but for the fact that the chronicler lived about two centuries *after* the fall of Samandar. Generally, between the fall of the Khazars and the composition of reports describing their greatness, decades or even centuries are allowed to lapse.

---

* Arthur Koestler, *The Thirteenth Tribe* (New York: Random House, 1976). Koestler was aware that his book would be used to delegitimize Israel, a result that did not please him. Israel's right to exist, he wrote, "is not based on the hypothetical origins of the Jewish people, nor on the mythological covenant of Abraham with God; it is based on international law. . . . Whatever the Israeli citizens' racial origins . . . their state exists de jure and de facto, and cannot be undone, except by genocide." I imagine he would be unhappy to see that his book has ended up on reading lists of individuals or groups advocating the unmaking of Israel.

While in Makhachkala, I went to see a distinguished Kumyk scholar, Gadzhi Saidovich Fedorov-Gusseinov, a professor of history at the local university whose book, *The Origins of the Kumyks*, was on display at the Tenglik convention. Fedorov-Gusseinov told me that he had studied the Khazars for thirty years, and he dismissed almost out of hand the Arab sources.

"Based on the coordinates Masudi provided us, Samandar may have been located in Tarki," he said. "It is a possibility, but not the only one. There are at least four other options. In any event, at the time he wrote, there were no longer any Khazars in Daghestan, and we have no real proof that there had ever been any. There is no archaeological evidence of it. Masudi's writings cannot be considered evidence. They were hearsay."

Why, then, do Aliyev and his supporters speak so earnestly of the Khazars? I asked.

"They are looking for a prehistorical motherland among the great nations," he said. "But this is entirely unnecessary. I am Kumyk, and I consider myself a member of the Daghestani family. I am no politician, I have never involved myself in politics. I am saddened by the political exploitation of history, particularly when it is so distorted. They are trying to tell all other Daghestanis, 'You are newcomers, you are the descendants of immigrants, not we. We are indigenous, we have always been here, we have always spoken this Turkic language of ours.'

"But isn't this silly? How can one know? You see, I live in a place called Alborkent, just outside of Makhachkala. There is a Mesolithic site over there, ten to fifteen thousand years old. Can we tell what language the Mesolithic people spoke? Can we tell, for that matter, what language God spoke to Adam after creating him? Some linguists have contended that twelve thousand years ago, all humans spoke the same language, and that language must have been Turkic.* Aliyev probably believes that God spoke Kumyk to Adam."

Did you ever try to dissuade Aliyev from preaching all this? I asked Fedorov-Gusseinov.

He nodded. "I did. I tried to speak to his brother Kamil. It was in December 1991, when they set an encampment in Khasavyurt [near the Chechen border] and halted all the trains from Daghestan to Russia [in protest against the settlement of the Laks on Kumyk lands]. I called on them. You see, there was an attempt to defuse tensions by inviting prominent people, including members of the intelligentsia. We were

---

* A reference to the "monogenetic theory of language" by the Soviet linguist Nikolai Marr (1864–1934). He theorized that all languages evolved from one original, made up of four basic elements. His theory was eventually ridiculed and discredited, but its residue is still evident, including among Turkic nationalists in the Caucasus.

squeezed in a little room, and Salau [Aliyev] delivered a speech. There were also peasants there, quite a few.

"One Kumyk journalist rose to speak after him. He began his speech with the following words: 'We, the Kumyks, number fifty million.' Members of the audience rose to their feet and applauded him. I was appalled.

"I then saw Kamil, Salau's brother. 'What is going on here?' I asked him. 'Does Salau agree with him? I would be happy if there were fifty million Kumyks, but this is idiocy.'

"'Leave him alone,' Kamil told me. 'Don't start a scandal.' Well, he dissuaded me from delivering a public rebuttal.

"After the journalist had finished his speech, I turned to him and asked him, in the Kumyk language, 'Why in the world are you deluding our people?' Somebody pulled my sleeve. 'Gadzhi Saidovich,' that person said, 'don't speak Kumyk to him. He doesn't understand.' I was furious. 'You don't speak Kumyk, and yet you dare speak for our people? Whoever gave you the right to do that?' That was my first and last foray into politics. I will never get involved again. When I see Salau, I say hello to him, nothing else."

So you think that Tenglik is deceiving the Kumyk nation? I asked.

"I do indeed. The Kumyks are not Turkic at all, and they cannot claim descent from Turks."

But is Tenglik actually dangerous? Should it cease to exist?

"No. It should exist. But they should not deal with history. They should talk about economics, about culture, about education. They should not spend time infuriating other nations. Our priorities are to build, create, develop, educate—not drive a wedge between nations, which they do."

Here is a piece of advice to a traveler in the Caucasus: each time you go to interview a nationalist leader, carry an encyclopedia, preferably all thirty-two volumes of it. Here politicians do not strive to benefit only those living in the present but also to redeem cultures and nations long extinct.

Salau Aliyev's Khazar pretensions are matched easily by Gadzhi Abduragimov's concept of "Lezgistan." The sixty-year-old electrophysicist who briefly claimed the leadership of the Lezgin people in the early 1990s has constructed an alternative history not only of the Caucasus but of the entire Southwest Asia region, at the center of which he places the Lezgins.

"We have a recorded history of 4,500 years," he argued when we met in an empty classroom at Makhachkala State University. "We existed in proximity to the time the world's first epos was composed and the world's first alphabet was created." Indeed, he claims that much of that alphabet was Lezgin, and to that alphabet later generations owed the Hebrew, Greek, Latin, and Cyrillic scripts.

The Lezgins first emerged around 2200 B.C. to become the ruling nation in large parts of Mesopotamia, he said. At that time, they were known by the name *Gutians*. They went on to change names and lands until they finally established, in the eighth century B.C., the quintessential Caucasian state known to the ancients as Albania (not to be confused with the later Albania in the Balkans).

There is a little problem here because Abduragimov is not the only Caucasian nationalist who claims Albanian ancestry. So do some Azeris, his sworn enemies. So important was their claim deemed, and so provocative was it, that it actually played a role in kindling the 1988 Karabakh war with the Armenians.

For two national movements at loggerheads with each other, identifying an alleged common ancestor is no cause for jubilation. On the contrary, it is cause for further conflict, since each group must now refute the ancestral claims of the other. In the Caucasus, both Azeris and Lezgins could not be right at the same time. The unanswered—perhaps unanswerable—question had to be answered.

Abduragimov announced the answer in 1995, in an impressive book, some six hundred pages long, in a handsome chestnut hard cover that was engraved with the name *Caucasian Albania—Lezgistan* in golden letters. *Lezgistan* means "land of the Lezgins," although no such state has ever existed.

I could not help but tell Abduragimov about an Israeli rabbi, Eliyahu Avichail, who started a movement in 1975 to gather all descendants of ancient Israelites, regardless of how far they might have spread or what their present religious persuasions were. The rabbi undertook to bring back to the fold the Pathans of Central Asia, Amerindian tribes in the Peruvian jungle, and hill people in northern India. He seriously planned for their relocation to Israel. In 1993 he told me of the next target on his agenda, the largest of ancient Israel's lost ten tribes.

"Who were they?" asked Abduragimov.

The Lezgins, I said. Abduragimov was not amused.

Reaching out to touch the most distant past is something over which neither Kumyks nor Lezgins hold a monopoly.

Soviet and post-Soviet historians have attempted a scientific codification of the evolution of nations. They have tried to show that nations are live organisms with childhood diseases, hormonal urges at adolescence, maturity accompanied by mellowness, and finally aging and death. A large number of academic conferences in the Soviet Union were devoted to the "origins" of nations, which often culminated with an actual resolution that immediately became a dogma. "Ethnogenesis," barely known in the West, became the alchemy of the historical discipline in the USSR, the humanities' equivalent of Lysenko's Marxist biology, an open invitation for state-funded charlatanism on a grand scale.

The Soviet system's elaborate theories on the "inception of nations" have survived Soviet Communism. When those who enjoy an academic aura and scientific authority occupy themselves with charts and formulae that purport to present history as a sequence of predictable and comprehensible events (and engage in the wildest speculations on prehistory as well), it is little wonder that nationalists resort to far-fetched theories in order to establish their nations' credentials.

"Modernity has made the entire question of antiquity divisive and painful," Timurlan Mutaliyev, the well-regarded Ingush historian and archivist, told me when I met him in Nazran. "The traditional character of historiography makes it impossible for us to rise above politics," he continued. "A new regime encourages the intelligentsia to 'prove' the antiquity of the state. Science and politics are so intertwined that we have no way of accomplishing much by way of independent research. It is preposterous to make history look more ancient than it is. For example, we were all very amused around 1992 or 1993, when two historians in North Ossetia [Ingushetia's western neighbor, with which a brief war was fought in 1992] published a booklet asserting that Jesus and Mary were Ossetian, and that eleven out of the twelve apostles were Ossetian. (The only one excluded was Judas.) They also claimed that Friedrich Barbarossa was Ossetian. Their proof? His name: *Barbar* stood for "barbarian," *Ossa* stood for "Ossetian." [*Barbarossa* is in fact Italian for "red-bearded." Friedrich, twelfth-century emperor of the Roman Holy Empire, was a native and hereditary ruler of the German duchy of Swabia.]

"This kind of aggressive ignorance did well especially in the days of *perestroika*. At that time, emotions flared, and no one tried to restrain them. For example, in 1989 the newspaper *Socialist Ossetia* carried in three of its issues 'historical evidence,' signed by fifteen leading historians of the republic, denying that Ingush people had ever lived there prior to 1920. That was so obnoxious, and contradicted facts so grossly, that the discontent here was enormous. After all, written sources, both Russian and Georgian, show that Ingush lived in what is now North Ossetia as early as the sixteenth century."

To Salau Aliyev, claiming antiquity for his own people was a matter not only of dignity but of survival. The "square inch in the sun" that the small nations seek is not merely a territorial place but a spot on a time continuum. To Aliyev, the Kumyks do not deserve a land only because they constitute a nation in the late twentieth century—they deserve it because they have given so much to the world that the world does not even realize.

Did "they" not stand between the Arabs and Europe, in the seventh century, when nobody else did? Would the Arabs not have taken over Europe through its eastern gate in one fell swoop, well before there was a Russia or a Charlemagne to fight for a European civilization, if it had not been for "our ancestors the Khazars"?

The parallels with Serb nationalism—though much older and better articulated—are no accident. The Serbs have also claimed credit for sparing Europe a long Ottoman yoke, by standing up to the Turkic hordes in Kosovo in the fourteenth century. The Ottomans finally prevailed, but by that time they had run out of steam and energy and did not attempt a takeover of Europe for another two centuries. The Serbs, even in defeat, were elevated (in their mind, at least) to saviors of Christendom. Aliyev was now claiming similar credit, but his pretension kindled little popular interest and was largely dismissed by historians. After all, unlike the Serbs, the Kumyks accepted Islam early on and were among its chief disseminators in the Caucasus.

Aliyev, in fact, was not *claiming* a past, he was *subverting* it. To create a distinct Kumyk identity, he had to do away with centuries of affinity and coexistence, marked primarily by a common religion. His best hope lay in the eighth century, and he was trying hard, if to little avail.

ALI ALIYEV, A HIGHLANDER

The aging Soviet car that took me to the mountains on an early September morning was a Daghestani microcosm on wheels. The driver was Lezgin, the guide was Lak, the interpreter was Kumyk. Their peoples have been cohabitants of this land for centuries, perhaps millennia, but the only language common to them now was Russian, which had been imposed by the bayonet a century and a half earlier.

The clear, warm weather of the Caspian coast was gradually giving way to the chilly mist of the highland. Forested slopes were transforming into barren hills as the car struggled toward Lakia. "You are probably wondering why our hills are treeless," Ali Aliyev, my Lak guide, anticipated my question. A retired Soviet naval officer, he was a self-styled custodian of the Lak spirit, a flowing fountain of historical data, oral traditions, myths, and speculations. "One legend has it," he continued,

"that many years ago, the villagers were losing their children to packs of wolves that were hiding in the woods. The survival of the nation was at stake. The elders gathered and determined that there was only one way out—to set fire to the trees and kill the wolves. The fire raged for days on end,

Ali Aliyev was a custodian of the Lak spirit, a flowing fountain of data, traditions, myths, and speculations.

spread all over the mountains, and wiped out the forest." Aliyev may have intended the fable as a metaphor for his people's present predicament, when the Laks' future is threatened by depopulation, urbanization, and modernity—wolves no less dangerous than those in the extinct forest. But he was willing to acknowledge that the deforestation here, as in other parts of the Caucasus, was probably accomplished through war and indiscriminate chopping for fuel.

The hillsides were strewn with patches of cabbage fields, the mainstay of the Lak economy. Peasants began to farm these terraces some eight thousand years ago, making it one of the most ancient agricultural civilizations anywhere, older even than those of the Middle East. "People can do well growing cabbages," Aliyev said. "Oh, yes, the nicest houses in Ghazi-Ghumuq are built on foundations of cabbage." He laughed heartily.

Ghazi-Ghumuq, where our little expedition was headed, was the heart of the Lak nation, the capital of the former Lak state. There a long line of warrior-dukes, or khans, reigned, whose military reputation transcended their principality's borders. Theirs was one of the ministates that endured for hundreds of years until overrun by Russian armies in the mid-nineteenth century.

My guide across mountain peaks and centuries, Aliyev was introducing me that day to the sites of his people's rise and decline. We were walking the hills overlooking Ghazi-Ghumuq, now a sleepy town hid-

The road to Ghazi-Ghumuq, the Lak capital

den in a crater. Atop Ghazi-Ghumuq lie the ruins of the khan's castle. Only a skeletal wall has survived, attesting to glory long gone. "When we were young, we used to fight here," Aliyev reminisced, gesturing toward a distant hill about two miles away. Young Aliyev used to lead his peers in a "Lak army" against the "Roman legion," composed of kids from the next block.

Romans? I interjected with surprise. Why Romans? Why not Mongols? Or Persians? Or Russians? All of whom have invaded the land in the past seven hundred years, left behind plenty of memories, mostly bad, and earned the well-deserved wrath of the highlanders.

"Oh"—he smiled—"who knows? Perhaps our genes carry the memory of a battle our ancient ancestors waged against the Romans."

Who knows indeed. It so happened that Pompey, the great Roman empire-builder, did venture into the Caucasus around the year 65 B.C. Whether he was specifically interested in the Lak land, we do not know.

For a Lak man immersed in his people's history, nothing was more natural than to choose a military career, which is what Aliyev did. Laks have provided an unusually high number of war heroes, including quite a few Soviet and Russian army generals, and even "one of *Ethiopia's* greatest heroes," as Aliyev insisted. While in Ghazi-Ghumuq, we took a little pilgrimage to the house of Musoi Manarov, a renowned Lak *kosmonavt* (astronaut), an exalted hero of the Soviet era.

The site of the khan's citadel offers a panoramic view of the mountains. "See?" Aliyev pointed to an empty hill a few miles away. "People used to live there, kids played in the fields, women washed clothes in the stream, men prayed in the mosque. . . . Nothing is left." He paused for a moment and took a drag on his cigarette. "Thirty-two Lak villages," he said, "depopulated or abandoned because of the Communists. My homeland is turning into a wasteland. For this alone, I would put the bastards on trial and have them shot. That is what the Soviet Union did to us."

A couple of hours earlier, en route to the Ghazi-Ghumuq valley, our car was stopped by uniformed Russian border guards. The nearest international frontier was many miles away, traffic on the road was very light, and border guards seemed a bit redundant. Perhaps the young Russian soldiers stopped us because they were bored, or under orders, or were just eager to remind us how unhappy they were, spending the prime of their youth in these godforsaken hills.

The fuming Aliyev was in no mood to empathize with the rude Russians. He leaped out of the car and confronted the uniformed men in an explosion of rage. "How dare you stop me here?!" he yelled, gesticulating angrily. "This is my *rodina* [motherland], this land belongs to me, you have no business bossing me around. You are visitors here—I am the

"See?" Aliyev pointed to an empty hill a few miles away. "People used to live there, kids played in the fields, women washed clothes in the stream, men prayed in the mosque. . . . Nothing is left."

master." He repeated the words many times, yet the targets of his fury seemed unmoved. They still insisted on examining our papers, which they ended up doing.

I was unsure whether they were remotely aware that this land was indeed not theirs, that its inhabitants had ferociously resisted their presence as late as the mid-nineteenth century, and that they had yielded only after one of history's longest anticolonial wars.

It was hard to figure out how much of Aliyev's outburst was a show of courage—after all, challenging a uniformed, armed Russian soldier in the Caucasus could be dangerous—and how much it was a spontaneous response to humiliation at the hands of an "occupation army." The spectacle of abandoned Lak villages helped convince me that Aliyev was indeed an angry man, with only memories of a better past to mollify him.

"If only you could go back in time," he said, pointing a yellowish, nicotine-tainted finger at me, "you should stop by in the eighteenth century and ask about the Laks. People would turn pale in fear!" He burst out laughing—or was it coughing? I was not quite sure.

Standing above his native Ghazi-Ghumuq, Aliyev continued our journey into the Lak past. "There, you see? There's a place we call Partavalo. We name it after Partu Pattima, our great heroine, the Lak *Jeanne d'Arc*. Laks have long believed she's buried there. When the Mongols arrived here, she headed a Ghazi-Ghumuq army against them. We have a poem extolling her courage. My father wrote an article about her, and last year her life was the theme of a national ballet performance." The notion of an army led by a woman stretches credulity in such a strongly patriarchal land, but as we have seen, some traditions hold that the Caucasus was the original home of the mythical Amazons, and one source dates the phenomenon of women warriors in the region to as late as the sixteenth century.

"**D**o you see that plateau?" Aliyev was now pointing out a bare, steep hill a few miles to the south. "There the battle against Nadir was fought. When I was young, I used to go there and collect war mementos."

Aliyev was not talking about World War II but about a war fought when Louis XV was king of France, George II reigned in London, and George Washington was a schoolboy. In 1742 Ali Aliyev's forefathers fought off an invasion by the great Nadir Shah, emperor of Persia, the Conqueror of Nations, Terror of the Universe, whose rule stretched from the Indian subcontinent to Central Asia, and whose army seemed invincible and the tide of his conquests unstemmable. "The new Nebuchadnezzar has been rendered quite mad by his triumphs," a Russian envoy reported from Tehran in 1741 following an imperial audience. He went on to quote the shah: "If I move with only one leg, I take India; if I move with both legs, I shall conquer the whole world."

The shah's troops were advancing northward unimpeded, hoping to accomplish something no one power had ever managed: bring the entire Caucasus under the will of a single state. The kings of Georgia could not halt his advance, nor could the Tatar khans along the Caspian Sea. But the ferocious Lak warriors of Ghazi-Ghumuq could and did, at the head of an all-Daghestani alliance. An exasperated Nadir, formerly imbued

Ali Aliyev (sharing bread with his cousins in Ghazi-Ghumuq), former Soviet colonel, former admiral of the Abkhaz fleet, speaker of the Caucasian parliament, a highlander. "Wherever I was," he says, "I always longed for the mountains."

with aspirations for world domination, was sinking so rapidly in the Dahestani quagmire that upon setting a camp in the highland not far from the Lak country he named it, bitterly, Ruined Persia.

In 1992 Aliyev had a large plaque installed in Ghazi-Ghumuq's main square, to commemorate the two hundred and fiftieth anniversary of the victory over the Persians. The words engraved in stone are his:

> *Daghestanis!*
> *Bow to this land, which is thickly impregnated*
> *with the blood of your famous and brave ancestors,*
> *and think: Is it not the friendship of our peoples,*
> *magnified by their courage,*
> *that helped them stand for the honor and freedom of Daghestan,*
> *to defeat the thousands of armies of foreign invaders.*
> *Remember this, and continue the brave tradition!*

These words are ambiguous. Their nationalistic tone is unmistakable, and yet interestingly, they hail unity, not separateness. Daghestan is home to thirty-two nationalities, some of which have strong grievances against each other—and yet Aliyev, the Lak patriot who bemoans the decline of his people, chose to accentuate a common purpose, not differences.

The 1742 victory over the Persians was the last scored by the independent highlanders prior to the Russian invasion—a fact not lost on Aleksey Yermolov, a battle-hardened czarist general, the first Russian supreme commander in the Caucasus. Fresh from his victories in the Napoleonic wars, during which he had marched his proud Cossack troops into Paris, Yermolov was dispatched to pacify the mountains—a task he undertook with exceptional gusto. "Bow down thy snowy head, O Caucasus / Submit! Yermolov comes," proclaimed an ecstatic Aleksandr Pushkin.

In June 1820, the czarist troops conquered Ghazi-Ghumuq, deposed the khan, and replaced him with a Russian lackey. A jubilant General Yermolov wrote to his emperor: "The subjugation of Daghestan is now complete; and this country, proud, warlike, and hitherto unconquered, has fallen at the sacred feet of your imperial majesty." Unusually strong words for a tiny mountainous tribe, spoken by a man who had just helped vanquish the most powerful army in Europe. Yermolov's self-congratulations turned out to be premature, however. Ghazi-Ghumuq would switch hands many times before a Russian flag would be hoisted over it for good. Twenty-two years after Yermolov's message to the czar, Imam Shamil sent a celebratory message of his own to his Chechen allies, notifying them of the liberation of Ghazi-Ghumuq. His words clearly testified to the exceptional importance of this tiny capital: "With God's help, I took with no difficulty at all the town of Ghazi-Ghumuq— *the mother of all towns.* . . . The khan's treasure and the most precious local treasures are the trophies of my victory. . . . I have taken thirty-five hostages from the rulers of Ghazi-Ghumuq." I wish I had recalled the imam's words when a Lak potentate, Magomed Khachilayev, invited me to have lunch with him one Friday afternoon at his sumptuous residence in Makhachkala. Fine wine was served, alongside the famed fresh vegetables of the Caucasus and fish from the nearby Caspian; then the man turned to me and asked why it is that Americans know so little of his land. Why, he asked, do Americans seem not to care at all that a terrible war was being waged by mighty Russia against the tiny Chechen nation, Daghestan's neighbor to the west?

I described the hurdles that small nations are likely to encounter while attempting to make their case in America's capital: the Beltway myopia of K Street lobbyists, short attention span as an American affliction, and the lack of a "North Caucasian vote" in critical states and congressional districts. "After all," I said matter-of-factly, "Washington *is* the most important capital city in the world."

My host frowned. "I think otherwise," he said quietly but intently. "To me, the most important capital city in the world is *Ghazi-Ghumuq.*"

It was a well-earned comment. A president in Washington may have nuclear buttons to push and satellite-transmitted importance to convey, but my host's favorite capital was older than Washington by a millennium and deserved greater respect than I had implied.

Khachilayev was born in 1957 in a village outside Ghazi-Ghumuq. His first name, Magomed, is a Russian form of Muhammad, and equally Russian by form is his last name. The Russification of forms has not spared even the name of Ghazi-Ghumuq. The Russians, unable to pronounce the original, settled for the diluted Kumukh, which is its official name to this day. Diluted forms of a heroic past account in some measure for the dwindling self-esteem of the highlanders.

Even so, Ghazi-Ghumuq has made a partial comeback in Daghestan's public life. In the late 1980s, when Mikhail Gorbachev's *glasnost* was in full swing, Soviet provincial bosses felt obliged to pretend to tolerate a degree of pluralism. Daghestan's government resolved that each of the province's "major nations" (those numbering more than 70,000 souls) would have a "national movement" to represent it. And yet, while opposition movements were shaking the foundations of many of the Soviet Union's constituent republics and autonomous regions, Daghestan's

"The houses of Ghazi-Ghumuq are founded on cabbage," Ali Aliyev laughed.

Communist leadership made sure that parochial agendas and interethnic rivalries nipped in the bud any attempt to unite opposition forces and unseat the deeply entrenched Soviet elite.

The national movements were thus allotted state funds; their leaders were put on the government payroll and were provided with offices and cars. Except for the Kumyk movement, the nationalists were gradually co-opted, though not entirely neutralized as a source of opposition to the government, which is otherwise based on a delicate ethnic balance and decision by consensus. The Laks were among the nations that qualified for their own movement; it was named Ghazi-Ghumuq, after the old capital, and Ali Aliyev became its first leader. A couple of years later, he stepped aside, and Magomed Khachilayev moved in to replace him.

Aliyev was a fiery intellectual, well read and well versed, a man driven by anger and idealism. Khachilayev, on the other hand, was a representative of what some Russians call "predatory capitalism," the class of relatively young people who have emerged from nowhere to amass huge fortunes and use them to buy political power as well. As a person, Khachilayev was low-key and premeditated, no match for Aliyev's rhetoric or learning.

Aliyev had emerged as a public figure in the heyday of Gorbachev's liberalization, when the intelligentsia was leading, or at least was viewed as leading, the process of change. Khachilayev rose after people had tired of the intelligentsia and shifted to survival mode. Aliyev knew every corner of the Caucasus, never running out of

Magomed Khachilayev frowned. "I think otherwise," he said. "To me, the most important capital city in the world is Ghazi-Ghumuq."

stories of wars long forgotten, languages long extinct, and kings long dethroned—but his demeanor seemed misplaced in a society increasingly enamored of material success, however ill-gotten. Khachilayev was a much abler representative of the emerging society.

One day at a kiosk on Lenin Avenue, Makhachkala's main thoroughfare, a young Lak man, a medical student who made ends meet by selling soft drinks and candies, upon hearing that I was writing about his nation, asked me, "Have you met Khachilayev?" and was absolutely thrilled to hear that I had. He did not ask about Aliyev; nor was it likely that he had ever heard his name.

Aliyev, nearly twenty years older than Khachilayev, was now a retired naval officer, holder of the seemingly important title "Chairman of the Parliament of the Confederation of the Peoples of the North Caucasus." Yet he was not whisked anywhere in black limousines; nor was he met by playing bands in distant airports. He was moving in the unrewarding realm of believers and idealists, a dwindling crowd in Russia. He believed in a North Caucasian common destiny. He believed that the multitude of tiny nations, many of them on the verge of extinction, could still be infused with life. He believed that ancestors could inspire their descendants to regeneration, both spiritual and political.

Aliyev could be said to be seeking a way to rescue the highlanders from the fate that has befallen American Indians. The indigenous people of the Caucasus met the might of Russia more or less at the same time that American Indians met that of the young United States. The commanding generals of the Russian and American armies, celebrated as heroes by their compatriots, were villains and butchers to the natives. Andrew Jackson's name evoked the same anguish and hatred along the

Mississippi that Aleksey Yermolov's did along the Terek River, which flows through much of the Northeast Caucasus. The "last frontiers" in North America and the North Caucasus were finally conquered in crushing defeats at the same time. But in the Caucasus, a century later, there was still hope.

In 1989 Ali Aliyev retired from the Soviet navy and went home to Daghestan. He had been away for some thirty-five years, had spent his shore leaves in dozens of ports worldwide, and had acquired a Russian speech so impeccable that no Russian ever mistook him for a *gorets* (highlander). Nonetheless, the diminutive man of fifty-five, with only a hint of his hair still intact, a deeply lined face, and a voice turned hoarse by chain-smoking, never forgot where he came from. "Wherever I was," he says, "I longed for the mountains, for the glaciers." Aliyev was determined to spend the rest of his life standing for the highlanders' cause.

Shortly after his retirement, he went to war against Georgia, becoming the commander of the tiny "Abkhazian navy"—two "military vessels" and a few civilian boats that served a pariah statelet of 90,000 that was recognized by no one.

Georgia had emerged from the ruins of the Soviet Union and then collapsed into civil war and was confronting actual and potential secessions virtually everywhere on its borders. The Abkhaz, a minority within their own autonomous province, won their war in 1993 and established their coveted statehood. The majority Georgians in Abkhazia, about a quarter million of them, were kicked out.

Aliyev's contribution to the war effort earned him Abkhazia's highest honor, a decoration named after the ancient King Leon, who had occupied the Abkhazian throne twelve hundred years ago. But Aliyev felt no hatred for the Georgians, with many of whom he used to share bunks in Soviet battleships and many bottles of cheap vodka, an ultimate token of interethnic solidarity in the old Union.

In his eagerness not to offend his former Georgian comrades-in-arms, Aliyev spent his Abkhazian admiralty under a nom de guerre, Aleksey Mikhailov, a most Russian name. Thanks to his Russian looks and unaccented speech, the Muslim Daghestani commander passed easily as a "Russian mercenary."

But Ali Aliyev was no regular mercenary. His service in somebody else's war was not motivated by profit. Unlike many hired guns of the Caucasus, he left Abkhazia empty-handed. At the time of my visit, he lived in a tiny apartment in a dilapidated building in Makhachkala, surviving on a meager Russian military pension, which was always late.

Aliyev waged a war he believed to be highly principled—in defense of a small nation, a quintessential victim of history, struggling to preserve its identity.

By the time the Abkhaz went to war, they had been reduced to a small minority in the land that bears their name. Their demographic decline began in the mid-nineteenth century, during Russia's expansion into the Caucasus. Most Abkhaz, who are Muslims, chose exile in Ottoman Turkey over life in the shadow of Christian Russia. The last Abkhaz hereditary ruler was dethroned by the Russians in the 1860s. The Soviet regime chose to make Abkhazia an "autonomous republic" within Georgia, which enjoyed the higher status of "Union republic." (The distinction may have mattered little at that time, but it made all the difference at the time of Soviet collapse. All Union republics automatically became independent, but no autonomous republic ever did.) To the Georgians, Abkhazia's inclusion within Georgia's borders was taken for granted. After all, they maintained, a Georgian dynasty had sat on Abkhazia's throne as early as the eighth century. The indigenous Abkhaz were less than happy, however, and their displeasure became evident years before the dissolution of the Soviet Union. As it dawned on them, in the dying days of the Soviet Union, that they were about to become subjects of a little state with limited importance and a mercurial temper, they became openly rebellious.

The Georgians insist that in Soviet times, they displayed enormous generosity toward their Abkhazian minority. The Abkhaz respond that Georgia encouraged mass migration of ethnic Georgian settlers into Abkhazia, thus dooming the indigenous Abkhaz to marginality. The debate over history was tedious and bitter and involved mutual attempts to discredit and to deny rights. Both parties have often resorted to the argument, couched in almost identical terms, that the other represents an "ahistorical" entity, and that its claim to distinct national existence is but a cynical ploy designed to advance the political agenda of a third party or parties.

Without passing a judgment on the merit of either case, it is clear that Abkhazia's freedom became a call to arms for thousands of North Caucasians, beginning in 1989–90. It was their first opportunity in many decades to raise again the banner of highlander solidarity.

As for Ali Aliyev, the crusade to restore Abkhazia to the Abkhaz served a spiritual need—it was a rite of passage of sorts. On the picturesque Abkhazian coastline, retired Captain of the First Degree Ali

Aliyev ceased to be a *sovetsky chelovek*, a Soviet Man, and reaffirmed his
true identity: a highlander.

On one late August day, Aliyev and I were sitting in the merciful shade
of a little park by Makhachkala's main square, escaping the humid heat,
enjoying homemade ice cream. I had just spoken at great length with
Rassul Magomedov, the octogenarian dean of Daghestani historians.
"There is not a *single* Caucasian identity, there are *many* identities," the
old scholar had said. I was now repeating those words to Aliyev.

"He's lying through his teeth," said Aliyev. "Of course a common
identity exists, no doubt of that. We are carrying it in our genes. Do you
know what anniversary we are celebrating today? That of the famous
Battle of Akhulgo. There, in 1839, for ninety days and nights, the Russian army tried to dislodge the highlanders. There were twenty-five
Russians for every highlander, and yet it took them a very long time to
seize the mountain, and they lost many troops. And do you know why I
mention it? Because there, in Akhulgo, in the distant east of the Caucasus, hundreds of miles from home, twelve Abkhaz fell in battle, defending our common identity. If indeed there were no North Caucasian
identity," Aliyev went on, reproaching me and the absent Professor
Magomedov, "why would so many young people, from the entire Caucasus, join Abkhazia's war of independence? And why would so many
give their lives in the process?"

He had not been the only non-Abkhaz on the Abkhazian front, he
said. "Abkhazia's defense minister was Kabardin, Sultan Saslanaliyev, a
retired Soviet colonel, just like me. His deputies were an Adyghe [Cir-
cassian from the province of Adygeiya] and a Chechen." As for Aliyev's
Laks, thirty-two of them volunteered to fight on Abkhazia's side—not a
bad ratio for a nation of 90,000—and two fell in battle.

Aliyev recalled a Lak who had come to Abkhazia's aid in the 1850s.
Muhammad Amin, an associate of Imam Shamil's, hoped to capitalize
on growing anti-Russian sentiments in Western Europe to get help for
the highlanders in resisting Russian subjugation. In 1853 the armies of a
mighty European coalition began a costly military campaign against
Russia in the Crimean Peninsula, not far from the Caucasus, and Amin
thought, not unreasonably, that the European allies and the highlanders
could help each other: while the Europeans engaged Russia on the
front, the highlanders, masters of speed and surprise, could launch an
attack against the vulnerable Russian rear. The end result might have
been to drive the czarist state back to its pre-eighteenth-century bor-

ders—far away from the Middle East. When Imam Shamil threatened to march on Tbilisi, which was occupied by the Russians, the Russian supreme commander was so unnerved that he proposed to withdraw his troops in haste across the mountains, to safety in Russia proper. (The czar refused and dismissed the coward.)

The Western European countries defeated Russia in 1856. In exchange for his help, Amin sought independence. But the Western Europeans refused to inflict such a severe punishment on Russia, and in any event, they did not think much of colonized peoples overthrowing the yoke of their European masters. After all, both Britain and France, the leaders of the anti-Russian coalition, were busy putting down rebellions in their own colonies. Amin's proposals, which his envoys conveyed to the British, came to naught. One can only speculate how different history might have been if a predominantly Muslim buffer state had emerged between Russia and the Middle East.

So well preserved is the memory of Amin among the Northwest Caucasians that in 1993 the victorious Abkhazian leader, Vladislav Ardzinba, fresh from his victory over Georgia, presented Aliyev with a book about Abkhazia's history, dedicated "to Ali Aliyev, the sea wolf of Abkhazia, the successor of the great Lak Muhammad Amin."

Now retired twice, first from the Soviet navy, then from the Abkhazian one, Aliyev sought justice for his fellow Laks.

The khan mosque, at the center of Ghazi-Ghumuq, is the only royal edifice still standing. When the Communists unleashed a fierce campaign against organized religion, Ghazi-Ghumuq's eight mosques, including the khan's, were converted for "socially useful" purposes. The khan's mosque became a cinema—a vulgar insult to believers. Laks would pass by the mosque with clenched fists, helpless witnesses to the undoing of their past.

"Fortunately, the bastards didn't touch the tombs," Aliyev related. He gestured toward two marble tablets just outside the mosque, covered with ornate Arabic inscriptions. They mark the resting places of the last two great dukes, Surkhai and his son Murtazali. The son had led the Daghestani army that, in the eighteenth century, beat off Persia's Nadir Shah.

The restoration of the khan mosque was one small step in the attempt to reawaken Lak national feelings. There are about 90,000 Laks currently living in Daghestan, but only one-fifth of them still inhabit the highland, where their forefathers had drawn a line in the hill before the great shah. Aliyev drove me along the deserted mountains, pointing out, every now and then, a ghost village, long abandoned by its residents. We passed by ancient settlements where houses had been stripped of building material until they were reduced to dust. In some places, only marked gravestones testified to a lasting human habitation.

The Lak flight out of the highlands was not just a matter of replacing one landscape for another. Dispersed in the plains and the cities, relegated to a minority position, the Laks will gradually cease to be who they are. In Makhachkala, where many of the Laks settled down, I met young Lak men and women who no longer speak their language and are likely to produce children to whom the Lak heritage will be anecdotal at best.

The exodus is inevitable. The poor cannot stay where they have been for centuries just to satisfy an accidental tourist or an occasional anthropologist. As elsewhere in the third world, the Laks have been leaving because the land can no longer sustain them. But the Lak exodus is also the result of Soviet ethnic engineering, which was intended to dislocate, assimilate, and phase out small nations.

In the 1920s, Aliyev told me, when the October Revolution was still young and inspired, thousands of Laks were transferred to the plains of Chechnya. They were stubborn highlanders, stiffened by a hard climate and hostile soil, unbent by foreign invaders. But the plains quite literally killed them.

In 1944 the Laks became hapless pawns in Stalin's grand design to reinvent the Caucasus. He deported the entire Chechen nation to Central Asia on account of its alleged collective collaboration with Nazi Germany, then ordered Laks off the mountains and into the deserted Chechen region in central Daghestan, newly christened Novaya Lakia ("New Lakia"). According to Aliyev and other Laks, 30 percent of the new settlers starved to death during the first year. In 1990, the surviving Laks were ordered to vacate the premises and allow the former Chechen owners to return. Many other Laks have been targeted for eviction elsewhere in the Daghestani plains. Unwanted where they are, unable to go back to their old highland homes, the Lak nation is teetering on the brink of extinction, another Caucasian tribe cheated by history.

The depopulation of the Lak highland was thus an intended result of Soviet policies. Daghestan may be an "autonomous republic," but in Soviet times its autonomy amounted to little. Moscow decided how much money should be disbursed and to whom. Suspicious of mountain dwellers, it spent on each highlander only one-third the amount it spent on each plain dweller.

In the mountains of Daghestan, a totalitarian ideology met and merged with a classical colonial practice. The ideology, says Aliyev, was the "insane attempt to create the Soviet Man, ignoring his national peculiarities."

Aliyev had few illusions that state assistance would be helpful in repairing any of the damage. Rather, he proposed that Laks pay a voluntary tax for the purpose of saving their own culture from extinction.

"I gave a speech in a congress of Lak youth. I said, 'Let us do something with our own hands. No one is helping us—let's help ourselves. We will register all the Laks, wherever they live, and ask them to cut their monthly vodka intake by a single bottle. There are 120,000 of us in the world—I'm talking also about our people who live outside of Daghestan. Let us assume that a quarter of us can pay—30,000 all together. That will give us 300 million rubles a month [about $60,000 at the time]. We will be healthier, and at the same time we will give ourselves financial ability.'

"Do you know what happened as soon as I finished speaking? People murmured, 'What is it with Aliyev? He has nothing better to do in life than rob 10,000 rubles from old pensioners?'"

Aliyev sighed and lit another cigarette. He knew very well that people were justified in suspecting his motives. In this poorest region of Russia, a handful of public servants have enriched themselves obscenely by securing access to public funds. I heard fantastic tales of government officials whose formal monthly salary was less than two hundred U.S. dollars, who were nonetheless residing in huge mansions. One need only walk the streets of Makhachkala to see for oneself. The poor capital was enjoying an amazing construction boom of red-brick villas, adorned by TV satellite dishes; their occupants were being driven around in shining Mercedes-Benzes. Against that background, who wouldn't suspect a man trying to raise some $700,000 a year for the sake of "national heritage"?

The rise of men like Magomed Khachilayev was not uncommon in the twilight years of the Soviet Union. On the old system's smoldering ruins, the fit survived but the manipulative thrived. Russians often argue that much of their society has been "criminalized" and that "Mafia structures" have taken over. In Moscow theater producers and mathematicians have emerged from nowhere to launch banking empires. But in the Caucasus, an old tradition has mounted a comeback: It was again time for the *abreks*, the Caucasus's own Robin Hoods, the ancient challengers of the prevailing order, to come down from the mountains and set new rules for the plains.

In some parts of the former Soviet Union, one's strength is often not only a reflection of one's social status and family connections but a direct result of one's physical prowess. Perhaps nowhere has this phenomenon been more pronounced than in the Northeast Caucasus, where a wrestler's physique, or a boxer's fists, or a weight lifter's biceps command unrivaled respect and earn one a huge advantage in the race to acquire new riches and influence. And so the four Khachilayev brothers moved swiftly from bodybuilders to bodyguards to bodyguarded. The karate masters of Ghazi-Ghumuq were quickly transformed into political masters of much of Daghestan and the North Caucasus.

A portrait of the brothers looms large in the dining room at Magomed Khachilayev's mansion, just above a small marble statue of Imam Shamil. Four lookalike hunks, they are shown seated on a bench, with barren mountains in the background. So closely do they resemble each other in the portrait—in their uptight posture, severe countenances, well-defined arms, square faces, pale features, and dark eyes—that I suspected the painter used only one of them as a model.

Magomed's oldest brother was killed in 1995 by a Chechen man, in a brawl widely rumored to have been related to matters of turf and seniority. "So," I suggested to Khachilayev, "you probably have an ax to grind with the Chechens," hinting at the notorious Caucasian tradition of blood feud. Khachilayev's expression did not change in the slightest when he said, very quietly, "Let us say that we are now even." No further questions, Your Honor.

Khachilayev is an imposing man, over six feet tall, his head completely shaven, pale skin, with a whitening black beard and wide-open dark eyes. He was twice karate champion of the entire Soviet Union, five times the champion of Russia, and, he says, "one of the first Eastern martial arts sportsmen in the country." When I visited him in 1996, Khachilayev was not only the leader of the Lak national movement Ghazi-Ghumuq but chairman of the coordinating council of Daghestan's national movements. He also ran the government agency that oversees the fishing industry. He is an exceptionally wealthy businessman. On top of everything else, he played a very important role in bringing the first round of the Chechen war (1994–96) to an end. Here was a man larger than life if ever I met one.

Khachilayev lives in untold splendor in the very heart of poverty-stricken Makhachkala. Russian newspapers portray him as a prominent godfather of organized crime. As a guest at his dinner table, I dared not ask about the origins of his wealth but noted that he made frequent allusions to the *Godfather* movies, which he had seen many times. It occurred to me that he was mimicking many of Marlon Brando's famous gestures, but then again, I had not met him before his acquaintance with the fictional Corleone family. Perhaps Khachilayev's body language and self-important moments of prolonged silence came to him naturally.

Martial arts provided him with a thorough preparation for his public role. The Communist authorities had frowned upon martial arts, considering them too intertwined with the clannish structure that they associated with the underworld. For two decades, no Daghestani was allowed to practice this form of self-empowerment, the nearest a highlander could get to his ancestors' combative traditions without wearing a Soviet military uniform.

As soon as the lid was lifted, many thousands of North Caucasian youths

Painted in oil is a Khachilayev brother, standing in his karate outfit on a Lak mountain. The bronze statue in the lower left corner is that of Imam Shamil. The imam just happened to adorn the shelf below the painting, he was not included in the frame, but the brothers did not appear too uncomfortable reducing the venerable nineteenth-century warrior to their feet.

sought out martial arts and excelled in them. The wrestler who won a gold medal for Russia in the Atlanta summer Olympics in 1996 was Chechen. I happened to arrive at Makhachkala's Kavkaz airport shortly after the end of the Olympics, within minutes of the Chechen champion's own triumphal return. Chechnya was still in a state of war, and Kavkaz was the nearest functioning airport. A huge crowd of flag-waving and horn-honking Chechens had gathered outside the terminal to welcome the athlete. The Chechen gold medalist provided his countrymen with a sense of victory and recognition, notwithstanding the irony that he had collected his medal under the Russian flag and had stood upright at the playing of the enemy anthem.

Khachilayev's glory and fame signified much the same sense of victory, specifically to his own Laks but also to Daghestan at large: a hometown boy recognized not only for his physical strength but also for the superiority of his tactics, the shrewdness of his moves, and his superb understanding of a rival's psychology, all resulting from the great discipline and relentless perseverance required of a successful karate master.

In November 1998, when Jesse Ventura won Minnesota's gubernatorial election, I could not help but think of Khachilayev, who is not only Ventura's age but has Ventura's body as well. I was imagining Khachilayev seated in front of his satellite-driven television set, surfing its international channels, and chancing upon Jesse's deep voice resonating from a CNN screen. Would his heart be filled with warmth and joy? Or would he grind his teeth in anger and frustration? I recalled what he told me so bitterly two years earlier: "Here, in Daghestan, even if the entire population supported me, I would never be allowed to become president [the local equivalent of a state governor in America]. Here people are not measured on the basis of their skills, but only on the basis of their ethnic affiliation. If I belong to a minority group, I can never hold power."

If Khachilayev had lived in the United States, he could have banked upon his reputation and name recognition the way American athletes do. But in poor Daghestan, however successful and adulated he was, Khachilayev could not win a million-per-endorsement contract from Nike or Wheaties. His best hope for parlaying his superb sportsmanship into wealth and prominence rested in crafting a public image for himself that joined the physical with the spiritual. After all, Daghestan is a land not only of military heroes but of saints and mystics. To win genuine acceptance, a leader must radiate a degree of inner strength. The power broker has to be seen to move not only in the unsavory company of goons but in the spiritual realm as well, seeking not just gunpowder but redemption.

In the former Soviet Union, there are many brutes around, people who would kill at will, plant a bomb, rob, and terrorize. But the Khachilayevs ascended despite their ethnic and geographic marginality, because they aroused not only fear but awe.

In reaching for power, Khachilayev and his brothers were well served by the discipline and patience that they had so masterfully acquired during years of rigorous training and self-deprivation. But his present domicile suggests little self-deprivation, as does that of his brother Nadir, founder and head of the Muslim Union of Russia. Both built themselves opulent mansions in the heart of what is inaptly called "the neighborhood of oil and chemical workers." In an astonishing construction boom, the dusty streets and old communal courtyards of the dominions of the poor were giving way to red-brick, one-family complexes whose walls enclose swimming pools, private mosques, and Mercedes-filled garages. Red bricks—said to be imported from Italy or the former Yugoslavia—have become new status symbols.

Magomed Khachilayev's mansion, alas, is mostly white, save for a new annex, still under construction, that one day will accommodate his two young sons. I asked him why, unaware that in raising the question, I was implying that my host was not as wealthy as the red-brick builders and therefore not as powerful. "I was one of the first Daghestanis to start construction, and there were no red bricks at that time," he explained almost inaudibly, like a man who is accustomed to complete silence around him when he opens his mouth.

I asked him about the history of the place. He hesitated. "As a matter of fact," he finally said, "this area had a lot of common yards, just like a ghetto. I consulted an architect, and such are the results."

Was it a Daghestani architect?

"Yes. His name was Ayub Mussayev."

Was?

"He was killed."

"**K**illed." That word has become a common epitaph on Daghestani tombs in the last few years. Makhachkala may now justifiably claim to be "the murder capital of Russia," at least relative to its population. Just two days before my interview with Magomed, a hand grenade had been hurled at two-thirty in the morning into his brother Nadir's residence a few blocks away. No one was hurt. A few hours later, a powerful explosion shook dozens of blocks in downtown Makhachkala, killing Daghestan's finance minister. Other government ministers have been at the receiving end. "This is very common here," Khachilayev said. "This is how the struggle for power is conducted."

We were interrupted by a man bringing Khachilayev a large, thick brown envelope, which he quickly inspected, then handed back, whispering brief oral instructions. "There is a disease spreading in the Daghestani body," Khachilayev continued. "We cannot cure it with balms, and we cannot pretend it doesn't exist. . . . We have lost our ancient spirituality, and we need to restore it. . . . A process of destruction is taking place here."

One could be forgiven for doubting Khachilayev's concern for spirituality. Living in his mansion, enjoying multicontinental TV signals beamed into his satellite dish, whisked about in foreign limousines and flown in a helicopter, sporting expensive jackets and Italian shoes, drinking imported wines of the best vintage, Khachilayev seems an unlikely preacher of righteousness.

My visit to Khachilayev's mansion had been arranged by a local government official who wanted me to hear the "other side" of the Daghestani story. Khachilayev was, after all, a government official. He ran the department of fisheries, a ministry in charge of one of this republic's few lucrative industries. Daghestan lies by the Caspian Sea, whose name is still synonymous with various fish delicacies, regardless of pollution and contamination.

Khachilayev's taste for the fruits of the sea notwithstanding, the barely reformed ex-Communists who run Daghestan needed him at least as much as he needed them. But they were unable to offer him a more prestigious post because the distribution of ministerial portfolios had to reflect the delicate ethnic balance.

"Look back at history," Khachilayev suggested to me, "and see for yourself. Lak dukes ruled not only Lakia but nearly the entire North Caucasus. They marshaled armies that were far larger than the entire Lak population! And they accomplished the impossible, repelling famous conquerors such as the great Timurlane, the great Nadir Shah, the Turks, and many others."

That Khachilayev saw himself as heir to the great Lak dynasties was clear. Given the chance, he would revolutionize Daghestan and the Caucasus. Even if he did not seek complete independence from Moscow or wish to lead armies in battle, he was nevertheless determined to extricate the republic from Russia's tight grip. "Everything here is controlled from Moscow, for the benefit of Moscow. This is leading nowhere. This is a sure route to disaster."

I visited Khachilayev on a Friday morning, the Muslim Sabbath, which means little in this Russified city. Khachilayev did beg our leave around noon and left the house, but if he was headed to the Friday noon prayer, he did not choose to share the information with me. He came back later and insisted that I join him for lunch. I was treated well, and he graciously opened two bottles of fine wine, the first with his own thumb. He pushed the cork into the bottle and then poured its content into my glass—probably not what the Tuscan winery had in mind. Like any *arriviste*, Khachilayev was still unsure what to do with the plenty that had befallen him.

The mansion was bustling with visitors, some of whom were paying homage to the lord of the manor, others attending to various kinds of business. A stocky, bearded man walked in and was introduced to me as Gussein, "our great karate master." Another guest, driven there in an official black Volga, the preferred limo of the Soviet era, was Ali Aliyev's brother Izaat, head of Daghestan's Journalists Association. He listened to my exchange with Khachilayev, interjecting learned observations on history and demography, such as the number of Laks who had perished in Russian-orchestrated deportations and resettlements in the previous 120 years (one-third of the nation, he maintained).

After the formal stage of our interview, we followed Khachilayev from his austere, dark study to an opulent living room, featuring brand-new imported furniture.

Almost hidden in a tall chair twice his size was a handsome boy, blond and pale—Khachilayev's youngest. At the time of my visit the boy was eight. Khochbar—named after the mythical hero of another Daghestani nation, the Avars—smiled at us mischievously. Turning to my Russian companion, a long-haired young Muscovite man, Khochbar asked, "Are you a man or a woman?" Khachilayev senior burst out laughing, and so did the rest of the crowd. The Muscovite, perhaps not so amused, maintained his self-composure. I inquired of Khochbar what language he spoke at home. "Lak," he shot back.

The boy was studying me with intelligent curiosity—or was it mocking benevolence?—leaning his little face against his palm, his dark brown eyes engaging mine. He was so comfortable in the midst of these recently acquired luxuries, so at ease with his father's guests and courtiers, that I could almost recognize a princely demeanor about him. Should he not be crippled by decadence, he could become a more natural claimant to the Lak mantle than his father or even his pious uncle, the head of the Muslim Union.

The Khachilayevs would probably have been confined to obscurity in Daghestan, had it not been for the Chechen war and its growing impact on Daghestani life. In the dead of winter 1996, Chechen fighters took over the large Daghestani village of Pyervomaiskoe. The Chechens were commanded by Jokar Dudayev's son-in-law, a flamboyant, immature man named Salman Raduyev, who had the mannerisms of a narcissistic gangster, and acted on behalf of his own ambitions, as he sought to position himself as a major warlord in his father-in-law's entourage.

The operation seemed extremely illogical, in that it inflicted misery on a non-Russian civilian population that was otherwise not unsympathetic to the Chechens. The operation won Raduyev nothing tangible but did expose the astonishing weakness and miserable combative skills of the Russian military. The Russians chose to level Pyervomaiskoe to the ground, primarily because they did not fancy hand-to-hand combat with the fanatic Chechens but also because they suspected the locals of collaboration with their enemies.

The Chechen war, never too far from the Daghestani mind or territory, now loomed closer than ever, less because anyone intended to get Daghestan involved than because the whims, bravado, and miscalculations of Chechen field commanders could result in a spillover. Magomed Khachilayev embarked on a mission of talking to the Chechens and dissuading them from pursuing independent miniwars in Daghestan. It was a highlander-to-highlander kind of talk, based on centuries of coexistence and partnership. This war, he told them, is yours. Make sure that it does not become ours. Khachilayev unquestionably deserved much of the credit for Daghestan's not getting embroiled in a war that rendered one-third of the Chechen population homeless.

The Khachilayevs' real flirtation with destiny came a few months later, in September 1996, when they facilitated the secret talks that brought to an astonishing end the first round of the Chechen war. Many Russians, as well as Russia's allies among the Chechens, were furious not only about the agreement itself, which practically recognized Chechnya's independence (and which Russia rose to undo three years later), but also about the prominence of the Khachilayevs in bringing it about. The prime minister in a short-lived government that Moscow installed in Chechnya complained that the angels of peace were in charge of Daghestan's "fish and oil mafia."

In my long conversations with Ali Aliyev, a clear Lak antithesis to Khachilayev, Aliyev repeatedly pointed out that the flight of his people from their historical mountain habitat to cities, where they were afflicted by massive unemployment and poverty, "creates a certain criminal atmosphere. A person who does not know how to keep himself busy can be introduced into criminal activity." Aliyev was mincing his words, but it was pretty clear what he was talking about and who he was referring to.

"Why is it," I asked him, "that you are trying to raise pennies to save your culture, when there are wealthy Lak individuals who could easily donate the money?" Aliyev smiled. "Let me repeat for the umpteenth time," he said. "No one is helping. . . . Unfortunately, the people you are talking about, those who would be expected to help a good cause, have displayed complete indifference. I have asked them openly, 'Why purchase a new Mercedes, or build a new palace, when you could actually erect a real monument, one that would outlast you by generations?' But look, it's entirely pointless. The so-called 'national leaders' have different interests in mind."

Aliyev has prepared an impressively realistic blueprint to save the Lak culture from extinction. He has compiled a guidebook on fifty traditional Lak games, so that Lak parents can teach them to their children in cities where the Laks are a small and easily assimilable minority. But he found no one to pay for the book's publication.

"We are the only Daghestani nation that has actually created a dictionary of our own, not Lak-Russian but Lak-Lak. The author was a well-known scientist, Ali Kayayev, who was deported to Kazakhstan in the 1930s and died in exile. His grandson has the manuscript, twelve hundred pages of it. We have established the Ali Kayayev Foundation to promote the dictionary's publication. We also wanted to publish Kayayev's grammar of the Lak language. We have failed.

"I have young children," said Aliyev. "At home I speak with them in their mother tongue. But then the children grow up and go to kindergarten, where the only language spoken is Russian. They walk the streets—they hear only Russian. They go to school, and there, as of the first grade, only Russian. Now, I'll tell you what the government has come up with. They say that children should be given the *option* of learning their national language, but they are not *required* to do so. A child who hardly ever hears his national language has few reasons to volunteer to study it. He doesn't need it in order to secure university admission, and it's not a skill expected of him in job hunting. The sole purpose of the language is to be spoken around the dinner table, at home, if at all. In no time, an ancient language is rendered a kitchen jargon. Even in the traditional Lak areas, Russian is taking over. Not a single Lak sign is visible." Not even in Ghazi-Ghumuq.

While in Ghazi-Ghumuq, Aliyev took me to the town's oldest mosque, where Jamal al-Din al-Ghazi-Ghumuqi used to pray in the 1830s. The foremost religious arbiter of the entire Caucasus, his authority was acknowledged even by Imam Shamil. It was at this mosque—a massive building, constructed in the late eighteenth century, with a vast dark interior—that Jamal al-Din hosted Imam Shamil. "Here," the mosque's

Lak women sitting at the mosque entrance, in Ghazi-Ghumuq. Conservative and pious as they might be, the Laks certainly do not qualify as "fundamentalists." Their Islam is broad and eclectic enough to accommodate even a portrait of the Madonna and Child.

prayer leader directed me to a remote corner of the mosque, where a door once existed. "Imam Shamil entered this door," he said. "Jamal al-Din, Shamil's teacher, our great Lak scholar, brought him here for prayer, and they walked through this door." The speaker, a stout, bearded man in his fifties, wearing a traditional Caucasian hat, was the first prayer leader at the mosque since it was restored in the declining days of the Soviet Union. (Before then, it had served as a government storage place for alcohol and pork, the two great taboos of Islamic dietary laws.)

Engraved on the outside wall were mysterious indents and notches believed to be part of an elaborate solar calendar system, used in the mountains in the pre-Islamic era.

The central mosque in Ghazi-Ghumuq housed the wisdom of the centuries.
Imam Shamil himself prayed and meditated here 160 years ago.

"When I was young," Aliyev related, "I saw how the Soviets stored food, including cases of vodka. Each time I visit the mosque, I am reminded of what they did and feel sick to my heart." He pointed out a crack in the ceiling. "This is a sign of the Bolshevik presence," he said. The prayer leader was quick to second him. "The stones successfully resisted the ages," he said. "But then came the Soviets, and they allowed the moisture to drip for twenty years."

The mosque building provides some evidence of the Laks' antiquity. Engraved on the outside wall, by the entrance, are mysterious indentations and notches that are believed to be part of an elaborate solar calendar system, used in the mountains in the pre-Islamic era. The mosque's site could have once been occupied by a pagan temple, probably for fire worshippers.

Gods and governors may have changed in the Caucasus, but the highlanders have never lost the urge to worship. To this day, they still celebrate the dawn of spring as their ancestors did a thousand years ago. In what they call *Intnil-khu* ("spring night"), the Laks spend a whole night on the peaks of their mountains, setting fires and eating *bartu*, a special bread shaped in a zodiac form. Similarly, they spend the first night of the summer on the peak of a sacred mountain called Vets'ilu, just outside of Ghazi-Ghumuq. When Aliyev was a child, people used to gather on the mountain and await the rise of the first summer sun, at which time they performed an ancient dance called *sappa*.

*Ali Aliyev (center) joins the imam of the newly reopened mosque in his native Ghazi-Ghumuq
for a noon prayer. The Soviets had turned it into a warehouse.*

Though proud of their Islamic traditions, the Laks do not fall into the
Western category of "fundamentalists." I accompanied Aliyev on a courtesy visit to an ailing aunt. A graceful lady, almost as old as the century,
she was lying in bed, speaking only Lak. So traditional was her Lak
speech that at times she could not understand her nephew, who liberally uses Russian words and expressions.

Throughout our visit, the aunt's fingers were constantly feeling a string
of beads, a traditional sign of piety among Muslims. This notwithstanding, the wall above the aunt's bed was adorned with a portrait of the
Blessed Virgin holding the baby Jesus in her arms. True, Jesus is recognized as prophet in the holy Qur'an, where he goes by the name Issa, and
Mary is acknowledged as his mother. Yet the portrait in the Lak woman's
home had little to do with Islam, if only because Islamic orthodoxy bars
the veneration of images, let alone those of prophets. Evidently, I had
stumbled upon an example of the eclectic Islam practiced in the mountains, where Muhammad the founder often competes with a host of other
claimants to divine inspiration.

I asked Aliyev about the unexpected presence of the Madonna at his
aunt's. He chuckled. There is a legend among the Laks, he said, about
the residents of the village of Ubra, a couple of miles north of Ghazi-
Ghumuq. Sometime in the early Middle Ages, Muslim missionaries
arrived there and advised the locals that the time had come to adopt

Islam. The congenial people of Ubra first inquired what Islam entailed. When they heard, they responded: "Fine, we'll all be Muslim in good time. But first we have to eat the salted and pickled pig heads that we have prepared."

No one should interpret these words as disrespectful of Islam, either on my part or Aliyev's or that of the proverbial villagers of Ubra. They are merely intended to suggest that the highlanders' state of mind at times defies classification. For ages their Islam was one of great tolerance—until the late eighteenth century, when their way of life clashed frontally with that of Russia, and an explosion of rage and zeal ensued.

Incidentally, Lak folk tradition has it that the people of Ubra all descended from Jews. If so, they were part of a large Jewish presence in the Caucasus, whose origins are the subject of speculations and myths.

I have already related the story of Eliyahu Avichail, an elderly Israeli rabbi who set out to discover lost Jewish tribes, and bring them back to the fold. He intended to travel to the North Caucasus to redeem the Lezgin people, who he believed were but "lost sheep of Israel."

If Rabbi Avichail were to follow my lead and look up the "Jews of Ubra," however, he would run into considerable difficulties. Ubra is one of the thirty-two Lak villages that were abandoned during the depopulations of the Soviet era. Lost sheep of Israel Ubra might have been, but it has now become the lost sheep of Lakia, an appropriate metaphor for a nation on the brink of vanishing.

SEE YOU AT LENIN,
BY THE SAMSUNG SIGN

The city of Makhachkala originally grew out of a czarist fortress, named Petrovskoye (later, Port Petrovsk), built in the mid-nineteenth century, during the long Caucasian War. Russia's expansion in the Caucasus, which began in the late eighteenth century and lasted about eighty years, required the maintenance of huge standing armies, which in turn required an extensive infrastructure, not only military but civilian as well.

Many of the cities of the North Caucasus—from Makhachkala on the Caspian, through Grozny, Vladikavkaz, and Nalchik, to Lazarevskoe on the Black Sea—began this way, as military encampments, and only later evolved into full-fledged towns, Russian by character and population. In most of them, native majorities did not emerge until well after the establishment of Soviet rule, if at all. In 1922 the Bolsheviks renamed Port Petrovsk "Makhachkala," after a local revolutionary hero who used Makhach as his nom de guerre. (His actual name was Ali Magomed Dakhadayev.)

There is little in Makhachkala to remind the visitor of Daghestan's rich history. Indeed, with the uncontested primacy of the Russian language and the public display of old Soviet icons, there is almost nothing to remind the visitor that the city is part of Daghestan. It is a quintessential Soviet city with a Leninesque core: a main boulevard named after Lenin, leading to a square named after Lenin, where a Lenin statue towers over government buildings. The Soviet founding father may be a bit rusty, and if left to his own devices, he would be likely to grow a thick cover of bird droppings around his bald scalp. But otherwise he is

Lenin is still there, in Makhachkala's main square, towering over the government of Daghestan.

still at the helm, overlooking a large vacant space that in the old days was reserved for worker parades.

Unlike Derbent, one of the world's oldest cities, about eighty miles to the south, Makhachkala is a nondescript place of 400,000 that bears many incomplete construction projects from the Soviet era, including a public library begun in the late 1970s. There is no sign of outdoor commercialism that has been so evident in Russia's main metropolitan centers since the demise of Communism.

As my eyes moved over Makhachkala from the top of the mosque in Tarki, the old Kumyk capital, two features of the city's architecture struck me.

Tiny patches of opulence were strewn at random around the city's center. The patches were marked by a pleasant red hue, the color of imported Italian bricks—a handful of ostentatious enclaves in an ocean of poverty.

When the sun sets on Makhachkala, another hue joins the skyline: a dim blue, hanging over Lenin Square, where the government of Daghestan has its seat. The blue comes from a huge, uninspiring neon sign advertising "Samsung." With admirable foresight, the South Korean industrial conglomerate installed itself in many cities in the southern tier of the former Soviet empire, where it opened digital telephone switchboards, in

joint ventures with local governments. At the time of my visit, the generally unreliable phone lines were still unreliable—through no fault of the
Koreans, who had not laid them. But dialing was no longer dependent on
the antiquated pulse system: each press of the button generated a tone
sound, the first time I heard it in the former Soviet Union. I had a sense of
joy at the sound of those tones, an affirmation of sorts that Daghestan was
really turning its back on the miseries of its centralized economy and
embracing the free market. To my disappointment, however, I soon found
out that touch-tone phones were still unavailable to the overwhelming
majority of residents.

The oversized Samsung sign was the only commercial display of its
kind in the entire city, and come night, it made every passing shadow in
Lenin Square a bit longer and slightly more ominous, including the
shadow of Vladimir Ilyich himself. Although his stony replicas have
been removed from main squares in Chechnya and Azerbaijan, Daghestan's two Muslim neighbors, the one in Makhachkala remains, either
because the Daghestanis are not vindictive toward statues of dead men,
or because there is no point in removing Lenin as long as Leninism is
still the order of the day.

A case in point is Daghestan's historical museum across the square
from Lenin, where any display related to the last eight decades was
"temporarily" suspended at the time of my visit, pending new funds and
perhaps a new authoritative interpretation of history. While certainly
people here are freer to express their views than they have been in a
century, there has been an enormous delay in introducing Daghestan to
the democratic trends of the north.

In the 1800s they were freer?

Across the square from Lenin is the only neon sign of the land, courtesy of Samsung.

Things that in the late 1980s seemed iconoclastic to party apparatchiks in Moscow but are now trifles were still perceived as unneces-
sarily controversial in the Daghestan of the late 1990s, including a more
balanced discussion of the ethnic engineering of Communist times.

In Daghestan, as in many other Russian provinces, the past is a Pan-
dora's box sealed many times over. Not only are the facts of the past
buried inside, but so are yesterday's interpretations of that past. History
has been tampered with so often that if total transparency were encouraged or tolerated, the very legitimacy of state structures might be called
into question. Who needs to know the truth about various acts of ethnic
cleansing and ethnic engineering, if the result will be greater mutual
suspicion, tribalization, and perhaps civil war?

In the latter years of the twentieth century, many nations became
increasingly interested in their past, ever more willing to delve into its
darker chapters, many of which occurred within the delvers' lifetimes.
"Truth commissions" became common, from South Africa to Guatemala.
But does the truth always liberate? Might it not be better to forget—or
even to induce forgetfulness?

I doubt that the barely reformed Communist leadership of Daghestan ever planned collective amnesia. But the official adherence to a
Soviet line is unmistakable, and some of its manifestations are almost
farcical. I noticed, with a mixture of amusement and discomfort, that
the only newspaper on display at the Daghestani parliament building,
just behind Lenin's statue, was *Sovetskaya Rossiia*, a fringe Communist rag
from Moscow whose contributors yearn for the restoration of the
Soviet Union and considered the Yeltsin government a disgraceful collection of sellouts.   *Is this not true?*

The paper's prominent display was all the more telling because only a
few weeks earlier, Daghestan had landed Yeltsin a handsome victory in
the second round of the 1996 presidential election. This victory was
universally ridiculed, as it came on the heels of a clear triumph of the
Communist candidate in the first round, only ten days before. It was as
though the government was openly apologizing to its staff and guests:
"Well, comrades, we had to deliver the republic to Boris Nikolayevich
because we need his subsidies—but everyone knows we would have
loved to see him drown in the Caspian."

Gussein Abuyev's worst nightmares have come true. Through the late
1980s and early 1990s, he watched bitterly and helplessly as the Soviet
Union slipped away. Now, he says, wherever he turns, he sees only
incompetence or fanaticism or outright criminality—or all of the above.

When I first met him, in midsummer 1996, he was well positioned to watch those post-Soviet activities. His modest office, on the second floor of the Council of Ministers building, was a little hub where prominent citizens of the Republic of Daghestan stopped by to solicit advice, or to seek access to the higher-ups, or to pour their hearts out—or just to shake hands and muse on times long gone, when political assassinations had not yet become common occurrences in the dusty streets of Makhachkala.

Abuyev, a tall man with stooping shoulders, carries himself with difficulty because of a serious injury to his leg. He was born to Soviet privilege—his father was an acting prime minister of the republic, and his family, he said, was "one of the most distinguished in Daghestan." A Lak, he is married to royalty: his wife is a descendant of the hereditary ruler of Ghazi-Ghumuq, the ancient Lak principality overrun by Russia in the mid-nineteenth century. Such aristocratic origins would not have been flaunted in public in Soviet times, when they were frowned upon, but now they are a welcome embellishment to any résumé.

In the old days, Abuyev's Lakness was of little consequence to him, a biographical anecdote at best, one that time and mixing of genes would have undone in any event. If the Soviet Union was a long train of nations, pulled by a huge and powerful Russian locomotive, then Abuyev was an eager passenger, even if his own wagon was far in the rear. The man's pale complexion and impeccable Russian speech ("I speak Russian better than most Russians," he reminded me) do not make him an obvious "member of a Caucasian nationality." The latter term is often used unflatteringly, since some ethnic Russians distrust and often detest the southerners, who are supposed to be of a darker pigmentation. The nickname *chornye*, or "blacks," is very much intended as a slight. But Abuyev, like most Daghestanis and other North Caucasians, is pale.

In the eyes of the Soviet regime, which affixed ethnic tags to every lapel, Abuyev's Lakness had more than anecdotal importance, however. A classification-for-life, it became a political glass ceiling to Abuyev's father. No Lak could aspire to the top job, normally reserved for members of the largest nations of Daghestan. Which is why the elder Abuyev had to settle for the title of "acting" prime minister.

As I traveled throughout Daghestan, I heard numerous complaints about this quota system, either from political players who were embittered about the dead-end they were bound to hit sooner or later, or from observers who bemoaned the system's lack of consideration for "merit." This is an argument that Americans will recognize from their own anguished public discourse over "affirmative action" and minority "quotas," except that in Daghestan everyone is a member of a "minority."

Had Abuyev had his way, Daghestan would have proceeded to full Russification. Despite the Lakness of both parents, his own children do not speak the Lak language. It was as though the Abuyevs asked themselves and each other, "Why bother?"

In Daghestan, where multiculturalism is not a matter of political correctness but is as ancient as the rocks and the rivers, cities have become merciless melting pots. Makhachkala is a case in point. Migration from the countryside has turned it into a grinding mill, where millennium-old distinctions are gradually reduced to folklore, while non-Russian languages and historical consciousness vanish forever.

The main cause is marriage between members of the numerous nationalities. A Lak husband and an Avar wife, or a Dargin wife and a Lezgin husband, are compelled to speak Russian to each other, thus making it unlikely that their children will learn a local language. The school system is so indifferent to indigenous tongues that a missed opportunity to absorb a language at home prior to school is an opportunity missed forever.

By title, Gussein Abuyev is only an "adviser on international economic relations to the prime minister." Daghestan's international economic relations are remarkable for their almost complete nonexistence. (A handful of South Koreans, Arabs, and Turks constituted the business expatriate community when I visited. The only Americans I ran into were members of Protestant sects bent on translating the Bible into the obscure languages of Daghestan.) In reality, Abuyev is an adviser on anything and everything. His credentials on the matter are impressive, and include a KGB uniform in his closet and the aura of an expert on Islam.

In his mid-fifties, Abuyev projects a laid-back posture, that of a man who has seen almost all that there is to see, has witnessed the parade of human frailties and vanities, has learned the great art of toning down rhetorical hyperbole (a matter of professional and intellectual survival in this part of the world), has studied mind and body language, and has finally established himself as the ultimate observer on Daghestan's life.

"I and my peers graduated from the best universities in the Soviet Union. My father did, my brother did," Abuyev said. "Culturally speaking, I am half Russian. Increasingly, Daghestan was becoming a part of Russia. Only ten years ago, the number of marriages involving Daghestanis and non-Daghestanis, Russians or otherwise, was on the rise. Look at my family—no ethnic classification will do to describe us. You might say that we are *Soviet,* even if some people no longer like the sound of the word. What else would you call a family in which an uncle is married to a Russian woman, and my cousin Murad is married to a Jewish woman, not to mention the fact that I have married one of my daughters to a Kumyk, and we have Lezgins and Georgians in the family as well?

"But this is now changing," Abuyev continued softly. "Russians are leaving in droves, and those Russians left behind—they are not as welcome as they used to be."

What brought about the sudden chill? The Daghestanis are so poorly treated these days in Russia proper that they can no longer show a smiling face to ethnic Russians in their midst. "Just this morning I met a man whose twenty-year-old nephew had been killed in some town in Siberia. My neighbor's son was stabbed at the Plekhanov Institute [in Moscow]. Another son was knifed inside the university dorm, also in Moscow.

"The inevitable result is that Russian universities have ceased to be the preferred destination of high school graduates. And the alternative?" Abuyev sighed. "Many young Daghestanis now go to Islamic religious schools in Pakistan, where graduates are expected to acquire basic skills not only in holy scriptures but in martial arts and machine-gun operation as well. So it's no longer Russia that young people look up to. It's Turkey, or the Arab countries, or the Islamic world—with dire consequences."

And yet, the growing role of Islam in Daghestan is not a transplant of alien ideas but the restoration of a very old heritage.

No other part of the Caucasus, possibly no other part of the Soviet Union, was as attached to Islam and to Arab culture as Daghestan. Daghestan's first encounter with the Arabs took place in the seventh century: an Arab army occupied the city of Derbent in A.D. 643, only twenty-one years after the official establishment of Islam and only five years after the takeover of Jerusalem.

The most daring and longest-lasting Muslim resistance to Christian European invaders anywhere in the world took place on Daghestani soil, in the first half of the nineteenth century. Unlike the guerrilla war against the Soviet occupation of Afghanistan, in the 1980s, the Daghestani resistance movement was entirely indigenous and went almost unsupported by the outside world, which was intrigued by its audacity but unwilling to take a stand. It is no exaggeration to say that Daghestan's resistance interfered with Russia's "manifest destiny." In the course of the Caucasian War (1830–59), it tied down a large Russian army, and slowed down the Russian advance toward the Middle East. Without

Daghestan, Russian soldiers would have marched on Constantinople and perhaps on Jerusalem.

Years after his final defeat, Imam Shamil visited Constantinople. One story has it that he was summoned to the Ottoman palace, where the sultan himself—as the Caliph of the Faithful, Islam's highest authority—kissed his hand.

Daghestan's claim to fame in the Islamic world in the nineteenth century was not confined to military heroes. As small and remote as it was, it also boasted some of Islam's greatest religious figures. To this day, it enjoys the status of a holy land of sorts to some followers of Sufism, an influential school of Islamic thought often described as "mystical." By the time of the Bolshevik Revolution, Daghestan boasted more than two thousand mosques and some eight hundred *medressehs*, or religious schools.

Daghestan's entire history under Russian rule was that of a weathervane pointing only in one direction, *north*, toward the Russian heartland. As was often the case in Russian and Soviet ideologies, geography and history were denied or banned altogether, to fit political needs. The very notion of "East" came to be considered subversive. Its restoration would amount to invalidation of two Russian centuries in the Caucasus.

Now that the notion of "East" is being reinstated, the large numbers of Russified Daghestanis of Abuyev's generation feel threatened by the transformation. At stake is not just their political allegiance but their notion of who they are. Imperial Russia had offered them not mere citizenship but membership in its cultural orbit; Soviet Russia extended the offer—and they accepted. No other colonial power (not even the French) has ever dealt with non-European and non-Christian native populations this way. Caucasians would be accepted as Russians as long as they were willing to shed their former identity and allegiance and assume Russian culture, Russian names, and a Russian worldview—namely, the belief in a Russian civilization that should be a light unto the nations. (Paradoxically, a Lak could have become, at least in theory, a prime minister of Russia even at a time when he was barred from the highest offices in Daghestan by virtue of a semiconstitutional arrangement.)

THE AUTONOMY NO DESPOT
SHOULD EVER RISK

Czarist methods were more consistent with the goal of establishing and maintaining one-nation-under-the-Russian-eagle than later Communist methods proved to be. Czardom saw no need of seeking earthly legitimacy and saw no reason to offer even a semblance of self-government to its subject peoples. The Communists, however, denounced old Russia as a "prison of nations" and promised to let the inmates out. Hence the autonomous republics and regions that the Soviet regime established in abundance, the nominal recognition it accorded local languages, and the ethnic classification it forced on every single individual, at times in a manner inconsistent with either history or common sense.

The early Soviet regime demonstrated considerable sympathy for the native nations and even, in the case of the Caucasus, hailed as "progressive" the local resistance to czarist expansion. It is of course not easy to distinguish sincere praise from propaganda. Whatever the case may be, Soviet historians in the years immediately subsequent to the 1917 revolution strove to establish a clear contrast between the new dogma and the one just repudiated. The czarist treatment of colonial nations was denounced wholesale and often described as genocide, "so cruel that its horrors surpassed those of all other colonial systems, which appeared benign in comparison."

Lenin—among whose ancestors Jews and Mongol Buddhists could be counted—warned sternly against the domination of the new state by "Great Russian chauvinism." Stalin was far less concerned. His famous toast "to the great Russian nation" at the end of World War II affirmed the chauvinism that Lenin had professed to abhor: non-

Russians, particularly non-Slavic peoples, were officially relegated to the status of sixteen moons to the Russian Jupiter. The various autonomies turned into enforcement agencies for the Communist center in Moscow. Local party bosses, eager to please the center, clamped down on serious education in local languages and turned it into window dressing.

A pointed illustration of Soviet duplicity on ethnic rights in the Caucasus comes from Zaur Naloyev, the prominent Kabardin intellectual and leading campaigner for ethnic rights whom we have previously met. He told me how Stalin stunned the Communist leadership of the Kabardin republic, in the Northwest Caucasus.

"In 1947, six years before his death, Stalin summoned the first secretary of the Kabardin party. His name was Mazin, and he was Cossack and so a Russian speaker. He was asked to discuss the leadership's policy on ethnic issues. A question was posed to him: 'What language is used to teach children at school? In what language are official documents written? What language is used in party meetings in the cities and in the countryside?'

"Mr. Mazin replied, 'Why, Russian of course.'

"Stalin thundered: 'Comrade Mazin, do you play with ethnic policies, or do you implement the ethnic policies of the Communist Party of the Soviet Union?'

"Poor Mazin. He turned paler than a blank paper. He rushed home and announced that henceforth all schools should teach in Kabardin through the tenth grade, that government correspondence should be conducted in Kabardin, and that the workforce should be subjected to 'Kabardinization.'

"But the policy was impossible to carry out. There were no trained teachers, no textbooks, and but few Kabardin speakers in the administration. . . . Luckily for Mazin, Stalin never came back to the issue, and the whole matter was soon forgotten."

To Western eyes, the autonomous leaders were but a collection of slavish yes-men, known for their total submissiveness and boundless flattery. (When Edvard Shevardnadze was Communist boss of Georgia, for example, he proclaimed, "Our sun rises in the north," in reference to his republic's northern border with Russia.)

The Economist magazine of London was so contemptuous of the Soviet Union's pretensions to federalism that it withheld recognition from the state so named and referred to it as "Russia." To its London editors, the USSR was no more a federation than Rome had been a republic after Julius Caesar, and its multiethnic structure was but a poorly woven disguise for a reconstructed Russian empire.

When various satrapies in the empire began to assume identities and wills of their own, the West hardly noticed, either because it genuinely lacked information, or because the Soviet monolith was easier to deal with at the time of the cold war. But well before the rise of Mikhail Gorbachev, autonomous republics became the breeding grounds for the regionalism and separatism that eventually unglued the empire. It happened not only in the big republics, such as Ukraine, where a local party chief in the 1960s openly championed Ukrainian rights vis-à-vis Russia, but also in the Caucasus, where nationalist sentiments erupted in mass demonstrations even under the unforgiving gaze of Leonid Brezhnev. A case in point is the North Caucasian republic of North Ossetia, where spontaneous rebellion engulfed the capital in 1981, an amazing episode that is almost completely unknown in the West to this day and little known in Russia itself. What Lenin and Stalin intended as a source of strength at best, or a propagandistic ploy at worst, turned into a catalyst of disintegration.

It most likely did not occur to the Soviet rulers that one day the nominal autonomies might make demands and even try to secede. Had it not been for the regime's insistence on presenting a facade of ethnic pluralism, we probably would not have witnessed the birth of an independent Belarus, or Turkmenistan, or Azerbaijan, or Kyrgyzstan or Kazakhstan, none of which existed as states prior to the twentieth century. Absent a nominal autonomy for the Chechens, however diluted, we might not have seen a Chechen independence movement, either.

By offering the nationalities their own institutions—parliaments, ministries, locally run police forces, national academies of science, local broadcasting—the system provided its future demolishers with precious launching pads. The nationalities did not have to call underground meetings of clandestine congresses or start an insurrection. They only had to put the existing structures to better use. They did not have to draw new borders—they had only to proclaim as "international" the existing inter-republican ones, however ill drawn, however ahistorical. Theirs were therefore not acts of rebellion, which the world might have been obliged to reject, but acts of reasonable divorce between civilized partners. In 1991, with flags and anthems and presidents and parliaments, the newly independent nations all looked solid, authentic, and well established.

Vladimir Zhirinovsky, the Russian nationalist demagogue, has advocated a restoration not of the Soviet Union but of the Russian empire. He wishes to return to the czarist system of *gubernii*, or provinces, whereby internal borders were drawn administratively, often oblivious to history and ethnography, and governors were appointed by the center, with no autonomy of any kind or local parliaments to answer to. For an advocate of Great Russia, Zhirinovsky drew the right lesson: federalizing an empire necessarily leads to its breakup, because federalism entails only voluntary acceptance of rule. Imperialism, by contrast, is predicated on universal submission to a single will.

The lesson all putative tyrants should draw is simple: never create even ostensibly independent structures if you do not want them someday to become actually independent, and never share your authority, not even with those who acclaim you as their leader. Even a mock devolution of power might get out of hand one day.

IMAM, COME BACK, BUT SMILE

Venerable holy men dominated Daghestani Islam for centuries. These holy men were scholars and teachers, theologians and priests; and they were at the center of the mountains' "free societies." Known by their Arabic name *jamaat*, these societies functioned as little republics, communities of equal men where decisions were reached by consensus and no blood aristocracy existed. The heads of the societies were elected, and before secularism and party politics, members of the societies turned for leadership to the holy men.

Imam Shamil, still unsmiling

Marxist historians considered the *jamaat* to be cases of arrested development, frozen in time before the onset of feudalism. For humanity to advance toward "scientific socialism," they argued, it had first to relieve itself of such primitive egalitarianism. But to the mountaineers, the *jamaat* were the essence of their freedom.

One of Daghestan's best-known "free societies" was that of Aqusha. In the mid-eighteenth century, Aqusha played a major role in the all-Daghestani coalition against the invading Persian army led by Nadir Shah, the Terror of the Universe. The Persians were beaten off and never came back. The fact that Persia was an Islamic power left no particular impression on the peoples of Daghestan. They craved freedom from any foreign interference, whatever its heavenly mandate.

During the Russian civil war, following the 1917 Bolshevik putsch, Ottoman Turkey dispatched emissaries to Daghestan, to seek an alliance against Soviet Russia. Sheikh Ali Haji of Aqusha, who was recognized as one of the foremost religious authorities in the mountains, turned them down. Like his predecessors, he was not impressed by his suitors' Islamic credentials. He thought his people would find greater freedom in a state controlled by the Bolsheviks, who, after all, were as egalitarian as he was. "Their doctrine certainly has some communist characteristics," one Bolshevik contemporary wrote of the *jamaat.* It was "ascetic communism comparable to that of the early Christians." Hence, rather than help prolong the life of the hopelessly corrupt Ottoman Empire, the holy man of Aqusha ordered his disciples to assist Lenin's armies.

Gussein Abuyev, the Daghestani official, smiled when he spoke to me of the venerable sheikh, a sage of the Sufi order. "After victory, the grateful Bolsheviks rewarded him with a golden watch. But it took him some time to realize that the Bolsheviks did not intend to leave him alone, and so he rose against them, too. Old people in the town of Aqusha—old enough to remember those days—told me how the sheikh, already very old, wearing *chalma* around his head [a green band signifying Muslim piety], used to stand in the main square and proclaim to the locals their new sacred duty: 'Everyone should kill at least one Bolshevik.'"

Sheikh Ali Haji of Aqusha—"Akushinsky," as he was known in Russian—was named in 1921 to head the People's Commissariat for the Shari'a, known by its Russian acronym *Narkomsharia. Shari'a* is the body of Islamic law upon which a proper Islamic state is to be based; *Narkom,* or *people's commissariat,* is how the Bolsheviks called their ministries for the first twenty-odd years of their revolution. The marriage of the two concepts is so improbable as to be almost funny.

Stalin, the commissar of nationalities in Lenin's cabinet, authored the idea in 1920—but his promise to uphold the will of Islamic scholars, delivered in person, was soon forgotten. By 1926 the last vestiges of a "people's *shari'a*" had been eradicated. Sheikh Ali Haji was arrested in 1928 and executed shortly thereafter. So were other holy men and religious leaders in Daghestan as well as Chechnya. The most common charges against them were "clerical bourgeois nationalism" and "economic sabotage."

"**H**ate thy expansionist neighbor" is a lofty principle among small, independence-craving peoples. But it is also a sure recipe for disaster.

During the two years after World War I, the Daghestanis, as well as their neighbors to the northwest, the Chechens, resisted Turkish approaches and fought White and Red Russians, never in concert with any other foe, never attempting to forge tactical alliances, always splendidly alone.

Peter the Great recognized that trait in the Daghestanis he met in the course of his abortive military campaign in the Caucasus in the 1720s: "When they are together, they do not hold at all, but run away, while separately each man resists so desperately that when he has thrown away his musket as if he were going to surrender, he begins to fight with his dagger."

And yet unlike the Chechens, the Daghestanis resigned themselves to defeat, twice within sixty years—and they have never attempted to rise again, not even when the Soviet Union collapsed and other nations with no record of resistance to Russian rule and no real national experience seized their independence and broke away. Daghestan did not even join the "march of sovereignties" in 1990, when a host of autonomous legislatures throughout the Soviet Union claimed the superiority of their own laws over those promulgated by Moscow.

Why were the Daghestanis so quiescent? Perhaps they had a greater sense of realism than their Chechen neighbors. Perhaps they were better sports, recognizing that their chance had come and gone. Unlike the Chechens, Daghestanis to whom I spoke expressed little hatred toward Russia and did not seek to settle old scores with it.

In this respect, the Daghestanis could have been inspired by Imam Shamil himself. That uncompromising warrior—who was ready to lay waste the entire region in pursuit of his radical social agenda—became a gracious loser in 1859. He could have made a heroic last stand against the infidels and fallen on his sword. He did not. He capitulated to the czar—a moment dramatically captured in a famous Russian painting—and was allowed to retire to the Russian city of Kaluga, where he received a reasonable Russian pension, kept a retinue, and maintained a little court. Shamil's Chechen deputy, who had lost an arm and a leg in the war, chose to resist a few months longer until brought down by Russian bullets.

Shamil's gentlemanly surrender launched the peoples of Daghestan on a long path of coexistence with Russia, which was only briefly interrupted during the civil war. Even then it was the Chechens who played the leading role.

At the end of World War II, the vindictive and ever-suspicious Stalin, ready to deport four Muslim nations from the North Caucasus to the steppes of Central Asia, barely touched Daghestan. Only Daghestani Chechens were loaded onto cattle cars and banished—nobody else. Even the Turkic-speaking peoples of Daghestan were spared Stalin's traditional Turkophobia. Apparently this shrewd son of the Caucasus concluded that the Daghestanis posed no danger to Moscow's realm. He has yet to be proven wrong.

In 1994, against the background of the Chechen war, some prophets of doom warned confidently that the war would inevitably spill over into Chechnya's North Caucasian Muslim neighbors, fomenting an "all-Caucasian war" against Russia.

Nowhere were these fears more pronounced than in Daghestan—after all, the Chechen frontier is only a three-hour drive from Makhachkala. The border is ill marked, and the populations are mixed—there is a significant Chechen minority in Daghestan, and a notable Daghestani Kumyk minority in Chechnya. Moreover, Daghestanis and Chechens had fought side by side before, not only under Imam Shamil. Word of the ravages of the Chechen war was passed along to Daghestan through extensive family channels, and a flood of refugees provided the Daghestanis with daily reminders of Russia's brutality.

All over Daghestan, people professed admiration for the Chechens. In one town in southern Daghestan, Magaramkent, populated by Lezgins, a five-year-old boy mounted the top of his father's parked truck and performed a dazzling war dance for me. The child leaped and hopped, waved his clenched fist, and recited Shamil Basayev's name as if it were a sacred mantra.

Basayev is the best-known Chechen military field commander and is deeply hated in Russia for his role in a 1995 raid on a Russian hospital. This episode resulted in a poorly executed rescue attempt and the death of many civilians. Basayev's boss and mentor, General Jokar Dudayev, was practically deified in the mind of many Daghestanis, who admired his contemptuous defiance of Russia's might. And yet hardly any Daghestani that I met ever raised the possibility of joining the battle alongside the Chechens. One night, in a remote Lak village, I sat down with dozens of men of all ages, to discuss life. One of them, in his mid-thirties, was particularly skeptical of me and of my profession. He turned to me and asked, "What do you tell your readers about Chechnya?" I stated my sympathy for the Chechens and my strong objections to Russia's methods. The man waited impatiently and finally shot back: "What is this crap. Russia has the right to do all that it needs to do in order to maintain law and order on its territory."

I waited for the other Laks to take issue with him. No one did. That is not to say that his view was unanimously held among the community. It is also possible that Laks hold a grudge against the Chechens because of bitter land disputes elsewhere in Daghestan. Still, I was struck by the silence. The Laks I spoke to that night did not appear to feel that they should expand the war and fight Russia in their highland, the way they had done 150 years earlier.

There is little doubt that various elements in Chechnya sought just such an expansion of the war and attempted to provoke it. In one unsavory example in early 1996, Chechen irregulars took over a Daghestani border town, Pyervomaiskoe ("First of May"); the ensuing Russian barrage leveled the place to the ground. In numerous other incidents, bombs went off in Russian military barracks in Daghestan, buses were hijacked, and security officials were shot—and yet any clamor to join the Chechens was negligible.

Dudayev was mystified. So many people in neighboring Caucasian nations had assured him that, should the Russians dare aim a single volley at him, the entire region would go up in flames. That the Kabardins or the Balkars did not close ranks behind him was to be expected: they had had almost no tradition of resistance to Russia. But the Daghestanis? Imam Shamil's own people? The ones who had forged such a powerful alliance with the Chechens in the thirty-year war against the czar's armies? How could they remain idle in face of the Russian onslaught against fraternal Chechnya?

Whether the Daghestanis should be condemned for their reticence or admired for their self-restraint is, of course, in the eye of the beholder. But their behavior in the late twentieth century seems to continue a pattern that emerged at the time of Shamil's surrender. If the venerable imam was willing to bow to a despised enemy and submit to his rule, then defeat—or at least acknowledgment of the futility of resistance—was no longer a source of shame. It is as though Shamil's testament, however unintended, were "Be realistic, my children," a message that few Chechens could countenance or heed but that Daghestanis, entirely dependent on Russian subsidies, could and would.

One of the most powerful men in Daghestan, Sa'id Amirov, Dargin by nationality, the first elected mayor of Makhachkala, told a Russian journalist in early 1996: "Daghestan did not voluntarily join Russia; nor will it voluntarily leave Russia."

He said in effect, No one can fault us for not resisting our incorporation into the Russian Empire 150 years ago. We gave the Russians a good fight. But if somebody expects us to dig trenches and mount a war now, he is entirely mistaken.

The message was clearly intended for the Chechens. In case they did not understand it, in April 1997 Daghestan's best-known federal politician, an occasional member of the Russian government, Ramazan Abdulatipov, wrote the Chechen president, Aslan Maskhadov: "Daghestan has made its choice—it will forever remain part of the Russian Federation."

The Chechens were unwilling to take the hint. Four months later, Chechnya's deputy prime minister, Movladi Udugov, who fancies himself an Islamic Che Guevara, convened a conference in Grozny of dozens of Islamic groupings from Chechnya and Daghestan. There he announced the establishment of a new movement aptly named Islamic Ummah. (*Ummah* is an Arabic word that combines the meanings of both "nation" and "community," the universal establishment of which is the ultimate goal of Islam.) Udugov told the delegates that the movement would struggle "to restore Daghestan within its historic boundaries," an allusion to the religious state that Imam Shamil established in Daghestan and Chechnya in the course of his long struggle against the Russians—the first Islamic republic of the modern era, with well-codified life, an organized military, and a meticulously managed treasury. The conference hall was decorated with the slogans "Chechnya, Daghestan Forever Together and Free" and "Freedom Is Not Granted, It Is Won."

In 1997 Daghestan officially marked the bicentennial of Imam Shamil's birth. The republican government wisely co-opted the imam and by doing so confirmed that his name was no longer associated with collective defiance. Indeed, the holy warrior of 150 years ago has now become something of a curiosity, almost a Father Christmas of the mountains.

When I first learned in 1990, through the Russian press, of the existence of a Shamil Liberation Front in Makhachkala, I immediately assumed that Daghestan would soon follow the Baltic states and Armenia down the path of confrontation and insurgence.

But the Shamil standard bearers had little to do with the imam. There were in fact two organizations named after Shamil. One was entirely benign, and its sole aim was the preservation of Daghestan's historical heritage.

The other organization, recognized by the Daghestani government as the representative of the Avar nation, was conceived in a more adversarial context. Its leader was a voluble, bearded man in his late thirties by the name of Gadzhi Makhachev. He promised to stand up to the Chechens living in western Daghestan (known as Akin Chechens), who became involved in land conflicts with members of other nationalities, and were perceived as aggressive and ruthless. It is a sad paradox that the name of Shamil, the great unifier of the North Caucasus, was now being used to accentuate differences between the two nations that had been most loyal to him.

As the head of the national movement of the largest nationality, Makhachev was quickly embraced by the Daghestani establishment. He was given one of the few plum jobs available in government: director of the republican oil company Dagneft. I visited him at his Dagneft headquarters. Seated at the far end of a large modern office, under a portrait of Imam Shamil, he behaved less as the director of a company

Gadzhi Makhachev claims the mantle of Imam Shamil (above his head). But he makes ends meet by running Daghestan's state oil company. It is barely enough to pay for a little mansion with a private mosque and then some.

than as a traditional chieftain in his court. An endless stream of people were coming and going, taking seats, listening and interjecting. I do not think they were there to discuss oil.

Every other minute, Makhachev would interrupt our interview and speak to his attendants in a mixture of Avar and Russian, raising his voice in anger, spewing out words at great speed. A few blocks away, he had an opulent mansion with his own private mosque and swimming pool, or so I was told. In early 1998, he became deputy prime minister of Daghestan in charge of energy. At the time of his appointment, the Russian press reported that he was a convicted felon who had served time in Soviet prison. I cannot corroborate this report, though it is commonly whispered in Makhachkala.

Expropriating Imam Shamil for Avar use is a bit like making Napoleon an exclusively Corsican hero, or portraying Saladin as a Kurdish chieftain, or describing Nelson Mandela as a Xhosa hereditary prince. All three rose far above their tribal roots, ascended to the leadership of continents, and are remembered as claimants to universal thrones, the disseminators of grand messianic notions of liberty and godliness. Reducing Shamil to his narrowest bloodline is, in essence, tantamount to stripping him of relevance and making him into a harmless Robin Hood of the highland.

That little is left of the imam's original agenda is attested to by the name of one of Makhachkala's largest department stores. I had to rub my eyes when I came across the sign on Lenin Avenue: *Imamat*, or "imamate," so named after the nineteenth-century state that Shamil established. In protocapitalist Makhachkala, Shamil's state is but a commercial logo. It was as if the French Revolution had become the name of a shoe store.

One day I was taken to meet a famous Kumyk hero, Haji Ismailov, in his native village in western Daghestan. He was one of the young soldiers who had hoisted the Soviet flag over the Reichstag in Berlin in 1945, an act that earned him the title "Hero of Russia," if only fifty years after the event. (He should have become a Hero of the Soviet Union if it had not been for the apparent absentmindedness of a Soviet-era bureaucrat.) Ismailov, a tall man in his seventies, with a broad smile and a hint of mischief in his eyes, gladly donned (for the benefit of my camera) his old military coat, resplendent with the medals he had received for participation in eighteen battles. He proudly displayed the shining rifle that the Daghestani police chief had awarded him on the occasion of his commendation. The wall in his living room featured portraits of

"Oh, him," retorted Haji Ismailov of the imam-on-the-wall. "I wouldn't know, really. I was born many years after his death."

his former Comrade-in-Chief Joseph Stalin, the C-in-C's own former C-in-C Lenin, and an artistic photo of the Reichstag takeover (black and white but for a red flag). The opposite wall showed only Imam Shamil.

Who is that person? I asked, pretending not to recognize the best-known face in the Caucasus.

"Oh, him." Ismailov smiled, showing a row of perfect teeth (which are uncommon, even if false, in a land where people's golden teeth glisten from great distances). "His name is Imam Shamil. He was a great Islamic, Arabic scholar." A somewhat unlikely description for a man better known for other skills, I thought.

Is that all he was? I asked. Did he not do other things?

"I wouldn't know, really." Ismailov smiled faintly. "I was born many years after his death."

So why is his picture hanging here? I asked.

"He believed in God, and I believe in God, and so I believe in him," the former Soviet hero replied.

He fought for the liberation of his people, didn't he? I persisted.

"Certainly, he fought for liberation." Ismailov continued our little game.

Whom did he fight against?

"I don't really know. That happened in the distant past."

Do the people today need another Imam Shamil to fight for their liberation?

"No, certainly not."

We stopped there, as the time came to sit down for lunch and to let the fabled Kumyk _khinkal_, the <u>dumplings</u> of the Caucasus, help us regain energy. Though Ismailov clearly exercised caution with me, it is also possible that the venerable imam has simply become a living-room fixture, a proverbial ancestor, his beard replacing the emblems of the Soviet regime.

If so, and if Daghestani conduct in the last century suggests peace, then why is Daghestan's future marred with so many doubts?

WILL A PECULIAR LAND SURVIVE?

"**Y**ou see," Magomed Ossmanov said, "when we meet each other, we identify ourselves as Avars, or Kumyks, or Lezgins. But when we talk to outsiders, we are all Daghestanis, first of all Daghestanis."

Professor Ossmanov is the head of Makhachkala's Institute of Ethnography, where a group of local historians assembled one morning to convince a foreign guest that Daghestan was more than a geographical concept, and that its inhabitants have too much in common to be driven apart.

The intellectual exercise in and of itself was a good indication of Daghestan's peculiarities. It is unlike any other former Soviet province, and there are few of its kind anywhere in the world: a land where no ethnic group comes close to claiming majority status (the largest falls short of 25 percent of the population); where six nations have the status of "constituent" (which makes them nominal co-owners of Daghestan); and where a collective presidency allows a single representative to each of fourteen ethnic groups, constitutent or otherwise. All in all, more than thirty ethnic groups, some of them numbering only a few thousands, vie for a place in the sun—and they do so in a territory about the size of Vermont and Maryland put together.

It is hard to escape Yugoslav parallels, imprecise as they may be. Tito's Yugoslavia was also a land of six constituent nations, none of which was in the majority. Tito held such a dim view of human nature that he forced upon his successors a constitutional arrangement that was intended to prevent the concentration of power into the hands of any one individual, and to spread it evenly among the constituent nations. He had in place to succeed him not one president but eight, seeking stability through immobility. But his system simply ground to a halt, and its collective weakness proved no obstacle to the ambitions of determined nationalist leaders from outside its ranks. Tito's vision of coexistence by mutual impotence is replicated in Daghestan, but will it meet the same cataclysmic fate?

In the mid-1990s, particularly in the wake of the savage war in neigh-boring Chechnya, quite a few Russians feared it would and delivered grave warnings of pending doom in Daghestan. Sure enough, there have been moments in which the worst seemed at hand, when spectacu-lar terrorist attacks have threatened to bring down the system, when ethnic groups have taken to the streets and resorted to violence, and when religious fanaticism has seemed to be rising. Notwithstanding the wounds, at the end of the fearful 1990s, Daghestan was still at relative peace.

Daghestanis I met did not appreciate even the slightest insinuation that their "multiethnic republic" was a Yugoslavia in the making, primar-ily—they argued—because there was nothing artificial about Daghes-tan. It may have never been a unified *state* (except for Imam Shamil's Islamic republic), but a common Daghestani *state of mind* had predated Russia's occupation by many centuries.

"As early as the fifteenth century, local scholars began to identify themselves as Daghestanis," said Amri Sheikhsaidov, an authority on ancient Islamic manuscripts in the Makhachkala Institute. "They would have first signed their given name, then their father's name, then the name of their village or region, and then 'of Daghestan.' It went like this: *Muhammad ibn Mussa al Quduqi ad-Daghestani.* That is to say, the person was Muhammad, the son of Mussa, of the village of Quduq, of Daghestan. The form of the name was of course Arabic—that was the language of literacy. Muhammad ibn Mussa happened to be Avar, and he lived in the seventeenth century. I can give you other prominent names of Laks, Lez-gins, and Kumyks who all signed 'the Daghestani' next to their names. . . . Daghestan was an integral part of people's identity."

Not only were they Daghestanis by preference, they were also bound together by virtue of their genes, or so contends archaeologist Magomed Gadzhiyev, another member of the Institute. "Nearly all of us had common ancestry," he said, "and then a process of divergence began, and the present nations started forming. Just think of Germany, where it took three hundred years for hundreds of principalities and duchies and free cities to arise. That period of time was sufficient for dialects to appear, so distinct and particular that northerners could no longer understand southerners. That is what happened to us. But in our case, the process continued unabated for four thousand years, and we finally reached a situation in which each village has its own dialect, its own vernacular, its own outlook."

After Islam arrived in the Middle Ages and was widely embraced, "an ideological cohesion was added to Daghestan as well," according to Professor Sheikhsaidov. It was a point that even the first Communist revolutionaries conceded. As late as 1925, Daghestan's first Communist leader, Najmuddin Samurski, wrote:

Daghestan has been for centuries the seat of Arab culture. Those Sheikhs, imams, alims and mutalims [all religious teachers of high and low rank] whom we meet in each *aul* [village] are scholars well versed in Arabic, who have thoroughly studied the ancient Arabic culture, science and philosophy and have penetrated all the subtleties of Muslim religion. Many among them are famous Arabists known throughout the entire Muslim world. Thousands of disciples from all Muslim lands of Russia, from Turkey and Persia used to visit them.

Samurski entertained the idea of making Daghestan a *meeting place* of Marxism and Islam, not necessarily a *battlefield* between them. His Daghestan might have exported progressive Islam to the countries of the Middle East and Central Asia, perhaps preventing the rise of the intolerant revolutionary Islam that so disturbed the West in the late twentieth century.

But Samurski met the only fate that original thinkers and noncomformists could have expected to meet in Stalin's days: the execution squad.

In the 1920s the Soviet regime attempted to secure for the Daghestanis a potentially unifying trait: a common language other than Russian. No indigenous Daghestani language could have played that role; the most obvious candidates were Arabic and a Turkic language (the one spoken now in Azerbaijan), each of which was tried briefly. But Stalin was not interested in establishing a viable regional identity. The idea of finding a lingua franca for the highlanders was dropped by 1928 and was replaced with a formula that took the notion of group rights to its extreme and thereby rendered the whole concept not only impractical but preposterous: tiny Daghestan, at that time home to a million people, was given eleven official languages. Not even India or Nigeria, which have dozens of viable languages, ever attempted to make so many of them official. The inevitable result was that artificially inflated diversity led, paradoxically, to uniformity.

The young and energetic Magomedsalikh Gusayev, Daghestan's

minister of nationalities at the time of my visit, told me: "In Daghestan there are only two official languages." When I raised my eyebrows, he smiled and explained, "Two languages per person. I am a member of the Agul nation [about 25,000 people], so to me Agul and Russian are the languages. To a Dargin, it will be Dargin and Russian, and so on." The end result of this bizarre formula was that local languages completely disappeared from public life. In Ireland you meet bilingual signs, even if only a tiny fraction of the population speaks Irish-Gaelic. In Canada federal legislators switch back and forth between English and French in parliamentary speeches. But in Daghestan, probably the most multilingual territory on earth, there is a virtual monolingualism. Daghestan's famed Tower of Babel is increasingly irrelevant.

Russian quickly became the "language of interethnic communication," to use a pet phrase of Soviet officialdom. Nowhere in Daghestan did I see a single public sign in any of the eleven official languages, not even in areas where a single ethnic group forms a majority: not in Tarki, the former Kumyk capital; not in Ghazi-Ghumuq, the former Lak capital; not in Magaramkent, the main administrative center in a district populated almost exclusively by Lezgins; not in Derbent, with its many Azeris; and not in Khasavyurt, with its large Chechen community.

To allow at least some of the local languages—say, the ones spoken by more than 100,000 people—a fighting chance, they would have to be taught at school. For that, curricula would have to be put in place, teachers would have to be trained, and textbooks published. It would be an enormous undertaking for any government, let alone for an impoverished province unable to secure employment for most of its residents.

Short of a massive infusion of external funds—say, from private philanthropists or from international organizations, such as UNESCO, that are interested in preserving ancient heritages—Daghestan faces an unstoppable exodus from its local languages into Russian.

Diversity in pursuit of uniformity is what the government of Daghestan sought—and seemingly accomplished also on the political level. It was the old Soviet idea in a modified form: institutionalize ethnic differences by encouraging the formation of "national movements" for all of Daghestan's main ethnic groups. Each of Daghestan's "constituent nations" therefore has a national movement—the Avars, the Dargins, the Lezgins, the Kumyks, the Laks, the Tabasarans—as well as the "nonconstituent" Noghai. The largest of them numbers about 600,000, and the smallest about 70,000.

These national movements, such as they are, have been largely discredited in the eyes of most Daghestanis, for they have all turned out to be vehicles by which unelected "national leaders" peddle their influence in exchange for material benefits and official perks. With the exception of the Kumyks, all of them have been more or less co-opted.

Since the dying days of the Soviet Union, not one major organization has come into being that is all-Daghestani in nature. Ethnicism has thus worked relatively well for the provincial government in that it serves to numb public opinion and perpetuate the status quo. Whether stagnation is the price a society should pay for stability is another matter.

One well-informed Daghestani told me: "I became involved with the national movements in the 1980s. At that time the movements were of interest only to intellectuals. But then the criminal world got interested. Shady figures, never before involved in politics or national culture, began to show up at rallies and deliver speeches. Why? It soon became clear. Their nationalist activities provided them with immunity of sorts. Each time they fell under suspicion because of criminal activities, they immediately threw their hands in the air and exclaimed: 'Look, we are persecuted because we are involved in the national movement. What kind of democracy is this?' Members of their movement would then hold demonstrations for their release, and the law-enforcement bodies would have no choice but to let them go.

"One particularly outrageous case involved the head of a branch of a national movement in an important provincial city. The security forces found illegal arms in his possession—AK-47 semiautomatics and pistols. He was arrested. Then members of the movement flocked to Makhachkala, abducted the state attorney, and took him along with them. They filled the main square in front of the government building, demanding the immediate release of the leader. I told the government not to surrender. That, I said, would be the end of any hope of applying the rule of law. He should at least have been put on trial, should have been fined, should have got a suspended sentence. Something! But the government got cold feet. They let him go. It happened a couple of years ago. And do you know what he's doing now? He's a member of parliament. Now he's got real immunity."*

My interlocutor went on to name names. One leader, he said, was convicted for robbery, while another did time for murder. Stories of this kind are whispered all over Daghestan and have two complementary results.

---

* Escaping prosecution by winning parliamentary immunity has become common throughout the former Soviet Union.

One is that they enhance the aura of the men concerned. Often in the history of the mountains, individuals with a healthy disdain for convention have been lionized. For generations, oral traditions have exalted the *abrek*, a law-enforcer and a law-breaker in one, a man who thrives on defiance of any prevailing order. It is easy to see why the prowess of a modern-day *abrek*—who has come from behind so swiftly that by sheer momentum alone he is reaching for the top—would appeal so much to people paralyzed by despair.

But many people, particularly among the well-educated, have not been able to adjust to the new economics and harbor a deep resentment against the modern-day *abreks*. Their helplessness drives them further into cynicism and further reduces the already-very-slim prospect that Daghestan will see the emergence of a civic society. For such a society to emerge, people must first feel that they have a stake in the system and that they may legitimately, without fear, affect the way it functions.

Daghestan may have witnessed more violent crime directed at public figures than any other part of troubled Russia. One day, only a few blocks away from where I was talking to an interviewee, a car bomb killed Daghestan's young finance minister, Gamid Gamidov, a rising star and member of the federal parliament, widely assumed to be in line for the post of republican prime minister. His body was blown to pieces. When I stopped by an hour or so later, the police had difficulty pointing out the remains of his car, so thorough and professional were the perpetrators. The minister had been Dargin, of the second-largest nation in Daghestan.

People all over Makhachkala were greatly shocked that day. This meticulously executed assassination—perhaps the most sensational against any political figure in Russia—seemed to confirm the popular suspicion that politics in Daghestan had been transformed into open gang warfare, and that decisions affecting the life of the people were no longer made in parliament or in any other governmental institution. People I spoke to responded with anxiety more acute than I had encountered anywhere else in Russia. "No one's life is safe anymore," I heard from a secretary in a newspaper office whose father, she said, had known the dead minister very well. Another man who had known Gamidov told me, ashen-faced, "Daghestan's last great hope is gone. He could have really turned things around." Another, less gracious, said: "He died the way he lived." Gamidov, like most leaders of the new ethnic elites in Daghestan, had emerged into politics out of the world of wrestling and in a short time accumulated a handsome fortune.

One man, involved neither in politics nor in government, told me, "Our Daghestan is the first component of the Russian Federation in which criminals do not run the show behind the scenes. They *are* the show."

With the failure of nationalism to provide an alternative to the sclerotic, corrupt system, the disaffected have only one remaining course: religion. Daghestan remains the most Muslim of all Russian lands, and Makhachkala boasts the largest mosque in Russia. (Its construction, completed in 1996, was funded by Turkish businessmen.) "We are experiencing a tremendous religious revival," Professor Sheikhsaidov said. "Just consider the numbers. Ten years ago, when Mikhail Gorbachev began his liberalization, there were only seventeen mosques in the entire republic. Now, no fewer than fifteen hundred mosques had been *officially* registered with the authorities, and I have no doubt that the actual number is much higher. Nowhere else in the former Soviet Union will you find such staggering growth. The same applies to the number of Daghestanis who have made the *hajj*. In 1985 only fifteen Daghestanis were allowed to travel. In 1996 the official quota was 6,600, but in reality 11,700 made it."

The reemergence of public religion has been accompanied by the rise of Daghestan's own fundamentalists. Some of them have resorted to coercion and violence. There have been attempts to inject religion into ethnic politics, as the case of the Khachilayev brothers demonstrated. But by and large, Daghestanis still follow a relaxed form of Islam, eclectic and idiosyncratic, replete with indigenous customs. (When foreign-educated militants, would-be reformers of Daghestani Islam, attempted a rebellion, most recently in 1999, the overwhelming majority of Daghestanis apparently turned against them.) Of course, such was also the case in Chechnya prior to the 1994–96 war with Russia, which suggests that the Daghestan equation could still change through missteps or sheer ineptitude.

READING A DAGHESTANI TEASPOON

Gussein Abuyev's study, next to the prime minister's office in the building overlooking Lenin Square in Makhachkala, has a large map of the Caucasus hanging on one of its walls. There is nothing unusual about a regional map in the office of a senior government official, except that in the Caucasus, such maps have never been available to the public at large.

Though it contains no military secret that I am aware of, the map conveys *knowledge*, and few commodities were more strictly rationed in Soviet times than knowledge. When knowledge could no longer be rationed, with the dawn of electronically retrievable information, the Soviet system was doomed. Pillars of the system, men like Gussein Abuyev, were no longer indispensable. And yet, Abuyev maintained half-smilingly, "you will not find a map as detailed and accurate as this almost anywhere else in the entire Caucasus."

Literally or figuratively, Abuyev's message was that openness and free travel notwithstanding, understanding of the Caucasus was still hard to come by. I asked the Daghestani sociologist Enver Kisriev to name a few influential Daghestanis to whom I should speak if I were to develop any grasp of the republic. He looked at me amused. "Those who would talk to you are not influential," he said, "and those who are influential would not talk to you." Happily he was proved wrong.

One day, after a series of attempts to get Daghestanis to speak, I sat down exhausted at a café table in a little park, just a few steps away from Lenin's statue, and wrote at a furious pace. After a few minutes, I realized that people were watching with intent curiosity. They were not curious about me—I had been there a few times before, and in any event the presence of Westerners, though not as common as in Moscow, is no longer exotic. It was that I was doing something few Daghestanis ever do in public.

Possibly what titillated the café onlookers was my apparent indiscretion: a foreigner evidently chronicling their unhappy life, perhaps shaming them in the process, much as the Lak man in the mountains had complained to me that foreign journalists "pretend to be friendly but describe us as backward when they go home."

This foreigner—they may have whispered in each other's ears—could not really like what he was seeing. But who is he to judge? Let him live here for a couple of years, endure what we have to endure, and then write.

It so happened that the subject of my café writing was this very gap in perception. I had already spent dozens of hours talking to a large number of Daghestanis, yet as I wrote a friend in Washington:

> I have never had greater difficulties interviewing people. They really do not appreciate an inquisitive style, they easily misunderstand the bluntness of Western questioning, they associate the questioner with his questions rather than understanding that the questioner is trying to get to the core of the issue, at times by playing the devil's advocate. For example, I had a long and tedious interview with [a senior government official], a youngish fellow. . . . It took me a while to realize that he was treating me not as a curious and open-minded journalist who was offering him a chance to think aloud about some fundamental problems bedeviling his land, but rather as a challenger, an opponent bent on discrediting him. Persistence is no great virtue in this land. . . . To people here, my persistence is often offensive, pushy, uncultured.

(I hasten to add that these words should not detract from the exquisite manners, lavish hospitality, and most genuine generosity displayed to me even by the poorest of the poor throughout my journey.)

Traveling in a region as tense as the Caucasus, using the least safe modes of transportation—tiny, aging buses or outrageously ill-maintained airplanes—guarantees constant friction with members of various law-enforcement agencies. Law enforcement is a relative term in the post-Soviet space, even in large metropolitan centers. The practices of many law enforcers range from relatively harmless incivility to harassment and extortion. On the Russian-Azeri frontier, I should have known better than to videotape the military encampment under the gaze of heavily armed soldiers. Similarly, nervous troopers may be expected to ask for and examine my ID all too often, especially in an area infested with refugees, where bombs have often gone off in crowded buses and bustling markets. I could even forgive the young and cocky Kabardin policeman who threatened to arrest me for the unforgivable sin of asking him for directions to the nearest post office.

But nothing prepared me for the subtlety of the Daghestani security services, subtlety such as belongs in a Gogol tale. It would be the tale of a spoon.

Throughout my journey to the Caucasus, I had to manage on a shoestring budget, so I economized as much as I could. When the generous publisher of *Severny Kavkaz* (North Caucasus) weekly invited me and my Russian companion to spend our nights at his Makhachkala office, I gratefully accepted. His head office was in Nalchik, the capital of Kabardino-Balkaria, but he maintained a tiny studio in Makhachkala for the benefit of his local correspondent. The studio gave us exactly what we needed under the circumstances: hot water for about two hours a day and a functioning phone line, an unheard-of luxury in the city's main hotel.

There was only one object I was missing: a spoon with which to eat a bowl of oatmeal in the morning, or its local sugary equivalent, something the Russians call Gerkules (Hercules). Any spoon would have done, even the easily bendable, funny-tasting copper spoon that is an integral part of dining life in Russia. But there were no spoons at the office. None.

I decided to buy one. Surely people use spoons at home—hence it should not be all that difficult to find a spoon in a store or at a street vendor, right?

It was our first full day in Makhachkala, a Monday, when we ventured into Lenin Boulevard in pursuit of a spoon. There was not one shop we spared in our diligent quest. We walked in, we looked around, we asked politely, but nowhere on Lenin Boulevard could we find a spoon. Gradually our spoon hunt gripped us as an obsession, blinded us to our other needs that day, made us oblivious to hunger or thirst.

From Lenin we moved on to the Baku Commissars Street, and from the Baku Commissars we walked to the market—but the spoon still eluded us. That is to say, a single, individual spoon, unaccompanied by a whole set of utensils.

Darkness finally set in, and it was time to head home, or to the office, as spoonless as we had left. We made a phone call to a businessman I was hoping to meet. I had seen him previously in Moscow, but he had no idea that I was now in Makhachkala; nor did I know for sure that he himself was back from the federal capital. It was by a stroke of luck that I found him. "So have you found a spoon?" he asked. No, no, I said, no spoon, thanks for asking. And after a few more words of courtesy, we bade each other good-bye. And hung up.

At which time the realization finally dawned on me. *He knew that I had gone looking for a spoon.* But how in the world could he have known? We had communicated our spoon wish to no one. Few people in town were even aware of our presence. But *he knew.* And he made a point of passing on his knowledge.

The man left Makhachkala the next day, and I have never had a chance to ask him about the source of his striking knowledge. Which was a pity, but at the same time it gave me license to speculate incessantly and reach the conclusion that the Daghestani authorities were sending me a message: *Slow down, esteemed guest, overcome the more intrusive aspects of your Western nature, do not ask unnecessary questions, never assume that you are alone.*

If so, it would mean that the best of Russian satirical literature has not been completely wasted on the Daghestani security apparatus. On the Caspian, in a distant corner of Russia, I finally heard an echo of the best of it.

A couple of days later, still spoonless, I offered to buy the spoon with which I had just finished eating ice cream in a downtown restaurant. "Keep it," smiled the manager, a pleasant Lak lady. I did. And it is still with me to this very day, quite possibly the only Daghestani spoon ever to have crossed the Atlantic.

KUNTA HAJI'S ROUTE TO MECCA

THE VAINAKH PEOPLE

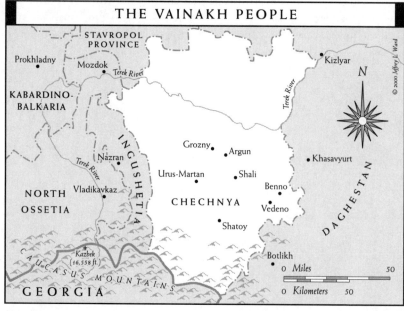

Part III

THE GODS
OF
THE MOUNTAINS

SHAME ON YOU, HAJI TOLSTOY   239

A prominent Russian anthropologist-turned-politician finds the true culprit. It is that hopeless romantic, the vegetarian one with the long beard, what's his name, Tolstoy. He dared tell Russians how brave and selfless Muslim Chechens are and intoxicated Russian minds irreversibly. He, a few drunk generals, and a pile of racist stereotypes.

BRINGING RANCOR TO THE ARSANOV COURT   242

All by myself, on a Friday afternoon, when the minds of believers should focus on God. After an ugly brawl breaks out about whose memory is best, old Ilyas (the son of Deni, a "bandit of honor") gives me a piece of his mind. In such godless times, he says, nothing could help us but a new imam.

HOW *ZIKR* SAVED THEIR ISLAM   246

"Religion?" the exasperated Moscow expert asked. "Haven't you ever heard of the Bolshevik Revolution?" But she never heard of religion that does not require institutions to survive. Just like the great martyr al-Hallaj once said, a believer's pilgrimage can take place without leaving home. You only need a *zikr*.

THE WAR ON THE *ZIKR*   249

But if zikr saved their faith, why is a cosmic war being waged on the zikr? Why did the Saudi religious patrol yell *"Haram! Haram! Haram!"* at pious Mariam? It all started with a desert preacher who did not like saints, dead or alive.

"WAHHABIS SEND SUFI SHEIKH TO HELL"   257

So there they are, the invisible ubiquitous devils. No Russia, no wine, no San Francisco fragrance, and most important of all—no chains of sages, please. It is time for the Eagles of the Ghazawat to rise again. But try telling that to the Wolof people of Senegal.

ABDUL WAHHAB THE JEW (AND MORE)   263

I should have known better: next to holiness dwells sheer madness. The man who repatriated the saintly genes now tells me that the Jews are to blame. America is Jewish, Russia is Jewish, you are Jewish (well, I am). And then a climax of compassion: if only Hitler had been allowed to finish . . .

ROMANTICIZING THE "BLACK FACES"   265

"Why do you like *these people?*" my Russian friend asked. "They are so obnoxious," those the Russians call "black faces," those who relish a good suicidal spasm once in a while. So how come they won a war instead of taking the booty and running? Do not seek the answers only in comparative military statistics, or in conspiracy theories. Perhaps they have something else, too metaphysical for a sound political analysis. But also remember what their own old Aydemirov said: "If only I could find a place in the world without Chechens . . ."

ABDUL-LATIF HAD A BEETLE AND TWO
HUNDRED TANKS   274

His ancestors left the Caucasus in ox-drawn carts to escape Russian favors. Exasperated Ottomans aimed rifles at them— loaded not with bullets but with medicine, to cure their madness. A century later, General Abdul-Latif (who used to ride tanks, to save his king) went home, riding a Volkswagen Beetle. Was he mad? "Absolutely," he says.

"THE GOLAN SHOULD BE CHECHEN"
(IT NEARLY WAS)   293

My journey to the Chechens took me farther than I had dared hope: to my own neighborhood, across a narrow river called Jordan. "Maybe this is your fate," Hashem told me on top of a hill overlooking a town his ancestors founded. But even more so, this is a Chechen fate: losing one home to build another, losing the beehive without losing the honey. And Dr. Daghestani cannot forget the buzz of his father's bees. Meanwhile he is helping build another country, nurture another peace. Will he be able to keep the line?

THE LAST PEOPLE OF THE SABBATH   302

Their ancestors settled the Caucasus some 170 years ago, banished from Russia for daring to pursue a sonless God and an Older Testament. "No one knows how it all began," said Avram, and raised his raspy voice in prayer one last time. Then we tried to figure out whose face old Mardofey had to smack to secure deliverance.

WRESTLING WITH THE SPIRITS 314

As we stroll in the cemetery, I tell Sasha Sheinin that I cannot see any Jewish names. "Why should you?" He shrugs. "They are not Jewish." When they left the holy church, they did not do so to be like the Jews, they only wanted the Jewish God. How so? Oh—they told the imperial grand inquisitors—a very old holy lady told us to, and she cannot even walk.

A HEBREW GOD ON THE IRANIAN BORDER 325

Just a few miles away from the border with the Islamic Republic, Dina Khaimovna still wrestles with ancient spirits—and observes every religious taboo she knows of. Her Hebrew God has survived Soviet atheism intact; not so Anatoly Aronovich's. He may be the last circumcised man in Yelenovka, but the only miracle he has contemplated recently is the revival of his ancient *Zaporozhyetz* car. "Tell me," he said in his raspy voice, "were my ancestors really so special?"

"MY COSSACKS? JEWS?" 336

They were. An incredulous czar spotted them dancing with Torah scrolls, waved his fist, then sat down murmuring. They showed up in a synagogue, the Jews trembled at their sight, but they only sought the rabbi's blessing. If this could happen, could not anything happen? And might new *Subbotniks* emerge from a Russian nowhere to claim a Hebrew God all over again?

EVERY MAN AND HIS GOD

One day in the early fall of 1994, I stood in the heart of Grozny, in the shade of a large and graceless building misnamed the "presidential palace." There was little of the palatial about it. It used to accommodate the local Communist Party, but now it was the seat of the rebel government of Chechnya; soon Russian artillery would level it. On that day, just a few feet from the entrance, a religious ritual was taking place, called *zikr*. It strongly resembled a dance, in that men were moving their bodies rhythmically, with great speed. Every now and then, almost as an afterthought, one of the participants would emit a long chant out of his strained lungs:

la ilaha illallah
la ilaha illallah

It was not a dance, though—it was more a dramatic enactment of an encounter with God. Not a warm embrace, not an unconditional offering of love, but a rigorous, manly, almost violent quest, with no guarantee of success—perhaps like the one described in the biblical tale of Jacob, when he is allowed to see "God face to face" after an all-night wrestling match with the angel, "until the breaking of the day."

I recall watching one young man, perhaps only eighteen or nineteen, his dark, short hair in vivid contrast with his pale complexion. His eyelids hardly opened for the duration of the ritual, and his head jerked in abrupt twitches that seemed out of control until a pattern emerged. Most of the time the only audible sounds were those of feet stomping and heavy breathing.

Chechens beating the drums in the course of a zikr procession (above). There are many kinds of zikr, and this one belongs to the "loud" variation. The cane-waving elder (below) is a leader of a zikr procession. He may have subsequently died in the war.

It has been almost six years since I first watched a *zikr*, and I have watched a recording of my first experience again and again on my video screen, enough to feel a close personal affinity with each of the nameless men involved in it, some of whom may have died in the war that devastated Grozny only three months later, or in another war, fought five years later over the ruins left by the first one. The majority of the dancers were in their twenties, lean, clean-shaven, casually dressed, yet strikingly intense. There was no hint of structure about their ritual. Their gathering seems to have been spontaneous, with no buffer between them and the crowd of onlookers. Unlike other dancers I was to observe in the following days, they took up very little space and spent the entire dance, well over an hour, jumping incessantly in place. I found out later that they belonged to a group named after its founder, Bammat Giray Haji, a disciple of one of the holiest men of the Caucasus, Kunta Haji, who is at the center of my story.

I ended up standing in their midst, at touching distance from them, their very loud exhalations amplified into a wailing wind by my camera's microphone.

Any elation they felt in the process was well hidden inside, befitting a culture that frowns on non-frowners. The *zikr* was not the "war dance" that Russian journalists imagined it to be. A battle was indeed taking place, but entirely within each dancer, pitting him against his flawed self, in quest of purification.

Waging wars against vastly superior enemies and beating the odds (or being beaten by them) is an old theme in Chechen history. But if military endeavors are carried out by the collective, the battles here were within each individual, to be won by drawing on hidden spirituality.

As the ritual was proceeding and streams of sweat poured off the dancers' foreheads, one man burst out crying; another sobbed. But most remained silent and grim.

Those moments were my introduction to the mystery of the Chechen psyche. Bulky academic papers had already been written on the motives of the Chechen rebellion—the only independence movement of its kind in post-Soviet Russia—but they dealt by and large with clannish loyalties, economic interests, and the spillover of internal Russian rivalries into Chechnya. Few if any had considered spirituality.

At that time, I knew little of the ritual, little of its historical and religious context, and not much about Sufism, the broad religious phenomenon to which the ritual belongs. I had no idea that a chain of saints was said to be guiding the *zikr* performers all the way from eleventh-century Baghdad, and beyond.

I spoke to some of the *zikr* practitioners after the event, after the sweat had been wiped off the brows, after the tears had dried, after a regular heartbeat had been regained, hoping that they would tell me what "precisely" happened to them in the course of the ritual. Advised by their elders "to help foreign journalists so as to present our just case to the outside world," they responded politely to all my questions, but no thought that they verbalized came close to peeling away the mystery.

What I could tell was that the experts in Moscow with whom I had talked a couple of weeks earlier were missing something that was beyond manpower statistics, beyond ethnic characterizations and mischaracterizations, beyond military science, anthropology, sociology, and criminology, all of which had served the Russians astoundingly poorly in shaping their idea of the "Chechen enemy."

To find so many young people in a backwater former Soviet province in such a religious state of mind did suggest that the Chechens might have missed something in the preceding seventy years: the chance to shed their most distinctive traits and keep but a few harmless customs and a couple of tasty dishes, embrace that which their colonizers assumed to be entirely irresistible: Russianness, sometimes disguised as "Soviet internationalism." Here—I thought—for better or worse, is a people with much of its memory still intact.

"NAUGHT BUT MY DESTITUTION TO PLEAD FOR ME"

The quest for Chechen memory begins with a North Caucasian goatherd, a resident of Chechnya by the name of Kunta, who some time in the early 1840s embarked on a long and eventful pilgrimage to Mecca. A believer's journey to Mecca is called *hajj* in Arabic, and Kunta's pilgrimage earned him the right to add *haji* to his given name.

Nowadays pilgrims can count on an airplane to carry them to and fro in a matter of hours, but Kunta Haji advanced toward Mecca very slowly. The entire journey may have taken a couple of years. For his was a journey not only to Islam's holiest shrine but also to the lands of Islam, across a marvelous spectrum of traditions and yearnings. There was no secular nationalism around to dilute it, no religious police to establish an unalterable dogma. Kunta benefited from his premodern era in a way that we, the inhabitants of virtual realities, can only try to simulate: he stopped at leisure, listened, and absorbed.

Along the way, something happened to Kunta, something so awesome as to be comparable with Paul's conversion on the road to Damascus. In Kunta's case, it occurred on the road to Baghdad. There one of Islam's most revered saints revealed himself to Kunta. His name was Abdul Qadir al-Geylani,* and he is believed by many to be second in holiness only to the Prophet Muhammad.

Even now a visitor to Baghdad would find it hard to escape Abdul Qadir's presence. A whole section in the downtown area is named

* This is how the name is pronounced to this day in Baghdad. A more common transliteration, if less accurate, is *Jilani* or *Gilani*, that is, of the city of Gilan, now in northern Iran.

after him, Bab al-Sheikh, Gate of the Sheikh.* In the sixteenth century, the greatest Ottoman sultan, Suleiman the Magnificent, commissioned his greatest architect, Sinan, to construct a huge mosque
on Abdul Qadir's grave. It is an astonishing architectural feat in that
it has no columns at all yet can accommodate tens of thousands
of people at any given time. Before all Iraqi religious activities
were centralized under the present regime, the mosque had one of
Islam's best-known theological schools, one which Kunta may have
visited.

Abdul Qadir, a native of Persia, lived in the eleventh century and
ministered to the poor and the meek. It was the poor and the meek to
whom Kunta Haji was also returning, in the midst of a losing war
against Russia, and they found his advocacy on their behalf to be a welcome change from the austere, harsh, legalistic and particularly unforgiving message of their own leaders.

In one verse attributed to Abdul Qadir, the saint of Baghdad carried
the poor's message to the Almighty:

> *I have naught but my destitution*
> *To plead for me with Thee.*
> *And in my poverty I put forward that destitution as my plea.*
> *I have no power save to knock at Thy door,*
> *And if I be turned away, at what door shall I knock?*
> *Or on whom shall I call, crying his name,*
> *If Thy generosity is refused to Thy destitute one?*

It was said of Abdul Qadir, "He was born in love, grew in perfection,
and met his Lord in the perfection of love." He was also known as "the
Supreme Helper" and "the Sultan of all Saints." His disciples, scattered
all over the Muslim world, from the western Mediterranean to Central
Asia to equatorial Africa, have felt his personal presence in their life in
much the same way Evangelical Christians experience their relationship
to their Lord. Indeed, Abdul Qadir has probably come closer than anyone within Islam to being deified, which has made strict observers of
Islamic law unhappy in the extreme.

"Slaughter a chicken where no one can see you," Abdul Qadir commanded his disciples, "and then bring it back to me." All obeyed but

---

* One usage of *sheikh* in Arabic is as an honorific title, conferred on high religious
authorities.

for one, who came back days later with a live chicken in his bag. "Oh, Sheikh," he said, "I have been unable to find a single place where no one can see me, because wherever I go, I cannot hide from Allah, and *you* are with me at all times."

Abdul Qadir immediately anointed that insightful disciple as his successor, or so legend has it. "Your brother knows that I am in his heart twenty-four hours a day, and that I never leave him," he explained to his other disciples. Thus arose the Sufi order known in Arabic as *Qadiriya*, so named in honor of Abdul Qadir, which has grown to be one of the world's largest religious mass movements.

Initiation into a Sufi order is no casual matter. It involves meticulous preparation, psychological as well as physical. Though little is known of Kunta's own experience in Baghdad, his initiation likely followed well-established patterns.

Around 1848, almost at the same time Kunta was initiated as a Sufi, so was the renowned British adventurer Richard Francis Burton, in Sind, now a constituent province of Pakistan. Burton later wrote that his preinitiation period, or *chillá*, consisted of a "quarantine of fasting and other exercises." *Chillá*, modeled on Moses' seclusion on top of Mount Sinai, normally lasts forty days but may be as long as ten months. Kunta Haji would have found no shortage of secluded places to retire to, either in the Iraqi desert or in the mountains north of Baghdad.

His rigorous regime, Burton reported, provided him with "complete mastery over his senses" and "an increased intensity of affection for the Supreme Being." The *zikr* was central to his ritual, as it is to that of any Sufi, but Burton described it merely as a repetition of God's name. The physical ritual was a sacred dance called *sama'*, which involved the self-infliction of pain by "glowing irons," cutlasses, and even swords. The cutlasses, peeled off the walls and heated, represented the mystical presence of Abdul Qadir. The local sheikh (the term used there is *pir*, a Persian word) would blow on a glowing cutlass, then pass it on to the adept who, by sticking it into his body, would absorb the saint's presence. At the time of Burton's death, some forty years later, his body was covered with numerous scars, the presumed result of *sama'*.

Whether Kunta Haji engaged in sword dancing, I do not know. Suffice it to say that self-inflicted pain is less common in the Arab world than it is among both Muslims and non-Muslims in the Indian subcontinent and among the Shi'i Muslims in Iran. But Arab Baghdad had a large

Shi'i population, and pain in one form or another could have been administered to Kunta in a process of soul-cleansing.

In Baghdad, Kunta Haji was one of many thousands, possibly tens of thousands, who, on their way back from Mecca, stopped over to make their supplications to Abdul Qadir. Kunta would have found the mosque and the grave bustling with activity, with men and women of all ages kneeling to kiss the tomb, offering their homage, and praying.

And there for the first time, he witnessed the *zikr*, *Qadiri* style. (*Qadiri* means "of Abdul Qadir.") He must have been familiar with the concept of the *zikr*, which means in Arabic "remembrance" or "testimony," in which the believer recites the names of God in an act of love and submission.* But the *zikr* Kunta knew was the one practiced at that time in his own Northeast Caucasus. The two forms of *zikr* could not have been more different. The one at home was voiceless, passive, and motionless; the dialogue with God was confined to one's heart; and few observers could guess the believer was in the midst of an ecstatic experience. The one Kunta saw in Baghdad, the *Qadiri zikr*, was loud, animated, and declaratory. It was also communal and mutually uplifting. The words, pronounced loudly, constituted a powerful summons, and their sound shook Kunta's heart:

> *la ilaha illallah*
> *la ilaha illallah*

"There is No God but Allah, there is No God but Allah."

Burton wrote that the final act of Sufi initiation was a private *zikr* assignment from his sheikh. Burton's "disciple certificate" instructed him to repeat the words *la ilaha illallah* no less than 825 times a day. Undoubtedly, Kunta also had a quota set for him by a sheikh. That is one reason Sufi adepts carry strings of beads, so they can actually count the recitations bead by bead and make sure they meet their daily target. Quotas aside, nothing in the *Qadiri* ritual matches the public, loud *zikr*. An important Sufi author, Muhammad Ali al-Sanusi, a contemporary of Kunta Haji's, described the *Qadiri zikr* this way:

> One puts one's hands open on the knees, so that they take the form of the word *God*. Then one speaks the name of God, prolonging it for a

---

* I prefer the spelling *zikr*, a near-phonetic transliteration from the Arabic. Scholars prefer the more precise form *dhikr*, "dh" being comparable with the English sound "th" in the word *this*.

time, and extending it with an emphatic pronunciation until the breath is cut off. . . . One continues that way until the heart is relaxed and the Divine Lights are revealed.

Having seen at last the Divine Lights, Kunta began his slow journey home to Chechnya. In all probability, he *walked* home, and months may have passed before he saw his native mountains again. His path must have taken him across the Kurdish-populated regions of present-day Iraq and Turkey, where he would have met a very large number of Abdul Qadir's adepts. The parallels between the Kurds and his own people were striking: both lived in isolated mountains, on the peripheries of two rival empires, zealously guarding their independence against the encroachment of an incomprehensible outside world, and steadily losing the battle. As he traveled from one Kurdish community to the next, he also saw how the Kurds made the loud *zikr* the focus of their ritual, an example he was determined to follow.

He then returned to the regions we now call Chechnya and Ingushetia—inhabited by people of the same stock, the Vainakh—and preached the gospel according to Abdul Qadir and taught people to dance.

Dancing in despair, substituting the ethereal for the real, is not a Caucasian invention. Other ethnic and religious groups in a state of deprivation, or on the verge of extinction, have acted similarly. In some cases, state repression has followed.

A case in point is the Ghost Dance religion, which spread with remarkable speed among the Indian nations of North America in the second half of the nineteenth century and reached its crescendo in the 1880s and 1890s. It was the centerpiece of a new religion whose messiah, the son of God, was sent to earth to deliver his people from the white man. The federal government (like the czarist regime a few years earlier) considered the Ghost Dance dangerous to public order. The 1890 massacre at Wounded Knee, the last bloody chapter of the Indian wars, was to some extent a result of the Ghost Dance.

Jews may recognize elements of the *zikr* in the dancing Hasidim, whose emergence in the eighteenth century scandalized the rabbinical establishment and created one of the most painful schisms in Jewish history.

The founder of Hasidism, Yisra'el ben Eli'ezer (known as the Ba'al Shem Tov), was no more a scholar and had no more theological authority than did Kunta Haji. If Kunta was virtually illiterate, so was Yisra'el. If Kunta was a goatherd, Yisra'el was a manual laborer and an innkeeper.

If Kunta cared little for the imposing self-righteousness and haughtiness of the religious authorities of his day, so did Yisra'el. Both were mystics, and both attributed to the scriptural text a meaning far greater than the mere sum of its letters. Kunta derived his legitimacy from his popularity with the uneducated masses, who—oppressed, defeated, humiliated, teetering on the verge of destruction—were in urgent need of a healer; so did Yisra'el.

The first generation of Hasidim worshipped outside the Jewish mainstream, both in terms of place and methods. An undisciplined lot, they marched into their fringe synagogues in rustic outfits, unwashed, unclean, often with a bottle of booze, often smoking pipes. Theirs was an almost anarchic challenge to the order of the day, an attempt by coarse peasants to expropriate holiness, which had hitherto been the domain of the few.

And what did they do in their synagogues? They sang and danced. This is how the *niggun,* or Hasidic tune, came into being, a proletarian antidote to the formal prayer. A Hasidic tale relates how a congregation of believers was mortified during a Yom Kippur service, the holiest of all observances, when a simpleminded shepherd boy strode into the synagogue sanctuary and emitted a loud, deafening whistle. Ready to kick out the profaner, the congregants were restrained by the presiding rabbi, who told them: "It is this boy's whistle that will reach God in heaven at our behest." A better metaphor for Hasidism may not exist.

Kunta Haji was, in many respects, a whistling shepherd in the heart of the sanctuary. While in Baghdad, he may have heard the famous story of Mansur al-Hallaj, a ninth-century Sufi devotee, who reached such high levels of spirituality in his quest for God as to question the need for formal religion. The true journey of the believer, he said, need not be taken to Mecca but can be successfully accomplished within his own room. Formalities do not matter so long as God is at hand. Al-Hallaj was tried for blasphemy and executed.

The social and political backdrop to Kunta's mission was cataclysmic. Chechnya had been at war with Russia since the 1820s, and Russian armies had not only obliterated whole villages but had employed methods of environmental warfare by destroying fields and forests to deny the Chechens their livelihood. In doing so they were following the advice of General Yermolov, the first of many Russian warlords assigned with the task of subduing the Caucasus, who had suggested around 1820: "Let the standing corn be destroyed each autumn as it ripens, and in five years they will be starved into submission."

Yermolov's benevolence was fully reciprocated. Lev Tolstoy recounted the Chechen feelings toward his nation that he encountered when he served as a young Russian officer in the Caucasus:

> It was not hatred, for they did not regard the Russian dogs as human beings, but it was such repulsion, disgust and perplexity at the senseless cruelty of these creatures, that the desire to exterminate them—like the desire to exterminate rats, poisonous spiders or wolves—was as natural an instinct as that of self-preservation.

Imam Shamil, the legendary leader of the Caucasian resistance to Russia, wanted the Chechens to become subjects of a strictly centralized religious state, in which Islamic law, not clan loyalties or local customs, would be the guiding principle. Though he himself was a Sufi adept, his was an austere Islam, with little tolerance for individual or local varieties. The imam wanted the community of believers, or *ummah*, placed in a state of total mobilization. To that effort, Kunta Haji, the obscure shepherd, posed a serious danger. He was carrying from Baghdad the idea of *zuhd*, or world renunciation, a throwback to a very early stage of Islamic mysticism that, by turning believers inward, in denial of "this world," threatened to undo the great accomplishments of Islam in the realms of war, politics, and economics.

Man, Kunta Haji said, can reach God, even if he is illiterate and unschooled in the ways of the Qur'an and the *shari'a*. He does not have to mount a horse and raise a sword in the process. He need only recite intently the Arabic words *la ilaha illallah*, "There is No God but Allah."

Kunta's lack of scholarly credentials was no impediment to the spread of his influence. He possessed, in the words of one scholar of Sufism elsewhere, "the charisma of the illiterate" (Joseph van Ess). The Chechens had followed simple men with messianic visions before. Some twenty years earlier, an illiterate man by the name of Howk became the leader of a revivalist movement; his followers considered him a saint "who attained all his knowledge not through religious learning but by direct inspiration from God."

It was also not uncommon for shepherds to engage in missionary activities, as their mobility made them the most effective disseminators of Islam in the North Caucasus.

To Shamil's horror, Kunta's message resonated with the people of the mountains, who then began to dance to the sound of that constant, monotonous, mesmerizing rendition,

la ilaha illallah
la ilaha illallah

Kunta Haji is seen here on the left. The identities of the other two are unknown to me, as are the age of the drawing and its authenticity. I came across it in Ingushetia.

They danced in their cemeteries, they danced in their village squares, they danced in their meadows, they danced in their courtyards, they danced to ecstasy, citing the name of God and His prophet Muhammad. They also cited the name of Kunta Haji, the Great Master.

Shamil's emissaries insisted that Kunta cease his proselytizing, and he did so for a few years. He could have been following the example of his own patron saint, Abdul Qadir al-Geylani, who had experienced a blunt rejection seven centuries earlier. Tradition has it that as Abdul Qadir was approaching Baghdad for the first time, a prominent Baghdadi sheikh, unhappy with the coming competition, sent him a cup full of water—a clear hint that Baghdad was well supplied with holy men and had little room for novices. Abdul Qadir, never at loss for words or gestures, reciprocated in kind: he sent the cup back with a rose stuck in it, indicating that as full as the city might have been, it could still do with more beauty. Abdul Qadir's disciples named him, after that story, "our rose."

Shamil was in no mood for roses, though, and Kunta had to bide his time. The imam, having been rebuffed by all the foreign powers whose aid he sought, finally surrendered to the czarist army in 1859, as we have seen, and left the Caucasus for a comfortable "internal exile" in Russia. It was time for Kunta's rose to bloom. He resurfaced, bringing the loud *zikr* with him.

Initially the Russians mistook the dance's message for one of peace. When it turned out that the *zikrists* (as they were now being called) were unwilling to submit, the Russians hastened to ban the *zikr*, and it remained virtually illegal for much of the next 120 years. But it was still performed discreetly in cemeteries, and it was kept alive on the steppes of Central Asia, where Chechens and Ingush were deported en masse in 1944. It is said that not even the ruthless agents of the Soviet secret police dared to interfere with it, so otherworldly and frightening was the spectacle.

One of the leading Islamic clerics of Chechnya, Meirbek Haji Nasukhanov, told me that throughout the Soviet period, people would gather twice a week in their homes and perform the *zikr*. "To many people, it was not just a religious ceremony but a reminder of Chechen culture, morality, lifestyle," Nasukhanov said. "It is common to see the most distinguished people, even religious scholars, burst into tears during the *zikr*." Indeed, among the *zikr* performers were leading members of the local Communist Party.

When the independence movement began in 1990, the *zikr* came out of the closet and spilled into the streets. In 1994 a baffled Russian press corps would watch the *zikrists* and report back that "the Chechens are again engaging in war dancing." When watching Chechens—adolescents and youngsters, middle-aged men and elders—jump in unison, shake their arms, jerk their heads back and forth in abrupt motions and run in circles, oblivious to the scorching sun or the freezing snow, television viewers worldwide mistook the ritual for an exotic dance.

But they were not really dancing. They were racing, struggling to deserve an ounce of godliness.

THE BEARER OF THE GENES

On a January night in Baghdad in 1992, Salih Khamkhoyev, a young Muslim cleric from Ingushetia, ran into an Iraqi general by the name of Faruq at an official reception. He and the general were countrymen of sorts, the general's ancestors having escaped Russian rule in the Caucasus a century earlier. Faruq was now a retired high-ranking officer in Saddam Hussein's army; Khamkhoyev was a North Caucasian delegate to an international Islamic conference in solidarity with Iraq. "I want to show you something," Faruq told Khamkhoyev, then drove the cleric to a little house somewhere in Baghdad.

"I did not know what to expect," Khamkhoyev reminisced over four years later, when I met him. Faruq walked him into a room, where strong scents of medicine were hanging in the air and an old lady was lying in bed, her face as pale as the whitewashed wall behind her. "This," Faruq announced solemnly, gesturing toward the woman, "is Badi'a, the daughter of Ibrahim, the son of Assiet, *the daughter of Kunta.*"

When Khamkhoyev heard the last name, he gasped. *Kunta* was an unmistakable reference to the holy man who had not only brought the *zikr* from Baghdad in the 1840s but introduced Khamkhoyev's people, the Ingush, to Islam. Kunta's name is almost as well known to the Ingush and the Chechens as that of the Prophet Muhammad. Some believe Kunta never died, only disappeared, and will one day return to redeem his people. Others feel already redeemed by his spirit and teachings. Now, in war-scarred Baghdad, Khamkhoyev was standing face to face with the bearer of Kunta Haji's genetic substance.

Badi'a was on her deathbed, drained and fragile, but her face lit up at the sight of "countrymen." "Have you really come from the *daimokhk* [homeland]?" she asked Khamkhoyev. She then went on to show her guests artifacts that had belonged to Kunta: his own copy of the Qur'an, a string of beads (which a Muslim believer would use to count the names and praises of God), and an overcoat.

To understand what it meant for an Ingush cleric to look at Kunta Haji's flesh and blood, a Christian would have to imagine meeting a direct descendant, say, of John the Baptist; an Orthodox Jew should imagine rubbing shoulders with a descendant of the Ba'al Shem Tov. Kunta Haji had been a combination of the two: he was an apostle to the faithless and the pagans, and he was also the popularizer of a religion and the restorer of hope. His followers were the desperate and the vanquished, those who were in greatest need of God yet unable to reach him within the strict form of Islam preached at that time by the great religious luminaries of the Caucasus. It was not at all accidental that such rigorous Islam had sanctioned thirty years of holy war, spurring new feats of heroism in the annals of anticolonial struggle but also exacting a great price from the population and the land. Kunta Haji had offered his contemporaries a way out of a futile war without compromising their identity and without bending their spirit.

As he stood respectfully by Badi'a's bed, Salih Khamkhoyev's knees trembled, not least because of the extraordinary coincidence: it was after all in Baghdad that Kunta's revelation had taken place. By Badi'a's bed, and later at the mausoleum over Abdul Qadir's grave, Salih Khamkhoyev could not help but think that what had been mysteriously awakened in Baghdad in the eleventh century, and what had been rekindled there in the mid-nineteenth century, was now coming full circle.

It was in 1845 or thereabouts that Kunta Haji, more or less Khamkhoyev's age, treaded the same narrow trails, eyed the same tombstones, and inhaled the same breeze blowing from the Tigris River. There Kunta conferred with the spirits of dead saints and drew on the wisdom of the uninterrupted *silsila*, the chain of Sufi sheikhs reaching across twelve Islamic centuries, all the way back to the dunes of Arabia, falling at the feet of Muhammad, the Messenger of God, Peace Be Upon Him.

If it had not been for Kunta's excursion to Baghdad in the mid-nineteenth century, Khamkhoyev himself would not have been there in 1992. Nor would he have been a teacher of faith and ethics to young Caucasian Muslims. Standing where Kunta had stood, it occurred to Khamkhoyev that he must have been picked up from his little Caucasian backyard for a reason. The soft-spoken cleric was not there merely to join in uniform applause for a beleaguered dictator. He was there to retrieve his people's memory, which had come close to obliteration under a century and a half of Russian imperial and Soviet rule. Few are the unintended results in the work of Allah, Khamkhoyev reminded himself.

Khamkhoyev's original assignment in Baghdad had little to do with ancestral spirits. Iraq's embassy in Moscow had picked him up at his Islamic college, in the sleepy North Caucasian town of Nazran, and invested him with the status of delegate to an Islamic conference in Baghdad on the first anniversary of the Gulf War. It was organized in solidarity with the current Iraqi ruler, whose record included demolishing mosques and killing imams in the Shi'i communities of his country's south.

Why were so many Muslims willing to oblige Saddam? An acute sense of vulnerability and frustration, perhaps sheer hypocrisy, may explain most cases. But the case of the Caucasian Muslims was different. They were newcomers to the "clash of civilizations" between Islam and the democratic West, viewing the Baghdad conference less as a political matter than as an opportunity to announce themselves to the world after seven decades of isolation and persecution.

Salih Khamkhoyev went to Baghdad to applaud Saddam—and came back with Kunta Haji's holy spirit, or at least its genetic extension.

"International solidarity" was one of the most widely used clichés in the Soviet lingo. The masses were to clamor in solidarity with the people of Santo Domingo, three oceans away, but hardly ever with those who shared their God, language, and history. Interest in the Middle East would not be unnatural for Northeast Caucasus people, whose first contact with Islam and Arab culture occurred in the seventh century A.D., long before the first Russian state was created. Daghestan was largely Muslim by the tenth century, even if Khamkhoyev's Ingushetia had to wait another eight hundred years. Thousands of religious schools familiarized a large section of the male population with the Arabic language, and a significant portion of the intelligentsia could actually converse and write in Arabic. After the Bolshevik Revolution, some even hoped to make Arabic an official language of Daghestan, but the regime eventually clamped down on all manifestations of religiosity, including schools and language. The Gulf War, highly unpopular among Muslims everywhere, gave the Muslims of the post-Soviet Caucasus a chance to affirm their reasserted identity, even if it required that they take the low road to Baghdad.

In choosing Khamkhoyev as a messenger of solidarity, the Iraqis opted for a man who was an unlikely candidate to be either a religious scholar or a holy warrior. He is clean shaven in a religion where beards, piety, and learning go hand in hand; he is boyish-looking in a culture where advanced age is often synonymous with authority. He has a casual demeanor and an earthy sense of humor—not traits that Westerners have come to associate with ascetic Islamic zealots.

One day in his comfortable study, as I was taking his picture, he quipped, "Oh, we Ingush men are used to having our pictures taken, but only in Moscow police precincts," a barb referring to the harsh treatment that Russia's law enforcers accord to those known as "members of Caucasian nationalities." As Khamkhoyev spoke, I watched his face for an overt sign of bitterness, but all I saw was the mischievous smile of a thirtysomething adolescent.

Nazran, where he serves as rector of the Islamic Institute, is the capital of Ingushetia, Russia's smallest autonomous republic. It is a lazy, overgrown village on a plateau that was transformed into a capital only in 1992, after the sudden divorce between the Ingush and the Chechens. Hitherto partners in the unified Checheno-Ingush Autonomous Republic within the Russian Federation, the two groups went their separate ways when the Chechens chose to secede from Russia in the fall of 1991. The Ingush preferred to stay. Not having a single city to their name, they had to invent a capital, and the choice fell on Nazran. Suddenly the nondescript place, which lacked even the most basic amenities, without so much as a single fleabag hotel or a properly paved road, had somehow to accommodate government ministries and a parliament, entertain official guests, and tolerate prying journalists.

The Ingush, who number fewer than a quarter of a million, are ethnic twins of the more numerous Chechens. They speak mutually intelligible languages and at times refer to themselves by the collective designation *Vainakh*, literally "our people." Yet one thing they do not seem to have in common is temperament. The Chechens are the warlike brothers, whose seemingly hopeless uprisings against Russian domination drew attention first in the mid-nineteenth century and again in the 1990s.

The Ingush have always admired their brave relatives but have been reluctant to join the battle. "We can do without this fame," one Ingush leader remarked angrily when I showed him a copy of John Le Carré's 1995 novel *Our Game*, which describes a fictitious Ingush insurrection against Moscow's rule.*

Unexpectedly, Khamkhoyev's political mission in support of Saddam Hussein had turned into a pilgrimage. Besides the political hyperboles—including anti-Semitic obscenities that he was to hurl at me four years later—he was to carry home a word of affirmation and validation about the descendants of Kunta Haji. He would call on his people to celebrate the double miracle of religious and genetic endurance.

At that time, he could not have imagined how close the parallels were between Kunta's situation and his own. Kunta had offered the message of finding God in oneself at a time when the world around him was crumbling and the Chechens were perishing by the thousands. As for Khamkhoyev, he was living in the last days of peace for the Vainakh nation. Ten months later the neighboring Ossetians, propped up by Russian tanks, would massacre hundreds of Ingush and render one-sixth of his people refugees. Starting in December 1994, the Russians would unleash a war against the city of Grozny, Chechnya's capital, that would equal in ferocity, and surpass in devastation, the war conducted by the Allies against Baghdad. The connection with Kunta Haji's bloodline could not have come at a more opportune time for Khamkhoyev and the Vainakh. They could use any uplifting message they could get.

To appreciate the relevance of the message, one should try to envision the Caucasus in which Kunta was born, the son of a Kumyk shepherd by the name of Kishi. The Kumyks, a Turkic people, were among the first in the Caucasus to convert to Islam, perhaps as early as the tenth century.

---

* Le Carré's novel, by no means his best, would have been far more credible had it substituted Chechen for Ingush. In seeking to convey the despair of a people under siege, Le Carré took a side in an ethnic conflict—the one between the Ingush and their Christian neighbors, the Ossetians—in a manner uncomfortably reminiscent of the excessive zeal displayed by many Western romantics, who, in encountering non-European cultures, quickly assume that one party is constantly right, preferably the one farthest removed from the West by virtue of tradition or religion, and the other constantly wrong. That has often been the case in various Middle East and Central American conflicts, as well as in Yugoslavia. I surely hope I do not commit this mistake in this book, at least not too often, but the reader is advised to remain cautious and skeptical at all times.

Kunta was only six when his mother Khedi moved the family away from the Kumyk plains of Daghestan. They settled in the mountains of southeastern Chechnya, in an area that was still thickly forested, where the great Imam Shamil, supreme leader of Muslim resistance to Russian occupation, had set one of his famous strongholds, the fortress of Vedeno.

There Kunta became a daily observer of the bloodbath of the Caucasian War. He was a young adult in 1840, when the Chechens suffered their defeat in the Battle of the River Death, an event immortalized in Mikhail Lermontov's famous poem "Valerik," a literary-political theme to which I will come back later. Kunta was a loner; "he spent most of his time walking in the mountains and in the valleys, watching life but getting as little involved in it as he could," according to a family tradition. Shortly after the disaster at Valerik, Kunta began his long excursion to Mecca, the one that took him to Baghdad and to the revelation over Abdul Qadir's grave. He returned to the Caucasus at a time that was not all that conducive to messages of peace. In 1845 the Russians suffered one of their worst defeats in the entire war—perhaps one of the worst defeats any colonial power ever suffered in a war with a native population. It was the Battle of Dargo (or Darghiya), in Daghestan, and Russian casualties exceeded fifteen hundred soldiers, including two dead generals. A Russian source described the survivors of the battle as "resembling a mare badly wounded by wolves."

The tide of war soon turned against the rebels, however, especially in Chechnya, whose territory was the main theater of operations for the Russian army's reenergized drive to crush Imam Shamil's movement. So enormous was the devastation that the Chechens, never known for faintness of heart, implored Shamil to let them sue for peace, if only "temporarily." The imam went into such a fit—even having his own mother flogged in public for the sin of passing on to him the Chechen request—that the elders left in greater fear of him than of their Russian enemies.

John F. Baddeley, whose history of Russian military campaigns in the Caucasus, published ninety years ago, is the seminal work on the subject in English, wrote that by the 1840s the war had evolved into a struggle between czar and imam *"for the bodily possession of these unhappy people,"* the Chechens.

By the time Kunta came back from his pilgrimage, these "unhappy people" had reached the end of their rope. Many of them readily settled in the Russian-dominated plains and even formed Russian-sanctioned militias. By 1852 the Russian commander in chief was able to parade his troops across Chechnya "without a shot being fired," such was the Chechens' war fatigue.

Shamil's agenda during the thirty-odd years of his uprising was multipronged. His was not a restoration movement, aiming at bringing back a pre-Russian past, but indeed a revolutionary movement aimed at expunging the vestiges of the old local order. He had no time for princely houses, steeped in corruption and petty rivalries. Varieties, so much on the mind of foreigners while observing the Caucasus, were abhorrent to him in that they interfered with his vision of the highland united by one creed and eventually, no doubt, by one language as well (Arabic). He could not tolerate pluralism of any kind, least of all religious. His official title was Commander of the Believers, and he expected his command to be obeyed. The state he gradually created was ruled heavy-handedly but with a degree of efficiency that earned Shamil a compliment from a Russian general: "We never had in the Caucasus an enemy so savage and dangerous. . . . The rulers [Shamil] has put over the different tribes are his unswerving loyal slaves. . . . The suppression of this terrible rule must be our first care." Russian sources, otherwise unsympathetic to Shamil, credited the imam in the early 1840s with raising the "moral standards" of the Chechens, whom the Russian already viewed as a collection of highway brigands.

Kunta Haji was not an easily identifiable enemy of Shamil's state. He was a commoner, a deeply religious person, one well known to and trusted by the Chechens. When he reappeared in the highland of his youth after his long trip to Mecca and Baghdad, he was wearing in his sheath not a manly sword but an ear of corn, a gesture clearly intended to set new priorities.* Salvation of the body was now taking precedence over freedom and honor, even over God. He is said to have preached, "Brothers, stop this war. We are being provoked to wage this war in order to be destroyed. . . . If you are forced to go to church, go. They are only walls. Still, may your souls remain Muslim. I will never believe that some Turks can help us. . . . So learn how to live with Russians."

Kunta's message of reconciliation naturally gratified the Russians. For years they had been trying to undermine Shamil by getting individual clerics to encourage religious dissent in his ranks, but never had their voices resonated with the masses. At last, they thought, a theological break had come their way.

In the mid-1990s, Russia's experts in Caucasian affairs summoned Kunta's spirit from the dead and evoked his "pacifism" again. But was he

---

* The story of Kunta's corn I heard from members of the Islamic Center in Makhachkala.

a pacifist? Kunta may have preached a conclusion to a losing battle, but he was not advocating surrender. He said: "But if you are forced to forget your language, your customs, then rise up in arms and perish, all of you." It was a call to arms that the newly initiated accepted promply. In the early 1860s, when Shamil was ensconced in comfortable Russian captivity, a spirit of rebellion swept through the Chechen land.

"THE STREAM WAS WARM,
THE STREAM WAS RED"

"Perish, all of you," Kunta Haji told his flock, "but only if you have no other choice." The Chechens threw themselves into the task in earnest, perishing time and again in the face of perceived choicelessness. In the eighty years that followed the suppression of the Shamil movement they would rise against the Russians perhaps ten times (even more, if localized rebellions are counted). No one else under Russian or Soviet rule came close to matching their record of resistance and defiance.

In 1944, when the Supreme Soviet of the Soviet Union convicted the Chechens collectively for collaboration with Nazi Germany, without trial, and deported them (along with others) to Central Asia, the notorious chief of the Soviet secret police, Lavrenty Beria, handled the logistics in person. He reported back with the relish of an accountant:

> The eviction of the Chechens and the Ingush is proceeding normally: 342,647 people were loaded onto special trains on February 25, and by [February 29] the number had risen to 478,479, of whom 91,250 were Ingush and 387,229 Chechens. . . . The operation proceeded in an organized fashion, with no serious instances of resistance, or other incidents. There were only isolated cases of attempted flights.

Beria's heroic effort at statistical precision would have surely been appreciated by a fellow secret policeman with a keen eye for precision, who was immersed at the very same time in similar statistics, similar cargo and similar transportation methods, one Adolf Eichmann, a master executor of the Jewish Holocaust.

The precise number of Chechens and Ingush lost in the course of the deportation has never been established. There seems to be a consensus that at least one-third of them perished, either in the course of the two-week-long journey, in sealed cattle cars, with no food or water, or after they had been dumped in the frozen steppes of Kazakhstan in the middle of a deadly winter. Very likely the actual numbers were higher because no one bothered to register the children born after the deportation who died in their infancy.

Whatever the actual numbers, the Chechens and the Ingush were the victims of a premeditated and well-documented genocide that coincided with the Holocaust and that came close to succeeding.

The years between the 1944 deportation and the 1991 rebellion was the longest period of Chechen military inactivity. Kunta Haji's advice on physical survival took precedence over anything else and was followed, knowingly or otherwise.

Ahmad Mudarov was a walking instance of the Kunta Haji–inspired choice. When I visited him in a small village outside of Grozny, he had just turned 102, or so his passport indicated. The Chechen who introduced me to him whispered in my ear: "He's cheating. He's actually 106."

Mudarov, surprisingly erect and lucid, wearing a red fez, talked about the day in February 1944 when Soviet officers came knocking, Stalin's deportation decree in hand. Five of Mudarov's children, too sick to travel, were executed on the spot. Calmly, he related how one son, bleeding to death, begged for his help. "I cannot help," replied the father, who was wounded but survived and was then deported himself. His wife and last surviving child vanished in exile.

Ahmad Mudarov lost six children to the Soviet genocide but, already in his seventies, fathered another eight. He was in his early 100s at the time this photo was taken (1994).

The survivors of Stalin's deportation were finally allowed to return in the late 1950s. Mudarov was nearly seventy when he remarried and went on to father eight more children. The entire nation, disarmed and demoralized, opted for a nonviolent form of defiance: it was busy reproducing, a traditional preparation for the next battle.

I had a foretaste of that battle in circumstances that could have been very poetic if it had not been for the bullets shot in affirmation of the recited verses.

In the fall of 1994, the Russians were still hoping to avoid direct intervention in Chechnya, even though their military chiefs and uncritical newspaper commentaries had promised a victory "in two hours" after any intervention began. Russia's security organs were arming opposition groups inside Chechnya and encouraging them to prepare for an assault on Grozny to remove the rebel government under President Jokar Dudayev, a former Soviet general.

One night an opposition warlord named Omar Avturkhanov launched an attack against a village outside Grozny. The warlord was driven in a black Mercedes to watch the battle. Dudayev loyalists, led by a nineteen-year-old sergeant, repelled the assailants. I went to see them a few hours later to hear about the course of the battle. The Chechens were euphoric and cocky and reconstructed the events in great detail for me. Finally one of the fighters, a man more than twice the sergeant's age, stood solemnly in front of my video camera and recited the following lines, in Russian, from Mikhail Lermontov:

> Wild are the tribes that in those gorges dwell
> Freedom their God is, war their law—and well
> They know of secret banditry and plot—
> Strange deeds and cruel are their daily lot. . . .
> To strike a foeman there, is never ill,
> Friendship is true—revenge is truer still;
> There good for good is paid, and blood for blood,
> And hate, like love, is boundless as the flood.
> (English translation by C. E. L'Ami and Alexander Welikotny)

His voice rose theatrically when he reached the words "blood for blood," at which time his fellow fighters raised their fists and blurted out *allahu akbar*, Arabic for "God is Great." They clearly found no contradiction between their admiration for a Russian poet, who had been an officer in an army that subdued their nation, and their submission to a wrathful, unforgiving God.

Within twenty-four hours, I was to hear more Lermontov from a well-armed Chechen. Maksharip Chadayev, twenty-six at that time, was a resident of the nearby village of Shalazhi, which, unlike him, was a bastion of opposition to General Dudayev. Maksharip took it upon himself to introduce foreign journalists to the history of his nation. He was not paid by anyone for his services, or for that matter for anything else. He belonged to the overwhelming majority of Chechens who had somehow managed to survive for years without drawing a salary.

One day Maksharip took me to the site of the Valerik River, where the Chechens had suffered such a devastating defeat at Russia's hands in 1840. (*Valerik* is a slight mispronunciation of the Chechen *Valarkhi*, literally "the river of man's death.") As we made our way slowly to the river, I felt a measure of excitement: after all, Valerik was the name, if not quite the subject, of one of Lermontov's greatest poems.

When finally I laid my eyes on Valerik, I felt a letdown not unlike that of a Christian pilgrim who travels for the first time to the Holy Land and realizes that the glorious Jordan River of the scriptures, which he had seen in so many paintings, barely qualifies as a creek. So with the Valerik, which I initially mistook for a muddy puddle hidden in the bush. It *was* a muddy puddle hidden in the bush. Could this be the place where

> *Like beasts, in silence, breast to breast,*
> *The corpses nearly dammed the water;*
> *I dipped my hand . . . I needed rest,*
> *Exhausted by the heat and slaughter.*
> *But from the bodies of the dead*
> *The stream was warm, the stream was red.*
> (English translation by Anatoly Liberman)

And yet this shallow stream has become synonymous in the Chechen mind with loss and humiliation. "This is our Alamo." Maksharip surprised me with an American historical metaphor, though a comparison with Wounded Knee would have been more appropriate. "The river was red with our blood, corpses were piling up. The dead were all buried across the road." He gestured toward the wood behind us.

The flow of poetics under such unlikely circumstances would have been startling almost anywhere but in the former Soviet Union. Nowhere in the world, I imagine, can one come across more people capable of citing more verses with greater precision and more profound feelings than among the graduates of Soviet high schools. Few Chechens can read their own language and literature, but Russian had been opened wide to them, courtesy of the Soviet melting pot, and they knew it well.

The two poems by Lermontov, "Valerik" and the much longer and more elaborate "Izmail Bey," apparently served to inculcate patriotism,

pride, and vengefulness in Chechen minds more than all the propaganda in General Dudayev's book, or any Islamic decree on the sacred
duty of raising the sword against the infidels. Oddly, much of the
Chechen state of mind on the eve of the war was Russified, and at times
the war itself resembled a civil conflict more than a nationalist rebellion
against an occupying power. No doubt exposure to the same school curriculum on both ends of the gun barrel helped.

Before the war, a Chechen historian and journalist, Murat Nashkhoyev, complained to me that the 130-year-old Russian design to melt the
Chechens in their imperial pot had finally succeeded. "In December
1864," he said, "Baron Ussler, a linguist, a general, a humanist much
admired in the Soviet Union, proposed the Russification of the
Chechens—by separation from Arab civilization, from the Qur'an; and
by introducing an alphabet based on the Cyrillic and teaching their language to children only for four years, then switching completely to
Russian. The Soviet government brilliantly applied his plan. And what
do we have today? What type of person? I call it 'the Russo-Chechen' or
'Checheno-Russian.'"

What Nashkhoyev seemed to miss was that the Chechens were turning the tables on the Russians: they were using the language and literature of their oppressors to mount a comeback. After all, was not the
Irish war of independence conducted in English?

Maksharip, my guide to Valerik, came from a family of Kunta Haji followers, but in 1994 there was little left of Kunta Haji's "pacifism" in him.
"If necessary," he said, tapping his AK-47 semiautomatic rifle, "there will
be another Valerik, and another, and another." The rifle had not been
supplied by anyone, Maksharip maintained. "My brother bought it in
the market."

Indeed, vendors in the marketplace in downtown Grozny offered
many kinds of arms. They were not on display—one had to accompany
the sellers to their warehouse to view the merchandise. But the loud,
friendly bargaining over lethal tools, available to all, blended well with
that of housewives hunting for cheap tomatoes, or blouses imported
from the Persian Gulf, or children's toys made in Turkey.

At times, Maksharip's bravado seemed something like that of a child
grabbing a toy and proudly displaying it. The next time I heard from
him was a few months later, on the Voice of America radio station. Both
of us were being interviewed about the Chechen war. I spoke from the
comfort of a Tel Aviv café, where I happened to be at the time. Maksharip was speaking from the basement of the constantly bombarded

presidential compound in Grozny, soon to be overrun and then leveled by the Russians.

He had his Valerik, after all, and lived to tell the story.

It took czarist Russia but a couple of years to change its mind about Kunta Haji. The Kumyk shepherd became an early victim of an infamous practice that lasted well into the Soviet era: in 1864 he was declared insane and was sent to prison without trial.*

In 1864, hundreds of Kunta's followers were massacred in one day in a village not far from Grozny. The first contingent of Chechens deportees, consisting of Kunta adepts, was then sent to exile in Siberia. The *zikr* was strictly banned, and the Russians encouraged the Chechens to leave the Caucasus altogether, much the same way the Circassians of the Northwest Caucasus left en masse for the Ottoman Empire in the preceding year. No mass exodus occurred in Chechnya, but thousands did leave, laying the foundations for the Chechen diaspora in the Middle East (which I discuss at length below).

As for Kunta Haji, he was said to have died in 1867, but his body was never seen and his place of burial remains unknown. The belief in his eventual return is a messianic expectation common to so many faiths. I asked Salih Khamkhoyev, the theologian from Nazran, whether he believed in Kunta's eventual return. "Kunta Haji cannot be considered dead," he said. "A few years after his reported 'death,' some Vainakh people ran into a Russian guard in the jail where Kunta had been held. He told a story of Kunta being walked out into the garden, watched by guards. A swarm of birds flocked around him. The guards told each other smilingly, 'You better keep an eye on him—the birds may take him away with them.' And that was it. No one ever saw him again. And all the files kept on him in the jail were transferred to St. Petersburg [the imperial capital] and were never seen again, either."

Khamkhoyev went on: "Kunta Haji had a cellmate in jail. He was a Syrian Muslim who later wrote about their joint experience. Kunta had told him to pass on his demand to his followers that they not mourn him even if they are told he is dead."

Might he reveal himself again? I asked.

"He might," Khamkhoyev answered. "But only to the godly ones, those who are clean enough."

* "Insanity" was a tag the Russians were fond of attaching to Sufi sages. They did the same to a Tatar sheikh of the *Naqshbandi* Path, Bahauddin Vaisov, who died in a psychiatric hospital later in the nineteenth century.

Kunta Haji's children, three sons and a daughter, joined a later wave of Chechen emigrants, en route to the safer, more hospitable lands ruled by the Ottomans. The sons are believed to have died without heirs in the city of Aleppo, now in northern Syria. The daughter, Assiet, was an exceptional woman. While still in the Caucasus, she had become her father's apostle, traveling widely and preaching Kunta's gospel. She was known as Assiet Haji.

Assiet eventually followed her husband, Kurqa, a Chechen war hero who received a commission in the Ottoman army. He was first sent to an area east of the Jordan River, a deserted wilderness at that time, where other North Caucasians settled in the thousands. (They laid the foundations for a few towns, one of which later became Amman, now capital of Jordan.)

Kurqa, already a man of advanced age, was later moved to the empire's easternmost province of Basra, in what is now Iraq. He was placed at the head of a battalion that, at his insistence, had only Chechen and Ingush soldiers. "I cannot fight as an Ottoman," he allegedly told the sultan, "but I will be honored to serve you as a Vainakh."

Special relations developed between the sultan and his "Vainakh army," and he rewarded his loyal Kurqa handsomely, by giving him as his personal possession two villages in Iraq, one outside of Baghdad and the other outside of Kirkuk, the major oil center in the north. "Not a single Arab house existed in either of them," I was told,* and the only languages spoken were Chechen and Ingush, which are virtually indistinguishable but for minor variations.

Kurqa lived to see the British triumph over the empire he served, and he died at the age of eighty-five. His and Assiet's son Ibrahim had a daughter named Badi'a, whom Salih Khamkhoyev met on her deathbed. Badi'a had a son named Waleed.

When Waleed was a little boy, his parents were so busy with their work in Baghdad that he had to move in with his grandfather Ibrahim. Ibrahim was a sick man; he carried the mark of a bullet that had nearly cost him his life. Young Waleed did not know the cause of "the hole Grandpa had at his side," but it was the result of an abortive attempt he had made to go back to the Caucasus after World War II. Soviet soldiers, or so the story has it, shot him in the process, and he escaped back to Iraq.

---

* In my interview with Kunta Haji's great-great-grandson in 1996.

"Come here, Waleed," Ibrahim used to implore his grandson. "Come and give me a massage, I'll give you candies in return." One day Waleed had enough of the candies and the chocolate and refused to render services to the old man. "Please come," Ibrahim smiled sweetly. "If you do, your reward will be a *house*."

"A house!" Waleed exclaimed. He gave the massage and was ready for the keys. "Where is my house?" he asked impatiently.

Ibrahim's face turned serious, almost harsh. "When you grow up," he said, "you will return to the *daimokhk* [homeland], and you will then go to our home village of Erten, and the house will be yours."

It took Kunta Haji's great-great-grandson forty years to carry out Ibrahim's wish. When he did, "it was as if in a dream, I recognized everything, as though I had already been there. I knew the people, the people knew me. 'Come with us, Waleed,' they said, 'we will take you to your house.'"

And so the genes of Kunta the son of Khedi and Kishi were finally reunited with the mountains.

KISHIYEV COMES HOME

The news that Kunta Haji's descendant was alive in Baghdad electrified the Vainakh. Shortly thereafter General Jokar Dudayev, the stubborn leader of the Chechen independence movement and never one to miss a symbolic opportunity, issued an invitation to Badi'a, Kunta's great-granddaughter, to "come home" and spend the rest of her days among her ancestors' flock.

Badi'a died the day the invitation reached Baghdad, but her son Waleed accepted. He settled down not in Grozny, the Chechen capital (which was still in existence, two and a half years before the Russians leveled most of it), but in tiny Nazran, the capital of Ingushetia. There was a good reason: unlike Chechnya, which had already been largely Muslim by Kunta's time, the Ingush, confined in their remote, barely reachable valley had still been worshipping trees and rocks as well as the spirits of their ancestors. Kunta introduced them to Islam, a leap they have never entirely completed but one that has left the deepest marks on them. At the time of my visit, Nazran was arguably the most religious provincial capital in the Caucasus, with shining new mosques and traditionally dressed pedestrians.

It is fairly safe to say that nearly all Ingush are followers of Kunta Haji, compared with roughly half of the population in Chechnya. (The proportion is highly tentative but is the most common estimate I heard.) Kunta Haji is to the Ingush what Saint Patrick is to the Irish, with one exception. The Ingush Saint Patrick is not hidden in the mist of time separating factual history and legend. On the contrary, his own flesh and blood had just been made available for the flock to see and marvel at.

Waleed performing the loud zikr his great-great-grandfather imported from Baghdad in the mid-nineteenth century. The glistening Mercedes behind him is a testament to the love and enthusiasm the Ingush have conferred on the bearer of Kunta's genes.

The beads of holiness: Waleed displaying Kunta Haji's original rosary. Sufis often use the beads to count the praises of God. The custom is anathema to purists, who consider it a dangerous "innovation," a reason for their war on Sufism.

At six feet, Kunta's great-great-grandson Waleed is head and shoulders above the North Caucasian average height. A large skullcap covers his thinning black hair, a cap that one can find among pious Muslims, notable for its richly variegated embroidery. His tinted thick glasses serve to accentuate the constant severity of his facial expression. I talked to him in the comfort of his two-story house, a couple of blocks away from the center of Nazran. The area was undergoing hectic development, with a row of handsome villas and what must be the most luxurious hotel in the entire Caucasus, as well as a Western-style ice cream parlor and a brightly colored children's playground. Nearby, the foundations for a new shopping center were being laid by bare-chested Slovak construction workers.

The placid setting was in striking contrast with the devastation and misery only an hour's drive to the east, across the Chechen border. Bestowing its largesse on Ingushetia was Russia's awkward way of showing the world and the Caucasus how well it can treat members of the same ethnic family if they stay loyal to Moscow. Ingushetia became a "free trade zone" in 1993, and money has seemed available in abundance ever since, at least for the purpose of construction, at times with incredible wastefulness (as in the project to build a new capital city, "in which no one but bureaucrats will live," as the deputy speaker of the Ingush parliament related to me proudly).

In Nazran, Waleed instantly became a national icon, and every aspect of his life became a matter of concern to the entire nation—all the way to his bedroom. The Ingush elders disapproved of his continuous bachelorhood at forty-five—after all, he had been brought back to the *daimokhk* as a living proof of genetic endurance. So they fixed him up with a much younger local beauty by the name of Zarita, who soon thereafter bore him a girl he named Assiet, after his great-grandmother, Kunta's daughter.

Uninterested in the fine details of his family tree, the Ingush insisted on attaching to him Kunta's own "family name," Kishiyev, which is not really a family name but simply the Russian form for "of Kishi," Kunta's father.

A man not easily given to smiling, Waleed came close to giggling when he related to me how the Ingush "Kishified" him, to make sure that they would be filled with awe each time "Waleed Kishiyev" was introduced in public. "I told them I was not Kishiyev, I was Archakov [the name of his father's clan], and in Iraq I was Waleed Abdulhamid

The Ingush elders disapproved of Waleed's continuous bachelorhood and fixed him up with a much younger local beauty by the name of Zarita, seen here shortly after she bore him a girl he named Assiet, after Kunta's own daughter.

Elias—we did not really have family names, and for the purpose of identification you would assume your father's name and his father's name. But they just laughed and said, 'To us, you *are* Kishiyev, and nothing could change it.' I said, 'Fine, so I shall be Kishiyev.'"

The appreciative Ingush government accommodated Waleed in a newly built cottage, painted white with red tiles. It packed his living room with imported furniture and plenty of electronic gadgets, and it installed in his courtyard a useful fixture, a glistening new Mercedes-Benz, though no local thoroughfare came close to matching the broad boulevards of Baghdad. When Waleed, a working man throughout his life ("I have had it hard since my childhood," he said), became unhappy about his involuntary idleness, the government purchased for him printing presses so he could pursue his old trade and greatest love. "In Iraq I worked in printing all day long, from morning to evening, from evening to morning."

Ah, I interjected, you are as fond of books as your late father was. (His father had spent thirty-five years composing "the most truthful and unbiased" history of the Caucasus Mountains, in Arabic, which unfortunately remains unpublished.)

"No," said Waleed nonchalantly. "I am interested only in the *technique*."

He lit a cigarette and hastened to say, "People here love me very much. They do not allow me to smoke. Smoking is an Arab habit I have. They are right of course. A good Muslim should not smoke, but I smoke secretly. They know but forgive me."

Waleed spoke to me in pidgin English, the likes of which I had never heard before, strewn as it was with dozens of Arabic words that he had always known and Russian words that he had absorbed since coming to the Caucasus. But he was perfectly understandable, and even when he groped for words, he made sense. His flow of thoughts was intelligent and logical, and at no time did he strike me as boastful or self-aggrandizing. His own version of events suggested that he was completely aware that he owed his comfort and social status to pure chance; that he was but a pawn on the chessboard of a national and religious revival in the Caucasus; and that various politicians and ethnic leaders were using him to propagate a message with which he had little to do other than by virtue of being the carrier of Kunta Haji's DNA.

I cannot say with any degree of certainty that I know what the message is, but the youthful Ingush president, a remarkable political acrobat and former Soviet general named Ruslan Aushev, probably felt that having Waleed around was an announcement that *his* government was now the *truer* custodian of Vainakh heritage, one in which holiness, or its genetic substance, is ensconced in a nice villa with a satellite dish on top rather than on a battlefield soaked in Vainakh blood. Or perhaps General Aushev, a practical man and a battle-hardened fighter in his own right (from the days of the Soviet war in Afghanistan, in the early 1980s), simply thought that to have a "Kishiyev" around brought good luck, even if he happened to be a towering, bespectacled Arab from Baghdad.

SHAME ON YOU, HAJI TOLSTOY

Russians have struggled hard over the last two centuries to figure out how to tell "good" Muslims from "bad" Muslims in the Caucasus. The task has proven difficult because the varying degrees of North Caucasian "friendship" toward Russia have reflected primarily survival needs rather than affinity.

The popular Russian notion of the Caucasus is highly romantic. Not only was the region a breeding ground for many of Russia's literary and poetic geniuses, it was also where Russian heroes rose and fell, where many Russian self-perceptions were conceived and nurtured, and where Russia's rendezvous with its manifest destiny took place. Their writers and poets introduced Russians to the Caucasus, and in the opinion of one Russian expert on national minorities, that did a great disservice to future Russian understanding of the region.

Valery Tishkov is a prominent Russian scholar who has been intimately involved in his country's decision-making process in the Caucasus: in the early 1990s, he was an official at the ministry of nationalities, then served briefly as a cabinet minister. A cultured man in his sixties, with good English and the mannerisms of a haughty intellectual, Tishkov berates a whole crowd of social scientists, mostly Russians, for engaging in "civilizational-ethnographic romanticism" and fabricating "a rich pseudoscientific mythology" of Chechen history. His long, accusatory finger points all the way back to the grand master of Russian literature, Lev Tolstoy, who, in Tishkov's view, fathered the "Chechen myth" in "Haji Murad," his famous tale of a North Caucasian hero. (Haji Murad, a historical figure, was actually an Avar from Daghestan, but the Chechens have come to think of him as one of their own.)

It is to Tolstoy, Tishkov argues, that Russians owe their belief in the congenital military skills of the Chechens, their stubbornness and

much-celebrated respect for their elders. So much so, Tishkov complains, "that in a Russian opinion poll, this novella by Tolstoy was rec-
ommended as primary material for those who take decisions on
Chechnya." An ironic twist, in that Tolstoy himself berated some of his
predecessors for over-romanticizing Russia's war in the Caucasus. Tolstoy's grievance ran contrary to Tishkov's: Russian writers and poets
were idealizing an atrocious war, waged largely against a civilian population, and dehumanizing the natives. Early Soviet historiography
embraced Tolstoy's reasoning, but soon thereafter renounced it, and
endorsed czarist practices as "the lesser of two evils."

Tishkov is a man who reveals little self-doubt or willingness to
acknowledge his own mistakes. "This is a scientific conference, not a
political rally," he once censured a questioner in Washington whose
comment about the persistence of ethnic stereotypes among Russian
experts Tishkov did not like. Apolitical as he might be, Tishkov says
that "it is a proven fact" that the most fateful decision of the war—
namely, to mount a massive attack on the city of Grozny on New Year's
Eve 1995—was taken during a late-night birthday party thrown in
honor of the minister of defense at a military base in southern Russia,
presumably while the celebrants were inebriated.

The fact is, Russia had been planning a violent solution to the Chechen
problem for months. Russia's leaders may well have been intoxicated, not
by alcohol, but by stereotypes and self-delusions, to which Valery
Tishkov and his colleagues—anthropologists installed in top advisory
positions to the president—contributed in no small measure.

One stereotype of the Chechens was that they are a collection of
clans, not a nation in a modern sense. A resulting self-delusion was that
Russia would be able to pit the clans of the plains against the clans of
the mountains, the clans of Greater Chechnya against the clans of
Lesser Chechnya, the proper Chechen clans against the Ingush clans,
even the clans of the loud *zikrists* against the clans of the silent *zikrists*.

The clan stereotype made it easier for Russians to portray Chechen
society as a Caucasian version of Sicily, Mafia and all. President Yeltsin
himself announced to the upper chamber of Russia's parliament, in the
third month of the war, that the "main interest of the [Chechen] bandit
formations in seizing power is to run their criminal business, despite the
false layer of appealing words about freedom."

Yeltsin even offered free passage to General Dudayev to a well-
financed life in exile (Turkey was Yeltsin's proposed destination), on the
assumption that the leader of the Chechen rebellion would be tempted
by such comfort. It seems not to have occurred to the hero of Russia's
own democratic resistance that a Chechen leader would be willing to

sacrifice his life in pursuit of a nationalist cause, unmoved by the temptations of peace and riches.

Russia's favorite Chechens are members of the Arsanov clan, who represent an alternative to the rebels, both in altitude and attitude. The Arsanovs live by and large in the plains, while the rebels count mostly on the highlanders. The Arsanovs are urbane and more thoroughly secularized—that is, more thoroughly Russified. In Soviet times, much of the local Communist elite was drawn from their ranks (though only in 1989 was an ethnic Chechen entrusted with the position of head of the local party branch). Chechnya may have been the only place in the entire former Soviet Union where Yeltsin and his anti-Communist reformers reached out to the discredited ancien régime in an attempt to stem nationalism and separatism. In November 1991, just weeks before the dissolution of the USSR, Yeltsin named an Arsanov as military governor of Chechnya and came close to installing him by force. He backed down at the last moment, but his anthropologist advisers kept alive the Arsanov option and revived it less than three years later. In the summer of 1994, an attempt to install a pro-Russian Arsanov-dominated administration in northern Chechnya started the slide toward war.

The Arsanovs differ from most of Dudayev's supporters in still another respect: they belong, or at least are associated with, the other kind of Sufism in the Northeast Caucasus, the *Naqshbandi* order. Historically at the vanguard of resistance to Russia—Imam Shamil answered to the *Naqshbandi* sages—the order's influence has been on the decline, and so has been its militancy.*

The most noticeable difference between *Naqshbandis* and *Qadiris*, if not necessarily the most important, is the formula of the *zikr*. The *Qadiri* ritual is loud and outward, while the *Naqshbandi* is usually silent and inward. I encountered groups of elders in downtown Grozny who were huddled in silence, apparently idle, but who were in fact in the midst of a sacred ritual.

Theologically the difference is of no consequence, for both forms of *zikr* reflect humble submission to God and celebration of His beauty. But politically the difference does matter. In the words of Salih Khamkhoyev, the Ingush *Qadiri* scholar, "Now the effect of the loud *zikr* is simply indispensable. We announce our love of God for the entire world to hear."

And so the loud *zikr* of Kunta Haji, even before the bullets, became the Chechens' best-known attribute, one of the first sounds that an outsider would have encountered in prewar Chechnya.

---

* *Naqshbandiya* was founded in the fourteenth century in Bukhara, which is now in modern Uzbekistan, by Muhammad Bahauddin Naqshband. Its eventual spread was unparalleled, reaching to the ends of the Islamic world. Though it has since fallen from its previous highs, *Naqshbandiya* still has tens of millions of followers.

BRINGING RANCOR TO THE
ARSANOV COURT

Just before the outbreak of the Chechen war, I called on the head of the Arsanov clan, the most venerable *Naqshbandi* elder in Chechnya. Ilias Arsanov, a wiry man in his late eighties, was preparing for the Friday prayer in a still-incomplete mosque that Turkish workers were busy constructing for him.

Ilias is the son of Sheikh Deni Arsanov, a fabled hero of the mountains. Tradition has it that at the age of nine, the father won the blessing of Kunta Haji himself, who laid his hands on Deni's shoulders and proclaimed his saintliness. Why Arsanov, blessed by the great *Qadiri* teacher, would end up a *Naqshbandi*, remains unclear to me. He later became an *abrek*, or "bandit of honor," and for years led raids against Cossack settlers along the Terek River.

"When my father received a telegram in 1917," Ilias told me, "informing him of the fall of the czar, he extended his arms in exasperation and said: 'The good has gone, the bad has come.'"

The father's judgment notwithstanding, his eldest son, Bahauddin, Ilias's brother, was accused twenty-seven years later of doing Stalin's bidding during the deportation of the entire Chechen nation to Central Asia. The Ingush scholar Khamkhoyev maintains that Bahauddin had the secret rank of colonel in the NKVD, as the Soviet secret police was known at the time.

To my surprise, Ilias did not take issue with the allegation when I asked him about it. "Yes, my brother worked with the NKVD. You must understand what was going on at that time. There was an army here that numbered around one million people. My brother did his utmost to make sure that our people did not get killed or burned alive in the mountains."

Ilias was clearly referring to the single most appalling episode of the deportation. In the mountainous village of Khaibakh, Soviet troops locked hundreds of peasants in a barn and set fire to it. A brief look at the list of victims sends a chill down one's spine: whole bloodlines were decimated. For example, those who perished from the Gayev family ranged from Tuta Gayev, the family's patriarch, who was reportedly 110 years old, his 100-year-old wife Saryad, and his 108-year-old brother Khatu, all the way to his 30-year-old nephew's wife, Khesa.

Horrendous and deadly as their banishment was, the Chechens survived it. Had they offered organized resistance—which some did—in all probability there would have been many more Khaibakhs.

The days leading to the 1994 war with Russia, however, were no time for impartiality or introspection among Chechens. Anyone belonging to a party other than one's own was fair game and deserved to be demonized in any way. Unmistakable was the mutual animosity between the Arsanovs and many of the *Qadiris*. My interpreter at the time was an urban *Qadiri*, a young professor of English at Grozny University, a modern-looking man, keen on Shakespeare. Chechen men, in my experience, often treat their elders with almost overstated respect. But not when my interpreter spoke to the ancient Arsanov. "I despise him," he told me. "He's contemptible."

At the time of my visit, Arsanov was proudly presiding over the construction of his new mosque. Despite the acute unemployment problem in Chechnya, the workers were all Turks—*Naqshbandi* Turks were the presumed source of the project's funding. Not since early in the century had minarets of *Naqshbandi* mosques been allowed to pierce Grozny's skyline, but even this thought failed to fill Arsanov with joy. "We no longer have pure Islam anywhere," he told me, "not even in the Arab world. We are supposed to teach the believers to live in accordance with the Law. Some people claim to do just that. But not even I can claim to follow the Law, not even I."

He sighed and wiped his beardless face with a handkerchief. Noticing my surprise at his confession, he paused a moment, and said, "The devil has won the upper hand. No human can change that. It is only for God to save us. It was prophesied that one day the people would stop listening to their sages, and it seems that this time has finally come. Nothing will change for the better without an imam. No new president, no new czar can help. Only an imam."

He then excused himself to lead the noon prayer and rose to his feet in the expectation, as it turned out, that we would take the cue and leave—the sanctuary of a mosque on the Muslim Sabbath is not a proper place for an infidel. But in my eagerness to converse with Ilias's flock, I stayed on, so we remained seated on a bench a few steps away from the sanctuary. One of the men who assembled there was ninety-four years old, his name was Deni Majiyev, and he remembered people who had fought on the side of Imam Shamil in the Caucasian War.

The conversation soon turned to the 1944 deportation, of which most of the men had a reasonably clear recollection. One told me of seventy-two hours he spent aboard a cattle car without food or water, and the humiliation of being ordered, at one train station, to relieve themselves in public, men and women together. One old man insisted on doing so behind the car. A Soviet soldier immediately shot him dead without warning. Once the train reached its destination, two weeks after departure, the speaker had to fend for himself. "I had to go and pick grass in the open field and eat it," he said. "Many did the same and went mad, and then died in agony."

Within a few minutes, to my great bewilderment, the Chechens around me came close to blows over trivialities such as whose memory was clearer. At the sound of the rising voices, Arsanov reemerged from the prayer, approached me, and said with evident displeasure, "You have brought rancor to my mosque." Indeed I had. But then the entire land was teetering on the brink of civil war and foreign intervention, and lowland Arsanovs were aiming submachine guns at highland Dudaye-vites. Apparently I inadvertently accomplished an even greater feat: pitting Arsanovs against Arsanovs.

February 1994 was the fiftieth anniversary of Stalin's deportation, and the Dudayev government did its best to reawaken memories and give them a fresh meaning in light of the ongoing conflict with Russia (though the war was still a few months away). Impressive signs adorned public places in Grozny, featuring the number "50" against the background of Khaibakh's flames and a wailing wolf. (The wolf is a Chechen national symbol.)

Moscow might have waited for the anniversary year to pass before striking Chechnya, if only for the sake of appearance. I had thought it would, but my expectation was founded on the erroneous assumption that the Russians had guilt feelings about 1944, the way, say, the Germans do about the Holocaust. Little did I know. By the end of the fiftieth year, the city of Grozny lay in smoldering ruins, and perhaps one-third of the Chechen population had been dislocated.

Shortly after the war started, Ilias Arsanov himself was taken prisoner by the "fighters," a common name for the rebels. According to Salih Khamkhoyev, Arsanov's Ingush detractor, only the most rigorous pleas for the old man's life led to his release in one piece.

HOW THE *ZIKR* SAVED
THEIR ISLAM

Russia's gamble on the Arsanovs was primarily a gamble that clan politics could tear Chechnya apart. Generally speaking, in the period leading to the war, Russia appeared to underestimate, if not altogether ignore, the religious factor. I am not entirely sure why this was the case. Perhaps it was the practical cynicism of people hardened by the struggle to endure a totalitarian system, who therefore tend to ignore matters as abstract as spirituality. Or perhaps it was the lingering residue of materialism and atheism that the defunct system had forced down their throats.

I had a good opportunity to gauge Russian attitudes toward Chechnya when I was in Moscow in the summer of 1994, as the crisis entered its final prewar phase. A few days before I was to leave Moscow for Grozny, I called on Irina Zviagelskaia, a reputed expert on Central Asia and the Caucasus and deputy head of the Center for Strategic Studies, an academic think tank that had provided many Western journalists with occasional authoritative comments on post-Soviet life. Dr. Zviagelskaia, young, urbane, highly articulate, was considered an expert on nationalities in the Caucasus, her article on the subject having just been published in a scientific compilation in the United States.

I asked her whether the religious factor was of any importance in Chechnya. She eyed me with a hint of exasperation. "Haven't you heard of the Bolshevik Revolution?" she asked, and went on to remind me that religious schools had been closed down long ago, that mosques had practically disappeared, that the only mullahs, or priests, were "complete amateurs"—and that General Dudayev's attempts to wrap himself in religious garb and derive legitimacy from the Qur'an simply did not resonate with his people.

Dr. Zviagelskaia's dismissal of religion was perfectly rational. She assumed that religion required organization and hierarchy as well as systematic education. But insofar as the Northeast Caucasus was concerned, she was wrong. Upon arriving in Grozny, it took me but a few hours to become acquainted with the form of religion that was still very much intact in Chechnya. Predicated neither on formal education nor on institutionalized prayer, it was constantly chanted from the main square, from private houses, and from cemeteries:

la ilaha illallah
la ilaha illallah

In remaining blind to the profound religiosity that permeated Chechen society, Dr. Zviagelskaia and others ensured that Russia—both its political system and its public opinion—would be taken by complete surprise when the Russian military began its disastrous campaign against the "bandits."[*]

One reason for the blindness may have been a terminological confusion, going back to the nineteenth century. The Chechens' Sufi practices had been simply called *zikrism*, after the *zikr*, creating the misleading impression that the dancers and hoppers were but the highland equivalent of many home-grown Russian sects, mostly Christian, that were named after their most conspicuous ritual. For example, one Christian sect was nicknamed "flagellants" because their ritual included self-flagellation; another was named "jumpers" for self-explanatory reasons; a third was named "people of milk" (or in some translations, "milk drinkers") because they drank milk during Lent; a fourth was named "Saturday people" because they preferred the Jewish Sabbath; and so on.[†]

In the nineteenth century, the various "sectaries" were seen as a threat to the Russian state and were prosecuted, punished, and banished. But by the 1990s, the "sectaries," including the *zikrists*, had become curiosities in the eyes of Russians. Soviet anthropologists were aware of the persistence of the *zikr*, even at a time when open religious activity was almost nonexistent. In 1975 a Soviet scholar reported the stunning fact that "more than half of the Muslim believers of the Checheno-Ingush Autonomous Republic are members of a *murid* brotherhood," that is,

---

[*] Dr. Zviagelskaia was neither the only one so certain of the unimportance of Chechen religion nor entirely ignorant of the dangers looming in the Caucasus. In fact, she sternly warned against the self-serving Russian official line that equated the Chechen struggle with criminality and that dismissed its nationalist aspects.

[†] I deal more with Russian sects in the chapters devoted to the Subbotniks, or "People of the Sabbath," on pages 320–47.

adherents of Sufi Islam who practice one form of *zikr* or another. The role of the *zikr*, particularly the loud *zikr*, in preserving Islam in the Caucasus was decisive. Practicing it did not require much theoretical knowledge, or organization, or even a house of prayer.

Yet in the course of my travels in the Northeast Caucasus, I was startled to hear much about the persistence of religious practices in people's private homes during the Soviet era, away from the ever-vigilant eyes of the authorities. One resident of Tarki, the Kumyk town overlooking Makhachkala, told me that throughout the month of Ramadan, the holiest in the Islamic calendar, he and his friends, as well as members of their families, would meet every night in a different house to celebrate their faith by performing the *zikr*. Unlike formal prayers, everyone was involved in this ritual, women as well as men, children as well as adults.*

My Kumyk interlocutor in Tarki knew little of theology, almost nothing about the disputes between Sufis and their critics, and not much about the various "paths" within Sufism. He knew very little Arabic, and the Qur'an was a closed book to him. But he did know the *zikr*, and he did know where the nearest saint was buried. And through the ecstatic ritual, and the discreet veneration of the dead sheikh, his Islam as well as that of so many others survived against the longest odds. This folk religion required little structure and hierarchy; it was *felt* rather than intellectualized. I have already related earlier what Mansur al-Hallaj, a famous renegade mystic of the ninth century, said of a Muslim's pilgrimage: It "can be accomplished within one's home." Al-Hallaj had to die on account of his heretical insight, but Caucasian Islam managed to live by practicing it.

If the *zikr* helped preserve the faith of captive Muslims in the world's longest-lasting atheist state, ought it not be universally praised, at least by Muslims?

Well, it is not. In fact, the *zikr* (or more precisely, the set of beliefs and practices that the *zikr* represents, called Sufism) is at the center of controversy over the structure and direction of Islam. Significantly, the loudest critics of the *zikr* and Sufism are those who never had to cope with a hostile non-Muslim government, and to whom the voice of the *mu'azzin* summoning the flock to the noon prayer from the top of his minaret is as natural as the sun and the wind.

---

* Their *zikr* is a hybrid and falls somewhere between the motionless *Naqshbandi* and the loud *Qadiri*: it involves no movement of the body but is recited aloud. I heard this *zikr* elsewhere in Daghestan, most commonly after funerals in the houses of the deceased.

THE WAR ON THE *ZIKR*

There is a religious war raging now in the Caucasus and elsewhere in the Muslim world, which might be called *the war on the zikr*. This, admittedly, is an oversimplification, and later I will try to help this collision between Sufism and puritanism regain some of its inherent complexity.

The *zikr* is the center of the Sufi ritual. To borrow an encyclopedic definition, "Sufism can be described as the interiorization and intensification of Islamic faith and practice" (*Oxford Encyclopedia of the Modern Islamic World*). Western observers have often characterized it as "Islamic mysticism," which in many respects it is, but it has also shown itself in the course of the centuries to be rational, rigorous, and uncompromising.

In many Muslim regions of the world, particularly in contexts of confrontation with the West or with Westernizers, revolutionary politics can be attributed to Sufi sages or to lay leaders inspired by them. In fact, it would be almost impossible to discuss the purported "clash of civilizations" between Islam and the West without referring frequently to Sufism.*

---

* Here is a partial list of major events in the history of relations between Islam and the West that were triggered or inspired by Sufis: The resistance to French colonization of Algeria (1830–47) was waged by *Qadiri* Sufis. The Caucasian war of resistance to Russian rule (1830–59) was launched by *Naqshbandi* Sufis. An anti-British uprising in Somaliland, in the late nineteenth century, was led by *Salihi* Sufi. *Naqshbandi* Sufis repeatedly challenged Dutch rule in Indonesia throughout the nineteenth century and early twentieth century. *Qadiri* sages led the uprising against Zulfiqar Ali Bhutto's government in Pakistan in 1977, which paved the way for a military coup and the Islamization of the judicial system. *Qadiri* and *Naqshbandi* Sufis were among the most important organizers of the resistance to Soviet rule in Afghanistan in the early 1980s. The resistance to Italy's occupation of Libya, after 1912, was waged by the Sufi *Sanusi* order, whose leader went on to become king upon independence. A Sufi sheikh was the main force behind

Unlike the revolutionary, confrontational Sufism described above, however, the Sufism of Kunta Haji, sparked by the gospel of the medieval saint Abdul Qadir al-Geylani, may appeal to New Age seekers in North America. Theirs is the Sufism of Rumi, the great medieval Persian poet, who read the scriptures very liberally and rarely sought God and his saints without the presence of a decanter ("A jug of wine, a loaf of bread—and thou," to quote Edward FitzGerald's translation of another Persian poet of the time, near-contemporary Omar Khayyam).

After Rumi's death, his disciples in what is now Turkey founded the *Mevlevi* Sufi order, better known in the West as the Whirling Dervishes because of the mystical dance central to their ritual. The Mevlevis have also done relatively well in North America, and their U.S. representative—the wonderfully named Sheikh Kabir Helminski—has even devised a "Ninety-Nine Day Program" of Sufi total immersion, with a "$40–60 donation suggested. . . . If you don't have a copy, we suggest you order from us ($11.95)."

New Age Sufism has little interest in waging angry crusades on behalf of God. At a Sufi conference in San Francisco, I found that many of the conferees were ethnic Jews. (One even wore a yarmulka and sported a small fringed vest underneath his shirt, a hallmark of piety among Orthodox Jews. He later told me he practices both Sufi Islam and Orthodox Judaism, submitting to a sheikh *and* a rabbi at the same time—a towering accomplishment in the annals of ecumenism that is possible only on either end of the Golden Gate Bridge.) Frustrated, I sought a platform to acquaint the delegates with the mounting Sufi casualties in Chechnya, but one of the organizers, a prominent campaigner for human rights in his *non*-Sufi life, reproached me: "People have come here to find flowers and love, while you want to talk to them about wars and death." He softened up a bit later when he had a chance to watch some of my videotapes from the Caucasus and recognized the *zikr*.

The Sufism of the Caucasus, unlike that of Rumi or Helminski, has been *frontier* Sufism, born in a defensive war, and it has remained militant. It is a bit hard to imagine the Three Imams, or supreme religious leaders, of the early nineteenth century doing well in the Bay Area other than in full battle gear, ready to unleash a holy war—though it is equally hard to imagine the great Sufi sages of India preaching anything but peace and love.

---

the military regime in Sudan, denounced as an accomplice and facilitator of "international terrorism" by the United States. Sufi orders are officially banned in Turkey, yet they are assumed to have played a major role in making possible the brief tenure of an Islamist prime minister, Necmettin Erbakan, in 1997. Indeed, many of his followers speak of him the way Sufi adepts speak of their sheikh.

This dichotomy within Sufism makes it all that much harder to define. By and large, however, the critics of Sufism have targeted the preachers of love, the men who dared violate one of Prophet Muhammad's most ominous and incomprehensible warnings to the believers: "Beware of matters newly begun, for every matter newly begun is innovation, every innovation is misguidance, and every misguidance is in Hell." Sufism, its enemies assert, is the mother of all "innovations."

Her people's pain was on Mariam Vakhidova's mind when she headed to Mecca for the first time in her life. A young Chechen journalist who used to work for General Dudayev, only to become disillusioned with his brand of self-destructive patriotism, she was born in Soviet exile: in Ka-

Mariam Vakhidova (seen here) set out to perform the zikr, *but the Saudi religious patrol yelled,* Haram! Haram!

zakhstan, the Central Asian republic where her parents, along with the entire Chechen and Ingush nations as well as others, were dumped in 1944 at Stalin's whim.

Vakhidova is a child of survivors, and for that matter she is a survivor herself. Having been raised in an environment in which children were severely reprimanded by teachers for uttering a single Chechen word in class, she knew precious little about her people's history of faith. She grew up a "Soviet Woman"—that is, a person without a memory, or at least with a memory that was strictly regulated.

Years later she decided to take the *hajj*, or pilgrimage, to Mecca with a group of fellow Chechens, all of them followers of Kunta Haji. "When we arrived in Mecca," she told me, "we immediately set out to perform the *zikr*. Saudi policemen interrupted us instantly. They said, '*Haram! Haram! Haram!*' [Forbidden! Forbidden! Forbidden!]."

Vakhidova could not fathom why the enforcers of religious law and piety should object to a ritual that, after all, seeks to refine piety and bring it to the highest level. But that was not the full scope of her ignorance. She had no idea what Sufism was either, or that her kind of *zikr* made her a disciple of the Abdul Qadir variety, the *Qadiriya*. Neither she nor her Chechen husband, Sultan, had ever heard the word *tariqa*, or "path," which designates various orientations of Sufism. Yet her attachment to her tradition and faith went far beyond methodical education and was not dependent on it. She had Kunta Haji's gift: self-reliance in quest of God.

The speed with which the Saudi religious police moved to nip Vakhidova's heresy in the bud confirmed for the North Caucasian pilgrims what they had been hearing at home for a while: that a war is being waged from within Islam against their traditions, funded by Saudi Arabia and carried out by the Wahhabis.

Along the southern tier of the former Soviet Union, the term *Wahhabi* is uttered with disdain and fear. Beleaguered rulers invoke the specter of *Wahhabism* to justify political repression, and religious leaders do the same to account for their own lack of influence on society. The president of Uzbekistan, for example, gave his people the following advice on how to tell a Wahhabi from a non-Wahhabi: "If you have noticed, Wahhabis have a characteristic feature—they have beards, untidy beards." Such people, he told his country's parliament, "must be shot in the head."

The Uzbek president, Islam Karimov, a heavy-handed autocrat who runs the most populous Muslim republic of the former Soviet Union, was the first one to outlaw the Wahhabis, deport their activists, bar Wahhabi visitors from abroad, and convince many in the West that he was in the forefront of a world crusade against Islamic fundamentalism.

But anyone familiar with the Caucasus, as well as Central Asia, would recognize that the term *Wahhabi* is being used so loosely and so inclusively as to undermine any ability to establish who the Wahhabis actually are. Much of the public discourse on the Wahhabis does not exceed the seriousness of President Karimov's beard-catching methods. The head of Grozny's Islamic University once told me, "Many Wahhabis do not even know they are Wahhabis," which brings to mind the images of the 1950s horror movie *Invasion of the Body Snatchers.*

The man who lent his name to this phenomenon was one Muhammad ibn Abdul Wahhab, who lived and preached in northeastern Arabia in the eighteenth century. He was a religious reformer who resolved to cleanse Islam of anything that did not directly emanate from the Qur'an. Unlike Kunta Haji, he favored the cerebral over the emotional.

Also unlike Kunta, Wahhab was a profoundly learned man. He was the ideological founder of Saudi Arabia in that his fervor provided the obscure Saud family with a powerful raison d'être that carried it, in the twentieth century, to absolute power in the world's leading oil-producing state. To borrow Machiavelli's apt definition, Abdul Wahhab was not only a successful "armed prophet" but also became, if only post-humously, a *funded* prophet. Through a combination of Saudi wealth and Saudi control over Islam's holy shrines, Abdul Wahhab's ghost has been propelled into a position of influence that he never enjoyed in his life-time. In the eighteenth century, he was involved in petty Bedouin poli-tics in the heart of the wilderness; two centuries later, he is perceived as a major threat to the prevailing political order throughout the Islamic world.*

Abdul Wahhab was to contemporary Islam what Martin Luther was to Christianity, seeking to overthrow an "artificial" hierarchy that stood between man and God. Luther had no use for a pope, or a confessing priest, or a culture of saints, or a regime of paid indulgences. Similarly, Abdul Wahhab had no use for dead saints (whose worship he consid-ered a form of idolatry) or live sheikhs who attracted loyal adherents, issued edicts, and made themselves God's intercessors.

What makes Abdul Wahhab such an important part of this story is that he declared war on Sufism, which he equated with evil. The com-pliment was reciprocated, and the battle joined. The war rages today across the full breadth of the Muslim world, but in the Caucasus it is waged against the highlanders' collective memory and self-perception. The message is clear: what you, North Caucasians, consider Islam is unworthy of that name. You are as good as pagans, and it is high time you were brought back to the fold.

On the eve of Chechnya's third Independence Day,[†] in September 1994, hundreds of Chechen villagers assembled in front of the parlia-ment building in central Grozny to perform the *zikr*. Those following the *Naqshbandi* path, predominant before Kunta Haji's ascent, carried out their *zikr* seated and in complete silence. The only sound heard was that of threaded beads clicking as the men, mostly elderly, moved their rosaries through their fingers, the very practice which Abdul Wahhab had denounced as an evil "innovation."

---

* The first Wahhabi-inspired uprising outside of Arabia took place in Sumatra, present-day Indonesia (1821–37). Pilgrims returning from Mecca carried the Wahhabi gospel and employed it against the local political and religious elite. The split in Indonesian Islam between Wahhabi-like militants and moderate Sufis persists to this day, and the site of the nineteenth-century war, Aceh, has recently clamored to secede from Indone-sia and establish an Islamic state.

† Independence was proclaimed unilaterally in 1991 and was recognized by none.

The long-bearded man was master of the ceremony, and I soon realized how charming and humorous he was, even in the midst of solemnity and supreme concentration.

The silent *zikrists* were in the distinct minority, however. The day clearly belonged to the various subgroups of whirling *Qadiri* who occupied large parts of the city center, some banging on their flat, circular drums, some running in circles to the point of exhaustion, some jumping in place. Presiding over them was a handsome old man with a long, well-trimmed beard, clothed in a magnificent robe, wearing a red fez, and waving a long cane. He was master of the ceremony, and I soon realized how charming and humorous he was, even in the midst of solemnity and supreme concentration. At least once, noticing me videotaping the ritual, he sought me out with his eyes, and upon making contact he winked and smiled. Some two years later, I was told that he was one the first casualties of the Russian bombing of Grozny.

Every now and then the whirlers would pause to catch their breath and be inspired by various speakers, who were impressing on them the need for Chechens to unite in the face of pending adversity. (A Russian military intervention was expected any day; it came three months later.) At one point, a scrawny boy, perhaps fifteen years old, wearing a large skullcap, his face drawn, pale, and blemished, rose to his feet with pronounced agitation. He spewed out a short monologue, warning his elders against the two greatest hazards looming over Chechnya: Communism and Wahhabism. As he spoke in a mountainous Chechen dialect called Shatoy, or so I was told by my interpreter, the boy's hands started trembling uncontrollably, and older men around him had to calm him down. The boy, in his all-white outfit, with flaming eyes and a hint of foam on his lips, had an eerie aura of saintliness about him, like a child-prophet transported to downtown Grozny out of the leaves of an ancient Etruscan myth, a Tages* of sorts, to announce the imminence of calamity brought by the intrusion of alien ideologies, one European and the other Arab.

Aversion to Wahhabi practices in Chechnya was widespread at the time. The Chechen social outlook may be more austere than that of

---

* Tages, a child with the features of a wise old man, was said by the Etruscans to communicate divine knowledge to humans. The Romans later absorbed his prophecy and called it *Etrusca Disciplina*.

their neighbors—from etiquette, to facial expressions, to clothing—but the strictness of orthodox Islam has been alien to them.

"We are not attempting to create here an Islamic state; nor do we believe that the faithful should be involved in politics," the rector of Grozny's then-thriving Islamic University, Meirbek Haji Nasukhanov, told me just before the war with Russia. "Our goal is to reconcile warring parties, not to incite them. Kunta Haji is our spiritual leader, and he taught us to unite, not divide. From time to time we hear of new schools of Islamic opinion whose aim is disunity. We reject them."

Restoration of Islam to prominence in Chechen political and social life was certainly a goal of the independence movement—it would be in any Muslim society, particularly one that had been denied its religious choice for so long—but the introduction of Islam did not necessarily imply stifling uniformity or the wholesale imposition of rigorous religious laws. For an independent Chechnya to acknowledge Islam was a matter of course; to submit to a sectarian interpretation of it was inconsistent with ancient customs and natural inclination.

The casual attitude toward alcohol was symptomatic of the condition of Islam in prewar Chechnya. No religious authority would have approved of its consumption, but few spoke of a prohibition. Alcohol and Islam coexisted peacefully and openly there, as well as in neighboring Daghestan.

One night in prewar Grozny, at an "independence day" party for foreigners, I saw the government's chief spokesperson, Movladi Udugov (a young nationalist whose trimmed beard and gray jeans suit gave him the appearance of a Western student), help himself to huge quantities of alcohol. He gulped vodka until his young body could take no more, then passed out on the floor of the barely finished Hotel Kavkaz.

As the war moved into high gear, however, a born-again Udugov was preaching complete abstinence to the Chechens. Later, upon becoming a presidential contender and deputy prime minister, he formed a political organization with the aim of recreating Imam Shamil's Islamic state. His beard seemed to get longer—most beards in Chechnya did at that time—and it was said that Udugov fancied himself the new imam. To use common jargon, he had become a Wahhabi, which is to say a practitioner of purist, ascetic Islam.

In 1996, after the nation was rid of the Russians, groups of "fighters" turned their attention to the state of national sobriety. Alcoholoclasts roamed the streets in quest of drunkards, raided warehouses and liquor stores, and meted out punishment in the name of Islamic law. Here is how *Severny Kavkaz*, the only regionwide publication in the North Caucasus, reported one such incident:

Last Friday, proponents of the self-declared Chechen Republic of Ichkeria* marked the end of the war and their day of independence. In many towns and villages, collective prayers were held and sacrifices offered. In the village of Naurskaya, the holiday had an unexpected end. A small table was set in the central square. As it turned out, the table played the role of the proverbial gallows. First announced were the names of the drunkards, petty thieves and hooligans to be punished by whipping, according to the norms of *shari'a* [Islamic law]. The culprits would lie down, get their "share" of wisdom, and then offer thanks for the information and promise to mend their ways in the future. The district mullah organized the administration of penalties. . . .

Concurrent with the floggings, raids were waged against all commercial kiosks and restaurants, resulting in the destruction of much liquor. The main streets were littered with the shattered glass of vodka bottles and empty beer cans. The proprietors of liquor stores counted their losses and wept. Some lost four million rubles [about $900], others three, two, etc. Buying vodka now is a big problem. The liquor salesmen disappeared, awaiting better times.

In July 1998, Aslan Maskhadov, the postwar president of Chechnya, finally decided to move against the *Wahhabis.* "The Chechens," he said, "from time immemorial are Muslims, have their history, national traditions and customs, and will never become either Arabs or Afghans. . . . We are not going to tolerate in our land any more foreign citizens who are trying to establish their ways here."

He was too late. The *Wahhabis* were to play a leading role in rekindling the war with Russia, in late 1999. A calamity followed.

---

* Ichkeria was the name General Dudayev added to the name of his republic, a controversial choice in that it emphasized the centrality of one region.

"WAHHABIS SEND SUFI SHEIKH TO HELL"

One Friday afternoon in Makhachkala, the capital of Daghestan, in a little apartment off a main street, I was introduced to about fifty young members of the Islamic Center.

If not for the anti-Russian rhetoric and the copies of the Qur'an, one could have easily mistaken the gathering for a revolutionary cell in czarist Russia. The language spoken was Russian; most of the faces were pale and beardless, ascetic and grim; and a certain intellectual intensity hung in the air. One could sense the excitement of young minds plotting the end of their failed world and its replacement by a new cosmic order.

Their discourse, delivered calmly and politely, left little doubt that they would like to see the termination of the present order in Daghestan. They would redraw the international borders to squeeze Russia out, and even more importantly, they would reshape the internal human borders to make way for their kind of Islam, which in the absence of a better term, we might call Wahhabi.

When I told them that most Daghestanis I had spoken to expressed a clear preference for continued life within the Russian Federation, as opposed to following the Chechen example, one sneered at me: "Yes, we know, they cannot live without Russia, exactly the same way a drunkard cannot do without a glass of wine."

Though it was midafternoon on a workday, about fifty able-bodied men, most of them not older than twenty-five, had crowded in two small rooms. Their leader, in his late forties, had just returned from an international Islamic conference in Khartoum, Sudan's capital and a new international bastion of "Islamic fundamentalism." His name was Murad, and he was the editor and publisher of an Islamic newspaper called *al-Mujahid* ("Holy Warrior"). The paper, written in Russian save for the logo, had been banned by the Daghestani authorities on the ground of "religious intolerance and incitement for the violent overthrow of the existing government." (The quotation is from Murad—I did not have the opportunity to study the official prosecutorial language.) Murad was duly indicted, but at the time of my visit, in late 1996, his trial had not yet started. In any event, he had been sternly warned not to publish ever again.

According to Murad, the passage that brought the prosecutor's wrath down on him was a poem composed more than a century and a half earlier by Ghazi Muhammad, the First Imam of Daghestan and the leader of the movement that later spearheaded the great rebellion against Russia. The original verse, translated for me on the spot, probably to the detriment of its literary qualities, read:

> *Rise, Daghestanis,*
> *Wake up* Alpan.
> *Should slavery be the destiny of the* Ghazawat *eagles?**

"If Ghazi Muhammad were to reappear today," one of the assembled youths interjected, "the authorities would undoubtedly order his immediate arrest for Wahhabism."

The room exploded in derisive laughter. After all, not only was Ghazi Muhammad not Wahhabi, he was in fact a venerable Sufi sheikh, a national icon of Daghestan, what Americans would call "a founding father." To suggest that he would be arrested if he cared to come back from the dead was to state that the system had gone mad.

Murad and his students did not represent a mass movement, and whatever danger they posed to the system was probably overstated both by the central government and by the local authorities. What the Wahhabis do have to offer, however, for the first time since Shamil's uprising in the 1830s, is a coherent ideology for individuals whose disaffection and bitterness remain unharnessed. Early signs indicate that a match-up of nonideological local potentates and powerless but ideologically motivated Islamic radicals is indeed taking place. But this development is still far from justifying the words of Russia's interior minister (who is in charge of internal security) in 1998: "We believe the greatest threat comes from Islamic fundamentalism, namely Wahhabism. It is a

---

* *Alpan* or *Alphan* may be Turkish for "divine leader" and *Ghazawat* is a derivative of an Arabic word used to describe the Prophet's raids against his enemies and detractors in the year 624. The Caucasian rebellion came to be known as the *Ghazawat* (or, in its slight Russian mispronunciation, *Gazavat*).

special form of political extremism similar to terrorism." The minister probably had in mind young Daghestanis who traveled to Pakistan to attend religious schools, in which—or so popular rumor had it—the art of handling a machine gun was an integral part of the curriculum. When I visited the main mosque of Makhachkala, my interlocutors invariably pointed out bearded youngsters wearing green skullcaps and whispered to me, "They are the 'Pakistanis.'"

(In 1998 the incidence of terrorist acts in Daghestan attributed to the Wahhabis increased dramatically. The most sensational was the assassination of the mufti of Daghestan, the highest-ranking religious official of the land, who was Sufi. The assassins have yet to be found, but while surfing the Internet a few days later, I came across the following message in a newsgroup that deals with Pakistan: "Wahhabis send Naqshbandi Shaykh to hell. . . . Insha'allah [God willing], we will see more such operations soon.")

Because Murad and his disciples would not confess to "Wahhabism" (few in the Caucasus ever do), I wanted to see how far they would go in disparaging Sufism, the nemesis of all Wahhabis. I asked a few questions, and their subsequent denunciations of dead sheikhs confirmed to me that they were out to dismantle the entire religious tradition of the land. Central to Sufism is the notion that learning passes from one generation to the next through a chain of sages (silsila in Arabic) that goes back all the way to the Prophet and is never interrupted. Interrupt it, and it is all over.

Therefore Murad's greatest goal was to interrupt a silsila that had passed through a Sufi named Hassan Kakhipsky (that is, Hassan of the village of Kakhip), one of the most fabled sheikhs of the early twentieth century. It was said of Kakhipsky that no train he ever boarded would start until he gave the command, no matter how hard the locomotive pulled. His reputation as a miracle worker has outlived him by many decades, especially among the Avars, Daghestan's largest ethnic group, to which Murad and his disciples belong. Interrupting Kakhipsky's chain by way of posthumous discreditation was a major goal of the Islamic Center's propaganda.

The war against the sheikhs has become one of the most divisive issues in Islam, even if it gains little attention in the West. It is divisive because it threatens the religious practices of many tens of millions of people, from the Far East to the Gulf of Guinea, from Central Asia to equatorial Africa to the southwestern shores of the Mediterranean, where the attachment to saints and the prominence of the zikr are extremely strong.

For example, in Egypt, where Sufism has its largest following in the Arab world, the birthdays of Sufi saints are celebrated regularly, in rituals attended by multitudes. Days of meticulous preparations reach their climax in what is called *Layla al Kabira,* or "The Great Night." A loud *zikr* is performed, to the sound of hypnotic religious music. So central is the ritual to Egyptian Islam that the most accomplished singers in these ceremonies often earn the honorific title *sheikh.*

In Baghdad, the grave of Abdul Qadir al-Geylani is a holy shrine, which in times of peace used to be visited by pilgrims from all over the world. Abdul Qadir's reach extends all the way to Senegal, in West Africa, where the indigenous Wolof people became Sufis of the *Qadiri* path more than a century before Kunta Haji had his revelation on the road to Baghdad. The Wolof *zikr* integrates elements of shamanistic African religions, including drum music called *tabala wolof* (which is now available on CD to Westerners as well).

What is at issue here is the idiom of religion and the relationship between the believer and God. Why humans seek God is a question that falls outside my assignment here, but it is fair to assume that people do not opt for religion because it requires them to abide by rigorous laws. They seek the mystery. Religious groups that overemphasize the rational do so at their own peril.

Islamic purists, Wahhabis or otherwise, consider the worship of dead saints a form of "polytheism," in that the saints are elevated to a divine status and probably play roles not unlike those of pre-Islamic pagan deities. Monotheism, to be sure, was born in an act of defiant iconoclasm, when the patriarch Abraham (according to the Jewish legend) destroyed his father's idols in a fit of anger, but iconoclasts have rarely carried the day in any religion. Eliminating the dead saints of the Egyptians, or the Wolof, or the Chechens, might kill their religion as well.

Can the scholar and the mystic not coexist? Sheikh Muhammad Hisham Kabbani, the American-based Sufi proponent of a kinder and gentler Islam, once told his disciples:

> You attract people by giving them a flower, not by brandishing a sword. Islam is a flower, scented with a nice fragrance for humanity. Ours is a message of purity; a message of light, not a message of hatred and enmity. Prophet Muhammad taught, "Treat all with goodness."

This "fragrant Islam" is remarkable considering the Sufi chain of sages to which Kabbani is the heir: it produced the rebel-imams of the Caucasus, including Shamil, the hero of Muslim resistance, the founder of a state where only one kind of fragrance was inhalable.

I spoke earlier of the schism that emerged in the Caucasus between Sufis of the *Naqshbandi* path and those belonging to the *Qadiri* path. Shamil, just like Kabbani, was *Naqshbandi*, while Kunta Haji was the apostle of *Qadiriya*. Shamil was committed to fighting a holy war, while Kunta wanted to put an end to a war that was bleeding his people to the verge of extinction.

And yet in 1859 Shamil surrendered to the Russians. It had already been clear for at least three years that his cause was lost, but surrender entailed the legitimation of Russian rule. Moreover, the terms of the surrender portrayed Russia as a benevolent victor: Shamil was offered, and accepted, a comfortable exile in the Russian city of Kaluga. All he had to do was lay down his arms, call on his disciples to follow suit, and depart the Caucasus forever. And he did all that.

Why? Why did the "Holy War Eagle" not apply to himself that which he had prescribed to a whole generation of Caucasian Muslims? According to Sheikh Kabbani, the real explanation lies in Shamil's violation of the sacred *silsila* principle of Sufism. "I will tell you a secret— you are going have a great scoop," the sheikh intimated when I spoke to him in 1996 in San Francisco, where he attended a Sufi conference during which he converted a sister of O.J. Simpson to Islam. "Shamil had three *murshids,* or great teachers. They were Ghazi Muhammad, Muhammad Efendi al-Yaragi, and Sayyed Jamaluddin al-Ghumuqi al-Husayni. They supported him in whatever he did, and it was thanks to them that for thirty years he was continuously triumphant in battle and was never defeated. After thirty years, he was filled with a sense of invincibility. He became arrogant and told himself, 'Who are these *dervishes* [a common synonym for Sufis] to tell me what to do?' And so he rejected their advice.

"In Islam, when somebody dies, you say *fatiha* [the first chapter of the Quran] after him. Those three sheikhs then said *fatiha* after Shamil. A week later he was captured by the Russians."

Sheikh Kabbani's historical "scoop" may be disputed,* yet it is interesting because it reflects an ambivalence about Shamil and could thus help explain the dramatic mellowing of the *Naqshbandis* in the Caucasus: this most militant of Sufi orders has become a paragon of peaceful coexistence with Russia.

---

* According to Kabbani, original documents corroborating the story are to be found in a vast archive the *Naqshbandi* order keeps in Lebanon. Still, it is problematic in that two out of the three *murshid* cited by Kabbani had been long dead by the time of Shamil's surrender and thus would have been unable to say *fatiha*. On the other hand, Sufis often believe that their sheikhs continue to protect them even posthumously and are therefore not quite dead.

As enmity between Sufis and purists has risen in recent decades, the latter have begun to claim Shamil as one of their own. The young Islamic activists whom I met in Makhachkala told me that Shamil, himself a Daghestani, had been "a great opponent of Sufism," who sought to establish Islam in its purest form. To my surprise, Sheikh Kabbani seemed to agree with this view, however subtly. He said in fact that Shamil, one of the greatest Muslim heroes of all times, had renounced one of the guiding principles of Sufism and thus had ceased to be Sufi.

To a Sufi, even the mighty Shamil had to answer to a higher human authority, a Sufi system, as it were, of sheikhs and balances.

ABDUL WAHHAB THE JEW
(AND MORE)

Salih Khamkhoyev, the rector of the Islamic Institute in Ingushetia who had rediscovered Kunta Haji's descendants in Baghdad, is, predictably, a sworn anti-Wahhabi. He enumerated for me all the Wahhabi sins against tradition, then added: "They do not protest the spread of alcohol, sexual perversion, Western music, or indecent women's dress." He was clearly wrong because much of the hostility toward "Wahhabis" in Chechnya was generated by their campaign against alcohol and their attempt to enforce an austere dress code for women. There was little point in arguing with him, however. Words in the Caucasus are often used metaphorically, and Wahhabi is but the newest vogue term for "bad people."

Khamkhoyev then fingered the ultimate Wahhabi sin. "They remain silent about the greatest threat to the foundations of Islam." He looked at me with a hint of a smile, as if to observe the pending change in my facial expression, inevitable upon hearing his subsequent words. "The greatest threat is the Jews. Only Jews can conduct this kind of propaganda against Islam. Only Jews can approve of drinking and all types of sexual behavior. Abdul Wahhab—he was a Jew and a British spy."

Khamkhoyev continued: "Jews are at the roots of all tragedies that have ever befallen humanity, all national calamities. You need only look at America. After all, *all* Americans are Jewish. Not only Americans, but also all the top decision-makers in Russia. Chubais is Jewish, Shakhrai is Jewish, I mean he is a Circassian Jew."

He was referring to Anatoly Chubais and Sergei Shakhrai, two former prominent members of the Yeltsin team, neither of whom is Jewish. Shakhrai is believed to have Cossack ancestry, but when I mentioned it to Khamkhoyev, he laughed and retorted: "If he were Cossack, he would be walking with a whip and be constantly drunk," an answer so persuasive as to leave me speechless.

Khamkhoyev then went on to credit "the Jews" with the bombing of Iraq in 1991.

That bombing was ordered by President Bush, I reminded him as uncontentiously as possible.

"Exactly," he said. "The Jew Bush."

The Jew? He is a practicing Christian.

"Christian?" Khamkhoyev responded with a smile, never departing from his friendly, casual demeanor. "There are no Christians, there is no Christianity. That is a complete misunderstanding. Christianity does not exist. It's all Jewish. All the so-called 'Christians' are Jewish. You look at Aleksey [the patriarch of the Russian Orthodox Church]. Do you think he is 'Christian'? He is a Jew from the Baltic region."*

I found myself asking an irrelevant question: "What of the Holocaust? Was it not perpetrated by Christians against Jews? Surely you do not think Hitler was Jewish."

"Hitler?" Khamkhoyev's eyes lit up. "Hitler deserved the support of all. If only he had been supported, if only he had not been prematurely stopped, everyone would have been better off. Hitler wanted to make the world happier. I do not approve of the death of people, but in order to remove evil, sacrifice is necessary. Every sacrifice is justified."

Khamkhoyev's charge against the Jews was the strongest I heard from a Caucasian Muslim, but it was by no means the only one. Svetlana Omarovna Aliyeva, a specialist in world literature in Russia's Academy of Science in Moscow, an ethnic Karachai (a Turkic people in the Northwest Caucasus), told me that Jews were to blame for the distortion of the Caucasus in the Russian mind "because they control the media." Haji-Murat Ibragimbeili, a distinguished and well-known scholar of Avar nationality (Avars being the largest nation in Daghestan), offered to help me obtain access to various Chechen leaders. "Call me when you get there," he said when I met him in Moscow. A few weeks later I did call him, and by way of refreshing his memory, I referred to myself as "the Israeli journalist" who had seen him in Moscow. He exploded in anger and berated me for "concealing your Jewishness from me in the first place," which I had never done. But I began to resort to more and more in my contact with Muslims in the North Caucasus. Vulgar anti-Semitism with medieval overtones is by no means a North Caucasian phenomenon—it is increasingly common in many Muslim countries, including those where Jews have never lived.

* Aleksey's family is indeed from the Baltic city of Riga, but he is of Christian German extraction.

ROMANTICIZING THE "BLACK FACES"

One day in Grozny's main square, I was talking with a crowd of men during their lunch break. Suddenly one, tall and trim, wearing a black-rimmed hat, drew a long Caucasian dagger, waved it at my video camera, and exclaimed: "I will aim this at the Russian tanks, if they dare come."

"What do you think will happen if you do that?" I asked. The man shot back without the slightest hesitation, "I will die. I, and the entire nation with me." Irked by his bravado, I turned to the dozens of men around us. "For two centuries you have been dying, and dying, and dying. Hasn't the time come to start living?" The men roared disapprovingly. "No one lets us!" snapped an elderly man.

The following day I related the episode to the head of Chechnya's national archive, Delkhan Khajayev, a historian in his mid-thirties. He smiled faintly and said in a resigned tone, "Someone from another culture always finds it difficult to understand why people who know they are bound to lose will still wage a war against a superior enemy. One has to be a Garibaldi, or a Tolstoy, or a Lord Byron to fully grasp it."

Maybe so, but the three belonged to an age that romanticized little-understood nations, at times to the detriment of the nations lionized. The Chechens may not need a Lord Byron to glorify their predicament as much as they need some constructive criticism of their own flaws. Murad Benno, scion of a famous Chechen family, warned me against romanticizing his people. "One day I hope to take you to a mountain village, to meet the greatest Chechen author alive, Abuzar Aydemirov, so you can hear from him how disillusioned he has become by 'the Chechen national character.'"

Murad Benno moved as a boy from Jordan to Chechnya. Now he warns against romanticization of his countrymen. He quotes Chechnya's greatest author, Abuzar Aydemirov. "If I were not so old," the exasperated author said, "I would leave this land, find a place where there are no Chechens at all, and spend my remaining years among them."

Right before the Russian attack, Benno called on Aydemirov and implored him to take a public stand to prevent a civil war among the Chechens. Aydemirov was exasperated. "If I were not so old," the author, then in his early seventies, told Benno, "I would leave this land, find a place where there are no Chechens at all, and spend my remaining years among them."

The Chechens' problem, Benno asserted, "is that we simply do not recognize the existence of a middle ground. We always drift to one extreme or the other."

Many Chechens with whom I met, both in Chechnya and in the diaspora, people with solid loyalty to their nation, voiced harsh criticism of General Dudayev's rebel government.

Dudayev's own former press secretary, Mariam Vakhidova, told me in Moscow that she had ceased being able to work with him—her admiration for his personal courage notwithstanding—because of the callous manner in which he spoke of the need to sacrifice hundreds of thousands of Chechens for *the cause.*

A young, pretty woman with raven hair and piercing dark eyes, born to Chechen deportees in Central Asian exile, Vakhidova had initially fallen for the excitement and the heroic halo of Dudayev's uprising. Though a virtual stranger to Chechnya and a halting speaker of the Chechen language, she cast her lot with the general in 1990. A black-and-white photo of Vakhidova and Dudayev still adorns one of the walls of her Moscow apartment.

The dapper, uncharacteristically relaxed Dudayev featured in the photo, with his elegant Panama hat and a black leather jacket, resembled an American gangster of the 1930s. When I made this observa-

Jokar Dudayev and Mariam Vakhidova, in an old photo hanging from Vakhidova's apart-
ment wall in Moscow. "I could have been a Bonnie to Dudayev's Clyde," Vakhidova laughed.

tion to Vakhidova, she burst out laughing. "I know," she said. "I could have been a Bonnie to Dudayev's Clyde."

"Jokar never made a secret of his intentions, even before he arrived in Chechnya," she said. "From 1990 on, he always said—whether privately or publicly, in intimate conversations or in outdoor rallies, in parliament, on television—'Freedom's price is high.' I once asked him how high, and he replied, 'Even if one-third of the population has to die.'

"He was convinced that for the people to gain true freedom, the legacy of the Soviet period had to be erased first. . . . Under the Communists, the Chechens had compromised their identity, he said. . . . They had conformed to the model of *sovetsky chelovek* ["Soviet Man"]. He said that we needed to cleanse the people.

"That is the reason I stopped working for him. You see, there is a continuous theme in Chechen life. Each time in our history the Chechen population reached the one million level, something catastrophic happened that reduced it all the way back to 300,000. I believe that the next four generations should be devoted to revival, replenishing the ranks. When Dudayev came to power, our population had just reached one million again, and he was going to reduce it.

"I told him, 'Jokar, this is too heavy a price to pay. Let the bad guys die—but why the innocents? I am not going to associate myself with

Jokar Dudayev celebrating Chechnya's last prewar Day of Independence. Behind him is the soon-to-disappear presidential palace. Russian firepower turned it into rubble.

this.' That is what I told him to his face. He responded: 'Mariam, you have weak nerves. You are not fit for grand politics.'

"I told him that I was going to tell the people what he had in mind for them, his freedom-by-blood program. He did not forbid it—quite to the contrary, he welcomed it. We parted as friends."

Ten months into the war, Dudayev, smug and pleased with himself, told a British television interviewer, Angus Roxburg, in his hideout:

Nov. 1995

I need this situation more than Russia does. Neither war nor peace. What would I do if the Russians suddenly pulled out? I've got 300,000 men, aged 17 to 50, homeless, jobless, embittered, and with nothing to do. All they can do is fight. I need a little war and an enemy to send them to battle against. I have a program, not to separate from Russia but to enter it and destroy it from within.

Three months later, in February 1996, Dudayev was dead, the victim of a well-orchestrated assassination, widely assumed to have been carried out by the Russians. The war drew to an end in September 1996. Dudayev's analysis was partly borne out: the heavily armed, unemployed, and impoverished Chechen population had proved a breeding ground for terrifying lawlessness that tragically cost the lives of many innocents, including International Red Cross workers and friends of the Chechens who came to help. Chechnya vanished into the black hole that Dudayev's zeal and Russia's blindness had helped create.

The advice not to overromanticize the Chechens is for foreigners. As for the Russians, particularly the ones living in major cities, they have developed what a Moscow sociologist, Aleksandr Iskanderian, calls Caucasophobia, or hostility toward Caucasian minorities. Iskanderian himself is an ethnic Armenian.

"Caucasophobia in official rhetoric," he told me, "has taken the place of the old Soviet anti-Semitism. America may have its own racism, but it has developed mechanisms to cope with it. Because Russia has no civil society and has no notion of 'political correctness,' the most outlandish racist statements from government officials go unchallenged. Think of it as a new virus for which no vaccine yet exists. People who move in my circles—in academe, in science—think they pay me a great compliment when they tell me how 'good' the Armenians are and how 'bad' the Azeris are because they cheat and harass women in the market."

The demonization of Caucasians in general and the Chechens in particular began only in late Soviet times, Iskanderian continued. "Of course, it had historical roots. Russians like their poets, and they have recited for a hundred and fifty years Lermontov's lines, *'And there the wicked Chechen creeps, / And whets his dagger keen.'* But for many years the good traits outweighed the bad. People spoke of the generosity of the Caucasians, their respect for their elders, and so on. The first opinion poll

Everyone has Soviet era stories of bullying Chechens. This fear is not new.

that I am aware of that reflected a change in the Russian attitude was conducted in 1994. It showed that 80 percent of the respondents feared the Chechens and hated them. Only a fraction of them had ever actually spoken to a live Chechen.

"Why did it happen? I think it was the result of post-Communist market conditions. Caucasians became enemies by virtue of their monopoly on much of the retail activity in food markets. The political and military crises just served to enhance an attitude that had already been shaping up for a few years. And the politicians were eager to exploit it. Imagine the mayor of Moscow throwing hundreds of Chechens out of the city the day after a bomb was planted in a tram car. No one had any idea who had done it, but the mayor was already moving to satisfy the stereotypes of his voters." (That mayor, Yuri Luzhkov, undoubtedly knew something about public opinion: he had just been reelected with an astonishing 90 percent of the vote, and was reelected four years later in the midst of another wave of anti-Chechen feelings.)

Hatred of Caucasians that is couched in political terms may have been late in coming, but a lot of anecdotal evidence suggests that casual contempt toward "blacks," as some Russians refer to Caucasians (many of whom are as pale as they are), predated the Soviet collapse by many years. Aleksandr Petrov, a human rights activist in Moscow, is a native of Ulianovsk, a provincial city on the Volga River, where, he recalls, in the 1960s Armenians were derisively referred to as *chernomazyiye*, or "black faces." Employed mostly in the construction industry, the "black faces" were rarely seen on social occasions because, Petrov says, "they would have been beaten up as soon as they walked in." At that time, few Russians bothered with distinctions between Caucasian Muslims and Caucasian Christians, between North Caucasians and Transcaucasians (that is, Armenians, Azeris, and Georgians), or between the various tiny nationalities of the North Caucasus. All were "blacks," and all were equally despised.

The extent of anti-"black" feeling was such that even other victims of ethnic discrimination joined the chorus. If Jews in the United States tend to identify with victims of discrimination because of their own experience of victimhood, evidence suggests otherwise in the case of Russian Jews. The sociologist Iskanderian contends that the right-wing sympathies of Russian Jewish immigrants in Israel have a lot to do with the transference of Soviet ethnic stereotypes to Israeli reality. When he interviewed some Russian Jews in Israel, he concluded that their former Moscow Caucasophobia turned into Arabophobia.

If Jews—members of a well-educated urban minority, quintessential victims of ethnic hostility—subscribe so eagerly to such stereotypes, then it is not all that surprising that xenophobia is prevalent among Russian intellectuals. After all, Russian national consciousness was largely shaped by a history of cataclysmic struggle with "Asia," going back to Holy Rus of the Middle Ages and to the desperate struggle of Muscovy to stem the Mongol and Tatar tides.

Just before I left for Chechnya, a young Russian intellectual who was otherwise liberal and open-minded asked me, "Why do you *like* these people? Don't you know how unpleasant they are?" My acquaintance had never been to Chechnya, and his idea of the Chechens had been shaped only by chance encounters in the streets and markets of Moscow.

I surely did not *like* or *dislike* the Chechens at that time, having never met any, but I found it increasingly difficult to accept the collective labels that so many Russians affixed to them. The gross caricature of the evil Chechen is undoubtedly so deeply ingrained in the Russian mind that it clouds the thinking of even the most astute Russians. Nikolai Barsukov, a former head of the FSB (a successor to the KGB), related the following story: "One local man told me that a Chechen may be a robber, a killer. In case he is neither, he is still a person ready for any other kind of crime."

A Chechen activist in Moscow, Sa'id-Usman Yakhiyev, told me that liberals in Moscow had begun to wage bitter attacks on "the Chechen character" almost as soon as Mikhail Gorbachev loosened the shackles on the press, in the late 1980s. "There was a newspaper in Moscow named *Glasnost*," Yakhiyev, a businessman who holds an academic degree in theology, told me, "that alleged that all 9,000 Chechens living in Moscow were bandits and criminals. We [a Chechen community organization in Moscow] sued the paper and demanded a retraction. They responded that the identity of the article's author was unknown to them. And that was the end of the affair."

Anatoly Shabad, a former legislator known for his support of human rights, whom I met in Moscow, recalls that it was the democratic press that attributed urban crime to "Caucasian nationalities." "They began to generate ethnic hatred," he told me. "Each time there was a crime and the perpetrator was from the Caucasus, the Moscow press would immediately mention the ethnic background in its reports. It never identified criminals as Russian, or Ukrainian, or Baltic; only 'a member of a Caucasian nationality' deserved to be identified."

(Disparaging remarks about the "Chechen character" could be heard not only from Russian Christians but also from Muslims who had served with Chechens in the Soviet military. They spoke disdainfully, almost in identical terms, of Chechen clannishness, which presented an ominous contrast to the loneliness and vulnerability of non-Chechen recruits.)

Aleksandr Solzhenitsyn, no advocate of Chechen rights, is nonetheless a grudging admirer of their tenacity. He would like to see a rump Chechen state, independent of Russia but permanently blockaded by it, thus rendering the Russian Federation effectively Chechen-free. And yet in *The Gulag Archipelago*, his powerful history of Stalinist oppression, he wrote of their conduct during their Central Asian banishment:

> The Chechens never sought to please, to ingratiate themselves with the bosses. . . . As far as they were concerned, the local inhabitants, and those exiles who submitted so readily, belonged more or less to the same breed as the bosses. They respected only rebels.
>
> And here is an extraordinary thing—everyone was afraid of them. No one could stop them from living as they did. The regime which had ruled the land for thirty years could not force them to respect its laws.

He related the story of a Chechen boy by the name of Abdul Khudayev, the only Chechen in his class: "He inspired no warm feelings and did not try to do so; he seemed to be afraid of demeaning himself by making himself pleasant. . . . But you could not help admiring his clear, precise mind."

One of my roommates in Frantsuzski Dom ("the French House"), a hotel of sorts in downtown Grozny, on the eve of the war, was a young, alert, and smart Russian journalist. At twenty-seven, handsome, blond, and blue-eyed with mild manners, he had come to Grozny for a couple of days to quickly prepare a "list of strategic reserves." He was driven every morning to various parts of Chechnya, where he made an inventory of all the armored vehicles, tanks, and pieces of artillery he spotted. By the end of the process, he contended, he would have conclusive findings about the ability of the Chechens to offer military resistance to Russia.

The journalist, bright and full of promise, never had the chance to test his scientific methods. Less than two months later he was blown to pieces in the editorial offices of *Moskovsky Komsomolets*, the popular Moscow newspaper for which he wrote, presumably in connection with an exposé he was researching on corruption in the top echelons of Russia's military. His name was Dmitri Kholodov, and he became probably the best-known martyr of Russian journalism in the 1990s. I have always admired his courage, but I think even Kholodov, like so many Russian military leaders, politicians, journalists, and academics, failed to grasp the core of Chechen strength.

Contrary to Kholodov's expectation, the coming Chechen resistance was not exclusively a matter of possessing certain amounts of military hardware. Nor was it a mere reflection of the number of trained soldiers under the rebel flag. (They were so few at the time that General Dudayev had had to give up control of towns he had just captured from his local opponents because he had to use the soldiers elsewhere.) Nor was the resistance a result of public support for Dudayev's antics. Yet once the battle was joined, the Chechens never lacked for men or arms.

National flaws aside, the Chechens' resistance to Russia reflected strength that could not be entirely quantified. Nor can their strength be explained by various other factors that have been proposed. Russia may well be in a state of decay, its military command consumed by corruption, its footsoldiers indifferent, poorly fed, and ill dressed; Chechens may well have been able to bribe their enemies away from the battlefield; veterans of the Afghan *mujahideen* from all over the Muslim world may well have swelled the Chechen ranks. And yet these factors do not provide a sufficient explanation for the ferocity of the Chechen resistance; nor do they account for the willingness of a nation to rise up once every generation, to suffer catastrophic defeats, and to try again thirty or fifty years later.

Nowhere is endurance tested more grievously than in exile. The Chechens have suffered two major exiles: the genocidal one of 1944, and the voluntary one of the late nineteenth century, which took many of them to the Ottoman-controlled Middle East. It was from Iraq that Salih Khamkhoyev had helped retrieve Kunta Haji's genes; I embarked on a journey to another part of the Middle East, Jordan, to seek more answers to the riddle of Chechen survival.

ABDUL LATIF HAD A BEETLE AND TWO HUNDRED TANKS

My interest in the Chechen diaspora was initially piqued in 1992 by the news that one Shamsuddin Yusef had been named foreign minister in Jokar Dudayev's rebel government. The new appointee was evidently a non-native because Arabic names such as his had not been used in the Caucasus since the Russians imposed their family name system in the mid-nineteenth century. Shamsuddin (which is how he was known, as Yusef did not quite constitute a family name) was a Jordanian by birth who had spent many years working as a mechanic in Jeddah, Saudi Arabia. Unknown to me at the time, his predecessor as foreign minister was also a Jordanian Chechen, by the name of Shamil Benno.

I met both men in Grozny in the summer of 1994, when the first winds of war were already blowing. Shamsuddin received me in his tiny ministry in the presidential compound. A smiling Russian receptionist let me in, a well-dressed lady who wore heavy makeup and spoke English quite well—a rarity among North Caucasian bureaucrats. Her linguistic skills were essential for the job, not so much because the minister had to see many diplomats—none were stationed in Grozny, and few bothered to stop by—but because that was the only medium of communication with her boss: she did not speak Chechen, while Shamsuddin spoke not a word of Russian, an indication of his irrelevance, given that virtually all correspondence and most political conversations had to be conducted in Russian. To the extent that any document was written in Chechen, it must have been in the only script available, Cyrillic, which the minister could not read.*

---

* Chechen, like most indigenous languages in the North Caucasus, had no written form prior to the Bolshevik Revolution. It remained largely underdeveloped under the

On the other hand, he spoke Arabic well, and his agreeable office was decorated with inscriptions of Qur'anic verses. Two beautifully bound, thick volumes of an Arabic-English dictionary lay heavy on his desk. While lobbying for the job, Shamsuddin is said to have promised Dudayev he would open Arab hearts and coffers for the cause of Chechen independence. He did not. Russian bombs eventually opened some hearts: A few veterans of the Afghan war against the Soviet Union (1980–89) joined the Chechens, trumpeting the gospel of a new, purer, and entirely alien Islamic dogma. Shamsuddin had predicted it, and warned against their radicalizing influence. "They will come here even if we don't ask them. We don't want them here—their presence will create problems for us. But if it happens, it will be Russia's fault," he told me.

A friendly man in his early fifties, Shamsuddin wore dark glasses at all times and sported a thin mustache, his smile revealing an upper row of bad teeth. He cut almost a comical figure, ignorant of both the West and of Russia. Inadvertently, he helped distort the meaning of the Chechen struggle and his people's image in the United States when, invited to address an academic conference in Washington shortly after the outbreak of the war, he told his bewildered audience, "We will burn Moscow." He burned nothing and, although his own office was consumed by fire, escaped unbruised to the comfort of Istanbul. There, as various Chechens told me, he accumulated considerable riches while Grozny was gasping for air and running out of standing buildings.

Dudayev's choice of a foreign minister illustrated how little the late president of Chechnya cared for intellectuals. Learned members of the Chechen diaspora, some of them graduates of leading Western universities, tried to talk to him about notions as unheroic as agrarian reform, the overhaul of education, and the rationalization of finance. They offered him a prescription for gradual growth, whose reward would be *real* independence rather than the spurious one feigned in military parades and public bravado. Unfortunately, *their* kind of independence would have been accomplished incrementally. Moreover, it would have required no *apocalypse now*. But Dudayev was a great believer in the virtue of rupture.

A prominent Jordanian Chechen, Abdul-Latif Benno, a retired general in King Hussein's army who knew Dudayev well, told me: "I have

---

Soviets—the language was taught as a subject, while Russian reigned supreme in all avenues of life—but a script was created, based on Cyrillic. General Dudayev announced a plan to Latinize the script, and though public signs in the new script mushroomed in Grozny, the low level of literacy in Chechen made the Latinization largely irrelevant.

no doubt at all that Dudayev has caused more damage to the Chechen people in five years than the Communists did in seventy years. Not since Yermolov has there been a deadlier enemy to the Chechen people." (Yermolov was the czarist general who led a bloody campaign to pacify Chechnya in the early 1820s, and whose name has since then been synonymous there with senseless butchery.) General Abdul-Latif's indictment of Dudayev's leadership notwithstanding, he still took pride in the Chechen resistance to the Russians. He calculated that Russia had used more firepower against the city of Grozny than the United States and its allies had used against Iraq during the entire Gulf War, "and yet they resist," he said of his people, "because it is better to die free than live like slaves," a contention with which Dudayev could not have agreed more heartily.

Shamil Benno, whose father is a cousin of General Abdul-Latif's, began to question Dudayev's ways early on, which is why he stepped down as foreign minister and became a vocal leader of the civic opposition. I use the term *civic* because to the best of my knowledge, Shamil Benno was never involved with the Russian-backed armed opposition; rather, he was a supporter of the Chechen right to independence, if not of the means by which Dudayev sought to bring it about.

Benno told me of a visit that a couple of Americans had paid him during his brief tenure at the foreign ministry. "They handed me two gifts—the Yellow Pages of the Washington political establishment and a collection of *The Federalist Papers.* I thanked them for the phone directory. As for the Federalists, I told them we had had a long experience with federation. The only federal choice the Russians had ever offered us was between assimilation and annihilation."

Benno, a gentle figure, mild-mannered and not easily given to hyperbole, was born in 1958 in Sweilih. Sweilih is now a suburb of Jordan's capital, Amman, but at the time an independent municipality populated mostly by people of North Caucasian ancestry.

General Abdul-Latif Benno, the first tank commander in the Jordanian army, a Chechen. He once turned down Dudayev's invitation to become Chechnya's defense minister.

Shamil is the bearer of one of the proudest Chechen family names. The Bennos originate from the mountainous village of Benno (which they sometimes transliterate as Bino or Beano), in southeastern Chechnya, and they form the largest Chechen *taip*, or clan. Benno estimates that over one-third of the entire Chechen people belong to his clan, a proportion impossible to corroborate. It was the support of his clan that Shamil Benno was trying to enlist in his futile attempt to remove Dudayev from the presidency by peaceful means.

The Bennos dominate the life of the 12,000-strong Chechen community in the Hashemite Kingdom of Jordan. Though the Chechens' share of the general population is minuscule (there are about four million people in Jordan altogether), they have been disproportionately represented in government service, particularly in the armed forces.

Amin Benno, Shamil's father, was the head of royal customs, a probable candidate for a ministerial position in the king's cabinet, and a man widely known and respected in the country. In 1970, however, Amin decided it was time "to go home"—home being a distant piece of land in an isolated corner of a Communist-controlled megastate.

"Going home" to the Caucasus was a practice that the Soviets had encouraged among Christian Armenians who were living in the Middle East. In the mid-1940s a few Armenians heeded the call and moved from Syria and Lebanon to a Soviet Armenia that they had never seen nor been connected to, hoping to help build a homeland for their scattered people. For the Armenians it was a natural choice, Russia having been a safe haven to them and a protector of their nationhood for two centuries; the Chechens, however, had viewed Russia, or the Soviet Union, as their nemesis.

Why, then, did Amin decide to "go back"? "Father hoped his children and grandchildren would be able to grow up as Chechens, *real* Chechens, and that could happen only if they lived among Chechens in their own country," Shamil Benno recalled. "My father recognized that Chechen psychology is incompatible with life in an Arab country. Arab policies and the Arab outlook make it impossible for a Chechen person to develop his distinctive features, though Jordan was much better than the others."

I am tempted to say that Amin Benno's almost irrational attachment to his ancestral land made him something of a Chechen Zionist, though I'm not sure the Bennos of Jordan would appreciate the analogy. To most Muslims, *Zionism* is a bad word. Amin Benno himself was the chief enforcer in Jordan of the Arab economic boycott against what was euphemistically known as "the Zionist entity," Israel. And yet it was his son Shamil who volunteered the Zionist analogy. "To a large extent," he told me, "my father was like Herzl and Jabotinsky," two founding fathers of Zionism. "Just like them, he concluded that the Chechens could not obtain spiritual satisfaction so long as they lived in a foreign land, even if they were offered a measure of equality."

The Benno ancestors had left Chechnya in 1897, in the aftermath of another failed uprising. Thousands of Chechens crossed the Caucasus by foot or ox wagons, into Turkey, and from there to the Holy Land (a term they applied much more broadly than either Christian or Jews, all the way from Arabia, the cradle of the Prophet, to Palestine, Jordan, and Syria).

Another Jordanian Benno, Dr. Murad Benno, a distinguished engineer and the director of the regional Islamic Network on Water Resources, related to me his grandmother's version of the origins of the Chechen presence in Jordan. She was a grown-up at the time of the Benno exodus and lived to be 110.

"Grandmother used to tell the story of how the Chechens—when they were coming out of the Caucasus—spent their first winter, their first year on the road. They reached Erzerum [in what is now eastern Turkey], were heartily welcomed by their fellow Muslims, and were offered good lands on which to settle. But the Chechens refused. They insisted they were headed for the Holy Land. The Ottoman governor implored them to stay, and still they refused. The governor was very upset. 'These people must be lunatic,' he said. 'They are offered the best lands, and they choose the deserts of the south!'

"When the Chechens were finally leaving, the Ottoman troops were ordered to shoot at them—but their rifles were not loaded with bullets, oh, no. The governor ordered that the guns be loaded with medicine, so the Chechens could be cured of their madness."

The old matron's embellishment of history provides us with a wonderful parable on a Chechen characteristic that few would ever question: obstinacy. Chechens appear to draw a certain mischievous satisfaction in their own references to their "madness." General Abdul-Latif Benno, Dr. Murad's first cousin, related to me with great relish the following anecdote.

"In the 1940s, while the British were fighting the [Vichy] French troops in Syria, the British barracks came under heavy shelling. Everyone ran out, with the exception of one man who ran in and who reemerged later with two wounded soldiers left behind by all the others. The British commanding officer stared at him incredulously. 'Are you crazy?' he asked. 'No, sir,' came the answer. *'I am Chechen.'"*

As the Chechens of the Middle East must have found out, their perceived "madness" became a desirable currency for various regimes, beginning with the Ottoman sultan. Not only was he not disappointed with their choice of the "desert lands of the south," but in fact he encouraged them to seek those lands. Then he tried to revive the dwindling fortunes of his empire by forming a military caste of his new North Caucasian subjects.

The first North Caucasians to serve under the Ottoman banner were the Circassians, who had mounted a mass exodus across the Black Sea in 1864 to escape Russian occupation. The circumstances of their departure suggested close collusion between the Russian and Turkish empires, which were otherwise deeply hostile to each other. Under whatever deal was made, Russia rid itself in one fell swoop of a belligerent and unassimilable ethnic group, while the Ottoman dynasty gained some of the most ferocious warriors of the day, whose decades-long resistance to the Russians had bled the czarist army heavily. The sultan grabbed the Circassians eagerly and a few years later used them against his rebellious Bulgarian subjects. The atrocities they inflicted on these Christian peasants appalled West Europe and were instrumental in reinforcing Western Turkophobia, which persists to this day.

The sultan also deployed some Circassians along the southern frontiers of his empire, settling them mostly in what is now Syria, where many tens of thousands still live. More Circassians were encouraged to settle the wilderness east of the Jordan River, where no community of humans, let alone a state, had existed since antiquity. In 1878, Circassians founded the town of Amman, the future capital of the yet-to-be-born kingdom of Jordan. The city remained largely Circassian until the mid-twentieth century. A street in downtown Amman today is named after the founders, *Muhajireen Shara'*, "the Immigrants Street." In a way, the Circassians were cofounders of modern Jordan. They also gave the kingdom its first and perhaps best-known prime minister, Sa'id al-Mufti, as well as an exceedingly large number of generals.

Many Chechens, and also some Ingush, followed in the Circassians' footsteps. That is how the family of Kunta Haji moved to Iraq, where two Chechen/Ingush villages still exist today, and where Chechens have excelled until very recently in the military trade. In Jordan the Chechens founded four towns, one of which evolved into the kingdom's second-largest city, Zarqa. There was a time when Chechen speech filled the streets of Zarqa and Sweilih, the Amman suburb from which many of the prominent Bennos of Jordan hailed. Chechens were mayors of both communities, they built the first mosques, and they buried the first dead in cemeteries that still bear their hallmarks. Both locales still have vibrant Chechen minorities—but the demography there as well as elsewhere in Jordan has changed fundamentally. Beginning in 1948, the establishment of the State of Israel drove a multitude of Palestinian refugees and deportees into the East Bank. Standing on the top of Sweilih's "West Mountain," one can see in the distance, down in the plain, the largest Palestinian refugee camp in Jordan, Baq'a, a sprawling slum, where perhaps 100,000 people live in dire poverty.

Almost overnight in 1948, the city of Zarqa also experienced a massive infusion of Palestinian refugees, and it is now predominantly Palestinian. In the late 1960s, it fell under the control of Yasser Arafat's PLO which came close to taking over the entire country. During a few weeks in 1970, which came to be known in the Palestinian lexicon as "Black September," the king struck back, killing many thousands of Palestinians in the process. Nowhere was the task of dislodging the PLO more urgent and crucial than in Zarqa. The king's army moved forcefully to reclaim the city under the firm command of Abdul-Latif Benno, Jordan's foremost tank officer, a Chechen. His ruthlessness is remembered fondly by few Palestinians.

I called on the general in his modest residence in a suburb of Amman in February 1995, shortly after the peace treaty had been signed between Jordan and Israel. A heavy-set man of sixty-one, bald, with a small gray mustache, he projected warmth and sincerity, using graceful body language to help his somewhat limited English, which he spoke in a thick Arabic accent.

"Believe me," he said, thumping a clenched fist against his chest, "if God were to tell me, 'You die so the King lives two more years,' I would happily give my life away. Because if I die, only my children lose a father, but if *he* dies, *everyone* loses a father: my children, all Jordanians, and I'll go even farther—all Arabs and all Muslims. They all need this man."

"This man," King Hussein, who ruled for nearly fifty years, had rewarded his faithful Abdul-Latif with plenty of royal affection. Three framed letters from the king adorned a wall in the general's living room, including one in the king's own handwriting, on stationery capped by a crown and signed simply "Hussein."

Abdul-Latif had initially joined the Arab Legion, as the army was then known, as a teenager, when its supreme commander was still a British general. He declined an invitation to attend the military academy, where graduation entailed automatic promotion to officer rank. Rather, he accomplished something fairly unique in the annals of modern armies: he rose to the rank of general simply by climbing the ladder, slowly and diligently, from private, through noncommissioned officer, to the higher ranks.

Abdul-Latif's first visit to Chechnya took place in 1968, when the Soviets partially lifted the iron curtain over the Caucasus and encouraged North Caucasians throughout the Middle East to visit their ancestral lands. They hoped some of them might be tempted to come back, but even more, they hoped to win the friendship of an active community with considerable clout in various Middle Eastern armies. The cold war was raging, and Soviet arms had just been beaten soundly in the 1967 Arab-Israeli war. Perhaps the Soviets entertained the notion that a young Jordanian officer with ethnic roots in the Caucasus could become an agent of influence. And so they granted Abdul-Latif the visa he had requested.

Abdul-Latif squeezed his entire family—his wife and four children—into a tiny ten-year-old Volkswagen Beetle and drove all the way from Amman to the Caucasus, across Syria, Turkey, Bulgaria, Romania, Ukraine, and Russia (the shorter route, across the Turkish-Soviet border, was off-limits), an adventure so amazing as to sound almost like a promotional stunt on behalf of the German auto manufacturer. It took the Bennos ten days and nights of nonstop driving across two continents before they saw the unassuming city of Grozny and took their first breaths of its air, fouled by an environmentally unfriendly petrochemical industry.

When I heard the story while standing in the general's living room, I felt a bit dizzy, former owner of a Beetle that I am.

Ten days in a Beetle? I asked. Would it not have been better to take an ox wagon? (The general keeps at home a miniature ox wagon, the like of which was used one hundred years ago by his ancestors on their way out of the Caucasus.)

The general laughed heartily. "Let me tell you something. Only when I finally arrived in Grozny did I begin to understand what I was doing. And I realized I was mad. Mad! Driving an old Beetle in the Soviet Union, without any spare parts available anywhere! And little kids inside!"

In 1979 King Hussein made Abdul-Latif Benno the first military attaché of Jordan in Moscow—an ironic twist, perhaps not entirely unintended, in that Benno was the first Chechen general ever seen in the Soviet capital. One evening at a military reception, Benno was approached by a dapper young Soviet air force colonel with a handsome mustache. "Are you really Chechen?" the colonel asked him in halting Chechen.

The general nodded. "And who might you be?" he asked.

"Dudayev," the colonel answered, "Jokar Dudayev, a fellow Chechen."

"If so, how come you speak Chechen so poorly?" the general snapped. He was to find out the reason later: Dudayev's interest in his people and his homeland had been limited. He had married a Russian woman, and Russian was the language spoken at home.

Exactly ten years later, Benno's and Dudayev's paths crossed again. By that time, both were retired generals, Dudayev having become the first-ever Chechen general in the Soviet army, the commander of an air force division. The venue of their meeting was Grozny, where the first Congress of the Chechen People was taking place. Dudayev, now a full convert to the nationalist cause, was voted leader of the Congress, a position from which he would launch himself into the presidency of rebellious Chechnya within the year.

General Abdul-Latif was a guest of honor at the Congress, one of many from the Chechen diaspora. He grimaced at the lack of linguistic skills among many of the local speakers, but at no time did he grimace more than when Dudayev rose to speak.

Later, he told me, Dudayev offered him the position of minister of defense in the first rebel government. "I asked him, 'Whom will I take orders from?' He answered, 'Why, from me of course.' I said, 'Jokar, how can I take orders from you? I do not speak Russian, and you do not speak Chechen.'"

Another prominent Jordanian Chechen who refused honors in the rebel government was the venerable Sheikh Abdul-Baqi Jammu, a religious figure who had served at one point as a minister in the Jordanian government. The sheikh's name was raised in 1991 as a candidate to become Chechnya's first president. Later he explained to a Jordanian newspaper why he turned down the offer:

> I thought that a religious, pious, and competent man would win the [1991] elections. I did not know that the elections would be won by a Russian agent named Jokar Dudayev. The election result was designed to prevent the Chechens from winning political independence, and, consequently, prevent the Islamic people from winning independence. . . . Dudayev damaged the country, harmed the Chechen people, and involved them in the woes of wars.

General Benno and Sheikh Jammu were not the only Jordanian Chechens who grew disenchanted with Dudayev's leadership. Another was Fakhruddin Daghestani, a brilliant scientist who became the president of Jordan's Royal Scientific Society, the director-general of the kingdom's Natural Resources Authority, and a founding fellow of the international Islamic Academy of Science. A former senior engineer at IBM in Minnesota and the holder of a Ph.D. from a major American university, Dr. Daghestani had many constructive ideas on how to prepare for independence, rather than proclaim it right away.

"If Dudayev had had brains, he would have called on people such as myself to set a path for true independence thirty years hence," Daghestani told me in his idiomatic, flawless English. "If he had issued a call on a Thursday, I would have been on my way by Sunday. We would have worked on infrastructure, on economic development, on obtaining foreign aid. In Jordan alone, I would have found him twenty experts on the level of World Bank consultants, people with enormous practical knowledge of agriculture, medicine, technology—modern nation-builders.

"After all, what have I been doing here since 1971? Exactly that. I helped build this institute [the Royal Scientific Society] from scratch. It is self-supported, it employs six hundred people, it has equipment worth $50 million, all obtained through international grants. . . . I could enlist hundreds like me. Do you know how many told us, 'Just give us a place to sleep in at night, and we'll go to Chechnya for three months, to lay the foundations for a new nation'?

"But that was not the case. Dudayev looked for bullets instead of builders."

Daghestani spoke these sorrowful words in early 1995, three months into the Chechen war, when people were expecting the worst and the notion of a military victory over Russia existed nowhere, not even in Dudayev's often-deluded mind.

The winter of 1995 represented a grim time for the Chechens. No longer anonymous and invisible on the world scene, they were counting their dead and missing. Before the war started, a number of Jordanian Chechens had moved to Grozny and were now trapped there. The Russian authorities made much of their presence and suggested that it was a proof that the resistance to the Russian onslaught was driven not by native Chechens but by "foreign mercenaries." King Hussein himself interceded with Moscow to obtain the release of some Jordanian Chechens held in Russian captivity. I visited one of them just a couple of days after his return to his family in Zarqa. He had been held in Russian prison for nearly two months, he said, and was repeatedly beaten and humiliated.

Many Jordanian Chechens told me they would gladly volunteer to fight if it were logistically possible. Absent that, members of the Chechen community in Amman would gather a few nights a week in a small apartment in Sweilih, where a committee of solidarity with the Chechen republic had its office. Sa'id Benno, a former cabinet minister, was the committee's head. The recipient of an engineering degree from Baghdad University, he was the community's elder, a gracious man, deeply religious and gravely concerned. Day in and day out he fired off letters of protest and exhortation to world leaders, which his son Hashem would type in Arabic and translate into English. "This is the least I can do," Sa'id Benno smiled. "I'd much rather be there fighting, but even if I am here I cannot sit idly by."

Here is how I got to know Dr. Daghestani and the Chechens of Jordan. In December 1994, just days after the outbreak of the war in Chechnya (the first round, as it turned out), an English-language newspaper in Amman reproduced an article I wrote for *The Washington Post* and the *International Herald Tribune* about Chechen history. The newspaper identified me as an Israeli journalist, which must have come as a surprise to Jordanian Chechens, given that the piece was not only sympathetic to their cause but ended with an uncommon note of empathy toward Muslims:

> The West will be told—and will be inclined to believe—that the oppression of the Chechens is part and parcel of a cosmic struggle against "Islamic extremism" that rages from Gaza to Algiers, from Tehran to Khartoum. Russians will seek Western sympathy. They should not be given it.

One day in early 1995, while I was in Tel Aviv, I received a phone call from the then-director-general of Israel's Ministry of Energy, Amos Ron. "I have just met a man in Amman by the name of Daghestani,"* the Israeli official told me. "He is of Chechen descent. He read your article about his people and asked me to extend an invitation to you to come and visit him in Amman."

I gasped. Only four months earlier, I had met Shamil Benno in

---

* Because family names, in the Western sense, are a novelty in the Middle East, many existing names were born as geographic attributes, with little attention paid to subtleties. Daghestani's ancestors were Chechen, all right, but insofar as the Arab environment was concerned, they came from the neighborhood of Daghestan, a term far better known to Arabs than the recently invented *Chechen*. (Later immigrants to Jordan claimed the name Sheshani, which is the Arabic pronunciation of *Chechen*. Others, such as the Bennos, are simply named after their original villages in the Chechen mountains.)

Grozny and told him how much I hoped that one day my Israeli passport would no longer prevent me from crossing the river into Jordan and visiting the Chechens and the Circassians there, of whom I heard so much. I had no way of knowing that six weeks later Israel and Jordan would terminate a forty-six-year-long state of war and exchange ambassadors, let alone that I would soon walk on the slopes of Sweilih's West Mountain, overlooking Amman, in the company of Hashem Benno, Shamil's first cousin and Daghestani's son-in-law, talking about the history of Chechen settlement in Jordan and hearing that "that is a Chechen house, and that is, and that, and that, and that one as well."

At one point I told Hashem incredulously how my pursuit of the Chechens had coincided with the transformation of the Middle East, and "here I am, switching from a Benno in Grozny to a Benno in Amman, which would have not been possible only a few weeks ago." Hashem, an articulate young man, laughed generously and said, "Well, Yo'av, this is your *fate*."

Indeed. Exactly at such moments, when roads long taken reach unexpected turns and dreams rarely verbalized assume concrete meaning, one runs out of sequential explanations and rationalizations and is left with the metaphysics of fate.

Three weeks after Amos Ron's phone call, at eight in the morning on a Thursday, in the Beit She'an valley, at the northernmost crossing point between Israel and Jordan, a smiling, bespectacled, stocky man wearing a tall Astrakhan hat typical of the Caucasus was awaiting me at the other end of the Hussein Bridge. It was Fakhruddin Daghestani in person who picked me up and drove me to his home in Amman.

But for the vicissitudes of Middle Eastern times, Dr. Daghestani might not have been a Jordanian scientist at all. He could have enjoyed the duller life of a country squire in the least probable of all places: the Golan Heights, which have been occupied by Israel since 1967. Daghestani was born in the Syrian town of Quneitra, the Golan provincial capital, in 1936. His father, he told me, was one of the largest private landowners in the Golan.

"In my youth," he reminisced, standing in the garden of his comfortable Amman villa against the backdrop of a hilly, undeveloped landscape, "every summer we were out in our farmland, near the western border [Syria's 1948 armistice line with Israel]. My father was quite well-to-do since his business included livestock, sheep, horses, camels, planting vegetables, wheat, corn, rice, trees, you name it—he had it, including even beekeeping. There were about six or seven thousand Chechens in Quneitra—they even had a special section of the town to themselves."

Daghestani the elder did not trust either money or gold. Whenever God smiled on his crop, he would take the money and invest it in real estate, always in the Golan. Money could depreciate in value, he reasoned, and governments came and went, but no one could take land from him. Little did he know.

"Soon after the occupation," Daghestani said, "the Golan Heights were emptied by the Israelis, an act of mass deportation similar to what has happened in history many times to many people."

Ten years before the loss, it was the Golan's plentiful soil that paid for young Fakhruddin's studies in the United States. He arrived in St. Louis in 1957, perhaps the first Chechen ever seen in the American Midwest. "I remember going into a class of thirty students, all Americans. I stood at the door and said in my mind, 'Well, you guys will hear a Chechen come. And I am going to be better than all of you.'" He paused to laugh, a twinkle of mischief in his eyes. "And my grades were consistently better throughout."

One day in 1959, a rare Soviet delegation paid a visit to the campus of his university in Missouri to cultivate the cause of early détente. So rare was such a visit, since the mild thaw of the post-Stalinist era had barely taken effect, that a full house was awaiting them. When the time came to pose questions to the Soviet guests, Daghestani took the floor. He wanted to know why his people had been deported en masse to the steppes of Central Asia. The deportation had taken place fifteen years earlier, but the outside world was still nearly unaware and uninterested.

The Soviet guests held an impromptu consultation, away from the microphones, and then, according to Daghestani, the head of the delegation replied tersely, "The questioner is in error. A nation such as the 'Chechens' does not exist, and the events described by him never took place."

Daghestani retorted angrily, "You have always been consistent in telling lies throughout the centuries, and this is just an additional small lie." Daghestani paused to accentuate the dramatic effect of the subsequent words. "*I am a Chechen,*" he said before reclaiming his seat. To his surprise, he says, "there was an uproar of applause from all the students who were listening to the exchange." Forty years later, Daghestani's hostility to Russia is undiminished. "We have had a holocaust—what else would you call those acts of genocide—once in a generation, losing each time 25 percent, 40 percent, or even 50 percent of our entire population? By the end of the great Caucasian War [in 1859] the nation had been reduced to old men, women, children, and only a handful of able-bodied men."

The result of repeated suicidal spasms, I murmured. Is that really necessary?

"Do not ask a Chechen this question," Daghestani snapped back. "Ask it of Russia. Russia is a country that had one million square kilometers in its possession and went on to expand and swallow another seventeen million square kilometers. Ask them why they occupy other peoples' lands. Colonialism is practically over in the world with one exception: Russia."

Daghestani lit another American cigarette. His old-fashioned chain smoking was relaxed, his motions measured and slow, almost gracious, as gentlemen of the Levant have smoked for generations. The habit nonetheless appeared to me a throwback to the American 1950s. A student from a remote Syrian province, the product of a pious, hierarchically conscious society, ever mindful of his minority status, never fully at ease with the permissiveness and indiscretion of American student culture, young Daghestani threw himself eagerly into at least one all-American activity, the consumption of nicotine.

America was good to him, and his doctorate *cum laude* launched him safely on the corporate ladder. He landed a plum job at IBM and could have looked forward to a rewarding career and material comfort. But after marrying his wife Na'imah-Polla,* a Chechen from Jordan, and fathering two of his six children on American soil, he resisted the melting pot. He was determined to bring up his children traditionally, as Chechens and Muslims, and America was simply not conducive to that.

"We know much about our history," Daghestani said in the solemn tone that he assumed each time he made a sweeping statement, "and it's a glorious history, in the sense that a whole nation was almost wiped out in the defense of land, country, identity, and so forth. So here we are, in affluence, luxury, peace. . . . We feel that we cannot break this bond, the continuation of the culture, because we are indebted to all the people who died in order to preserve something.

"Let all that go without any resistance? It is a chain, and we are a link in the chain. Personally, I have no right to take that away or produce children who are not directly linked to our history."

* "Na'imah" being the commonly used Arab name, "Polla" the intimate Chechen name, meaning "butterfly."

Na'imah-Polla and Fakhruddin Daghestani pose by a patriotic mural featuring the Vainakh towers, a symbol of antiquity common to the Chechens and the Ingush. "It is a chain," Dr. Daghestani says, "and we are a link in the chain."

And so Daghestani had to decide where to go. His native Quneitra was not only under occupation but in fact simply was no more. Shortly after the 1967 war, Israeli bulldozers leveled Quneitra to the ground in an act of senseless vandalism with odd echoes of the Old Testament. (Quneitra was returned to Syria in 1974, under the terms of a new ceasefire agreement. The Syrians have chosen not to rebuild it but to leave the town in ruins as a testament to Israel's misconduct.) Finally, because his wife Na'imah was a native of Jordan and had many relatives there, the young family headed to Amman.

Na'imah brought to the marriage not only her natural beauty and grace but also impeccable education and immersion in all matters Chechen. As her husband acknowledges, Na'imah's Chechen speech was superior to his at the time of their marriage, and her knowledge of Chechen traditions was also greater.

One reason is that Jordan has encouraged its North Caucasian minorities to maintain their distinct identity. They have been given seats in parliament (three for the Circassians and one for the Chechens, under the present electoral law) and at least one cabinet seat, which usually rotates between the two communities.

Many Jordanians have argued recently that this quota system is obsolete and divisive. Perhaps. And yet this system, which costs Jordan so little (what is one portfolio in a cabinet which consisted in 1999 of twenty-six departments and fifty-three subdepartments? What are a handful of secure parliamentary seats in a legislature of eighty?) has helped preserve human diversity, one that is frowned upon elsewhere in the intolerant Middle East. The Circassian school in Amman is the envy of Circassians the world over, the Chechen speech of Sweilih is a yardstick for purity and precision. There may be more values and certainly greater historical and cultural awareness among Jordanian North Caucasians than there is in any part of the Circassian diaspora and perhaps most parts of the North Caucasus itself. Survival of human diversity has been on my mind throughout my excursions to the peoples of the Caucasus, and I found more of it in Amman than I have in Nalchik, or Makhachkala, or indeed Grozny.

One evening I had the pleasure of visiting Fat'hi Taifan, a young Chechen businessman, formerly a dancing instructor. Fat'hi was a walking mosaic of the Middle East: his mother was Chechen, and his father was half-Palestinian and half-Kurdish. The father was born in the formerly Arab town of Beit She'an, now inhabited mostly by North African Jews. The family fled Israeli occupation in 1948. Fat'hi was therefore a result of three cataclysms that had involved mass uprooting: the loss of the Caucasus to Russia in the mid-nineteenth century, the loss of Kurdish freedom to Turkey, Iraq, and Iran in the early twentieth century, and the loss of much of Palestine to the Jews in the mid-twentieth century.

He harbored little overt resentment and even surprised me with a few Hebrew words (which many Jordanians have picked up from Israeli television broadcasts, easily viewable in Amman). After giving me a guided nocturnal tour of the Chechen neighborhoods, he took me to his home in Sweilih, where I met his three-year-old nephew Abdallah. Strikingly, the little boy could speak not a word of Arabic—his entire vocabulary consisted of a few dozen Chechen words. That was common among Chechens in Jordan, Fat'hi and others told me. "You first teach your children Chechen, because no one else will; Arabic they will pick up at school." But Fat'hi's brother had been refused admission to the first grade of elementary school because he had no working knowledge of Arabic. He had to go home, acquire the skills, and come back a year later.

Fat'hi had an impressive library of Chechen music cassettes from Grozny, and he used to listen to them avidly at home and while driving his van. "Fat'hi," I asked him, "why do you Chechens try so hard? Why is it so important to remain Chechen?"

Fat'hi smiled broadly. "Why? Because we are always *homesick for Chechnya.* We want to go home."

The history of North Caucasians in the service of the Hashemite dynasty goes back to its very first years, shortly after the British, in 1921, created a little fiefdom for Prince Abdallah of Arabia east of the Jordan River, halfway from Mecca to Damascus. He had little to sustain him in power, save for his sponsors and bodyguards. At one point in 1921, the British had to dispatch airplanes and tanks to check a drive from the south against the Hashemites by the rival Saudis. Similarly, nationalists in Syria, then under French control, were eager to treat themselves to the northern parts of the Hashemite state, which they considered an artificial creation of a colonialist mind bent on dividing the Arab house against itself.

Who saved the fertile north, with its precious water resources, for the dynasty? Who but a Chechen officer named Ahmad Ramzi. Murad Benno, the Jordanian-Chechen geophysicist, says that Ramzi, a former officer in the Ottoman army, was put in charge of subordinating the north of Jordan to the rule of the Hashemites. "Ahmad Ramzi was so tough that even today the Arab women in the villages tell their children when they want them to go to bed, 'If you don't go to bed, I'll call Ahmad Ramzi.' He earned that notoriety among the Arabs of the north because he was very harsh with their big chiefs. He told them time and again that if they didn't do it right, if they were not loyal, if they didn't pay their dues to the government, he would treat them very badly. That is how the Chechens got the reputation of being very loyal and became so prominent in Jordanian life."

Loyalty was also offered in abundance by the more numerous Circassians. A case in point is the Shurdum family, where two brothers, Ihsan and Tahsin, rose to the rank of general. Ihsan was commander of the Jordanian air force and is said to have battled Israeli aircraft in the late 1960s while flying his British-made Hawker-Hunter. Tahsin was head of Jordan's military intelligence and led the Jordanian delegation in the military talks that preceded the signing of the peace treaty with Israel, in October 1994.

I asked General Ihsan why the North Caucasians have done so well in Jordan. "Well," he replied in fine, cultivated English, "perhaps we started early, and we kept steady at our jobs, and we did not bend with all the currents that went around in the Middle East, especially the political currents. . . . We did not sway with the winds of those days. And I think that was, to a great degree, credited to our belief in the country, our belief in its leadership."

One evening I sat down with General Ihsan and others at the office of a Circassian cultural organization in Amman, surrounded by framed photos of Kabardin princes and Shapsug folk dancers. The general, a handsome man in his early fifties, an immaculate dresser with a well-groomed handlebar mustache, spoke to me about the North Caucasians' spiritual attachment to Jordan. "Remember that people emigrated from the Caucasus also for religious reasons. In their mind, they were going to the Holy Land. In fact, when Circassians arrived in Aleppo [in northern Syria], they took off their shoes, so sacred was the ground to them."

Religious sentiments were also at the core of the North Caucasians' attachment to the Jordanian crown. The Hashemites claim direct lineage from the Prophet, a distinction that all Muslims value highly in light of Muhammad's announcement to his disciples before his death that he was "giving" them his family. Not only was the land holy, but now its rulers had a measure of holiness as well.

The list of North Caucasians in Jordanian public service is remarkably long given their tiny numbers. (Taken together, the Chechens and the Circassians fall short of 100,000, not even 3 percent of the overall population.)

"It is simply in their blood," Dr. Daghestani says of the militarily inclined Chechens of the Middle East. "A Chechen cannot afford to be a coward. If he were, he would simply be disowned by his people. That is how men are expected to live—not to sit behind a stall in the market and weigh tomatoes on scales. That is a matter for women. Service in the armed forces is always a Chechen's first option. And it has nothing to do with whose army they serve in. If Chechens served, say, in the Vietnamese army, they would still behave the same. It is a sense of patriotism and duty toward the country of their residence."

Which is why Chechens have excelled throughout the Middle East. In Turkey, where tens of thousands of ethnic Chechens live,* officers of Chechen extraction have reached the highest echelons in the military. Even in Iraq, where only a couple thousand live, half a dozen Chechen (or by some designation, Ingush) generals served Saddam Hussein during the war with Iran in the 1980s. The same applies to the Circassians,

---

* Estimates of the North Caucasian populations in Turkey are highly tentative. The Turkish state does not recognize ethnic varieties among its Muslims, and all are considered Turkish. There may be, however, millions of Turks who have at least some North Caucasian ancestry.

whose presence in various Middle Eastern armies has been exceedingly large.

The Chechens in exile also retain a temperamental volatility that has gotten them in trouble in the past and might still again. Their belligerence was on open display in the spring of 1995, when the campus of the University of Amman became a battlefield between a handful of Chechen and Circassian students on the one hand and hundreds of their Arab peers on the other. The North Caucasians carried the day, and only an intervention of the royal family and elders of the community brought to an end a bloody incident that could easily have spilled over into nonacademic spheres.

Among the Chechens fighting were sons of prominent figures, even former cabinet ministers. I talked to some of them after the event and was amazed by their audacity and apparent lack of self-restraint. They insisted that they had merely defended the slighted honor of a North Caucasian woman. Others told me tensions of a more profound nature had percolated for a long while, and it had been only a matter of time before they surfaced violently.

It appeared to me that the elders were treating their young with forgiving smiles. I do not know if the Chechen language has a phrase remotely like "boys will be boys," but that notion was implicit in our exchange on the matter.

"THE GOLAN SHOULD BE CHECHEN" (IT NEARLY WAS)

The astonishing pace of Middle East events landed Fakhruddin Daghestani the most improbable of assignments. In 1995, twenty-seven years after the loss of his family's Golan estates to Israel, he was seated in the lobby of a Tel Aviv hotel, sipping Israeli juice, and discussing with Israeli officials the one issue in the Middle East that is truly a matter of life and death: water.

The irony was almost perfect. Control of water resources was a major factor in the escalation that led to the 1967 Arab-Israeli war, which led in turn to Israel's occupation of the Golan. Daghestani was now the head of Jordan's Energy and Mineral Resources Authority. Israel and Jordan had just concluded peace, and the fair allocation of meager water resources now topped the agenda. Dr. Daghestani's presence at the talks made some of his Israeli counterparts uncomfortable. One can imagine them thinking to themselves, "Why in the world would Jordan send this *Syrian* to talk to us? Are there not enough Jordanians?" One Israeli source described Daghestani to me as a "tough negotiator," so tough that some Israelis privately suspected him of deliberate obstructionism.

Daghestani had no such intentions. His commitment to Jordan and the Arab cause struck me as honorable, not intransigent. He had little love for what Israelis are fond of calling "the Zionist enterprise"—and why would he, having been disinherited as a result of Zionism's success? But his belief in the advantages of peace was as strong as anyone's. Moreover, it was enshrined in pragmatism and rationalism, rare commodities between the Mediterranean Sea and the desert. He drew a distinction between his private experience and his public duties, and he pursued his new assignment with the same enthusiasm that had characterized his previous undertakings.

To Daghestani, peace was not optional—it was a requirement of life. Each foray he made across the border, whether to the bustling commercial centers of Tel Aviv or to a kibbutz in the heart of the wilderness, he confronted Israeli success. He was a remarkably perceptive visitor, with a keen eye for methodology, who unsentimentally, if unhappily, recognized Israel's gigantic technological advantage over the Arabs, both in planning and in execution.

As I listened to him in three separate meetings, two in Amman and one in Tel Aviv, I could not help but feel the utmost admiration for this renaissance man. His penchant for learning had not mellowed as he inched toward sixty, and he rarely let the inevitable human prejudices interfere with his ability to observe and absorb.

Shortly after my return from Amman, the main foreign affairs program on Israeli television commissioned from me a report on the Chechens of Jordan, an unexpected local angle to a conflict in a faraway land. I ended my piece with Fakhruddin Daghestani's recollections of his youth in the Golan. As it happened, the most contentious subject at the time in the Israeli public arena was the future of the Golan. An extraparliamentary movement had been formed to oppose any Israeli territorial concessions, which the late Yitzhak Rabin, then prime minister, was widely assumed to favor. The program's editor and anchor, Immanuel Halperin, a sharp-eyed observer of human events, signed off with the following tongue-in-cheek comment: "Here we argue about whether the Golan ought to be Israeli or Syrian. Perhaps it should be neither. Perhaps it should simply be Chechen."

Indeed, one cannot help but reflect on history's sense of humor, or lack of it: Chechen deportees, ejected from their land by Russia in the late nineteenth century, sought and found security and prosperity in the ancient mountains of basalt overlooking the Sea of Galilee—only to be ejected again by a nation of ejectees, deportees, and refugees. I sensed no bitterness in Daghestani's words about the Golan, even though Israel had rendered his family penniless and reduced his old father from a proud proprietor to the ranks of the dispossessed.

"I always knew the occupation was temporary and that peace would prevail," Daghestani said. "Sad as I was at the loss, I knew that someday it would come back. When the Golan is liberated, I hope I will return, get my father's lands, and try to develop them, continue what my family had started before."

A long interview on Israeli television was not a risk-free exercise for
Dr. Daghestani. The peace with Israel was not popular in Jordan—the
majority Palestinian population there believed they had little to gain
from it, and felt betrayed that the king seemed to allow the Israelis to
continuously occupy the West Bank and deny Palestinian rights. Most
Jordanians continued to treat Israelis such as myself with a measure of
suspicion and discomfort.

Eventually, as the Israeli-Jordanian peace turned stale and rewardless
and a new government in Israel dispatched Mossad agents to the streets
of Amman to assassinate hostile Palestinians, the spirit of reconciliation
weakened, and contacts with Israelis became a considerable liability to
the dwindling numbers of Jordanians who initiated them or reciprocated Israeli interest.

My Chechen friends, by inviting me to Jordan, by treating me as well
as they did, and by appearing on Israeli television, were placing themselves in the line of fire, figuratively but perhaps literally as well. Exposure of that nature could easily destroy a man's career and deprive him
of his well-being.

On a February day in 1995, when the peace was still young and winter
snow was still mixed with an ounce of euphoria and hope, the Daghestani family assembled in its kitchen to welcome me, with every member
doing his bit. Dr. Fakhruddin fried the eggs, Mrs. Daghestani poured
the orange juice, their son-in-law Hashem sliced the bread. (I was the
only beneficiary of all this endeavor, for it was the holy fasting month of
Ramadan.) Talal, the youngest, was running errands around the house in
a frenzy. Soon three daughters would show up.

The only absentees were the second-eldest daughter and the eldest
son, both of whom were in the United States. The daughter was accompanying her husband (a captain in Jordan's Royal Air Force), and the son
was completing his studies in a Virginia university, largely paid for by a
"bicycle scholarship" he had won on account of his cycling excellence.
"I strictly forbade him to take his bicycle along with him to the States,"
Daghestani related with a grin. "I told him he had to go and study, not
ride around. He disobeyed me, and by doing so saved me a fortune."
The disobeyed father shook his head with mock disapproval.

The youngest son, Talal, was named after King Hussein's father, Talal
bin-Abdallah, and the one who had named him was none other than the
king's brother and then-designated heir, Crown Prince Hassan. When
Na'imah was pregnant with Talal, the crown prince visited the house,
looked at her, and said: "You are going to have a baby boy, and you

should name him after my father." How did the prince know? I asked. The Daghestanis smiled. "Oh, well, he is after all of the Prophet's Holy Family."

At the time of my visit, Talal was fourteen years old, a handsome adolescent with thickening soft down above his upper lip; a speaker of excellent English; faithful to his ancestral legacy but also a great fan of hard rock music; a "baby brother" who was giving his older sisters a hard time. At the same time, he seemed to be as loyal to the Chechen cause as any of his elders. "Of course," he said when I asked him whether he would like to fight for his people's independence.

Talal had already visited Chechnya in 1991, accompanying his parents on one of their three forays to the old country. The Daghestanis had done it the Chechen way: by driving the family car across eight nations. The first time, in 1983, was a moving journey in search of roots and meaning. Na'imah Daghestani went looking for a great-uncle with whom her family had had no contact for over eighty years. The uncle, living in a remote village in the mountains, recognized her instantly, even though he had never seen even a picture of her. "I was waiting," he said. "I knew you would come." He died shortly thereafter.

The second trip came close to being a journey of loss. One day, on a narrow mountain road overlooking a magnificent valley, Dr. Daghestani

How do you say in Chechen "Boys will be boys"? A youthful moment in the Benno residence in Amman. Featuring (left to right): Talal Daghestani, his brother-in-law Hashem Benno, and Hashem's younger brothers, Muhammad and Ala'uddin

stopped his old Mercedes, and the family members got out to get a bird's-eye view of the landscape. By the time they had inhaled enough mountain air and were ready to proceed, Talal was missing. He had wanted to have a better look at the river below, and had gone for a little unauthorized walk. He lost his balance and dropped off the rock's edge into the ravine. His scream was drowned out by the loud sound of the river flow. The free fall would have taken Talal all the way to the bottom, but he managed to grab a little tree and hold on to it, bleeding and in great pain.

Horrified, members of his family spotted him there, but none of them was particularly dextrous or accomplished enough in mountain climbing to extricate Talal from what seemed to be his destiny. Local villagers who arrived on the scene offered Na'imah Daghestani words of wise fatalism. "Thirty people have fallen into the ravine in the course of the years," they told her. "No one has ever been rescued alive. This is the will of God." Would this tall, beautiful woman, who had never stopped yearning for the land of her ancestors, have to sacrifice her youngest to that land?

And then with unsettling suddenness, a car appeared and stopped. Three young men got out and immediately let themselves down the rock by rope. An hour later they reappeared with Talal in their arms— and almost instantly disappeared, before the stunned Daghestanis even had the opportunity to thank them.

Such was the miracle of Talal's life. The chain that his father had spoken of would continue. My first glimpse of Talal was on the fringes of his parents' kitchen, away from the table, totally submissive to his elders, as would be expected of a young Chechen.

Dr. Daghestani intimated that he was in charge of breakfast once a week, on Fridays, but that it was highly unusual. "Chechen men are never to be seen in the kitchen," he laughed. Hashem seconded his father-in-law, "My grandmother used to say, 'Blessed be the house where the man cooks.'"

Dr. Daghestani's willingness to break with tradition, however, went only so far. His large family was run the way Chechen families had always been run: by sticking to a strict hierarchical discipline, in which the father-husband is the sole source of authority. Though every member of the family spoke excellent English, replete with American colloquialisms, and though everyone had a good notion of the outside world and Western culture, everyone was still bound by tradition.

I asked them about the odds of the survival of Chechen culture and tradition in their diaspora and was told that the preservation of the language was the best guarantee. Na'imah Daghestani admitted that she was not always able to force linguistic discipline on her children, the three who were still at home. "It's amazing," Na'imah said. "At home we tell them, 'Speak your language, speak Chechen.' Sometimes they do, sometimes they don't. But once we go out, walking in the street, they automatically start speaking it, so the people around us do not understand." The daughters burst out laughing. "It has become our secret language," they said.

I turned to the younger daughter, Suha, a short-haired brunette with pretty if frail features, and asked her whether *her* children would speak Chechen.

"Of course they will," she replied.

You have no doubt of that? I persisted.

"No," she said, "not at all."

I know it is a bit early for you, Suha, I asked. You are only eighteen. But do you assume you'll be marrying a Chechen man?

She giggled with evident embarrassment. "Yes, of course," she said.

Is it absolutely impossible that you will fall in love and marry somebody who is not Chechen?

She giggled again, covered her brow with her hand, and lowered her eyes. I was sorry to make her so uncomfortable.

Her mother came to her rescue. "Her father will have to make sure that she does not fall in love," Na'imah Daghestani said, with only a faint hint of a smile. I do not think she was kidding.

I turned to her husband. How will you make sure, Dr. Daghestani?

Na'imah interjected, "He will put his foot down."

Dr. Daghestani's body language testified to his displeasure at this turn of the conversation. Leaning away from me, he was clearly struggling to maintain his composure, "They will never get married until they get my blessing," he finally let out, calmly but firmly. "And they know precisely *how* they will get my blessing."

I turned to Najwa, the elder of the two daughters still living at home. What about you? I asked. Will *your* children speak Chechen?

Najwa, brown-haired and blue-eyed, betrayed not the slightest sign of confusion or uneasiness. She was clearly blessed with an independent spirit. "I will never go against his will," she said, gesturing toward her father, "but personally I am never going to get married." Loud laughter filled the room, a welcome relief from the tense moments. Najwa added, "So you see, for me the question of my children's language does not even exist."

We then had a lighthearted exchange in which Dr. Daghestani pretended to bargain with his rebellious daughter over her future marriage. "You will not get married until you have finished your master's degree," he suggested. Najwa, energized by her own audacity, counterbargained. "Until I have got my Ph.D.," she said, hinting at her own academic preference to study overseas, in America.

Months later I came back to Amman with my friend Amit Breuer, an Israeli film producer who had become interested in the Chechens of Jordan and entertained the idea of featuring them in a documentary we thought we might call *Mother, Why Am I So Chechen?* Amit, as a woman, gained Najwa's confidence far more easily than I could. I hope I do not show myself to be entirely indiscreet in quoting Najwa's "secret wish," expressed to Amit, "to be a racing car driver." I thought that Najwa's freedom craving was a credit, however unintended or undesirable, to Dr. Daghestani and his wife, who had managed to raise children with so much strength of character. Perhaps that trait more than any other would help them perpetuate "the chain" of Chechen existence.

I have chosen to relate the story of the Jordanian Chechens at some length primarily because I think it is an extraordinary illustration of the nation's tenacity and as such may help to shed light on the enigma of Chechen survival in Russia's shadow. Group survival in dispersion is always more remarkable than survival in one's homeland because the temptation to extricate oneself from a minority status and assimilate is often irresistible. Some Chechens have indeed assimilated.

And yet a majority of Chechens seem to have opted *in* rather than *out*, seeming to operate under a yet-to-be-passed Preservation of Small Nations Act. Their perseverance offers hope and inspiration to other beleaguered groups that endeavor to survive. Few nations, however, have managed to come back from the dead as often as the Chechens. The remarkable pool of their peaceful talents in Jordan suggests at least the possibility that they may choose life over death next time around. The Chechens, who have excelled in battle and excited the imagination of so many romantics worldwide, may now need a thousand Daghestanis and Bennos to lead them to the last decisive battle, the one that might culminate in a genuine national independence.

One who is conspicuously absent from the Jordanian Chechen spiritual landscape is Kunta Haji. The overwhelming majority of Jordanian Chechens are descendants of *Naqshbandi* Sufis, Kunta's opposite numbers. Hence, one hears no loud *zikr* here. The Chechens of Jordan gave up Sufism long ago. The last *Naqshbandi* sheikh, an uncle of General Abdul-Latif Benno's, was already a very old man in the 1950s, and a joint photo of him with a young King Hussein, perhaps only a teenager, adorns the general's living room. It is said that the *zikr* is still performed at funerals, but I have not witnessed it.

One evening I shared with my Jordanian Chechen hosts hundreds of slide photos that I had taken in Chechnya, including many of the *zikr*. None of them had any difficulty recognizing the ritual, and some even speculated about the variations in form and style among the different *zikrists*. But I thought I detected a hint of discomfort about their people's close association with what they considered, as it turned out, an esoteric practice.

One Jordanian Chechen appeared to mince his words when he offered a somewhat apologetic explanation. "Sufism," he said, "is good for Muslims who must struggle to keep their religion when they are faced with a hostile government. It is unnecessary in normal circumstances, when a Muslim is free to worship. Here we belong to the mainstream."

Which is to say, at least one element in "the chain" linking the present with the distant past, the intergenerational chain of which Dr. Daghestani spoke with so much eloquence, has been severed, probably for good.

A CHECHEN LULLABY

My visits to the Chechens of Jordan were an intensive time of learning, on many levels, one of them about music. I came back to Israel with a bundle of taped Chechen folk songs. My ailing mother instantly became an avid fan. Most of all she liked the song about Zelimkhan Kharachoyevski, a legendary *abrek* of the early twentieth century whose greatest claim to fame was the robbery of a Russian bank in the Caucasus in 1908. He also used to attack Russian military columns single-handedly, or so the story goes.

The song about Zelimkhan is actually a lullaby. After relating tales of his gallantry in the service of his nation, it addresses the child-listener and beseeches him to "grow up fast so you may serve your homeland. . . . Be dauntless and selfless just like Zelimkhan." Na'imah Daghestani had been kind enough to translate the lyrics for me, and I delighted my mother by reciting them to her, at her bedside in the dialysis unit of the Sheeba Medical Center near Tel Aviv. My mother was dying at that time in great agony, her frail body parting each day with one more ounce of life, yet she insisted I play the Chechen music to her whenever I drove her to the hospital. A couple of days after she died, a bouquet of yellow flowers arrived at her home in the town of Ramat Gan, outside Tel Aviv. It was the only bouquet my brother Ehud and I received, and both of us were reduced to tears when we opened the accompanying letter and read the name of the sender: Dr. Fakhruddin Daghestani.

It so happened that that very day Dr. Daghestani had been in Tel Aviv on official business (the joint Israeli-Jordanian committee on energy and natural resources was holding its periodic meeting) when one of his hosts came across the death notice we had run in a local newspaper, a couple of days earlier. Knowing of my contacts with Dr. Daghestani, the Israeli official drew his attention to the death notice. I was later told that Dr. Daghestani insisted on taking a break from his tight schedule to look for a florist. He was not entirely sure whether Jewish traditions allow flowers in memory of the dead, but he was determined to extend a hand of friendship to me.

"You are my brother," he told me when I met him later that day in his Tel Aviv hotel, and offered me the warmest embrace of my entire mourning period. I was astounded by the sincerity of the moment. I do not at all exaggerate when I say that no one came as close to feeling my pain as Dr. Daghestani did—he who had nursed his own dying father, already in his nineties and in a state of total disintegration, for many months in his own home in Amman. At no time did it occur to him to commit his father to an institution. Members of the family would rotate at night in bathing the old man or quenching his thirst. This was a matter of course for the Daghestanis, not an act of sacrifice. And I admired them for that.

I also recognized that the fear of death so common in Western cultures did not register with the Daghestanis. They confronted it without inhibitions, without filters—which is why their empathy was so great and their expression of sorrow so genuine.

To me, it was only fitting that my journey to the Caucasus finally brought me home to the landscapes of my youth, to the bittersweet taste of my people's triumph, to the pain of my people's victims, to the sadness of my mother's death, to the void that followed, and a bouquet of yellow flowers, delivered over a fragile bridge suddenly open to two men once separated by enmity.

THE LAST PEOPLE OF THE SABBATH

Farewell, unwashed Russia
Land of slaves, land of lords,
And you blue uniforms,
And you submissive hordes.

Perhaps beyond Caucasian peaks,
I'll find a peace from tears,
From Tsars' all seeing eyes,
From their all hearing ears.

(LERMONTOV, 1837, ENGLISH TRANSLATION BY JOHN MERSEREAU)

On an arid mountain overlooking a lake in central Armenia, I bade farewell to a remarkable phenomenon in the history of religion. It was a mid-October day, 1994, and at Maria Solovyova's modest house, the Subbotniks of Yelenovka had gathered to pray, probably for the last time in the 170 years of their existence. Avram Karalov, a man in his early seventies, wearing a black beret, presided. His audience of four elderly women followed in respectful silence as he recited the words of the Fifty-third Psalm, once spoken in the Israelite temple in Jerusalem.

God looked down from heaven upon the children of men,
to see if there were any that did understand,
that did seek God.

Avram went on to read more psalms; it took him about half an hour to exhaust the day's repertoire. Then and only then did the Subbotnik man and women sit down. It was the women's turn, and Maria Solovyova burst out in a song of sorts. The little room, whose walls were covered with a fading tapestry, filled with the cacophonous chorus of high-pitched, shrill voices, joining in a long ululation

Yaaaaaa yeeee, yaaa yaaaaa yeee yaaaa
Heeeeee haaaa, hee, haa, heeeeeeheeeee ha.

Avram Karalov then recited the words once spoken in King Solomon's temple:
"God looked down from heaven upon the children of men, to see if there were any
that did understand, that did seek God."

They were all ethnic Russians, with Russian looks and Russian names; they spoke only Russian; and their prayer books were exclusively in Russian. The entire scene would have been indistinguishable from that of any other group of peasants gathered in a Russian Orthodox church on a Sunday—but for the fact that the day was *Saturday*, and no crucifix or icons of Russian saints were to be seen, and the man and women prayed only to a father, never to a son.

Unlike a Christian, Avram Karalov kept his hat on throughout the ceremony. He had a deeply lined face, a bulbous nose, thick glasses, and a pleasant if somewhat rasping voice—and he was the senior man in the community, one of a handful of men left, along with a slightly larger group of widows. Karalov had not led a prayer in many months; nor would he have, on that October afternoon in 1994, if not for my pleas.

I wish to hear you, I told them, I wish to videotape you. Otherwise people might not believe that this ever happened, that the People of the Sabbath ever came so mysteriously and suddenly to life, restored an ancient god, defied emperors and secret policemen, mounted an exodus in quest of a promised land, settled in the South Caucasian wilderness, worshipped and labored, earned the admiration of strangers, endured Stalinism—and are now dissolving.

Soon the dominant culture—Armenia's, as it were—would claim the little old houses, the apple trees, the prayer books left behind, the cemetery above the lake where cows were now grazing at leisure. Another memory would then overlie the mountain.

Just one more time, I implored Maria Solovyova, who complained that she had an excruciating headache and was feverish, and that her voice was not as strong as it used to be, and that "there are too few of us anyway." She finally relented but remained distinctly unsentimental about it all, suggesting I should address most of my questions to Avram. But Avram could not answer the one question I was most interested in.

Avram, I said, I do not understand at all. Why did your ancestors choose the God of Israel? They had never seen Jews. They lived in the most oppressively anti-Semitic state in the world. They were severely punished for their choice. So why did they do it?

"No one knows," Avram said impassively. "No one knows how it all began."

This is a tale of extraordinary audacity, of simple Russian Christian peasants, who one day, under obscure circumstances and against common sense, concluded that they had been worshipping the wrong God. So they switched, unprompted, and then addressed an appeal to a distant czar, imploring him to affirm their freedom of choice.

The czar was furious. They were given a choice, all right: repent—or suffer. Many chose to suffer. That czar, as well as his successor, inflicted great misery on the unrepentant, took their children away, and finally had them banished. They were meant to disappear so that the contagion they carried would disappear with them. But they did not.

Many of them ended up in the Caucasus around 1830, where they built houses, planted crops, lived exemplary lives—and worshipped the God of their choice. Throughout the nineteenth century, travelers from Europe en route to Persia crossed their settlements often and related stories of enigmatic people of faith whose industriousness and cleanliness were unmatched. Then came the Bolshevik Revolution, and a curtain was pulled across them. For seven decades they were assumed dead, an extinct species drowned in the deluge of politics and social experimentation.

I began to hear about the Subbotniks when I first arrived in the Caucasus in 1991. A year later I met them, and in the course of the next four years visited them three more times. Unlike the other characters in this book, they do not represent a Caucasian nationality and do not qualify as "indigenous"—although some might be justified in thinking that 170 years of uninterrupted habitation make any bloodline worthy of the distinction "native."

I write about them because they belong in a broader category common to the Caucasus, one that transcends ethnic delineation: the freedom seekers, people who seceded from the mainstream to pursue their own way of life, wishing nothing more than to be left to themselves. They are the spice of any civilization, and their streak of rebelliousness has catapulted our world time and again to new heights of spiritual development, from the early Christians, to the fifteenth-century followers of Jan Hus, to the American Puritans, to the modern-day champions of liberation theology in South and Central America. Their contributions should be measured not in terms of their theological proclivities alone but in terms of their daring to challenge a prevailing order. In this, they have left a legacy that is bound to outlast any concrete set of beliefs they might have espoused.

I chose for my epigraph in this chapter Lermontov's farewell to Russia, which the young poet-warrior composed en route to the Caucasian front. He was not the only Russian hoping to find freedom in the Caucasus. Since the sixteenth century, a multitude of fugitives had taken that route, escaping either serfdom (which was abolished only in 1863), or state Christianity, or both. Whole colonies of Old Believers and Schismatics sprang up, people whose fierce individualism and profound hostility to official doctrines belied some of the conventional wisdom about Russia being a "nation of slaves."

The Subbotniks did not choose to live in the Caucasus but were pushed there, at times with the greatest cruelty. Yet they made their land of banishment a refuge from the Russian state. As I write these words, their last remaining members are either dying or scattering. I was one of their last visitors, and I bear witness to the final chapter of their journey.

Maria Mikhailovna Kondratova had just turned ninety when I came to see her in the fall of 1992. Her appearance and demeanor were those of a quintessential old Russian peasant, her complexion fair, and her facial features unmistakably Slavic. Her accent was that of a provincial from Russia's south. After all, she was born in Russia and had never left it. It was Russia that had left Maria Mikhailovna. She was now a resident of a new state, barely one year old, called Armenia—a twist of fate that her great-grandparents could never have anticipated when they were sent away from their villages a thousand miles to the north, in the heart of Russia.

At ninety-two, Maria Mikhailovna Kondratova, the matron of Yelenovka, was ready to go. Soon Yelenovka itself would follow.

A brown, treeless mountain hung over the street, which was lined with neat little houses, painted white and light blue. The apple trees in the residents' private gardens were still holding out against the chill. On the day of my visit, early autumnal winds were blowing cold through the barren highland, and with the young state's energy resources depleted, the prospect of six freezing, dark months was looming large. "When a person reaches the age of sixty," Maria Mikhailovna said, "he has to start collecting the clothes in which he will be buried. So I am ready." There was no hint of self-pity in her voice. It was as if she were speaking of the changing leaves.

The old woman was seated motionless at the doorstep of a one-story house, her home for many decades. Her head was framed in a tight headscarf, and almost half the length of her small body was covered by a fading green apron. Her browless, deeply sunken eyes observed me with apparent distrust, as if unsure why this unannounced foreigner would pose questions on matters that were either self-evident or purposeless and obscure. Her nose, broad at its base, was so narrow at its tip that it resembled a beak pointing at her drawn upper lip. A lifetime of frowning had rendered the bridge of her nose a plump band of flesh protruding in sharp relief. Her years notwithstanding, Maria Mikhailovna's brow was not heavily furrowed. The skin of her uncovered forearm was surprisingly smooth, her voice was firm, her motions were vigorous, and the clarity of her thought was never in doubt. In the mountains of Armenia, she was a walking testament to the legendary longevity of highlanders, even if her own roots belonged in the plains of central Russia.

Three years later, about two hundred miles to the east, in the southern plains of Azerbaijan, I called on Yakov Iseyevich Zababurin. He was eighty-three at the time of my visit and cut a striking figure with his long, bushy white beard, which evoked not just pre-Communist Russia but the Russia of the seventeenth century, before the country's soul was exposed to the contamination of foreign ways. Zababurin, a wiry, shrinking man, carried his years with difficulty; his steps were hesitant, and his feet met the ground almost tentatively. Nonetheless his weakening voice was still audible, and his memory was sound. Like Maria

Mikhailovna, he was a native of an empire twice removed—that of the czars. It was a czarist command that had dispatched his Subbotnik ancestors as well as hers to this distant frontier.

Theirs is a tale replete with paradoxes. The most obvious one is that their ancestors, distinguished and admired servants of the empire that they were, would have never had the chance to claim a new frontier for the Romanov dynasty if they had not first aroused the ugliest suspicions of czars, priests, and bureaucrats, who desperately wanted them out of sight. Extraordinarily, they were fully expected to serve the good of the country that had so mistreated them. Even more extraordinarily, they ended up fulfilling these expectations.

Another paradox: in the Communist era, they were far more success-ful in retaining features of the traditional Russian village against Soviet interference than were most villages in Russia proper. Outside the impe-rial autocrat's line of vision, they remained pretty much outside the Communist autocrat's line of vision as well. The collectivization that swept the old Russian village out of existence by the 1930s and cost the lives of millions did not entirely spare them, but it left at least some of their traditions intact.

The greatest paradox was that, although the Subbotniks carried the Russian banner to lands where no Russian had ever lived before, they

An angry czar dumped his ancestors on the Iranian border, but so happy were they that they called the place Privolnoye, "the free place." Yakov Iseyevich Zababurin

fell short of Russia's own definition of Russianness. Though they looked like Russians, walked like Russians, and spoke like Russians, they were not quite Russians in at least one major sense: they had turned their backs on the cross, refused to accept the divinity of Jesus Christ, denied Russia's pretension to be the "Third Rome," and declared themselves fearers of the *Hebrew* God.

Moreover, they did so while living under a state that barred Jews from settling until the late eighteenth century, where the people were said to "dread no one more than the Jews"; where an empress turned down badly needed economic services because they were rendered by Jewish merchants, exclaiming, "From the enemies of Christ I desire no benefits"; where a Russian convert to Judaism was burned alive at the stake, in the heart of the imperial capital, as late as 1738.

The Subbotniks, unlikely agents of Russian influence in the Caucasus, were not embittered by their experience. "My ancestors were sent here as if to be held in prison," Yakov Zababurin said. "When they arrived, they found a forest and nothing else. They cleared it, they planted wheat and potatoes, they had plenty of harvest, they were free to worship, they were left alone." So happy were they that they called the place Privolnoye, roughly "the free place." Perhaps like the Puritans in the Massachusetts Bay Colony, they were intent on pursuing religious freedoms denied them at home and on marrying their religious preferences to a life of hard labor and dedication unknown to most of their contemporaries. There is no telling what might have happened if a vast ocean had separated them from the mother country the way it did the English and Scottish colonizers of America. They might have become the founders of a new nation.

The shade of Yakov Zababurin's oak trees offered a welcome relief from the scorching heat of the late July day. "They are older than I," he said of the trees, remnants of the forest that predated the Subbotniks' arrival. Zababurin and his wife of sixty years lived in a long and narrow wooden house, its outside painted a soft blue. Despite the Zababurins' growing frailty and apparent poverty, the place was flawlessly clean, if run-down. A couple of chickens announced themselves from time to time, but the Zababurins had long given up their animal stock and agricultural work. Their five children now lived in Ukraine, and it had been two years since they were last heard from. "Not even a letter," the old man remarked with sad resignation. The knowledge that mail delivery in large parts of the Caucasus had ground to a halt around the time of the Soviet collapse, and that whole nations struggling to survive had

given up on the niceties of a fully functioning society, held little consolation for him.

"I was born here," Zababurin said. "So were my parents and my
grandparents. But my great-grandparents came from Russia. Catherine
the Great expelled them because they had accepted the God of Israel."

Curiously, Catherine featured prominently in all my conversations
with the Subbotniks. It was to her that they attributed the upheaval that
drove their ancestors out of Russia and into the Caucasus. Catherine's
culpability seems unlikely, however. The empress died in 1796, well
before the conclusion of the Persian War in 1813 that delivered the
Southeast Caucasus into Russian hands. Unless the Subbotniks arrived
in Privolnoye twenty years *before* the Russian army, Catherine, guilty of
so much, was innocent on this account.

Why then would two groups of people who had nothing to do with
each other—the Subbotniks of Yelenovka had never heard of Privolnoye, and vice versa—invoke Catherine? We simply do not know. The
early history of the Subbotniks remains a mystery. Mark Kupovietsky, a
Jewish scholar from Moscow, one of the few who have devoted time
and scarce resources to studying the Subbotniks, told me, "The only
written documents we have about their origins are the protocols of
investigations by czarist prosecutors in the nineteenth century. There
are no other sources that allow us to analyze their ideology or beginnings. Anything else we know, we know from their detractors and per-
secutors in the Russian Orthodox Church."

What can be stated with a high degree of certainty is that the Subbotniks originated in central Russia, mainly from three cities and their
environs: Tambov, Saratov, and Voronezh. Tambov was a fountain of
religious nonconformism for two centuries, so much so that it earned
the nickname Tambog, *bog* being Russian for God, *tam* being Russian for
"there [is]." It was in Voronezh that church officials spotted the first
group of Subbotniks, apparently in 1796. The Zababurins were sent
packing from a village in the Saratov area, in the lower Volga region.
When they arrived, "they started exploring the land," Yakov Zababurin
said, and because they came from the Volga, "they looked for another
river to settle by." The first one they came across was the site upon
which Privolnoye was eventually built. "First only ten families came,
then the whole village followed, then all the Subbotniks of Russia. Each
time Catherine heard of a Subbotnik, she ordered him away, to Privolnoye." Zababurin was clearly taking liberties with facts, but his belief
that "all the Subbotniks" of Russia ended up in Privolnoye suggests a
lifetime of splendid isolation, perhaps much like the life that his great-
grandparents had intended for their descendants after they realized that

Privolnoye, founded by banished Judaizers from the Russian hinterland, was intended to fortify Russia's southern frontier. Now an Azeri town, it has still preserved the simple grace of a Russian agricultural colony.

little good could be expected from the imperial crown. Zababurin had never heard of Subbotniks outside his native district, either in Armenia or the rest of the Caucasus, or in Russia.

"To begin with," he said, "there were two streets here. One ran up the river, and the other ran down the river. In the street that ran up, we built ourselves a house of prayer."

Was that your synagogue? I asked.

"No," he said, "we never called it that." He used the Russian word *sobranie*, which could be translated here as "congregation." Zababurin's entire religious vocabulary consisted almost exclusively of Russian terms. One curious exception was a minor Jewish festival, the Feast of Lots, which he referred to by its original Hebrew (or to be precise, Persian) name, Purim.

The Subbotniks I met in Yelenovka spoke no Hebrew at all. When I asked them about Rosh Hashana, Yom Kippur, Sukkot, Shavu'ot—all household names even among Jews who speak no Hebrew—the Subbotniks shrugged and said, almost to a woman, "I have never heard of them." But when I asked them to name their holidays, it became clear that they celebrated the very same holidays, with some embellishments, but called

It used to be the main street of Yelenovka, which the Judaizers founded in the 1830s. Time has finally caught up with the Subbotnik town; it is now a section of Sevan, an Armenian city.

them by their Russian names. Rosh Hashana, or New Year, is simply *Novyi God;* Yom Kippur, which they recognize along with Jews as the holiest of the entire year, is *Sudnyi Dyen,* Russian for "day of judgment." Sukkot is *Kushi,* and Passover is *Paskha* (which is also Russian for "Easter"). I struggled a bit with the meaning of *Troitsa,* a festival they celebrate in the early summer. After all, the word means "trinity" and sounds hopelessly un-Jewish. But they assured me that *Troitsa* was just the informal name they accorded to a festival they knew as "the fiftieth day," an unmistakable reference to that which Jews call Shavu'ot, or "the feast of weeks," and Christians call Pentecost. In the Russian Orthodox calendar, it is known as *Troitsa.* So steeped were the Subbotniks of Yelenovka in Russian traditions that they did not mind the silly plagiarism, even if it entailed a challenge to their own theology. After all, it was their very opposition to the Holy Trinity that had made them break with the Russian Church.

More perplexing was the "festival of *Mardofey.*" I first heard about it from Maria Solovyova. What is Mardofey? I asked her. She turned to her

Singing was not Maria Solovyova's strongest suit, but she deserved encouragement for trying. After all, the mystery of Mardofey was at stake.

son and her daughter-in-law and came back to me slightly embarrassed. "No one knows," she said, smiling.

I thought it might be another name crudely borrowed from Orthodoxy—perhaps Mardofey was a saint or even a pagan deity. Maria Solovyova closed her eyes intently as if attempting to squeeze from her system the last drops of memory. After a long pause, her face lit up with a twinkle.

"Amman . . . Amman . . . ," she repeated a few times, and then began to sing. "Ahmaaaahaahn . . . Ahmmmmaaan . . ." Singing was not Maria Solovyova's strongest suit, and this little tune fared no better than others, but she deserved encouragement for trying. I complimented her, and she warmed to the challenge. "I used to hear my father sing it," she said, displaying a bit of nostalgia, the only time she seemed moved by religious talk. "It was such a happy holiday. We would gather, we would sing, we would drink."

Amman? I was ready to guess that she had in mind Haman, the evil chief minister of the Persian king Ahasuerus in a famous biblical tale, who plotted to exterminate the entire Jewish population of the kingdom but for the courage of the king's newly wedded Jewish wife Esther. The story is related in the Old Testament book that bears Esther's name, but nowhere else.

The Mardofey mystery deepened, however, when Maria's younger brother, Aleksandr Karavayev, injected a new possibility. *Mardofey*, he announced, was derived from the Russian *mordoboy*, which means "smack your mug," in the sense that during the festival, the celebrating youth get drunk, lose control, and smack each other on the face. Happily, Karavayev's banter turned out to be unfounded, though it suggested a moral decline among the Subbotniks of his generation. Previous generations had prided themselves on little drinking and much self-restraint.

The next comment on the meaning of *Mardofey* came from Avram Karalov, the prayer leader: "Mardofey was an Egyptian king who conspired to kill the Jews. Esfir got rid of him." Avram's was a mind-boggling mixture, a merger of a major myth and a minor myth, though both had a common theme—miraculous delivery from the hands of a powerful enemy. (The Egyptian king was, of course, Pharaoh, who sought to limit the Hebrews' reproduction by casting the newly born into the river.) What finally betrayed the secret of Mardofey was Avram's mention of the rescue of Esfir, the Russian version of Esther. As for *Mardofey*, it must have been a slight mispronunciation of Mardokhey, Russian for Mordecai, uncle of the said Esther, whose resourcefulness saved the day for Persia's Jews. Indeed, the Subbotniks may be right in naming the festival after him.

The story of Purim/Mardofey may have had a special significance for the Subbotniks. The Book of Esther's author, after relating the convoluted tale of near-holocaust followed by miraculous salvation, brings the triumph to a climax unheard of elsewhere in the Bible: so complete was Mordecai's victory over Haman that "many of the people of the land became Jews; for the fear of the Jews fell upon them." Because none of the characters in the Book of Esther are thought to have existed, the "Judaization" of the Persian empire must be treated as a metaphor or wishful thinking on the part of the anonymous author. But a Subbotnik of the first generation might well have treated the Old Testament words as foreshadowing the events taking place in central Russia.

And yet the Judaization that took place in Esther's Persia because "the fear of the Jews fell upon them," was clearly different from Judaization that was entirely voluntary, as was the case of the Subbotniks. The latter were *Jews by choice*, a proposition almost incomprehensible in later centuries of pogroms and holocaust. Why would anyone want to join a faith so widely detested, one that brought down so much misery on its members?

Jewish incredulity in the face of voluntary Judaization is illustrated in the memoirs of the Russian Jewish merchant Zvi Kasdoi, a tea importer who traveled extensively in Russia during the first years of the twentieth century. In the Ukrainian city of Cherkassi in 1908, Kasdoi recalls, a new Russian garrison arrived, consisting of dozens of Subbotnik soldiers. The local Jews felt amazement, then consternation. Taking for granted their own hopeless plight, they could not fathom why

> those strange Russians—for the sake of a Judaism which had not been revealed to [their ancestors] on Mount Sinai—would have relinquished their own rights and left the ranks of the ruling nation, in exchange for persecution and the loss of civil rights, only to be held in contempt and suffer humiliation.

According to Kasdoi, the local Jews decided to avoid the incomprehensible creatures; so low was their own self-esteem, so clear to them was the unalterable Jewish condition of inferiority, that they projected it onto the newcomers.

WRESTLING WITH THE SPIRITS

September 1992. I walk between rows of tombstones in Yelenovka's cemetery on a hill overlooking Lake Sevan. My guide is Aleksandr Sheinin, a thirty-seven-year-old electronic engineer, a native of Yelenovka who now lives in Yerevan, the Armenian capital, twenty miles to the southwest. He is half-Jewish. His father, who had just died, was the only Jew in Yelenovka.

The *only* Jew? I wonder aloud. But I thought everyone was Jewish.

"Ah." Sheinin smiles.

He suggests I concentrate on reading the names that are engraved on the stones. He points to one stone on which miniature tables of the Mosaic Law are replicated. The language is Russian; there is not a single Hebrew character to be seen, which is unheard of in Jewish cemeteries. Still, nearly all the tombs feature a Star of David. This one reads, "Here was laid to rest Isaya Makashamov, 1884," nothing more. A neighboring tomb, progressively invaded by acid and mold, dates back to 1881: "Here was laid Yekaterina Leontovna Karakinyeva." Other tombs state dates in conformity with the Jewish calendar, like the one under which Yakov, the son of Zakhar Yershov, was laid to rest in "5674" (1903–1904).*

Not one Jewish name, I say in my surprise to Sheinin.

* A calendar system counting the years since Creation was in force in Russia until 1699 (though the Russian numbers were ahead of the Jews' by 1,748 years), at which time Peter the Great switched Russia to the common European calendar. Up to that time, the Russians celebrated New Year on September 1, more or less at the same time as the Jews, believing as they did that the world was created in the autumn. At the time the first Subbotniks emerged, memories of the old calendar were still relatively fresh. To many Russians, the retreat from the Creation calendar was another manifestation of the dangerous "new ways" that were forced on the believers, beginning in the mid-seventeenth century.

In death, as in their life, they were Russian peasants who happened to worship an Old Testament God, which is why their tombstones never bore a single Hebrew sign. Even the Star of David was almost an afterthought.

"See?" he says. "They were *Russians*. Why would there be Jewish names?" Which is the gist of my story. It is not so much their choice of God that intrigues me, as their doing so on their own terms. The Subbotniks broke new ground in modern Jewish history: they demonstrated the possibility of accepting Judaism without assuming Jewishness, changing faith without changing nation. Many Jews, possibly a majority, perceive themselves not merely as coreligionists but as a *people* (America may be a partial exception).

In few places is the *peoplehood* of the Jews taken for granted as naturally as it is in Russia—and not for benevolent reasons. Until very recently, "Jew" has been an ethnic classification that Jewish citizens, however irreligious, were required to acknowledge in their internal passports, a legacy of the Soviet period and also of pre-Soviet perceptions. (Some Russians still rankle at the English expression "Russian Jews." One can be either Russian *or* Jew but not both, they argue.)

The inseparability of religion and ethnicity in Jewish history has contributed to the sense of tribalism that has certainly played a crucial role in preserving the Jews as a collective, but that may also have stood between Judaism and a true universal status. After all, how can a member of another nation join a religion so ethnocentric, so territorially based, without ceasing to be who he is?

The Subbotniks offered an alternative. Their switch to the God of the Old Testament was entirely self-induced—no rabbis or "conversion courts" (as they are known in Jewish religious practice) were involved. They did not care in the least about *Halakha*, the Jewish rabbinical law, nor could they have—*Halakha* not being part of the Bible, they were entirely unaware of it. They stepped out of the church they were repudiating and into the temple they were embracing for one reason: the Israelite creed *appealed* to them.

This is a mind-boggling idea to many Jews, who are resigned to the inferiority of their religion in the marketplace. It is as though Jews hold it to be self-evident that missionaries may carry Bibles on behalf of evangelical sects, or Books of Mormon, or Islamic Qur'ans, or scriptures of Eastern holy men—but Judaism is somehow congenitally barred from spiritual expansion. Yet if Judaism is so noncompetitive, so poorly packaged, how can one account for its spontaneous emergence and subsequent growth in central and southern Russia? Why would people have gone out of their way to adopt it? Certainly not because of coercion, and definitely not because they were locked behind the walls of a ghetto with fellow Jews or barred from joining the outside world. There were *no* Jews around them at all, because no Jews were allowed to live in Russia until the 1770s, and even then only in strict confinement.

The road leading to the rise of the Subbotniks was admittedly a bizarre one, paved with 150 years of Russian messianic agitation. Nineteenth-century Russians were remarkably receptive to religious speculations, so much so that an exasperated czarist bureaucrat remarked in 1853, "The *still* usual simple-mindedness of our people is well-known: there is no absurdity which could not make an impression on them; there is no foolishness of which you could not convince them."

More gracious was the Russian populist writer V. I. Kelsiev, who considered Russian nonconformity an

> honor to the Russian people, showing that they do not sleep, that every intelligent peasant himself wants to test the dogmas of faith, wants to think about the truth for himself, that *the ordinary Russian seeks the truth*, that whatever truth he finds, by that he marches forward, not fearing the stake.

Both men wrote not about the Subbotniks but about the Old Believers, yet their words could have applied to the entire period of religious changes from the seventeenth century on. Though their judgments are contradictory, they are describing the same phenomenon. Russian rebelliousness (and not only in matters of religion) has always been audacious and inspiring and at the same time astonishingly senseless, as testified by the many vagabonds and cynics who assumed the identities of dead czars, won tremendous followings, and almost brought down the Russian state in the process. (In all fairness, Western rebels, from the Middle Ages through the eve of modernity, often displayed similar qualities. It seems that there were times when the free spirit could break loose only by total defiance not only of political, religious, and social norms but, also, of what was perceived as sanity.)

The Subbotniks may have had distant predecessors in the late fifteenth century, when a movement of "Judaizers" is said to have swept the Grand Duchy of Muscovy, czarist Russia's precursor, carrying along with it members of the ducal family and top Christian clergy. Its exact nature is in dispute among historians. Some believe that it really aimed at converting the entire Russian population, or at least the elite—a staggering thought, raising one of the most fascinating "what-if" questions of all time. Others suggest it sought to "rationalize" existing dogmas, primarily doing away with the doctrine of the Holy Trinity—which would have dramatically reduced the gap between Christianity and Judaism, without entirely closing it. It is even possible that the Judaizers were so named simply to discredit them in the eyes of a largely Judeophobic population. Denunciations of theological reformers as "Jew lovers" go back to the early days of Christianity.*

* Such was the case of one Bishop Ibas of Eddessa, in what is now southern Turkey, in the fifth century. When he returned from an ecclesiastic council in which he was willing to compromise over Jesus' divine nature, an indignant mob was awaiting him in the streets. "The Christ-Hater to the arena," they shouted. "Down with the Judeophile."

Whoever they were, the Judaizers of Muscovy came tantalizingly close to taking the reins of power, converting the grand duke's own sister in the process. Her name was Yelena, and she was locked up in a monastery for the rest of her life on account of her heresy. (Many others were tortured and burned.) Was it a complete coincidence that the Subbotniks named their village in the Armenian mountains *Yelenovka?* Probably, but the thought that they might have considered themselves heirs to the fifteenth-century Judaizers, and therefore must have been aware of the tragic fate which could await them, is intriguing. One historian of religion in Russia, Serge Bolshakoff, believes that the Judaizers, after their suppression in Muscovy, were never completely eliminated; they only went underground and waited for an opportune moment to reemerge.

The seventeenth century saw a tremendous religious upheaval in Russia, again over the issue of church reform. The dispute, which had early Byzantine undertones, centered on seemingly trivial issues like ornaments and shapes of icons, even the number of fingers one should use in making the sign of the cross. The anti-reformers—or Old Believers, as they came to be known—were Russia's first recorded dissidents. They had an apocalyptic idea of the world and anticipated its imminent end. "The Old Believers believed that heaven had moved irretrievably beyond reach," in the words of one historian, J. Sévérac.

It was a time when tongues were turned loose and extraordinary departures from sacred doctrines occurred. At one point a metropolitan, or archbishop, of the Orthodox Church declared, "The Jews were right to crucify Christ for his revolt." He probably meant it as a blunt call for the restoration of order, but given that the period was rife with millenarian expectations, and the Anti-Christ was lurking behind every corner, words often assumed a role and weight that had been unintended by their speakers. Beliefs began to spread that Jesus was about to renounce His throne, and that God no longer wished to dwell on earth.

With the religious marketplace wide open, a collection of self-anointed saviors stepped in. In 1645 in the Volga region, one Daniel Filippov announced himself as nothing less than *Yahweh Sabaoth,* the God of the Old Testament. Filippov had a slightly updated testament at hand: he offered *twelve* as opposed to the original *ten* commandments. He called on the Russians to quit the church, rid themselves of secular books, and vow never to drink alcohol or have sex. He also revealed that he himself had fathered a son, who, by virtue of Filippov's own divinity, became the son of God.

The "son," a peasant by the name of Suslov, is considered the founder of Russia's first religious sect. They are known as the Khlysty, or "flagellants," because self-flagellation, literal rather than metaphoric, was central to their ecstatic ritual. They had an eclectic set of beliefs in which pagan traditions and Hindu teachings existed side by side with a diluted Jesus, who was the son of God only figuratively.

The Khlysty fathered many subsects, the best known of which was the Dukhobors, or "spirit wrestlers." They continued to downgrade Jesus: he was still respected, but only as an inspired mortal. The Dukhobors may have fathered, or at least greatly influenced, the next sectarian wave, known as the Molokans. Their most distinctive feature, in the eyes of the church, was their rejection of the fast during Lent. Still, they refrained from eating meat and limited themselves to milk; hence their name, *Molokans*, Russian for "milk people." Later on they introduced the full set of Old Testament dietary laws. Eventually, but well after the appearance of the Subbotniks, the Molokans gave up all major Christian holidays as "inventions of the ecumenical councils" and reverted to Old Testament holidays. Yet they insisted that they remained Christian and continued to believe in the Holy Trinity.

In the 1760s, encouraged by Catherine the Great, members of various German Protestant sects poured into Russia in large numbers, importing with them not only their religious dissidence but also their notions of close-knit community where redemptive labor and abstinence were the paramount virtues. Their ideology, known as Pietism, eschewed church dogmas in favor of a thorough study of the Bible. Popular editions of the Bible made their debut in Russia in the 1750s, and "biblical" communities began to emerge along the southern Russia frontier, guided by literal interpretations of the scriptures.

With the Molokans' open flirtation with the Old Testament, the road was short to complete abandonment of Christianity. A Molokan peasant by the name of Sundukov, from the central Russian province of Saratov, preached the superiority of Moses to Jesus, and with the approach of the nineteenth century, the first report emerged that the "Judaizers" had reared their heads again.

The recent general availability of the bible in Russia was decisive, as is illustrated by the interrogation of the first Subbotniks before a commission of inquiry in the city of Voronezh.

> One peasant informed the commission that he and his fellow Judaizers were induced to change their faith by "a holy lady."
> "Bring her here," the commissioners ordered.
> "She is very old, and cannot walk," came the answer.
> "Then carry her in."
> A few minutes later the peasant reappeared with an old Bible wrapped in a napkin and presented it with the words: "This is the holy old lady who pleaded with us to become Judeans."

The Orthodox Church, alarmed at the mass defection of the rural population to the camp of "Christ's enemies," set about checking it first by repression and then by persuasion. Evoking the religious disputations of the Middle Ages, priests of the church held meetings to argue the case of Christianity. The traveler Kasdoi reported that

> In opposition to [the priests] would rise simple peasants, the soil tillers, who had studied the bible *in toto*, [hidden] in cellars. . . . The public debates had a thorough influence over the masses and provided further stimuli to Bible instruction. Elders and youth, even women and children, studied, ready to be engaged any moment. And the more they came to know the [Old Testament], the more they rejected the [New Testament], began to believe in one God, observe the Jewish Sabbath, and convert. Events unfolded so quickly that in a single day a whole village, forty-family strong, converted en masse.

The sequence of events leading up to the birth of the Subbotniks may in fact suggest evolution rather than revolution, in that each cycle seemed to drop one more ounce of radicalism into the expanding pool of Christian nonconformity. The first Molokan-Subbotniks may have been more interested in what they were leaving than in what they were joining: they were eager to turn their backs on the established church and perhaps on the entire polity it represented and legitimized.* At times accounts of the early Subbotnik movement, however indirect and however questionable their reliability, suggest nihilism more than profound theological commitment. A case in point is the story of an unnamed Subbotnik, as recorded by Kasdoi, that a Christian reader may find disagreeable in its openly blasphemous tone:

> Judas Iscariot came to me in my dream, he looked exactly the way he is depicted and painted on the wall in our monastery, grinding his teeth at me and preventing me from making the sign of the cross on my chest and heart, as required of the Orthodox. I woke up anxious and moved in the extreme. The dream haunted me for many days and took away my peace of mind, until I revealed its details to an acquaintance of mine, a Molokan-Subbotnik who lived around us, and he

---

* Which is indeed the contention of a Soviet-era scholar, A. I. Klibanov, who studied Russian sects in the 1950s and 1960s. To him, the Subbotniks "appeared as a peculiar form of social protest of peasants, directed against the ruling church." But his utter disregard for spiritual motivations was to be expected of a Marxist-Leninist.

resolved it: It was time for both of us to convert to Judaism! And so did we, on the very same day.

An element of peasant down-to-earth common sense, which found Trinity theology a bit too intricate, may also have been involved. The Russian author Maksim Gorky once encountered a peasant in a village near Kazan, in the Volga region, who believed in God but not quite the way the church expected. He told Gorky: "I can't understand Christ at all! He serves no purpose as far as I'm concerned. There is God and that's enough. But now there's another! The son, they say. So what if he's God's son. God is not dead, not that I know of." Gorky did not indicate the man's religious affiliation, but he might well have been a Subbotnik, or en route to becoming one.

It is impossible to determine whether the first Subbotniks—or as they are sometimes called, Molokan-Subbotniks—wanted to break completely with Christianity, or whether they would have been happy to remain nonconformist *Christians* and be left alone by the mainstream—say, in the way the Amish of Pennsylvania are treated by larger Protestant denominations. Mark Kupovietsky, the Jewish scholar from Moscow who has studied the Subbotniks, suggests that "they were by and large a phenomenon within Russian *Protestantism.*" In many respects the Russia of the second half of the eighteenth century resembled Central Europe two centuries earlier, when in a single village in Moravia no fewer than thirteen religious sects were discerned, "all drawing up catechisms, all desiring to be ministers, all pulling in different directions, all claiming to be the true church," in the words of a Venetian contemporary, Marcantonio Varotto. In 1573 the Holy Inquisition reported the existence of forty sects, among them the Adamists (who ran naked), the Devillers (who believed in the Devil's ultimate salvation), Antichristians (who worshipped a sacred harlot), and Judaizers, who were so named not because they professed Judaism but because they reverted to heresies that had threatened the unity of the church in the fourth and fifth centuries: the denial of Jesus' divinity, though accepting him as a messiah.

Russia's Judaizers might have been relegated to exactly the same position: heretics within the church. But their future choices were largely decided by powers and circumstances outside their control. This was Russia, after all—a land where mystics and brutish policemen often had the ear of the sovereign, or indeed *were* the sovereign.

The brutish mystic to whom the Caucasus owes the Subbotniks was Alexander I, possibly the most complex czar ever to have mounted the

Russian throne. Implicated in the assassination of his own father, he initially favored a constitutional order and genuine popular participation in government. He showed favor to the Catholic Church, a much-maligned enemy of Russian Orthodoxy for centuries. He played a leading role in liberating Europe from Napoleon's yoke, and he demanded that postrevolutionary France be a democratic state. He offered to restore a large measure of autonomy to Poland, Europe's most unfortunate victim. He even promised to put an end to the mistreatment of the Jews in his realm. Alexander was a man immersed in messianic religiosity. In the words of his trusted adviser, Prince Golitsyn, the czar "related all his actions to the Divine Power, and attributed his victory to God alone."

Alexander rendered the Judaizers in his realm an unintended service: he made both testaments of the Bible immensely popular in Russia. Ironically, this "rod of God's anger" never actually read the Bible himself until he was well into his reign; nor had his closest adviser and future religious affairs minister, Prince Golytsin. Once they did, however, en route to the final round of the Napoleonic war, their entire worldview changed overnight. They proved quite impressionable, so much so that Alexander drew inspiration from the Hebrew prophet Daniel to form the "Holy Alliance" with his fellow monarchs in order to exorcise the revolutionary demon from Europe. He was confident he was establishing a new world order "which shall never be destroyed" (Daniel 2:44). It was under Alexander that a complete edition of the Bible first enjoyed wide distribution in Russia, and he established a Biblical Society to familiarize the masses with the scriptures.

The masses, as it turned out, were a bit too interested.

For Alexander, everything fell into place in the grand scheme of things, including his own historical mission as the redeemer of Christianity. The czar's mind became increasingly responsive to apocalyptic visions. He fancied himself the "defender of all the religions" and became enamored of one Karl von Eckartshausen, a minor German religious thinker who preached the restoration of early Christian amity, in which consensus and harmony would replace competition and division. Alexander fell under the spell of a German baroness, Barbara Juliane Krüdener, who expected the world to come to an end with "an explosion of love." She reinforced in him the sense that he had been elected by God to transform Christianity and lead it to a final triumph.

Such millenarian expectations brought to the fore an old Christian hangup: that deliverance of the Jews to the true God would coincide with the final act of salvation (as in Paul's exhortation, "And so all Israel shall be saved," Romans 11:26). In other words, the conversion of the

Jews should facilitate Christ's Second Coming. This message, never alien to the Catholic Church, was taught with increasing vigor by certain Protestant sects, and it penetrated Russia in earnest during Alexander's final years in power. Equipped with the Bible, the emperor turned to the Millennium.

In early 1817 Alexander established a Society of Christian Israelites, which was intended to ease the Jews out of their faith. Jews were not offered outright financial rewards for doing so, but they were assured that the state would take the place of the Jewish communal organizations in providing them with an economic safety net. It was announced that the Society would help all those Jews "prompted by reverent obedience to the Voice of Bliss which calleth unto the scattered sheep of Israel to join the faith of Christ."

But shortly after Alexander had reached out to the Jews with such unparalleled generosity and warmth, offering to make them full human beings if only they ceased first to be who they were, he was notified that at least 1,500 Christian Russian peasants were moving in the opposite direction, possibly taking many more along with them. Not only did they betray him, they were now petitioning him to grant them full religious freedoms, and to extend to them the recognition any Orthodox congregation would have enjoyed. "How very naive they were!" Simon Dubnow, the great historian of Jews in Russia, was to exclaim eighty years later.

The czar's fury was boundless. To thwart this Alexander-Ahasuerus, the Subbotniks could surely have used a "Mardofey" and "Esfir," but only Hamans existed in the imperial court. Government ministers as well as bishops of the Holy Church urged the czar to "uproot the Judean sect" by whatever means it would take. Subbotnik leaders were to be conscripted to the military, and the unfit were to be deported. Any contact between them and their Orthodox neighbors was barred. Their worst punishment—or so believed the authorities—was that they would be exposed for what they were: not mere "People of the Sabbath" but "Zhidy [Yids]," in the elegant wording of one imperial minister.

Evidently, few terms in contemporary Russian were more dishonoring to their recipients, even in the vast areas where few Jews had ever lived.

The fate of the Subbotniks was decided in 1825. In the words of Dubnow,

> Entire settlements were laid waste, thousands of sectarians were banished to Siberia and the Caucasus. Many of them, unable to endure the persecution, returned to the Orthodox faith, but in many cases they did so outwardly, continuing in secret to cling to their sectarian tenets.

The Subbotniks' choice was no whim or religious fad. These Russian peasants not only chose to challenge the dogmas but remained faithful to their choice despite tremendous suffering that involved forced separation of parents from their children. Their persecutions in Alexander's reign entered the collective memory of the Subbotniks as a formative religious experience unto itself, on a par with the momentous nation-forming tribulations of the ancient Israelites. When I asked Maria Solovyova, the Subbotnik woman in Yelenovka, about the significance of the unleavened bread they ate during *Paskha* (Passover), which Jews call matzah, she responded without the slightest hesitation: "Our ancestors had to leave their villages in haste, and they had no time to finish baking their bread. They had to feed themselves with this half-baked dough."

Her words filled me with awe. She may have been ignorant of Jewish religious history, but she claimed a stake in an act of self-affirmation and survival no less miraculous than that of the Israelites coming out of Egypt. Indeed, she may even have had an advantage: her ancestors' exodus and heroic endurance did not belong to ancient, ahistorical myth but are known to have happened. After I told Maria Solovyova what the original *Paskha* was all about, she shrugged and said: "But *they* were not *our* ancestors." She gave Passover her own people's coloring without losing one iota of its original meaning. As a matter of fact, she may have demonstrated Passover's universal applicability and detribalized it.

On Passover night, while reading their Haggadah, the narration of the Exodus, Jews are reminded of God's commandment to celebrate Passover, "that you may remember the day you left Egypt all the days of your life." But Maria Solovyova never celebrated another *Paskha* in Yelenovka. By the time of my next visit, two years later, she and her family, as well as most of the Subbotniks, had left. And yet, in relating to me the story of her family's exodus from central Russia to the Caucasus, she became an active practitioner, however unknowingly, of the Haggadic exhortation.

A HEBREW GOD ON THE
IRANIAN BORDER

In banishing his Judaizers to the Caucasus, the czar could have hardly chosen better, on two accounts. One was its isolation, secured through topography and the scarcity of passable roads. A simmering conflict in the North Caucasus, which would soon escalate to a full war, rendered the South Caucasus even less reachable. In their new confinement, there was little danger that the Subbotniks would spread the Judaizing contagion further.

The second reason for sending the Judaizers southward was the war of expansion Russia was waging against its southern Muslim neighbors. By 1829, Russia had acquired new lands in the Caucasus that were the size of Indiana, and it had to pacify and secure them. The Judaizers may have been traitors to Christ, but there was no reason they could not be made into vehicles of consolidation of their country's new borders. Alexander I and his successors were to find out that the Subbotniks were industrious and law-abiding, refrained from smuggling, and even paid their taxes on time. One official report, commissioned by the imperial government, wrote so sympathetically of them that in 1887 the state lifted all restrictions on the movement of Subbotniks, as well as members of other heretical sects. They were now free to roam the Russian interior and settle wherever they liked. This sudden benevolence, however, changed little for the Subbotniks of the Caucasus. They had already struck deep roots in the mountains and did not clamor to go back home.

In 1995, when I visited, Privolnoye was a large village, mostly populated by Turkic Azeris, in Azerbaijan's district of Jalilabad, only fifteen miles from the Iranian border. So tight was the security in and around the village that I had to obtain a written permission from the office of

Azerbaijan's prime minister to carry a video camera, even though my interest was solely cultural and historical. A century and a half after the Subbotniks had claimed their place in its sun, Privolnoye was still treated as a frontier fortress.

Unlike Privolnoye, the Subbotnik colony of Yelenovka, in Armenia, had long ago been rebaptized. It is now called Sevan, after the large lake nearby, and it boasts the status of a major Armenian town. (Lake Sevan is one of the world's highest lakes, at an altitude of about six thousand feet. It is Armenia's main reservoir of potable water.) Just a mile away, on a little patch of land off the lake shore, lie the ruins of an ancient Armenian monastery, reinforcing the impression of Armenian antiquity. Yet at the time the first settlers arrived, around 1830, few Armenians were to be found. The Yerevan area had been a Persian-controlled province, and the overwhelming majority of its residents were Turkic "Tatars" (now designated "Azeris"). Russia had just won the territory as part of the Treaty of Turkmenchai, which delivered into its hands the last remaining Persian possessions in the Caucasus.

Persia had been so weakened in the process that it ceased to be an enemy, but the Ottoman Empire still was; its huge domains were an inviting target, and Russia was to fight three more major wars against the Ottomans in the following eighty-five years. The Turkish border was only sixty-five miles away from Yelenovka and a borderland full of Muslims was not considered safe. Here, unlike the Northwest Caucasus in the 1860s, Russia did not resort to wholesale deportation of indigenous populations and preferred ethnic *engineering* to ethnic *cleansing*. It invited a large number of Christian Armenians from Persia to settle the new lands—and it issued an invitation for Russian settlers as well.

Alas, the empire was expanding so rapidly—in the four decades preceding 1830, Russia had added territory the size of Western Europe—that there was simply not a large enough reservoir of pure Russian stock for the purpose of colonization. In the Caucasus, the only available colonists were the Cossacks, who settled mostly in the north, and members of the heretical sects, who were sent to the south. The majority of the sectaries were Molokans, the "milk people," who were related to the Subbotniks by way of cohabitation, or customs, or genes. It was almost a rule that whenever there were Subbotniks, one would come across Molokans as well, though not always the other way around.

According to a Molokan calculation, on the eve of World War I, there were no fewer than forty-three Molokan villages in the South Caucasus. (Yelenovka was probably the only joint Molokan-Subbotnik settlement in which the Subbotniks were in the majority.) Most of the villages had two traits in common: they were located at high altitudes (as high as seven thousand feet, in 25 percent of the cases), and they were established along the borders of Persia and Ottoman Turkey. Indeed, eleven of them were located in an area that was reincorporated into Turkey in the aftermath of the Bolshevik Revolution. By any measure, the religious heretics whom Czar Alexander so feared became leaders in Russian colonial expansion.

The Subbotniks of the Caucasus were by no means a cohesive group. Having come to life spontaneously, they often evolved independently of each other, at times entirely unaware of each other's existence. Accordingly, their degree of immersion in the new faith, or renunciation of the old, varied. The Subbotniks of Yelenovka remained staunchly Russian, and as a result they were often confused with the Molokans or even referred to as a Molokan subgroup. Those of Privolnoye moved farther: there the division was not between Subbotniks and Molokans but between Subbotniks and *geyrim* (Hebrew for "converts")—that is, Subbotniks who decided to go all the way to Judaism. Their embrace of Jewish law went beyond the Bible to include Talmudic law, and in some cases it led to emigration to Palestine. The *geyrim* I met, however, were Jewish only in a religious sense.

"I am Russian," Dina Khaimovna Kalachkova of Privolnoye told me. She opened her old Soviet identity document ("internal passport"). On its second page, under "nationality," the Cyrillic script of a local bureaucrat was unmistakable: *russkaya*. "I am *geyrka*," she hastened to add, attaching a Russian form onto a Hebrew root, meaning "female convert." "My religion is *yudeiskaya*," which is translated "Jewish" but does not have the same connotations as *yevrei*, the standard Russian word for "Jew."

Dina Khaimovna, a pudgy woman with enormous energy and a smiling face, initially professed ignorance to most of my questions, but gradually she warmed to the occasion and displayed an amazing knowledge of the Jewish religion. Her knowledge was amazing, partly be-

"I am geyrka," she introduced herself to me, donning a Russian form on a Hebrew root meaning "female convert."

cause of the venue of our interview, an isolated town by the Iranian border, but even more so because this peasant woman was born in 1936, at
the height of the Stalinist terror, when no religious propaganda or education were tolerated, and for many years she had no contact with outside Jews. When I complimented her on the unlikely endurance of her
historical memory, she said, "I learned it from my grandmother and
from my mother, and I have read the Bible time and again [by which she
meant the Old Testament]. Every Saturday I read the *parsha*," or weekly
portion of the Pentateuch.

She kept at home a curious collection of religious literature, including the Pentateuch, the book of First Prophets, and one Talmudic trac-
tate (befittingly, the one dealing with Sabbath customs). "This is the
written Torah," she said of the book of Pentateuch, "and this is the *oral*
Torah," she added, pointing the Talmud. I shook my head incredulously.
Few Soviet Jews would have known the difference. Indeed, many American Jews would not.

I followed Dina Khaimovna to her kitchen, where the sink was over-
flowing with fresh red grapes. For one reason or another, there was no
running water in Privolnoye that morning, evidently not a rare event
because water was stored in large dispensers in the room. She dipped a
bowl in a dispenser, then poured the water over the grapes four times. "I
have two sinks here," she said. "One is for meat, the other for dairy. I
never mix them."

A duckling joined us in the kitchen, earning Dina Khaimovna's
friendly nod.

She then turned to me in earnest. "I must ask you a question."

I was all ears.

"Somebody has died recently. His body was lying at home, and I
touched it. Should I have washed right away?"

I was struck. This would have been the fear or concern of a deeply
religious woman of the Eastern European Jewish diaspora a century earlier. One may still encounter such doubts in the Hasidic neighborhoods
of Brooklyn, or in the Orthodox boroughs of Jerusalem—or indeed fifteen miles away, among the Shi'i Muslims across the Iranian border.
But in this case, anxiety over ancient purity laws and tribal taboos
emanated from a hospitable, good-natured Russian peasant woman,
with the mildest demeanor, who had spent most of her life in a God-
hating state.

"I do not know," I replied with a sense of acute helplessness. Such
questions never cross my mind, but I realized I had let my hostess down.
She had had to struggle so hard and for so long to cling to her ancestors'

adopted traditions—while I, born in freedom and affluence, had not found a moment to study a basic law so easily available to me.

Dina Khaimovna's question illustrated the greater importance that the Subbotniks attached to ritual over theology. That was natural: their faith was not a matter of tribal affiliation, they could have alluded to the "God of our fathers" only in the narrowest sense, they could not share in the ethnic experience, and they were unable to relate to mythical patriarchs or common tribulations of a distant past. So they manifested their religious choice by dwelling on the law, often with extreme attention to almost legalistic minutiae. Festivals interested them mostly in the details of their celebration, not so much their theological meaning. Time and again, when I asked my interlocutors to describe differences between various groups of Judaizers, the answers dealt with matters of ritual, like the proper way to treat corpses. "Oh, we leave the dead at home, the *geyrim* take them out right away," one Subbotnik said; or, "Oh, the Subbotniks bury their dead in regular cloths, we use special shrouds," a *geyr* said. And so forth.

Some Subbotniks, who otherwise knew little of Jewish theology or history, talked to me at length about the thoroughness of their preparations for Jewish festivals. Aleksandr Karavayev, the Subbotnik from Yelenovka who thought *Mardofey* (Purim) meant "smack your mug," was an accomplished baker of unleavened bread for Passover. He had a special stove in

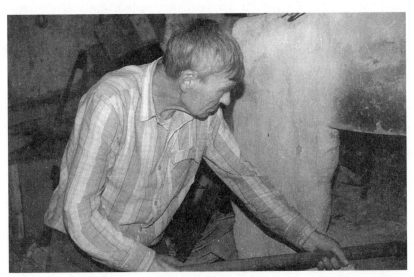

True, Aleksandr Karavayev thought that Mardofey *(Purim) meant "smack your mug," but he was an accomplished baker of unleavened bread for Passover (which Jews, but not Subbotniks, call* matzah*). He is seen here attending to the special matzah stove in his Yelenovka courtyard.*

his courtyard, one that had served the community since much earlier days. The Subbotniks were strict, he told me, in observing the rule against buying ritual wine from non-Subbotniks (thus abiding by the legal prohibition against "impure" wine), or never letting a non-Subbotnik slaughter an animal for a festival meal. They had no idea what the word *kosher* stood for, but they observed dietary laws with zeal.

Their strict adherence to the law was demonstrated to me once more when Dina Khaimovna's sister, Estra, showed me into a room in her house that was still functioning as an informal synagogue sanctuary. But she would not let me open the small Holy Ark where a Torah scroll was kept. First, she explained, "a woman is not allowed to attend," and then, "we need at least ten men in the room," the quorum required for a formal religious ceremony.

"My children implored me to move with them to Russia," Dina Khaimovna mused. "But I refused because of my religion. I do not think I would be able to follow it if I lived among the *Pravoslavnye*," or Russian Orthodox. She had never thought of emigrating to Israel, she said, though her great-uncle, Moises Iseyevich Sapunkov, did so in 1918.*

Out of a hidden drawer in her bedroom, Dina Khaimovna pulled an old prayer book that she correctly named *siddur* (which she pronounced the Eastern European Jewish way, "SEE-der," with the stress on the first syllable). When I asked her to recite a prayer for me, she deferred to her husband, Leonid Yosipovich, six years her senior. He was thin and lanky, his face was covered by white stubble, and his gestures were unsure. He could not find a recitable prayer, and Dina Khaimovna had to come to the rescue. "Here," she said, fixing her headscarf, and sat behind him in the half-covered balcony of their kitchen, as if to follow the text. But she required no text, for she knew the prayer by heart.

> "The Lord eternal reigned before the birth of every living thing. When all was made, as He ordained, then only was He known as king."

Oblivious to our presence, seven domesticated geese kept themselves busy and noisy, plunging into a puddle, splashing about and earning the reluctant attention of an old gray cat.

---

* Hundreds, possibly thousands of Subbotniks, mostly of the *geyrim* subgroup, emigrated to Palestine beginning in the late nineteenth century. Perhaps the best known of them was Efraim Dubrovin, a wealthy farmer from the Astrakhan region of southern Russia, a Molokan by birth who later fully converted. He emigrated in 1906 at the age of sixty-seven with his large family and settled in the Upper Galilee village of Yesod HaMa'ala, a preferred destination of many Subbotniks. His descendants, as well those of others, still live in Israel, entirely integrated, distinguishable only by their "non-Jewish" Russian family names. In the early 1990s, the entire population of Yelinka, a *geyr* village in the Voronezh *oblast* (district) of Russia, moved to Israel en masse.

"When I wake, as when I sleep, my spirit in His care I place. Body and spirit in His keep, I have no fear, held in His grace."

"We used to have fear," Dina Khaimovna said. "We used to be followed, to have our movements restricted, but no more. We are now free to pray, free to go about our life. . . . If only life were not so difficult."

Privolnoye, and even more so Yelenovka, lived in the shadow of the Nagorno-Karabakh conflict, which has pitted Armenia and Azerbaijan against each other since 1988. Subbotnik men were drafted into rival armies, perhaps even faced each other in battle. Maria Solovyova's son Anatoly was summoned to military service at the age of thirty-nine and was sent to the Karabakh front (belying the official claim, oft repeated, that Armenian regulars never participated in the war). He went missing for three months, then reappeared, as if from nowhere, the day before my second visit to his mother. He said he had spent that time as a prisoner of the Azeris. "I had no doubt that he would be back," Maria Solovyova said, surprisingly self-composed. "I prayed, and God heeded my prayers."

Anatoly's good fortune was his Russianness. Had he been an ethnic Armenian, the Azeris might have held him in captivity for years, pending an exchange of hostages, a common practice in the Caucasus. By the same token, the Azeris could also have labeled him "mercenary," which would have absolved them from the need to observe international law regarding prisoners of war. In that case he might have met a fate worse than long incarceration. Thankfully, Anatoly Aronovich was back home to embrace his Subbotnik mother, his Subbotnik wife, and his little Subbotnik girl, but what-might-have-been was constantly on his mind.

The Subbotniks were a phenomenon of the colonial era, even if they were involuntary colonizers. But now that most of Russia's colonies are finally on their own, they are running out of reasons to stay. Unlike Dina Khaimovna in Privolnoye, the religious identity of the Yelenovka Subbotniks was secondary to their ethnicity. Whereas Dina Khaimovna was still a quintessential *sektant* (sectary), in quest of a little oasis where she would be left alone to face her God, the Subbotniks of Yelenovka were Russian expatriates left stranded behind the receding imperial borders. With the memory of their ancestors' persecution and banishment fading or nonexistent, only one route was open to them: return home, to Russia.

By the time of my last visit, in late 1996, the handful of Subbotniks still left in Yelenovka told me that the Solovyovs were gone. They had joined

Three Solovyov generations pose for the camera shortly before the exodus from Yelenovka: Maria Solovyova and her son Anatoly hold the last Subbotnik to be born on Yelenovka's soil, Anyushka.

other Subbotnik families to live in the province of Krasnodar, in southwestern Russia, just north of the Caucasus. Many of them continued to live in compact communities, but there was virtually no hope that the physical ambience would facilitate spiritual survival. Very little about the younger generation in Yelenovka could have qualified them as Subbotniks in the sense of their ancestors, and their children were likely to have even less.

Anatoly was one of the last Subbotnik men to be circumcised in Yelenovka, but even he knew almost nothing of the past. "Tell me," he said in his raspy voice, "were my ancestors really so special that you'd come all the way from America to talk to us?"

As pleased as I was by the opportunity to restore some of Anatoly's memory, I felt saddened by the realization that this middle-aged man had never asked his elders about his ancestors, or if he had, had never received an informative answer. My travels in the Caucasus took me time and again to distant villages where cultural memory was being challenged by a combination of poverty, modernity, and indifference induced by Soviet assimilating practices. Nowhere, however, had I come as close to the end of memory lane as on the shore of Lake Sevan.

I took my time with Anatoly and spoke to him at some length about the courage and idealism of his ancestors. He listened politely and asked no questions. He was a friendly man, who smoked and drank and cursed, wore a short brown beard, and was fond of a particular genre of popular Russian music, the one associated with singers his age, who grew his kind of beard, who allowed nicotine to claim the clearness of their deep, manly voices, and whose repertoire consisted mostly of songs that told the stories of outcasts and left-behinds who ran afoul of norms and bolted out of mainstreams. My friend Aleksandr Mnatsakanyan, a Moscow-based writer with an observant eye, who traveled with me in the Caucasus, took a liking to Anatoly's easygoing manner. "He is what Russians used to call an *urka* [Soviet prison argot for 'criminal']," Alek said, intending the term in a folksy rather than a literal way. Anatoly had indeed served a period of time in prison, of which he spoke only fleetingly but almost fondly.

Anatoly may have been oblivious to Subbotnik history, but he offered to drive Alek and me to the Subbotnik cemetery outside of town. "We'll have a little picnic," he said, and loaded his little car with the necessary ingredients: *lavash*, the pitalike Armenian bread that, if properly baked, is rivaled for good taste by no other dough; fresh vegetables and garlic (a lot of it); as well as two bottles of cheap vodka and one of Armenian cognac, to warm us on the blustery, midautumn day.

Cemetery visits do not normally call for picniclike preparations, but in this part of the world the two are not at all irreconcilable. Perhaps by conferring with the dead regularly and at length, and by engaging concurrently in activities intended to sustain life and gratify (eating, drinking), the bereaved rid death of its evil mystique.

Anatoly's brother, Yuri, once drove an old car up the mountain—the one that rises so close to his mother's home, it could almost be touched from her window—when the vehicle's brakes gave out. The car quickly rolled back, and "Yura," thirty-six at the time, became the last Solovyov to be buried in Yelenovka's soil, in 1988. His grave was our first stop in the cemetery. I was interested in its design. Unlike all the older tombstones, it contained no hint of the Hebrew religion: no Star of David, no image of the Mosaic tablets, no counting of the years since Creation. Its central piece was a black granite tablet engraved with an impression of Yura's face, which made it entirely indistinguishable from tens of thousands of Christian and Muslim graves across the Caucasus and probably hundreds of thousands across Russia. I have encountered such images even in Jewish cemeteries, and they are to be seen increasingly outside the former Soviet Union, where ex-Soviet immigrant communities have sprouted. Earlier generations of the Solovyov family would surely have frowned on the reproduction of their descendant's facial features, as they were bound by the biblical prohibition, "Thou shall not make unto thee any graven image." No Subbotniks would have done so prior to the 1970s. Yura-turned-icon reinforced the impression that the age of the Subbotnik was indeed over.

The cemetery was in a pathetic state: If two years earlier I had been able to read most of the inscriptions, this time only a handful were still legible. Two cows were grazing at leisure, walking over the lopsided tablets, shaking the few that were still erect. The local authorities could easily have prevented this profanity. Yes, I know, Armenians had better things to worry about—they were struggling to survive, and the living

Anatoly Solovyov standing by his brother Yuri's grave. That the age of the Subbotnik was over was evident by the burial style. Throughout the Caucasus facial images of the dead adorn gray marble tablets like Yuri's, regardless of ethnic or religious background. For the Subbotniks, biblical taboos were the gist of the faith, but Anatoly never heard of the Mosaic ban on "any graven image."

unquestionably take precedence over the dead. But there were no cows in the neighboring Armenian cemetery, just a couple of hundred yards away. A few years hence, with the neglect and the cows (and the goats as well), not to mention the harsh winter climate, not only would the surviving Subbotniks have vanished from Yelenovka, but so would the dead ones as well.

Aleksandr Karavayev, Anatoly's uncle, took me to his great-grandfather's grave.

> Here lies
> the body
> of the Lord's servant
> Yakov
> the son of Avram
> Nevirov
> Died in 5659 [1898/1899].

Despite the Jewish ring of the names, both Avram and Yakov were common names among Russian Christians at the time. Yakov Avramovich lived to nearly one hundred, which means that he had been born in Russia proper and was a grown man, with a fully developed conscience, when the deportation of the Subbotniks began.

Anatoly's paternal grandmother, Rakhila Finayedovna, was buried nearby. She was born in 1873 and lived to the age of ninety-six. If only these parts of the Soviet Union had not been cut off from the outside world for seven decades, one might have been able to retrieve the oral traditions that still lived in old Rakhila's mind. It appears that she did not pass them on to her children. She may have thought the preservation of collective memory was too risky for Soviet times. And so she left Anatoly with no notion of who he was. The chain was broken.

"MY COSSACKS? JEWS?"

In 1992, just before I bade Maria Kondratova a final good-bye, the matriarch of Yelenovka sighed heavily. "I am concerned only about one thing," she said. "Who is going to take care of our holy scroll after we are gone?" The phrase "holy scroll" had an Arthurian ring to it, as if it were a cousin of the "holy grail," but she was referring to something much less metaphysical: the Torah scroll of Yelenovka.

Maria Kondratova could not read it, and it had been many years since anyone in Yelenovka could. Even at the height of the community's prosperity, Hebrew had played no role in prayer or education. Perhaps the scroll had been donated by an out-of-town Jewish merchant, or perhaps it was bought with local money. Though it was a sealed book to the Subbotniks, they still recognized it as a sacred object of great importance. What would become of it now? the old woman asked. "Do not worry," Aleksandr Sheinin, the half-Jewish engineer from Yerevan, attempted to cheer her up. "I will take care of it."

In 1994, however, the Torah was gone, and the few remaining Subbotniks were furious about the circumstances under which it had left them. "We were deceived," said Avram Karalov, the old man who served as prayer leader. A rabbi had visited them from Yerevan—a Lubavitcher missionary to the handful of urban Jews in Armenia—and had convinced the old Subbotniks that the scroll had to be "repaired." He took it away with him, promising to return it, but he never did. Apparently, he was not all that moved by the Subbotnik tale, and the obligation to preserve the parchment, important as it is in Judaism, superseded any other consideration.

But the rabbi had left untouched an old book that was solidly bound, if somewhat worn. Oddly, though printed in Russian, it read "backward," that is from right to left, the first page opening in what readers of Latin and Cyrillic-scripted texts would consider the "back" of the book. Its first page proclaimed, in Russian:

MOLITVY
Yudeiskoi Obshchiny

meaning "Prayers of the Judean Community," not employing the standard Russian term for Jew, *yevrei.*

Compiled from different sources
by Lazar Aronovich Semyonov
of Yelenovka, Guberbniya* of Yerevan, 1908

These few lines tell an important story about Yelenovka on the eve of World War I, just before the entire Russian imperial order came tumbling down. For the first time in their existence, the Subbotniks had raised their heads fearlessly. In the aftermath of the failed 1905–1906 revolution, the czar reluctantly promulgated an act that granted full religious freedoms to all residents of the empire. The Subbotniks were now free to go to a Yerevan printer and have him roll out a thick volume of prayers, compiled by one of their own, especially for them, and based on their own preferences and criteria. They could have had prayer books shipped to them from Vilnius for less money and less trouble— and many Subbotniks elsewhere, such as those in Privolnoye, did so— but the Yelenovka Subbotniks chose to maintain their independence vis-à-vis the outside world, whether Jewish or Gentile.

The physical quality of the prayer book suggested that the Subbotniks of Yelenovka were well off and could afford the luxury. Western travelers who passed through Yelenovka in the late nineteenth century heaped praise on its inhabitants for their economic success, often without having the faintest idea that they worshipped the God of Israel. "It is a pity they are not more of them in the country," wrote a British aristocrat en route to Mount Ararat.† A British general, Viscount James Bryce, e⟨qⁱually unaware of the nature of the Subbotniks' beliefs, emitted the following sigh of relief: "I very much regretted that we could not remain

---

* Administrative term from the czarist era, the equivalent of *province.*
† His compliment was addressed to all Molokan settlements he had encountered.

"Prayers of the Judean Community," proclaims the front page. It was compiled by and published especially for the Subbotniks of Yelenovka in 1908, at the height of their economic and cultural prosperity. The hands holding it ever so gently are the author's.

for some days at Elianofskia [sic], a flourishing Russian settlement . . . where the station-house appeared better than usual, and the post-master and others were very civil." Expressed in the understated manner of an upper-class Englishman, these words probably qualified as an enthusiastic endorsement.

Another British traveler, Douglas Freshfield, who wrote a magnificent two-volume book about mountaineering in the Caucasus, reported that Yelenovka's "postmaster was a Jew, and talked a little German," by which he may have meant Yiddish.

Yelenovka's economic success was largely based on fishing, Lake Sevan being renowned for its trout. At the time of Freshfield's visit, in the late 1860s, Lake Sevan still bore its historical name, Gokcha. Freshfield wrote: "A strong odour of dried fish revealed at once the staple of industry; the salmon-trout of the Gokcha lake are famous, and are sent both to Tiflis [Tbilisi] and Erivan [Yerevan]." Another British traveler, Commander John Buchan Telfer, who visited Yelenovka a decade or so later, found "an extensive fish mart, where we purchased some of the fine trout for which the lake has been celebrated from all time."

Yelenovka's prosperity and resulting spiritual self-sufficiency made it an autonomous "Judean" community in the South Caucasus, a minire-

public of what the ancient Greeks had called God Fearers, a term
employed precisely for Gentiles who became interested in the God of
Israel but preferred not to go all the way and abandon their original
identity.

Maria Mikhailovna Kondratova, the ninety-two-year-old matriarch,
died soon after my 1992 visit, one of many elderly victims of Armenia's
most disastrous winter, when oil and gas reserves ran dry, electric power
was available only one hour a day, and people were feeding precious
books to the fire merely to keep the temperature of their bodies at a life-
sustaining level.

In 1996, when I made my last visit to Yelenovka, Armenian speech
filled the former Subbotnik yards. (A community used to be counted by
its yards, and at its heyday, before World War I, Yelenovka was said to
have seven hundred.) Few of the new Armenian occupants had the
faintest idea of their predecessors, as in all fairness they could hardly
have been expected to. A dozen elderly Subbotnik women were still
left, some desperate to join friends and family in Russia, others resigned
to spending their declining years in Yelenovka, too poor or too sick to
seek another home.

I encountered Yelena Aronovna Zhatukhina in front of her house. At
sixty-five, she was one of the last few Subbotniks left in Yelenovka. Her
three children had long ago relocated to other parts of the former
Soviet Union: her elder daughter, an economist, now lived in Minsk,
the capital of Belarus; another daughter was a physician in Novosibirsk,
in western Siberia; and her son, a pilot, was now unemployed in
Moscow, having lost his home and old job in the Black Sea City of
Sukhumi during the Abkhaz war.

And your children? I asked. Are they Subbotniks?

"No," she said. "All of them have been baptized. As soon as they
moved to Russia, they went to church and had themselves baptized.
They are Christian."

I was struck. Why? I asked.

"Why!" she exclaimed, surprised at my surprise. "They live in Russia,
and Jews are not allowed to live there. So what choice did they have?"
(Needless to say, she was wrong on this point, at least for now.)

Were you saddened by their decision? I asked.

"Sad?" Yelena Aronovna frowned. She was evidently taken aback.
"Why would I be sad? It is a matter of adaptation. You live in a place,
you'd better adjust to its environment. If they were in Armenia, they
would be like the Armenians. In Russia, better be like the Russians."

Didn't you think they were turning their back on their ancestors in doing so? I persisted. After all that their ancestors had endured in order to maintain their faith?

"Oh, they will never forget their ancestors, never."

But they will, I thought. And so turned the wheel.

There is a story about the Subbotniks that is worth relating, not for its historicity—it bears the marks of a legend—but because it is an exceptional illustration of the chasm that separated these people from their Jewish contemporaries.

Unlike the Jews, the Subbotniks were so self-confident, so unapologetic about their religious preferences, that even in the heart of Russia, even in the face of a government that instigated massacres of Jews till the eve of World War I, these proud practitioners of the despised religion wore their faith on their sleeves.

In 1851, according to this story, at the height of the Caucasian War, Czar Nicholas I took a trip to inspect his Cossack troops along the front. He traveled to the three main concentrations of Cossack population, along the rivers Don, Kuban, and Terek. As Nicholas was passing by one *stanitsa*, or Cossack village,

the peasants came out, as was customary, to greet the czar "with bread and [salt]." And then appeared one group, seemingly as Cossack as the others—tall, heroic, virile—save for the fact that in their hands they were carrying not only the traditional "bread and [salt]" but Torah scrolls as well, as was customary among the Jews. The provincial governor stood them among the rest of the Cossacks [for the czar to review]. And yet, when the czar finally arrived, they did not take off their hats.

The czar, who was always anxious about a possible rebellion against him (since the time of the Decembrists*), noticed that instantly and turned to the governor in rage: "Is this a plot? A rebellion? How come they are not taking off their hats?"

The governor replied in a tremble: "Your majesty! It is no plot. Their religion does not permit them to stand bareheaded, these are members of the Israelite faith."

"My Cossacks are Jewish?" The emperor was stunned. "This is not in the realm of possibility."

"They used to be *Pravoslavnye* [Russian Orthodox]. But since the ranks of the Judaizers have swelled here, with the arrival of deportees

---

* The Decembrists were radical military officers who had plotted to establish a constitutional state in Russia twenty-five years earlier.

in the newly occupied districts across the Caucasus, they have also assumed the faith of Israel and converted," the governor struggled to explain the matter away.

His words, however, incensed the emperor even more until he rose off his carriage seat, shook his fists, and screamed in fury: "I shall show these dogs what Judaism and the faith of Israel are! I'll teach them to kick Holy Orthodoxy! Have them picked up instantly and place them in shackles—"

"But the emperor could not finish the sentence," told me old Judaizers who witnessed the event as it was unfolding, "and the last word stuck in his mouth. He turned pale as the whitewashed wall, returned to his seat, held both sides of the carriage with his hands, and sank in deep thought for a whole hour, mumbling to himself. He then raised his head, stared for a while at the Torah scroll held by the Cossacks nearest to him, and recoiled."

Some of the elders in Caucasian Stavropol [a major city in southern Russia, just north of the Caucasus] told me they overheard him recite to himself in Russian the verse, "The Lord at thy right hand shall strike through kings in the day of his wrath," and he commanded "not to harm these converts, only to transfer them to remote villages, the farthest from the main highway, so they do not spread the disease of Judaization."

The source for this tale by no means has impeccable credentials. Zvi Kasdoi (who later adopted a Hebraized version of his name, Kasda'i), born in Ukraine in 1862, was for many years a traveling salesman of Wisotzky, a tea marketing company owned by a Russian Jew and based in London. He crossed the Russian Empire time and again and is said to have traveled extensively in Siberia as well as the Caucasus. But he was a romantic and mystic who, like many Jewish travelers during the centuries, was in perpetual quest for the lost ten tribes of Israel. In his book, it is not easy to distinguish gross exaggerations from factual eyewitness accounts, particularly when both occur in the same paragraph.

Nonetheless, the tale of Nicholas I and the Torah scrolls, fantastic as it may sound, may not be entirely unfounded, at least in one respect: large numbers of Cossacks did indeed join the Subbotnik ranks.

Elsewhere in his book, Kasdoi reproduces another story he heard around 1910 from a prominent Hebrew author, Y. L. Katzenelson (also known by his nom de plume Buki Ben Yagli). The author visited the imperial capital St. Petersburg, where he came across two hundred Cossack Subbotniks stationed in the local military garrison. One day on the eve of Passover, they appeared unannounced in a local synagogue and demanded to see the rabbi. The Jews were naturally intimidated both by the visitors' military outfits and by the date they chose. (Passover was

a traditional time for blood libels against the Jews, which often generated massacres.) When it turned out that those Cossacks were brothers
in faith and all they wanted was to celebrate Passover, the rabbi, whose
name was Eisenstadt, inquired whether they had a permit from their
superiors.

"Oh, our dear rabbi," the Subbotnik Cossacks answered, "please do
not worry. We *shall* have a permit because no one dares slight *our* honor,
the honor of Cossacks." One could not have invented a less typical
answer from an adherent of the Jewish faith in Russia. Jews and self-
confidence? Jews and defiance? Jews and proud assertiveness? That is
what Zionism was created to reintroduce into Jewish life, but it was
assumed this could happen only outside of Europe.

Mark Kupovietsky, the Jewish ethnographer who has studied the
Subbotniks, views Kasdoi's book with great skepticism. "He was a good,
enthusiastic man, but was not a professional," Kupovietsky told me in a
long conversation on a bench in Moscow across the street from the
Kremlin wall.

Nevertheless, Kupovietsky confirmed that whole regiments of Cossack Judaizers (a term he prefers to the less inclusive *Subbotniks*) existed
before the revolution. He once met a man from Kuban in southern Russia who told him that 5,000 Cossack Judaizers used to live in his village.
During the 1905 upheaval, as well as the civil war (1918–20), those
Cossacks came to the rescue of local Jews. The irony could hardly have
been more pronounced, as so many *Christian* Cossacks, at the very same
time, were at the forefront of hordes that devastated Jewish communities throughout Ukraine and massacred many thousands.

The Kuban Judaizers of yore, Kupovietsky told me, are all gone.
Most of them were deported or died during Stalin's collectivization
drive in the 1920s and 1930s, while a minority left for Palestine even
before World War I. I met in Moscow an Israeli-born woman who was a
descendant of the Cossack converts.

Kupovietsky went looking for descendants of the Subbotniks in eastern Siberia, not far from Lake Baikal. He was particularly interested in a
village that was called Yudina before the revolution. Travelers who visited Yudina at that time conveyed extraordinary reports to the outside
world of a self-sufficient Subbotnik community that was both affluent
and deeply religious.

Kupovietsky arrived there in 1986, as the Gorbachev thaw was under
way but before it seriously affected the life of the most distant provinces.
His information, he says, was that 2,000 people lived in Yudina before the
revolution, half Subbotniks and half Molokans.

"I spent a whole day there," he told me. "I called on almost every single house. I spoke to anyone I could find. People had no problem with questions about the Molokans. They directed me to the Molokan house of prayer, told me where the Molokans' descendants were, and so forth. But when it came to the Subbotniks—complete silence. No one was, no one knew, as though they had never existed.

"I finally gave up and left. A local truck driver offered me a ride to the nearest city. He was a young peasant. He asked me who I was and what I was doing there, and I told him about the Subbotniks, and how much I had hoped to find some, and how disappointed I was to leave empty-handed because no one knew about them.

"The young peasant lit a cigarette, smiled, and said, 'They lied through their teeth without understanding that people are punished for lying.' And he went on to tell me that people in the village had just celebrated Passover, and he even used the Hebrew word, *Pesach*. But he wouldn't say anything else. I implored him, but he wouldn't. He said only that they baked *lepyoshki pekni*, special bread."

The last visitor to the old Yudina managed to get there in 1920, just before the Soviets lowered the curtain. He reported later that the Subbotniks were totally indifferent to the life of Jews elsewhere in Russia. They were primarily interested in matters of Jewish ritual:

> All the laws of Passover were observed with special vigor, and they are haunted by the slightest doubt about unleavened bread. [Jews are expected not only to refrain from eating leavened bread during the festival but indeed purge it from houses and neighborhoods.] . . . For two weeks all residents of the village, from the youngest to the oldest, were preoccupied with this matter as well as the baking of *matzah* [unleavened bread].

The similarities between Yudina's brand of Judaism and Yelenovka's is remarkable: the same zeal in practicing the rituals, the same obliviousness to ethnic Jews, the same geographic isolation, the same cohabitation with Molokans. The significance of the latter lies in the fact that Molokanism was the final link between the Subbotniks and their Christian Russian origins. In many cases, those who lived in joint settlements with Molokans were less likely to move beyond their status of Russians of the Old Testament persuasion. They were the Subbotniks least touched by the outside world and the least influenced by ethnic Jews. To the end of their collective existence, they served as an intriguing reminder of what Judaism might have become if it had not been for the unremitting hostility of the world without and the Jews' lack of self-confidence within.

The Subbotniks' exact numbers at the heyday of their existence, around the turn of the twentieth century, are virtually impossible to establish. Mark Kupovietsky, a cautious minimalist, thinks they added up to only 30,000. Zvi Kasdoi, the euphoric triumphalist, contended there were up to two million of them. (He probably used very inclusive figures and counted all the Molokans, who claimed a million followers in Russia around 1900, as well as members of other heretical sects.) One Jewish scholar from Moscow, who had done some research on Subbotniks in Ukraine, told me that in 1917 there were fifty or sixty villages in Russia that were "entirely Subbotnik," with an overall population of 60,000 to 70,000. However, she says, even that was a far cry from their peak in the mid-nineteenth century. By the end of the Soviet period, she believes, about 5,000 or 6,000 Subbotniks still lived in the country, though most of them preferred to hide their identity.

The Soviet ethnographer Klibanov reported meeting Subbotniks in the Tambov and Voronezh districts, south of Moscow, in 1959 and 1964, respectively. Forty years into the Soviet period, when Nikita Khrushchev was waging an unrelenting campaign against all forms of religion, Klibanov still found people immersed in religion, "who give primary importance to its rituals and customary side."

As the story of the Subbotniks comes to an end, one remaining question begs to be asked: Could it ever happen again? Given that the Subbotniks emerged from nowhere over two centuries ago, is it not possible that new Subbotniks might emerge with the same suddenness and spontaneity?

Kupovietsky did not dismiss my question out of hand. In the 1960s, he said, Russia experienced heightened activity on the part of indigenous religious sects, the harshness of Soviet rule notwithstanding. The most celebrated case was that of the Pentecostalists, also known in the United States as Charismatic Christians, whose immense personal courage won them considerable international attention. Interested in the Old Testament and preoccupied by millenarian visions of the "triumph of Israel" (the ancient nation, not the modern state), they inspired an offshoot in the North Caucasus that bore the hallmarks of the Subbotniks. According to Kupovietsky, the group's leader took a major step beyond the Subbotniks in proclaiming himself Messiah, which brought him close to "the establishment of a new religion." But otherwise, the group rejected the New Testament, celebrated Jewish festivals, and even established contact with the Israeli embassy, something ethnic Jews at the time would not have dared to do. (Western Jews referred to the quiescent, voiceless Soviet Jews of the pre-1967 era as "Jews of Silence," a polite synonym for timidity.) Just like the Subbotniks in the early nineteenth century, the new group refused to be intimidated into conformity. They were later accused by Soviet propaganda of being "Zionist agents," Kupovietsky added. The group eventually dissolved, and its leader emigrated to Israel.

Kupovietsky said that groups of "new Judaizers" had emerged elsewhere in the former Soviet Union, at times thousands of miles apart: from Riga and Tallinn on the Baltic to Ashkabad, the capital of Turkmenistan, in Central Asia.* Their numbers are small, perhaps 2,000 in all, in Kupovietsky's estimate. He doubts that anything remotely resembling the Subbotnik movement would ever result from the "new Judaizers."

But then, could anyone have predicted the rise of the Subbotniks two centuries ago? Can we really apply entirely rational expectations to spirituality? Can we foresee people's divine needs?

The appearance of the Subbotniks left rabbinical authorities with mixed feelings, and only in the early twentieth century was there any systematic attempt on the part of organized Judaism to engage with them or help them. The reluctance was dictated largely by fear. Not until 1905 did the czar promulgate an edict on freedom of worship, and for Jews to become actively involved in proselytizing might well have incurred the holy wrath of both crown and church.

But fear of the authorities could not have been the sole reason, for in the 1920s, a wave of would-be converts knocked on the doors of synagogues in Poland and Lithuania, perhaps influenced by the Subbotniks, perhaps as spontaneous as the first Subbotniks had been. The applicants were shown a cold shoulder by a suspicious, unaccommodating Jewish leadership, and with a naïveté that equaled that of the Subbotniks a century earlier, the scorned ones petitioned the local governments to help them exercise their religious choice. Then an event of an almost farcical nature ensued. In Lithuania, where nationalism and anti-Semitism were often closely related, the authorities took up the case of the defectors from Christianity and reproached the local Jewish community for its unfair treatment of those seeking conversion.

---

* Molokan villages were known to have existed near Ashkabad in the late nineteenth century. I have found no evidence of Subbotnik settlements, but their presence in Molokan communities is not only possible but in fact highly probable, given what is known of the schism among Molokans that gave rise to the first Subbotniks in the nineteenth century.

One might assume that a minority so despised and persecuted as the Jews of Eastern Europe would have welcomed the opportunity to accept converts. But old habits die hard, and the Jews' built-in resistance and skepticism outweighed any other sentiment. The words of a Talmudic sage no doubt were still reverberating in the ears of Lithuanian Jews some eighteen hundred years after they had first been uttered:

> If at the present time a man desires to become a proselyte, he is to be addressed as follows: "What reason have you for desiring to become a proselyte; do you not know that Israel at the present time is persecuted and oppressed, despised, harassed and overcome by afflictions?"

Or indeed much worse, as in the stunning words of the ancient Rabbi Helbo: "Proselytes are as hard on Israel as leprosy."

Given the centuries-old reluctance about converts, it is no surprise that the story of the Subbotniks is so little known to Jews worldwide and that few lessons have ever been drawn from it. Judaism as a religion is still probably more inward-looking than any other major faith. This shyness is all the more remarkable in that religions assume the truthfulness and the universal applicability of their respective formulae. Yet there has been no Jewish "evangelism" to speak of, save for one Jewish group: the Reform movement in America, led by its former president, Rabbi Alexander Schindler. Perhaps it is no coincidence that Rabbi Schindler was inspired to a very large extent by the Subbotnik experience.

The rabbi's late father, he told me, a renowned Yiddish poet, Eli'ezer Schindler, was a soldier in the Austro-Hungarian army during World War I. He was taken prisoner by the Russians and spent his captivity in Siberia. When Russia collapsed in late 1917, Schindler, like tens of thousands of POWs, began the long trip home, a journey through many time zones that was often undertaken by foot. On his way, in the steppes of Central Asia, Schindler one day stumbled upon a strange village, populated by distinctly non-Jewish-looking people, who professed to believe in the Mosaic laws.

Schindler, a scion of a respected Hasidic dynasty, was astounded. He had never met the Subbotniks. They were not only ethnic Russians but also Mordvinians (members of a small Finno-Ugric nation who live mostly in Russia's Volga region). The Subbotniks welcomed their unexpected guest with jubilation. They urged him to stay as long as he wished. He became their teacher in Judaism and even acquainted them with Hebrew and Yiddish.

"During that very time of his stay in their midst," Alexander Schindler reminisced about his father a few years ago, "when these Russian Jews-by-choice heard that a pogrom was planned against the Jews of the region's capital, they took their farm implements in hand, marched there, and successfully defended their coreligionists."

When Rabbi Schindler was still a child, his father "entranced" him with tales about the Subbotniks. One point he made was that Judaism would never have become accessible to them if it had not been for their Russian prayer books. The father's lesson was not wasted on his son: he developed a profound interest in broadening Judaism's horizons and reaching out beyond what Jews are fond of calling "members of the tribe."

As leader of the largest Jewish denomination in America, Schindler launched the optimistic, inclusive, and highly controversial Outreach program to the non-Jewish spouses of Reform Jews, with the idea of easing their entry into Judaism. His many detractors among Orthodox Jews, and among the more moderate Conservatives as well, accuse him of splitting the Jewish people by creating Jews-by-convenience, whose switch of allegiance was not thought through or well prepared.

"All my life," Schindler explained in an address on the tenth anniversary of Outreach, "my father reminded me that people who have no mission are suspected of having no message, of possessing nothing that is sufficiently worthy to share with others. He was also the first to tell me what Albert Einstein said: 'I am sorry that I was *born* a Jew, for it kept me from *choosing* to be a Jew.'" (The same words have also been attributed to Justice Louis Brandeis.)

The lucky Subbotniks had a choice to stay where they were or wander in the wilderness. Two hundred years ago, they plunged into the wilderness, and in 1830 their wholesale deportation to the Caucasus began. They thereby joined a long line of religious and political fugitives throughout the generations who have sought haven on the unreachable summits of the Caucasus. Only a handful of those have left any traces; all the rest merely added a couple of genes to the pool, inserted a word or two to an orally transmitted myth—and then vanished. This need not be the case of the Subbotniks, whose story is still awaiting its ultimate chronicler and explainer.

THE GHOSTS OF THE CAUCASUS

RUSSIAN FEDERATION

STAVROPOL
PROVINCE

Prokhladny

KABARDINO-
BALKARIA • Nalchik

• Khabaz

INGUSHETIA

CHECHNYA

NORTH
OSSETIA

CAUCASUS

SOUTH
OSSETIA

MOUNTAINS

DAGHESTAN

AJARIA

GEORGIA • Tbilisi

TURKEY

ARMENIA

Sevan (Yelenovka) •

Yerevan •

Lake Sevan

Ararat (16,946 ft.) +

NAKHICHEVAN
(AZER.)

Quba •

Khynalug •

AZERBAIJAN

Sumgait •
Baku •

NAGORNO-
KARABAKH

• Stepanakert

Privolnoye •

IRAN

Caspian
Sea

N

0 Miles   300

0 Kilometers   300

© 2000 Jeffrey L. Ward

Part IV

REMEMBER AND FORGET: THE POLITICS OF MEMORY

THE DARK SIDE OF ELBRUS

On a midsummer day in 1996, I traveled to a remote village, not far from Europe's tallest mountain, Elbrus, in the central section of the Caucasus range. To ancient Middle Eastern and Mediterranean civilizations, Elbrus signified the end of the world, beyond which darkness prevailed. The village I was visiting, Khabaz, was one of the nearest human settlements on Elbrus's "dark side." It is situated in a land called Balkaria, populated by the descendants of goatherds who are said to have occupied this land since antiquity. I went to Khabaz looking for the memory of the Balkars. I wanted to know how those destitute farmers, living in an alpine environment at the far end of Europe, related to a terrible tragedy that had befallen their people only half a century earlier.

The land around Khabaz is synonymous in the Russian mind with health and pristine beauty. In the old Soviet days, when life was orderly and predictable, vacationers would flock to the area in the summer to inhale its pure air and drink its water, said to be blessed with curative powers. But the only tourists we came across that day were a father and his two teenage boys on a day trip from Stavropol, capital of Russia's main southern province. They filled empty vodka bottles with spring water in order to sell them back home. In the city, we were told, spring water's market worth was roughly thirty U.S. cents a bottle.

Khabaz was slogging its way through mud that day, a mild reminder of what the village could expect come winter. No asphalt roads were to be found, and local transportation was confined to a few tractors and horse-drawn carts. Families shared their fenced yards with domestic animals, and at the outskirts of the village, poorly dressed, wet-nosed kids—all-too-familiar representatives of rural poverty worldwide—

welcomed us: myself and two friendly members of the neighboring nation of Kabarda, with whom the Balkars share the lilliputian semi-autonomous province called Kabardino-Balkaria, a constituent republic of the Russian Federation.

"Look at that hill," my older companion said. We had stopped the car to do just that when a seven-year-old boy approached us. His name was Albert. He was wearing a cheap baseball cap and an old windbreaker featuring a fading image of a panda bear. Albert seemed eager to engage the foreigner, so we challenged him to run as quickly as he possibly could to the top of the hill, about five hundred feet above us. Albert snickered and flew upward so fast that he was smiling and waving at us from the summit by the time I had my video camera focused and ready to go.

Albert then briefly disappeared into a dark cave, which was the reason for our stopover. "That cave," my Kabardin companion said, "served as the last point of resistance when the Germans moved to occupy Khabaz. The partisans entrenched themselves in the cave and kept shooting at the German column for three days, until they ran out of ammunition and had to withdraw." During World War II, Adolf Hitler's army established a garrison in Khabaz in December 1942, in order to secure the great prize: the oil fields lying east of Balkaria, in Chechnya and Azerbaijan.

When I traveled to the Balkar land, I expected to hear of cowardice and submission to the Germans. The Soviet regime later denounced the Balkars for collective collaboration with the Nazis and banished them en masse to Central Asia. At least one-third of them perished in the process. But my companion's account of the cave suggested that the tale of the Balkars' "betrayal of the fatherland" was incomplete at best.

My companions drove me to the house of an elderly friend who, they promised, would tell me everything that I cared to know about "the nightmare of 1944." His name was Magomed Kaygermazov. The old Balkar welcomed us with a mixture of amusement and incredulity. *Amerikanyetz?* American? Kaygermazov kept asking, pointing his finger at me and laughing heartily. My many years in the United States convinced most of my Caucasian interlocutors that I was American, my Israeli passport notwithstanding.

The poverty around me was so striking that I told my companion we had better not stay there too long, lest the old man insist on treating us the way highlanders treat their guests: slaughtering an animal, uncorking bottles of booze, and depleting the family's meager resources. My concern turned into open anxiety when I heard that Kaygermazov's grandchildren, two boys aged seven and eleven, might not be able to go to school come fall because there was not enough money to buy them boots. "Don't worry," said my Kabardin companion. "There isn't a greater honor and joy for them in the world than the visit of a foreigner."

En route to the house, we had to cross a muddy stable, treading carefully between puddles and small piles of horse manure. A pale young woman, wearing a scarf around her head—probably our host's daughter—was seated on a stool in the yard, stirring what seemed to be a large pot of soup. She nodded at us reservedly, evidently shy and perhaps not unmindful of the extra work that our unexpected visit was certain to generate.

We ate and drank and chatted amicably about matters of greater and lesser importance. Kaygermazov was wearing a gray hat, which he never took off.

When I raised the subject of the Balkars' near-extermination at the hands of the Soviet Union, I was startled to learn that Kaygermazov's grandchildren had not the faintest idea of what I was talking about. I could not help but think of my own childhood in a country of genocide survivors, where the lingering shadow of a bloody past was a matter of

There are still Balkars on the mountains of Balkaria, but little Balkar memory.

Magomed Kaygermazov, seen here in his courtyard in the village of Khabaz, would not tell his grandchildren, for now. But who will?

course and where the word *sho'a*, Hebrew for Holocaust, entered my vocabulary almost at the same time *tree* and *sky* and *car* did.

"How is it possible?" I asked their grandfather. "Why don't they know anything about your own experience? After all, *you* were only slightly older at the time of the deportation, and they could easily identify with the tribulations of a boy their age."

"They have time," the old man mused, "they have time. They will go to school, there they will hear about it from their teacher. When they come home and ask questions, we will reply. All in good time."

A few days later, in the open market of Nalchik, the provincial capital, I came across a popular school textbook for ninth graders, *Russia's History in the Twentieth Century*. Presumably, this was the book Kaygermazov's grandchildren would use one day. In three hundred pages of the book, I found a single reference, one sentence long, to the deportations of seven nations at the end of World War II.

"Did you collaborate with the Germans?" I asked Kaygermazov. "Sure," he laughed, as if relating an anecdote. "We gave them food, drink. . . . We obeyed their orders. . . . Who didn't? The Ukrainians did, the Belorussians did. . . . But they could not be deported—there were too many of them and not enough trains. For us, a single train was sufficient. We were the scapegoats."

He recalled the day the first Axis troops appeared in Khabaz. "First came the Romanians," he recalled. "They were short and dark-haired. Only then came the Germans. They stayed three months, ate our cows whenever they felt like, and dissolved our *kolkhoz*," the Soviet-installed collective farm.

German rule in the Caucasus lasted less than six months. Because the Caucasus was a combat area, the more dreadful aspects of the Nazi "Eastern policy" were not put into effect there, and the peoples of the Caucasus were generally spared atrocities, with the exception of Ashkenazi Jews (not Mountain Jews, who were deemed racially fit to live). The tone was set by the German military, not by the SS or the civilian Nazi viceroys who devastated large parts of Eastern Europe. Consequently, the reserve of goodwill and optimism in the North Caucasus, which would have awaited any liberator from the Soviet yoke, did not evaporate as quickly as it did in other German-occupied areas. Hitler, in fact, authorized the establishment of vassal statelets in the Caucasus, something he was never willing to contemplate anywhere else in the East.

"Primitive tribes," the historian Gerald Reitlinger observed astutely if condescendingly,

> have an irresistible appeal for the professional soldier. While it is the dream of Civil Servants to turn primitive tribes into urban communities, it is the professional soldier's dream to turn urbanized men into a primitive tribal society. . . . Thus there emerged [in the Northwest Caucasus] something that resembles the native protectorates of South Africa [under apartheid]. For the few weeks or months that they lasted, these little autonomies functioned without friction.

The highlanders knew little of Nazi philosophy or goals. They did have an intimate knowledge, however, of Stalinist practices. The Balkars themselves had experienced Stalinist justice a few days before the Germans arrived. On November 28, 1942, in an atrocity that remained unknown to the outside world until recently, Red Army soldiers entered two Balkar villages with clear instructions: "Take drastic measures against the [Balkar] bandits and their accomplices. Kill them on the spot. Burn their dwellings and their possessions, destroy everything that can give rise to future banditry. Under no circumstances is mercy to be shown." The soldiers, who were attached to the NKVD, the Soviet secret police, proceeded to slaughter the entire civilian population. The villages were Sautu and Glashevo, on the Cherek River. An eyewitness from a neighboring village prepared a list of 323 dead, all of them old men, women, and children, as the able-bodied had been drafted to the front.*

Just a few days later, the Germans appeared. The contrast with the Soviets could not have been more striking.

The full story of German rule in the Caucasus is still awaiting its chronicler; local historians treat the subject with trepidation. Alexander Dallin, who wrote a seminal book about the history of German occupation in the Soviet Union, concluded that in Kabardino-Balkaria, the "Balkars were particularly cooperative." The German supreme commander in the Caucasus, General (later Field Marshal) Ewald von Kleist, visited the Balkars in person and allowed them complete freedom in running their cultural and religious affairs. High-ranking German officers attended the festivities in honor of the Qurban, a major Muslim holiday. The highlanders presented the Germans with specimens of the famous Kabardin horse of the Caucasus and were rewarded with copies of the Qur'an as well as arms and ammunition. Observing their religion and bearing arms were two fundamental rights the Balkars had upheld for centuries, were denied them by the Soviets, and were now fully restored by the Germans. At the same time, the Germans encouraged the Balkars to join a North Caucasian Legion formed within the German armed forces, which, alongside a multitude of ethnic formations, was to participate in the liberation of the Soviet Union. By the end of 1944, 13,000 North Caucasians served under the German flag.

The question therefore is not whether the Balkars collaborated with the Germans; it is not even whether collaborators deserved to be prosecuted or punished. The question is whether the Balkars deserved a collective punishment on the account of the conduct of individuals— punishment that came close to destroying their nationhood.

"In early March of 1944," recalled Magomed Kaygermazov, "young Red Army soldiers arrived in Khabaz. They spent a week here. We were under the impression that they had come for a rest, before continuing to the front. Then one evening we noticed that two armed soldiers were guarding our house. 'What's going on?' we asked them. They remained silent."

A few hours later, the mystery was resolved. The Kaygermazovs were ordered to pack some food and blankets, then were directed to waiting trucks.

* Only in 1989 did the massacre of the Balkars gain any public recognition, when Balkar nationalists erected a commemorative sign next to the ruins of one of the villages.

Did they seek any explanations? "What explanations? That was it. Law is law."

Was there any resistance? "No resistance. We were loaded on the trucks at gunpoint. How could we have resisted arms with bare hands?"

And the women and children, how did they respond? "They cried, of course. And the cows mooed. And the dogs howled."

So fanatic was Moscow's determination to find a lasting solution to the Balkar problem that even Balkar soldiers serving in the Red Army, some of them decorated heroes, were taken from the front and sent to Central Asia. Accounts by the deportees of their grueling journey often read like Elie Wiesel's *Night*. In testimony published recently by North Caucasian activists in a trilogy called *Tak Eto Bylo (The Way It Was)*, Rades Kuliyev, nine years old at the time of the deportation, related:

> My father was fighting at the time in Leningrad [against the Germans]. The rest of us were transported in a truck to Nalchik and were then loaded on a freight car. Each car had seventy people squeezed into it, almost no men. The old people said we would be drowned in the sea. For half a day the train was moved back and forth on a bridge. Years later we found out it was a new bridge, just completed, and they were testing the bridge's endurance.

Kuliyev and his village were taken to the Kirgiz Soviet Republic in Central Asia, now independent Kyrgyzstan, and were divided among local collective farms as a slave labor force. Within two or three years, about half of them perished in the fields. Seven years later Kuliyev, having come of age, was granted his "passport," or identification card, and was told never to leave the farm without the commander's explicit permission. An illegal trip to the nearest town was punishable by six months confinement. A trip outside the republic would result in an automatic twenty-to-twenty-five-year term in a forced labor camp, without trial or the right of appeal.

Another deportee, Vladimir Lukayev, testified that during the journey to the east, bodies of the dead had to be thrown out of the train cars. Lukayev's old aunt Aba recalled that when the deportees reached their final destination in the heart of Kazakhstan, another Central Asian republic, a "welcoming committee" was awaiting them. An NKVD colonel, mounted on a beautiful white horse, inspected their party and presided over a selection process. At hand were also cranky chairmen of collective farms in search of laborers. Aunt Aba overheard the angry exchanges among the selectors. One was shouting, "Don't burden me with this family. There's only one worker in it, and the other eight are all dependents, an old lady and little children. Why should I feed them?" "Oh, is that it?" came the answer. "Should I take them? I'm up to my neck in dependents on my farm. I don't need these bandits anyway."

"And so," related Aunt Aba, "we were all standing there, listening, standing and waiting." The bickering was finally interrupted.

"Calm down all of you, don't shout," a solid and confident man laughingly assured the chairmen. "What's all this about dependents? Take them all! Take them all! They have been sent here for good. This is not the Caucasus, and in our climate the dependents will not last for long. They will all soon be dead, and you'll be left with the workers."

"He turned out to be right, as though he were looking through a crystal ball, the bastard," Aunt Aba recalled. "So many of our people died over there!"

The day of the Balkar deportation happened to be International Women's Day, an important festival in the Soviet calendar. Perhaps it was thanks to a peculiar Soviet sense of decorum that all the deportations were effected on important civic holidays. (The Karachai, the Balkars' ethnic brethren, were deported on Revolution Day; the Chechens and the Ingush on Red Army Day.) Late winter of 1944 was a hectic time for the wholesale-deportation industry in Europe. German trains were busy transporting Jews to death camps, and at almost exactly the same time that the Balkars began their journey to the east, final preparations began for the liquidation of hundreds of thousands of Hungarian Jews.

No gas chambers were awaiting the Balkars, but the circumstances of their deportation left little doubt about the intended results. Deported in the dead of winter, in the middle of a world war, without food supplies, to a strange land where no logistical measures were taken to absorb them, the Balkars and others were being led, if not into a Final Solution, then definitely into a Final Dissolution.

While accounts of Soviet atrocities under Stalin no longer surprise us, and even the lowest estimates acknowledge that millions perished, the case of the Caucasian nations (and three equally tiny and obscure nations outside of the Caucasus) was unique: this was the only instance in Soviet history in which entire nations were targeted. The Balkars, the Karachai, the Ingush, and the Chechens, as well as the Tatars of Crimea, the Kalmyks of southern Russia, and the Meskhetian Turks of Georgia:

the seven nations deported by the Soviets between 1943 and 1944 were the victims of an attempt to obliterate them as ethnic entities and to erase their collective memory.

While the Balkars were gone, the Soviets not only took their property but disinherited them in another characteristically Soviet way: they blotted out ancient Balkar names of settlements and rivers and expunged all references to the past existence of a Balkar nation from the official literature. Stalin was rewriting not only history but also archaeology.

Luckily, Stalin died in the spring of 1953, and his chief executioner Beria soon followed suit. By the decade's end, most of the Balkars returned and were generally allowed to reclaim their property. But how successful were they in reclaiming their memory?

For Magomed Kaygermazov and his grandchildren, the memory of 1944 itself had largely faded—not so much the fact of the catastrophe as its significance. In the frosty plains of Central Asia, not only did a third (some argue half) of the Balkar nation perish, but so did much of its character and heritage. In the words of Svetlana Akiyeva, a Balkar historian, "the links between generations were destroyed. Many elders died before they had the opportunity to pass on oral traditions to the young."

The "killer of nations," as historian Robert Conquest has called Stalin, was also the killer of nations' collective memories. He waged war against the Balkars' memory by banning the basic rituals of communal life: traditional wedding ceremonies were outlawed, and folk music and dancing were prohibited. The weak would die of hardships, and the strong survivors, having lost access to their heritage, would cease to be Balkar.

Magomed Kaygermazov related to me at length the horrors of the three-week-long train ride to Central Asia in a sealed car with little food or water, as the old and young were dying in agony in front of him. I then asked him what he thought of the Soviet regime. "Much better than the present 'democracy,'" he retorted without hesitation, pronouncing "democracy" with evident contempt. "I wish Stalin could rise from the dead and restore law and order."

When I suggested that Stalin's "law and order" had not quite benefited the Balkars, the highlander offered a resolute defense of the dead dictator. "He did not know, he did not see the decree. . . . He was manipulated. . . . Let us leave him in peace."

I met with identical responses from other deportation survivors. Older Balkars were far less eager to discuss with me their national tragedy than were, for example, the Chechens.

A case in point was Vassily Ulbashev, a Balkar driver who was living in the provincial capital of Nalchik. Himself a child of deportees, born in Kazakhstan, he defended the deportation by making a battlefield analogy. "Think of a general who has to sacrifice a platoon, or even a battalion, in order to secure victory over the enemy," he told me. "That is what Stalin had to do with us in order to obtain victory over the German Fascists."

I shared my amazement at the nature of the responses with Svetlana Akiyeva, the thirty-seven-year-old Balkar historian. "Forgiveness is embedded in our character," she asserted. "Besides, the Balkars abhor self-pity, and they are reluctant to talk about that period. My own father would boast about beating the hell out of a neighborhood bully when he was young—but never, never about his own humiliation at the hands of others."

While I was at Kaygermazov's house, the old Balkar sent for a neighbor's son. "He's a colleague of yours," he told me. I thought my host was taking liberties with professional definitions and that the neighbor's son was at best the editor of the collective farm newsletter.

A young man in his mid-twenties walked in, sporting the uncommon beard that in the Caucasus is presently associated with Muslim defiance. He turned out to be a reporter for a popular news program on Russian national television. He lived in Moscow but was spending a summer vacation in his native village on his way back from the battlefields of Chechnya. During most of my conversation with Kaygermazov, he was subdued. "I am sorry," he told me in completely understandable English, "we have a tradition here—young people do not speak in the presence of their elders. Doing so is a sign of disrespect." But the journalist was evidently unhappy with Kaygermazov's forgiveness toward Stalin and his lack of national ardor. When he finally did interject a few words, he spoke admiringly of the Chechens' courage.

It was exactly at that time that the Chechen rebels were mounting the most amazing coup of the war: their irregular units had pushed back into the capital Grozny and were driving the Russians out, inflicting the most stunning defeat upon the Russian army. Nothing of the sort had been seen in the Caucasus since Imam Shamil's great victories in the 1840s, in the triumphant phase of his rebellion against the czarist government. The young Balkar journalist had just spent a couple of days in and around Grozny and was entirely convinced that the Chechens were winning the war.

And here—I asked him as discreetly as possible—in the mountains of Balkaria? Could anything like the Chechen rebellion ever happen?

"Who knows?" he responded. "We surely have some good reasons, but I'm not sure we have the strength or the will."

The contrast between the Balkars and the Chechens could not be more striking. Here are two mountain nations, both with claims to antiquity, both of which fell under Russian rule more or less at the same time in the nineteenth century. Both were accused in 1944 of collective collaboration with the Nazis, and deported en masse within two weeks of each other; both suffered catastrophic losses. Yet the Chechens never forgot, nor did they ever forgive. Given the chance, they rose up in arms, in a rebellion that stood absolutely no chance of succeeding, lost tens of thousands of people, and never recoiled. That they finally overcame the longest odds and handed the Russians a defeat (in 1996) testifies less to their common sense than to their improbable audacity.

To the question "Why then not the Balkars?" the not-so-simple answer is that the Chechens are indeed different. They are comparable with no other people in the Caucasus and for that matter with no other people in the entire Russian Federation. Russia never understood this. Much like America in Vietnam, it was driven by a false "domino theory," which held that the fall of minuscule Chechnya would generate a mass defection and subsequent disintegration of the entire Russian state, across eleven time zones.

Shortly before Russia attacked the Chechens in December 1994, warnings abounded about "a new Caucasian war," from the Black Sea to the Caspian. Such was not the case, neither in 1994 nor in 1999. A certain Balkar army officer, a former general in the Soviet army, became a symbol of the impotence that gripped the nationalities of the Caucasus. A couple of days after the beginning of the Chechen war, Russian intelligence eavesdropped on a telephone conversation between this general, Sufyan Beppayev, and his former comrade-in-arms in the Soviet army, the Chechen leader, General Jokar Dudayev.

Dudayev implored Beppayev to organize military actions against the Russian rear: "Fire, fire, fire, fire, Sufyan, fire. In the heart, while they're messing around here. It would be good to give them a jolt there."

The exchange continued:

Dudayev: They're beasts of prey that don't know when to stop. Mean-..ess, treachery, and sheer violence—we'll probably have to use the same methods against them, Sufyan. They won't understand anything else.
Beppayev: Yes, it'll come to that.

Dudayev: It will. I can supply strategic data on the makeup of these groups, how many and where. And the same goes for how they will move, where in the rear they need to attack from, the best places in the rear to wade into them. The age-old tactic of the highlander is raid and retreat, raid and retreat, wear them down until they're so terrified and scared that they croak. Raid and retreat, raid and retreat.

At the end of their conversation, a besieged Dudayev again pleaded with the Balkar general: "Take up a little bit of leadership there, Sufyan, so that it means business. When it starts there, we will feel easier here."

Beppayev had little to say in response. "Let us see," he murmured. "We are also trying our best. We have already launched rallies. We staged a protest rally today. But to our great regret, these rallies lead nowhere. . . . But anyway, in fact, the people are rising."

In fact the people were not.

In November 1996, nearly two years after that conversation, General Beppayev was proclaimed "president" of a Balkar "republic." The proclamation initially terrified many Russians. The "Balkar Republic" turned out to be short-lived. Within days of assuming its "presidency," General Beppayev retracted, and was happily coopted into the Kabardin-dominated government of Kabardino-Balkaria. Knowing little about the Caucasus, many Russians saw in Beppayev a potential new Dudayev: an ill-tempered former general of a small Muslim nation attempting to capitalize on Russia's woes and setting another part of the Caucasus ablaze. To hard-line nationalists in Moscow, that was the ultimate proof that the peace treaty in Chechnya, concluded in August 1996, had been a colossal mistake, and that now the disintegration of the motherland was gathering unstoppable momentum.

Russian media outlets outdid each other in making learned speculations about foreign hands pulling the Balkar strings. The president of Kabardino-Balkaria, Valery Kokov, a typical Communist boss of the Soviet era, blamed Turkey. Indeed, the Balkars being Turkic, Turkey was the foreign country most widely suspected. Blame Turkey First has been a guiding principle of Russian and Soviet policies in the Caucasus for nearly two hundred years.

General Beppayev had been an unlikely convert to nationalism: in Soviet times he won notoriety as the hunter of nationalist agitators in the South Caucasus, and he was implicated in some of the bloodiest acts of repression against independent movements in Azerbaijan, Armenia, and Georgia. The man mostly responsible for Beppayev's brief conversion was one Bahauddin Etezov. Etezov is a middle-aged radio journalist with dignified, gentlemanly features; he is also the founder of a Balkar nationalist organization called Türé ("Assembly"). I met him in late summer 1996, a few weeks before Beppayev was proclaimed "president." Indeed, the general had just left Türé's modest office when I walked in on that sunny, pleasant Saturday morning. Etezov's demeanor was not that of a revolutionary. He spoke calmly, his eyes flickered with slight irony, and even when he was sharing with me the grimmest prognostications about the future of his people, a hint of a smile never left his lips.

A Russian, suspicious of Balkar intentions, would probably have felt vindicated upon entering Türé's office, located in a remote section of Nalchik. He would have seen on one wall a smiling portrait of Jokar Dudayev (by the time of my visit Dudayev had already been assassinated, most probably by the Russians); another wall was adorned with a map of all the Turkic nations, from northern China to the Balkans, including a few that are not quite Turkic. I asked Etezov to pose for my camera next to Dudayev's poster. "Ah," he half-smiled. "You are going to write that I am a separatist who wants to be a Balkar Dudayev."

*Bahauddin Etezov has a famous Chechen rebel hanging on the wall—
but he has no intention of leaving Russia.*

Do you? I asked.

"Dudayev was a paragon of honesty, morality, and masculinity," said Etezov. "But we admire him not because he wanted to secede from Russia. We want our rights to be upheld *within* Russia, based on the Russian constitution and solely through peaceful means." Etezov subscribed to the notion, popular among some Turkic intelligentsia in Russia, that the Russian state "was founded by two nations, Slavs and Turks." He, being a Turk, was therefore no less a Russian than any Slav around.* I imagine very few Russian nationalists would concur in this heretical interpretation of the birth of Holy Rus, but that is a different issue. What matters is Etezov's own lack of animosity toward the very Russia whose Soviet government brought his people to the verge of extinction.

It is not Russia from which he wants the Balkars to secede, but rather Kabardino-Balkaria, the political union in which the Balkars are only nominal partners alongside the more numerous and politically dominant Kabardins. If he had his way, a tiny patch of land would be carved out for the Balkars (who do not have a single town or city to their name), and a "Balkar autonomous republic" would be established on it.

An outsider could be forgiven for thinking that the Caucasus has gone out of its mind. There are already seven autonomous republics between the Caspian and the Black Sea, providing self-determination of sorts to fifteen nations. (How seven can serve fifteen is another matter, a specialty of Soviet arithmetic that earns attention elsewhere in this book.) But the existing ones, with their "sovereign laws" and "presidents" and "national security councils" and virtual one-party state systems, offer a strong challenge to the Balkans when it comes to Ruritanian diversity.

One might wonder: Who needs a Balkar republic on top of this ethnic mélange? Well, the Balkars may need one. It is indeed tragic that group grievances sometimes cannot be addressed within the geographic boundaries of a multiethnic entity and that minorities may feel they need extra protection. But Americans—unsympathetic toward secession in the light of their own civil war, and culturally partial toward ethnic melting pots—may find it easier to understand Etezov's agenda for his people by comparing it with that of various social and racial groups

---

* Etezov was probably inspired by "the Bulgar thesis," which sought to relate some Turkic peoples in the former Soviet Union to an early medieval Turkic tribe called "Bulgars." Some "Bulgarists" contend that members of the tribe were founders, or at least co-founders, of most state structures between the Danube and the Pacific Ocean, including the first three Russian principalities. For reasons too arcane to enumerate, some Turkic intellectuals would rather claim Bulgar genes than share ancestors with the Turks of Anatolia. For more of the curiosities of Turkic historiography in the former Soviet Union, see the next chapter, "The Ghosts of Caucasian Albania."

in the United States from the 1960s onward. For a melting pot to work, without producing alienation and disenfranchisement, individual identities need to be recognized. To borrow a term from the civil rights campaign in the United States, the Balkars need *empowerment*.

An episode that took place in 1986 may shed some light on the differences in American and Russian perceptions on how best to treat minorities. Mikhail Gorbachev, still in the early days of his rule, hosted a delegation of black leaders from the United States. As polemical and argumentative as he was, Gorbachev lectured his guests on how much better minority groups were treated in the Soviet Union. "Why don't blacks have their own separate state in America?" he retorted triumphantly when he was asked about his country's own human rights record. Needless to say, the Americans were taken aback. Separate development is not what the civil rights movement was all about. But in the Soviet-Russian context, respect for minorities is incomplete if the minority is not offered its own autonomy. Hence the Balkars think that their turn has come for the same form of empowerment.

It took the Soviets thirteen years to allow the repatriation of the Balkars. It took a Russian government fifty years to express remorse for the near-destruction of the Balkar people. Finally, in 1994, on the eve of the anniversary of the deportation, President Boris Yeltsin issued a solemn decree "On Measures for the Rehabilitation of the Balkar People and State Support for Its Revival and Development." He proclaimed: "The Balkars drank to the full from the cup of humiliation. I bow my head in memory of the dead." The proclamation was rich in exclamations, metaphors, and promises to indemnify the Balkars for their suffering. Sadly, at that time, the Russian government was not generally in an introspective mood concerning its policies toward the native peoples of the Caucasus. In lieu of measures to correct the fifty-year-old injustice, the Kremlin escalated the war of words against the Chechens, the Balkars' fellow victims. By the fifty-first anniversary of the deportation, thousands of Chechens were dead, their capital lay in ruins, and the specter of 1944 was casting a new shadow over the Caucasus.

Yeltsin's edict on the rehabilitation of the Balkars bore no more fruit than thousands of other presidential decrees he issued on any number of matters. The Russian state was simply too weak, and its attempt to reassert itself by waging a war on the Chechens only provided further evidence of its weakness.

According to Etezov, perhaps 85 percent of the funds allocated under the rehabilitation decree never reached their intended destination. "The rest ended up in the lowland, in Kabardin hands—and that was no surprise. In seventy-five years of Kabardino-Balkaria's existence, not one factory has been constructed in our mountainous regions, and 98 percent of the highlanders are unemployed." Etezov appreciates the expression of regret from Moscow, but he believes that undoing the damage of 1944 will require more than giving the Balkars a patronizing slap on the back. It will require a *purpose*, a sense of direction. Hence the idea of an autonomous Balkar republic within the Russian Federation.

Creating one would necessitate the breakup of an existing republic: a divorce between the Balkars and the Kabardins. It is doubtful that such a divorce could be accomplished through mutual consent, as was divorce between the Chechens and the Ingush, who had formed a joint autonomous republic before the Chechens first raised the banner of secession from Russia, in 1991. Back in the early 1990s, Kabardin nationalists, in opposition to the republican government, campaigned for such a dissolution. But President Kokov's government would never sponsor an act that would render the minuscule republic even more minuscule. Russia's constitution does not allow for the breakup of an existing territory. Civil strife, pitting armed Balkars against armed Kabardins, could of course change the situation, but for that to happen, ethnic hostility would have to exist, such as that which, elsewhere in the region, has pitted Armenians against Azeris or Abkhaz against Georgians. Traveling across the Kabardin-Balkar republic, I encountered no evidence of such hostility.

Still, the Balkars sounded a strong note of unhappiness with the status quo when they voted overwhelmingly against Boris Yeltsin in the first round of the Russian presidential election in 1996. Yeltsin was startled. The vice president of Kabardino-Balkaria, Gennady Gubin, an ethnic Russian, reproached the Balkars for their ingratitude. "It is unexpected and incomprehensible for the republic's leadership," he wrote in a local newspaper. "Boris Yeltsin was the first official person in Russia who publicly apologized to the Balkar people for the deportations." Much to the incredulity of most observers, Yeltsin went on to win Kabardino-Balkaria in the second round with a solid majority, showing that Bill Clinton is not the only "comeback kid." Few people I met, whatever their nationality, believed the official tally. (Yeltsin's successor, Vladimir Putin, encountered no such problem. He won the first and only round in Kabardino-Balkaria, in March 2000, by a whopping 74.42 percent.)

When I visited the republic three months after the election, huge campaign posters of Yeltsin were still hanging from billboards. They were perfectly preserved, even so long after the completion of the campaign in which they were used—no simple feat given the summer's scorching sun and early fall's drenching rain. Posters are, after all, made of paper. The miraculous survival of the election posters seemed to me a bit farcical. It was as if President Kokov were replicating Lenin's mausoleum in his own tiny capital, with the slight difference that in Moscow a team of bright scientists had managed to embalm a corpse, while in Nalchik an all-too-eager team of provincial bureaucrats had accomplished the miracle of extending the life of posterboard.

President Kokov himself was reelected rather comfortably in early 1997. His margin of victory: 99.37 percent, letting us know that Kabardino-Balkaria is still run by acclamation.

Bahauddin Etezov was born six years before the deportation of his people. He came of age in a distant Kyrgyz village, not far from the border with China. He was twenty at the time of his return to Balkaria, when he started a long career as a radio broadcaster. When I met him, he was the editor of a Balkar-language program that the official Nalchik radio transmitted to an "overseas audience," on shortwaves.

I could not help a smile when I heard that. You? I asked him with disbelief. A subversive nationalist agitator? They trust *you* with an official radio program? Etezov chuckled. "They don't really trust me," he said. "They just never listen to my programs." Fair enough, I thought. Such little absurdities make life under authoritarian systems a bit more livable.

If the authorities do not take Etezov's radio commentaries very seriously, however, they take his political activities all too seriously. Well before the proclamation of a Balkar "republic," the local prosecutor, hand-picked by President Kokov, served Etezov with a court order requiring him to drop "offensive" clauses from Türé's political program. The order, which I saw and photographed, was written on official stationery. One clause that the government found particularly offensive was the one that called for the repatriation of the thousands of Balkars who still languish in the poverty of their Kyrgyz exile, unable to afford the trip back home. Why would that be judged offensive? "They simply don't want more of us around here," Etezov explained.

After the proclamation of the "republic," Türé was banned altogether. What will happen to the Balkar people if they do not get a republic? I asked Etezov. "We will die as a people," he said.

"Balkars do not like to pity themselves," historian Akiyeva told me. "They do not like it when a stranger tries to understand what happens in the depths of their psyche. They are a proud lot, and the deportation period is a constant source of pain and humiliation for them. They were entirely helpless—there was nothing they could do to change their situation."

Akiyeva, who was born in exile, is a modern-looking woman, the only Balkar on the staff of Nalchik's leading academic research center. Her parents were born in two different villages that ceased to exist in 1944 and were never reclaimed for human habitation, Balkar or otherwise. In terms of her biography and her education, she would be a natural articulator of her nation's suffering as well as an ideologue of empowerment. But she is neither. She offers a smiling apology. "It is a matter of national character," she said. "Is there really a compelling need to change it? The Balkars do not like to be perceived as weak. They like to think of themselves as strong. And if they want to be strong, why would I impose weakness on them?"

And so, as I was coming closer to completing my journey to the Caucasus in quest of memory, the question I had been asking repeatedly, "Why forget?", was now being turned on its head. The Balkars of the Elbrus lands were, in fact, retorting, "But why remember?"

THE GHOSTS OF
CAUCASIAN ALBANIA

In fact, the whole of Japan is pure invention.
There is no such country, there are
no such people.
OSCAR WILDE

One would expect people to remember the past
and to imagine the future, [b]ut in fact . . . they
imagine the past and remember the future.
LEWIS NAMIER

To remember also means to invent,
and the one who remembers is also an inventor.
OSIP MANDELSTAM

On a late July afternoon, on a distant peak in the mountains of northern Azerbaijan, two courteous young men led me to an ancient brick wall next to their village mosque and pointed to an inscription. "No one has ever managed to read it," they said. "Perhaps you might?"

I looked at the sequence of hieroglyphic signs engraved in an old stone.

"Sorry," I said, half-smiling. "I wish I could."

The following day I was led to a heap of stones in an isolated valley, about three miles away. A local saying has it that "no one can claim to have visited us without first seeing the stones." Unassuming from a distance, the stones reveal on closer inspection a natural phenomenon. A steady stream of gas flows from below them, sustaining a small flame that local ingenuity has turned into an ever-running stove. There, on the stones, the freshly cut meat of a slaughtered sheep is fried in an instant. How long has this flame been burning? I asked my host's son. He was young and modern-looking, wearing a T-shirt featuring the Golden Gate Bridge and the words SAN FRANCISCO. The man chuckled. "Here," he said, "you assume that everything has existed since God created the earth."

Yet even God has changed quite a bit around this flame. Many centuries ago, long before the first Muslim warriors emerged from the Arabian Desert, this stream of natural gas was almost certainly a shrine for

There, on the stones, the freshly cut meat of a slaughtered sheep is fried in an instant.

local fire-worshippers—an offshoot of the Zoroastrian religion, which had a huge following all over the mountains, along the full length of the Caspian coast, across modern Azerbaijan and Armenia, and as far away as Iran and India.

Fire and the Caucasus are solemnly wedded. About two hundred miles west of where I was walking stands Mount Kazbek, the presumed site of Prometheus' exile. It was there that the angry gods of Greek mythology banished the best-known renegade of all times for stealing fire from Olympus and sharing its secrets with mortals.

Vague recollections of a half-mythical past abound in the mountains. They used to be the stuff of harmless folk legends or the object of archaeological curiosity. But with the rise of nationalism in the dying years of the Soviet Union, the speculations were benign no longer. Indecipherable inscriptions and ancient sites of worship have become factors in a new Caucasian equation, where facts and fiction are often indistinguishable, where history is but the slave of politics.

About two thousand years ago, Greek geographer Strabo wrote that twenty-six tribes, forming a loose confederation, lived in this region. So zealously did they observe their ancient liberties that their king was merely first among equals. Though the names by which Strabo knew the tribes are long forgotten, many of the local ethnic groups, at times confined to a single village, claim those ancient tribes as ancestors.

Khynalug, northern Azerbaijan. Is this nation-village, speaking a distinct archaic language, an offshoot of ancient Albania?

Such is the case of Khynalug, the village I was visiting south of the Daghestan-Azerbaijan border. Perhaps "village" is not an accurate designation for a community that really constitutes a nation, with a distinct language so elaborate that it requires fifty-nine consonants and eighteen vowels to be written properly, and whose speakers use no fewer than nineteen grammatical cases. The entire Khynalug nation consists of about 2,000 people, all concentrated in this village, offering a remarkable illustration of why a medieval Arab geographer once called the Caucasus "the mountain of languages."

Perhaps the inscription that I failed to decipher could tell us where exactly the Khynalug came from. One possibility is that they are a surviving fragment of a long-forgotten nation that dominated the mountains until about a millennium ago. Its name was Albania, as if we needed further proof of how evocative the Caucasus is of the Balkans. The name notwithstanding, the two Albanias have nothing at all in common, and in any event the Caucasian one no longer exists.

Or does it?

The quest for Albania could have made a good *Indiana Jones*–style movie, complete with action scenes through narrow alpine passages and hitherto unvisited caves haunted by ancient demons. But pending an

Street scenes from Khynalug, whose architecture is uniquely mountainous.
One indecipherable inscription on a Khynalug wall might have made a difference
(or might not).

outburst of Hollywood interest in the Caucasus, we will have to settle for the unlikely drama that the Albanian enigma has already generated. It began as an obscure quarrel among scholars and ended up as a catalyst to a devastating war and appalling human misery and, along the way, played a role in the breakup of the Soviet Union.

The twists of the Albanian story are extreme even in the bizarre context of Old World tribal rivalries. An outsider uncoached in the ways of the Caucasus may be forgiven for feeling that the parties involved would be better left to their own devices, so hopeless are their irrational enmities and fears.

Do not blame the Albanians. They serve merely as a metaphor for nationalism gone berserk, for legitimate aspirations turned ugly and deadly. This is a tale about the ghosts of Albania, their invokers, and their exorcists.

Standing in front of the inscription in Khynalug, I hoped that the language was indeed the mysterious Albanian and that one day it would turn out to proclaim, "Please, take it easy. It has already happened. You cannot change it. Why try?" Unfortunately, interjections of humor are few in the Caucasian war over history. Welcome to the lands of grim exclamation points.

Ziya Buniyatov had come a long way from his personal triumph in Berlin in 1945, which earned him the Soviet Union's highest decoration. He was one of the young Red Army soldiers who raised the ham-

mer and sickle over the top of the vanquished Reichstag, symbolizing the
end of World War II.

I met this multimedaled "Hero of
the Soviet Union" exactly fifty years
later, in an apartment overlooking the
city of Baku. With oil money beginning to flow into Azerbaijan's capital,
the standards for material success were
quickly rising. Nevertheless, Buniyatov's two-bedroom apartment proclaimed to the world his continuing
high status: such space and comfort,
however modest by Western measures,
were a luxury unheard of in Soviet
times, a clear indication that the fortunate resident was a favorite son of the
system.

At the time of my visit, Buniyatov
was a prominent historian, a vice president of Azerbaijan's Academy of Science, and a member of parliament.

*This Khynalug boy followed our little
retinue in the mountains, whistling a
Turkish shepherd song (or so I was
told). He finally caught up with us and
introduced himself as "Socrates." My
first ever.*

Under the Communists, the acade-
mies—a national one for the entire Soviet Union, and one for each of
the fifteen "Union republics"—carried weight unmatched by similar
academies in the West. They were elevated into superministries of educational and technological advancement and became chief arbiters of
cultural policy. Their ranking members were lionized pillars of society,
bearing the revered title *academician*.

Academician Buniyatov was caught off guard when the state that had
so pampered him dissolved. He had few reasons to rejoice at the sudden
transformation of Baku from the Soviet Union's "finger pointing to Asia"
(in the words of an early Soviet foreign minister) into the capital of a
backwater state.

One day Azerbaijan may well become a Kuwait-on-the-Caspian, and
untold riches may fill its coffers—but for now it had little to show for its
sudden independence. The poorly fought war against the Armenians
over Nagorno-Karabakh (1988–93) cost it many thousands of lives as
well as one-fifth of its territory and tremendous human suffering.
Upward of 800,000 people, more than a tenth of the population, were
rendered homeless. The country's ever-bickering politicians had accomplished little in the way of improving the people's lot, but a lot by way

of manipulating each other into and out of power. Within the first nineteen months of its independence, Azerbaijan witnessed two armed rebellions and three state presidents, as well as a brief attempt at secession and the constant specter of civil conflict. This was a particularly gloomy record, even in the post-Soviet order.

That twilight period, when the old had not quite died and the new had not yet been born, offered few rewards to intellectual. Distinguished professors of yesteryear were reduced to selling shoelaces on street corners, it was said. But that was not Buniyatov's fate. The old warrior was still soldiering on. He had an important mission: endowing Azerbaijan with a history. Bolshevik theorists had prepared a melting pot for the nationalities, intending them to forget their past or at least to embrace a diluted version of it, so as to facilitate the emergence of a homogenized "Soviet people." But nationalism did not give in to Soviet internationalism. It remained active if disguised, enjoying a comeback in the 1960s (then referred to as "national Communism") and reemerged in earnest in the declining years of the Union, when the reawakening of memory became a high priority for the individual republics. Buniyatov's task was particularly daunting: his nation's very name had not existed only seventy-five years earlier, and its enemies were still assailing its "artificiality."

The quest for Azerbaijan's antiquity had actually begun well before Soviet collapse and reached its climax in the late 1980s. The fierce debates it generated had an eerily existential, rather than scholarly, quality. They were conducted along the lines of "I am, therefore *you* are not," or better, "You *were* not, therefore I am." The debaters locked horns with an intensity that outsiders might find bizarre and futile.

Lionel Trilling, the eminent American literary critic, once wrote of the "dark and bloody crossroads where literature and politics meet." Buniyatov seems to have spent a lifetime in the politico-literary trenches, earning both adulation and resentment in the process. His most daring thesis is thought to have played a role in kindling the Azeri-Armenian conflict, which precipitated the collapse of the Soviet Union—a remarkable turn of events for a young Soviet hero who stomped his feet on Nazi Germany's grave in 1945. At that time, he helped announce to the world the rise of a new superpower; fifty years later, he unwittingly became one of that superpower's undertakers.

A tall man, whose trim mustache was still resisting the discoloring of age, Buniyatov was an unlikely ideologue for Azeri national identity, since his mother was born a Subbotnik, and hence was an ethnic Russian.

At the time of my visit in the summer of 1995, he was busy time-traveling. Current politics evidently bored him, and he responded impatiently to my questions about the present. "Everyone asks me such questions," he snapped. "Why don't *you* ask me something *else?*" He told me he was researching a book about "Azerbaijan in the eighth century." A few might find the subject thus described somewhat oxymoronic. After all, nothing remotely reminiscent of "Azerbaijan" existed twelve hundred years ago.

It soon turned out that Buniyatov really meant not Azerbaijan but Albania. That long-extinct kingdom—Buniyatov contended—was related to Azerbaijan the way Gaul was related to France, or Roman Britain to England: that is to say, not exactly the same, but pretty close, with a lot of genes passed on, as well as traditions and traits of character; and even more important, with claims to continuity. If the modern Azeris are descendants of the ancient Albanians, then they are entitled to be considered indigenous, not the Johnnies-come-lately that they would be if their ancestors were sixteenth-century North Asian migrants.

Little is known of ancient Albania. In the second century A.D., the Romans, in need of local allies along their Parthian frontier, became interested and made Albania a province, but they stayed for only three years, thus depriving posterity of the opportunity to know more than Strabo had recorded a century or so earlier (in a couple of pages in his famous *Geography*, probably based on secondhand information).

Albania's later history is better known, thanks to Armenian and Arab sources. For more than four hundred years, between the fifth century and the ninth century A.D., a loose Albanian state was a vassal, in turn, of Parthia, Persia, and the Arab caliphate. Its borders roughly equaled those of modern Azerbaijan, and under the Arabs it enjoyed considerable commercial prosperity. It adopted Christianity as early as the fourth century through the activity of Armenian missionaries—but gradually reverted to Islam as a result of centuries of Muslim occupation (by Arabs, Mongols, Turks, and Persians). The last Christian Albanian state ceased to exist in 821.

Even though the ancient Albanians earned some disparaging remarks about their culture and degree of learning—it was said that they could not count to one hundred—they seem to have left behind some indications of literacy, such as the stone in Khynalug. The existence of an Albanian script was established in 1938, but unlike the Rosetta stone of Egypt, the Albanian hieroglyphs, in Khynalug and elsewhere, are still awaiting their Champollion. Until then, Albania remains an inviting mystery, an irresistible target for Caucasians in quest of a distant past.

In most places, speculations such as Buniyatov's on the origins of the Azeris would belong in high-minded academic seminars, not in real life. The Caucasus begs to differ.

This is why the Albanian theory gained so much attention—not only in the Caucasus but also as far away as Moscow. Azerbaijan already began teaching Buniyatov's alternative history to schoolchildren under the Soviet regime. Members of minorities living in Azerbaijan had to clench their teeth when their children were treated to historical narratives describing everyone in Azerbaijan as the descendants of the Albanians— somewhat evocative of the incongruous way in which local children in France's African colonies had to recite the line "Our Ancestors, the Gauls."

But what in colonial Africa was considered harmless, even silly, was perceived in the emerging Azerbaijan as evidence of the majority's desire to impose its ways on minorities. What better way to do it than to repackage everyone's history?

Buniyatov's thesis sat well with the Soviet attempt to discredit and preempt "pan-Turkism," the notion of unity among the numerous Turkic-speaking peoples, who live in areas ranging from China's Xinjiang province in Central Asia to the outskirts of the Balkans. For most of the twentieth century, pan-Turkism was a favorite bogeyman not only of Russians but also of Greeks, Armenians, Serbs, and other unhappy subjects of the former Ottoman Empire.

The Soviet campaign against the Turks (or "Tatars") assumed various forms. One was the wholesale expulsion of small Turkic nations to Central Asia during World War II. (Many Azeris believe that Stalin intended to deport them as well and refrained only at the last moment.) Another was the Soviet encouragement of Armenian nationalists, right after the war, to claim for Soviet Armenia considerable chunks of Turkish territory. Within months of the deportations, in August 1944, the Communist Party's Central Committee practically ordered a non-deported Turkic group, the Volga Tatars, to renounce their Mongol ancestry, particularly the Golden Horde, which dominated much of the future Russian Empire through the sixteenth century. The party was not all that interested in archaeological truths; rather it hoped that by exorcising evil Mongol spirits it would fatally undermine pan-Turkism. Astonishing alternative histories for the hapless Tatars were commissioned and concocted, which still prevail today.

Ziya Buniyatov's scholarly endeavors offered another platform in the Soviets' ongoing campaign against "pan-Turkism." Thanks to Marxism-Leninism's infatuation with polemics and its never-ending quest for "conclusive scientific evidence," they treated the news that the Azeris' "non-Turkishness" had been "scientifically proven" with the utmost seriousness.

Such "evidence" could not reduce the actual Turkishness of much of Azerbaijan's culture, or alter the fact that the Azeri tongue remained the closest to Turkish of any major Turkic language. Nonetheless, Buniya-tov's speculations provided Soviet ideologues with another opportunity to affect the present by remolding the past.

Buniyatov's alternative history did not stop with redefining the Azeris. He ascribed Albanian origins to many Armenians as well. Until 1990 about half a million Armenians lived in Azerbaijan, mostly in the Baku area and in a remote province that is known by its Russian name, Nagorno-Karabakh, or "mountainous Karabakh."

The Armenians of Baku were recent immigrants, having moved to Azerbaijan in the nineteenth century, and contributed enormously to the city's development. The Karabakh Armenians, however, thought of themselves as the heirs to an ancient Armenian community that had occupied the highlands for many centuries, even millennia. Armenians never fail to remind foreign visitors that an imposing old church in the northern part of Nagorno-Karabakh was constructed in the twelfth century, adding pointedly that Armenians were praying in that church while the Azeris' ancestors were still grazing their cattle in the steppes of Central Asia, many hundreds of miles away.

No way, said Ziya Buniyatov, the perennial rebel against conventional wisdom. To him, the Armenians of Karabakh were simply *Albanians* who had been forcibly converted to the Armenian Church as late as the nineteenth century.

What about the old Armenian church?

"Albanian."

And the famous Armenian princes of Karabakh over many centuries?

"Why, Albanian of course."

The Albanianness of the Caucasus, Buniyatov argued, had fallen victim to a conspiracy led by three elements who were interested in taking the Caucasus away from its indigenous population. It took a while to expose the conspiracy—some eight hundred years, to be precise—but Buniyatov had finally revealed the conspirators: the Arabs, the Armenians, and the czarist Russians. Each of them resolved, for their own reasons, that the Armenians should become the leading Christian nation of the Southeast Caucasus. The Southwest Caucasus belonged to the Georgians.

Under Arab auspices, in the Middle Ages, monks and priests of the Armenian national church had translated the entire body of Albanian ecclesiastic literature into Armenian, destroyed the Albanian original, then integrated it into the Armenian Church. From that point onward, the Albanians were persecuted and forcibly assimilated. The Albanian Church, formerly independent, was downgraded to a subdivision of the Armenian Church. Finally, in the nineteenth century, Russia, the new mistress of the Caucasus, dissolved this last modest vestige of Albania.

Buniyatov's most explosive contention, the one that impregnated his academic thesis with so much political significance, was that the wholesale expropriation of the Albanian past made it possible for the Armenians to cover up the fact that they were not an indigenous nation of the Caucasus.

In 1987, twenty-two years after the publication of Buniyatov's work on the Albanians, his young disciple, Farida Mamedova, took the hypothesis a step further. In a doctoral dissertation presented to the Academy of Science of Azerbaijan, she contended that the Armenians had been transplanted to the Caucasus by Russian officials in the early nineteenth century in order to strengthen Russia's foothold in areas it had just taken over from Ottoman Turkey and Persia. The earlier inhabitants of Nagorno-Karabakh who were considered "Armenians" were not Armenians at all—they were Albanians. If anything, they were the kin of those we now call Azeris.

The Armenians, whose claims to antiquity are rivaled only by those of the Chinese and the Jews, were being told that in this neighborhood called the Caucasus, they were the new kids on the block and should behave accordingly.*

When I asked Buniyatov whether politics played a part in his controversial contentions, he insisted that he advanced his ideas in good faith. "I am a scientist, you know," he said, frowning. I got a similar response from Farida Mamedova, Buniyatov's disciple and the heiress to his Albanian heresy.

Does it really make any difference, in today's world, whether the Armenians arrived here 150 years ago or 1,700 years ago? I asked her, during an interview at her modest apartment in Baku.

"It may or may not," she answered, "but that is none of my business. I am a scholar, and I am trying to find out what happened. It is for others to determine the relevance."

Within moments of protesting her political innocence, however, she did make the politics of the present her business. "So," she said sardonically of the Armenians, looking straight at my video camera, "anywhere *they* go and settle, *they* think *they* deserve a state of their own?"

She was aiming her volleys at the Armenian rebels in Nagorno-Karabakh, who had recently made a unilateral declaration of independence. Unable to win international recognition for unification with

---

* The Armenians trace themselves to the landing of Noah's ark. They were first observed by others around the seventh century B.C. and though their main centers of population were located in Asia Minor—from which they were ejected between 1915 and 1923—they may have appeared in the South Caucasus as early as the fifth or sixth century B.C.

Armenia, which had been their initial goal in 1988, they began to claim, in 1991, the right to secede from Azerbaijan and be on their own—a speck of a territory with 150,000 inhabitants.

Mamedova was contemptuous. "They say that wherever there is a territory densely populated by them, they deserve to have an independent state. But then what of California? There are areas of California in which the Armenians are in the majority. Should they get their independence there, too?"*

To Mamedova, the Armenians are a people without a land. "Every people in the world has a history based on land," she said. "You have the 'history of France,' or the 'history of England,' or the 'history of Italy.' Every people—except the Armenians. In their case, it is the 'history of the Armenians,' because 'Armenia' as such never existed."

But, I protested, you also have the "history of the Jews."

"Fine, and the Jews, too. But only these two peoples have been landless."

When I raised the subject with Buniyatov in a separate interview, he gave me an amused look through thick, black-rimmed glasses. "King Solomon," he said cryptically.

I was mystified. Were we now going to involve the Davidic dynasty in this?

"Did he have coins?" asked Buniyatov, of the biblical monarch. "Of course he did. And why did he? Because he had a state to govern. Why haven't the Armenians had any coins since the time of King Tigran [the great Armenian monarch of the first century B.C.]? I'll tell you why. They didn't have coins because they didn't have states!"†

Peter the Great, the first Russian emperor who attempted a takeover of the Caucasus, was also the first to entertain the idea of inviting Arme-

---

* She had in mind California's Central Valley. Facetious warnings against the pending "Armenianization" of California became quite common among Azeris in the early 1990s. For example, in 1992 Azerbaijan's defense minister, Meerzalik Arwadov, was quoted: "The Armenians had to be stopped in Karabakh, otherwise they would come east. . . . In addition, other countries would not be free from Armenian expansion. . . . They would like to make a separate state within California." But the notion that "Armenia is where there are Armenians" is much older than that. Armenian presence in the southeast of the Crimean Peninsula was described back in the fourteenth century as "maritime Armenia," though at no time had it ever constituted part of Greater Armenia. At the end of World War I, a frustrated Georgian diplomat complained that Armenians were claiming historical Georgian territory that had been settled by recent Armenian emigrants from Turkey. "This meant, 'where Armenians have settled even as recently as the nineteenth century—that is Armenia.'"

† In fact, no coins attributable to King Solomon have ever been found.

nian colonists from Muslim lands to settle his new Caucasian domains. In 1724 he wrote to one of his field commanders, Major-General Kropotov: "The Armenian people have asked us to take them into our protection, so order suitable places to be made available in our newly acquired Persian provinces for settlement." Peter's grand design was picked up fifty years later by one of Russia's most able and far-sighted statesmen, Grigory Potyomkin, chief minister and onetime lover of Empress Catherine the Great, a master not only of politics but of human vanities as well. Potyomkin promised Catherine that one of her grandsons would sit on the throne of Constantine the Great, the fourth-century founder of Christian Constantinople. Fulfilling the promise, to be sure, would have required a modest cartographic change: the dissolution of the Ottoman Empire. The grateful empress made Potyomkin a prince, and he went looking for local allies on Russia's southern borders.

In 1782 he reached out to Iosif Argutinskii-Dolgorukov, a bishop of the Armenian national church, an indefatigable lobbyist for his people's cause. Argutinskii, whose Russified name clearly suggested where his sympathies lay, aspired to create an Armenian state under Russian protection, and Potyomkin issued a solemn promise that such a state would indeed be created. Argutinskii assured Potyomkin that, should Russia attempt to expand into the Caucasus—at the expense of the two great Muslim powers of the day, Ottoman Turkey and Persia—the Armenians would flock to the czarist banner in droves, and the rich Armenian merchants of Persia and Turkey would help finance the war.

Argutinskii became a main adviser to the empress on all matters Caucasian, and the Russians eventually propelled him into the office of *catholicos,* or pope, of the Armenian Church. Argutinskii's advice to the imperial throne was "that the security of the proposed Christian protectorate necessitated the acquisition of all the [Muslim states of the Transcaucaus], even those with few Christians."

It is interesting that in recognition of Argutinskii's importance, Potyomkin officially sanctioned the publication of the bishop's history of Russian-Armenian relations. The shrewd prince appreciated early on that in planning for the future, one had to engage in some remolding of the past.

During her research on this episode, Farida Mamedova claims she came across a letter that Prince Potyomkin wrote to Catherine. "He reported that Armenians from Crimea had approached him and asked him to give them 'a capital.'" Potyomkin went on to propose that Russia should grant them the city of Yerevan, which at that time was controlled by allies of Persia. According to Mamedova, Catherine wondered, "Why give them a capital if they have no state?" Potyomkin answered, "*Now* they have no state, but one day they will."

Russia's ambitions in the Caucasus were put on hold because of the Napoleonic wars. Then between 1813 and 1829, the czarist armies soundly defeated both the Persians and the Ottomans. The former ceased to be a factor in the Caucasus. The Persians also lost their local allies, the khans, petty dukes who ruled many obscure principalities and paid their dues to the shah in Tehran. One of the duchies that the Persians lost to the Russians was Karabakh, which included what we now know as Nagorno-Karabakh. Another was Yerevan.

At the time of the Russian occupation, the future capital of independent Armenia had an overwhelming Turkish-speaking Muslim majority. It took the Armenians another fifty years, and two mass migrations from the Ottoman Empire, to establish their own majority in the province of Yerevan, "for the first time in centuries," according to an Armenian-American scholar, George A. Bournoutian.

The year 1829 saw the climax of what Buniyatov and Mamedova consider a Russian-Armenian plot against the Azeri people. A victorious Russia imposed harsh peace terms on Persia, one of which required the shah to allow the mass migration of his Armenian subjects to Russia. To oversee the exodus, senior Russian military officers were dispatched to Persia. No fewer than 45,000 Persian Armenians heeded the call.

Over the course of the nineteenth century, Russia fought three wars against Ottoman Turkey, at times penetrating deep into Ottoman territory. "Ordinary Armenians," writes an Armenian historian, "welcomed each appearance of the Russian army . . . with demonstrations of joy, followed by more or less sizeable migrations in the direction of Transcaucasia after its incorporation into the Russian Empire."

The Armenian newcomers constituted the new imperial elite not only in the future Armenia but in the future Azerbaijan and Georgia as well. They were to dominate the commercial life of Baku, and by the end of World War I, they were the majority in Tbilisi. Indeed Tbilisi, the capital of Georgia, was seen as the largest Armenian metropolis of the time. To Armenian nationalists, the notion that "bleak, unimposing" Yerevan was their "national capital" remained preposterous until 1918, when it was forced upon them by the disintegration of the czarist state and the subsequent failure to form a South Caucasian federation of Georgia, Armenia, and Azerbaijan. The Armenian leadership of the time was appalled by the need to sacrifice the comforts of cultured, aesthetic Tbilisi, which would have been the natural capital of a unified Caucasian state.

The relative newness of the Armenian presence in Yerevan is an uncontested fact, even among those Armenians who may feel unhappy about its implications for their cause. But not so in Nagorno-Karabakh. There, both the effect of the Armenian migration and its possible ramifications are debated and challenged with the utmost ferocity. The Armenians may feel that they can afford to concede nineteenth-century Yerevan, but to abandon the pre-1830s slopes of Karabakh? Oh, no. That would threaten the foundations of their national consciousness.

According to Mamedova, the first two hundred Armenian families arrived in Nagorno-Karabakh in 1828. There they established a village and named it Maragashen, after Maraga, their native town in Persia. A century and a half later, in 1978, the Karabakh Armenians raised a monument in Maragashen to commemorate the anniversary of their ancestors' arrival. In 1988 they demolished the monument, Mamedova told me. Why did they do that? Because, she insisted, the Armenians were bent on rewriting their own history. They pretended to the world that they had been in Karabakh since time immemorial; in reality, they are descendants of the Persian colonists. When I asked Buniyatov how many Armenians had lived in Karabakh prior to 1828, he said, "Perhaps two percent of the general population. All the rest were Albanians."

Eight years after the beginning of the Armenian migration, in 1836, the czarist government dissolved the Albanian Church district and brought it under the complete control of the Armenian national church. To Armenian historians that was a purely administrative move, which simply did away with an unnecessary anachronism, in that the Albanian Church had been Armenian in all but name. Mamedova strongly disagrees. "That was an autonomous church which had existed since the fifth century," she said of the Albanian diocese. "Since 1836, all references to the Albanians were blotted out, and an order was issued to substitute 'Armenian' for 'Albanian.'"

In the ensuing eight decades, many Armenians sided with Russia in its attempt to establish hegemony over the declining Ottoman Empire, where the majority of Armenians still lived. Prince Potyomkin's solemn vow to install a Romanov czar in Constantinople tantalized the Armenians until World War I.

In 1916, shortly before the collapse of the Romanov dynasty, Russian armies pushed deep into Turkey. But even if they had succeeded in driving all the way to Constantinople, it would have been too late for most

Armenians. Their pro-Russian orientation, in the eyes of the Ottoman government, qualified them as "a treacherous nation." It made them the target of the twentieth century's first genocidal ethnic cleansing. Between 1915 and 1923, the entire Armenian population of eastern Turkey was forcibly displaced. Up to 1.5 million perished in the process, and others were dispersed all over the planet, from the Caucasus to Rio Del Plata, from Jerusalem to Fresno.

Whether Russia ever intended to carry out its promise to the Armenians is highly questionable. In the first years of this century, Czar Nicholas II was ready to do to the Armenian Church what his great-grandfather had done to the Albanian. A Russian governor-general in the Caucasus, Prince Golitsyn, is reported to have threatened, "In a short time there will be no Armenians left in the Caucasus, save a few specimens for the museum." He was planning, not a physical annihilation, but a thorough Russification. The authorities were well on their way to dismantling the entire Armenian educational system and assimilating the Armenian Church into Russian Orthodoxy. Only the vicissitudes of history saved the Armenians from cultural extinction.

A year after my interviews with Buniyatov and Mamedova, in late 1996, I was in Yerevan, drinking tea with Babken Harutunian, one of Armenia's foremost scholars and dean of the faculty of history at Yerevan University. Were you very upset at the time the Albanian hypothesis was made public? I asked him.

"We were fuming!" he replied. "But our hands were effectively tied. In Soviet times, scholars from one republic could not discuss the history of a territory belonging to another. We had no right to engage the Azeris head-on. Besides, the Azeri government was pampering the authors of these theories. Not so the Armenian government. It took us a huge effort to publish a single critique of Buniyatov in the late 1960s."

Harutunian recalled a conference in Moscow in 1981, at which the matter of Caucasian maps in the historical atlas of the Soviet Union was discussed. "It became clear to us that the Azeris were not interested in historical sources. Whatever the disagreement with them was, they replied, 'That's it, that's how it is.' And under the system, they had the final say—there was nothing we could do."

Then came Gorbachev and freer speech, and Armenian hands were no longer tied. When Farida Mamedova presented her dissertation on the Albanian Church in 1987, the Armenians let off their steam. "Her book was nothing. Scientifically speaking, it was bunk," Harutunian told me. "But we understood that her goals were political and ideological, and we reacted accordingly. She was scheduled to defend her dissertation in Baku, and we wanted one of us to attend the deliberations, to make sure that the right objections were raised. But it was too dangerous for an Armenian to go. As soon as we heard that she had won her Ph.D. in Baku, we appealed to the scientific inspection committee of the USSR Council of Ministers."

The obscure academic dispute now moved into center stage. Mamedova told me with a clear sense of pride: "A copy of my book was placed on Gorbachev's desk, at his own request. He wanted to see what it was all about."

Farida Mamedova, a petite woman in her fifties, is affable and smiling, pretty and pale, with short-trimmed raven black hair. It is difficult to believe that this lover of obscure manuscripts and avid collector of ancient maps has driven so many Armenians to bouts of rage. Her long romance with ancient Albania began in 1972, when few could have imagined that the Soviet Caucasus would ever again be divided among its constituent nationalities.

For this young Azeri student, with impeccable Russian and a soft spot for archaeological mysteries, there could hardly have been a more benign topic than Caucasian Albania. And yet when she submitted her first monograph on the Albanians for publication in 1975, strange things began to happen. First, the manuscript was held over for a year. "Then," she told me, "I ran into Armenia's greatest historian, Suren Yeremian, a member of the Academy of Science, a scholar with an international reputation. He cautioned me never to get involved with Caucasian Albania or with the history of the Albanian Church, because Armenian scholars would never accept anything I might have to say. He then turned to me and said, 'If you do pursue this course, I'll have to pity you as a scholar. You will break your own neck.'"

Mamedova was shocked. Why would a prominent Armenian academician feel so strongly about the writings of a young Azeri woman who was only just making her debut in the world of Soviet academe? "I told myself that this reaction alone, this aversion to the truth, is enough of a reason for me to get interested in the history of Albania."

And so she did. The Armenian antipathy toward her rose accordingly. At one conference, in Berlin, shortly before the collapse of the Soviet Union, Mamedova presented a paper in which she argued that an Armenian state as such had never existed in history. Soon after her lecture, Mamedova ran into an Armenian scholar whom she named to me. "He looked at me and said, 'Women like you should be killed.' I replied, 'Woe to the Armenian people if it needs to kill women like me.'"

The worst confrontation occurred under the auspices of the ultimate arbiter of learning, the USSR Academy of Science in Moscow, in 1987, shortly after Mamedova's doctoral dissertation on the Albanian Church had been accepted in Baku. "The Armenians," she recalled, "petitioned the Central Committee of the Soviet Community Party incessantly. People in Moscow began to perceive my book as 'very dangerous' to the harmony between nations. So Moscow asked the Communist Party in Azerbaijan to look into it. Our officials read the book but could not figure out why Moscow was so upset."

The Azeri Communists decided to follow the common Soviet practice: when in doubt, let Moscow decide. Mamedova was summoned to the Soviet Academy of Science to defend her dissertation. "I did just that, for five hours, in the presence of seventy scientists. No one raised any objection to the concept of my book. I replied to all their questions, to their satisfaction. But the Armenian wounds were not healed."

When Mamedova interrupted my flow of questions, politely but firmly, to make sure that "our guest please not forget that I am a scholar, not a politician," she was probably being sincere. Elsewhere in the Caucasus, however, other experts on antiquity were willing and eager to use Mamedova's work to further their political ends.

It is interesting and perhaps telling that, while in Moscow and Leningrad the most prominent Soviet-era dissidents emerged from faculties of physics and mathematics, in the Caucasus opponents of the Soviet system chose to flee to the bosom of the humanities. "There were two kinds of emigration available to us," I heard from Suren Zolian, a linguist and historian who played an important role in the overthrow of Communism in Armenia. "One option was to escape oppression by leaving the country and establishing *geographic* distance. Another option was to leave the present and establish a distance of *time*. We emigrated to the past."

It was in departments of ancient languages and early medieval history that many of the future leaders of the Caucasus were being trained. Levon Ter-Petrossian, a young linguist with an extensive knowledge of extinct Middle Eastern tongues, is a case in point. A native of Syria, he was the son of a founder of Syria's Communist Party. Ter-Petrossian found the perfect haven for a man of his generation and his intellect in the Matenadaran, Armenia's depository of ancient manuscripts and the sacred heart of Armenian civilization. Few matched his supreme knowledge of such

Levon Ter-Petrossian

illustrious figures as Abraham the Confessor, a fifth-century Syrian hermit. His command of Syriac, a tongue widely spoken in the eighth century, was almost unparalleled. His articles on Armenian-Syrian relations in the early Middle Ages won him high acclaim.

Many, including his former comrades-in-arms, mistook Ter-Petrossian's professorial aloofness for a lack of political acumen or a paucity of personal ambition. They did so at their peril. The man so infatuated with the distant past was to play a pivotal role in the destruction of the Soviet Union and would become Armenia's first president (1989–98). Indeed, he was the longest-serving Armenian head of state since Constantine III, the king of Armenian Cilicia, in what is now southern Turkey, in the mid-fourteenth century.

Ter-Petrossian's amazing ascent owed something to Farida Mamedova, in that her controversial alternative history helped inspire a small group of intellectuals to challenge the legitimacy of the Soviet system. They did so by claiming victim status for their nation, a traditional prerequisite for any national revolution. It was not an easy course to follow, for Armenians had hitherto enjoyed the status of favored sons under the old regime, and they had been allowed certain liberties unheard of elsewhere in the Soviet universe. Yerevan boasted the only international airport of any non-Russian city, a clear indication of Moscow's trust. Some Armenians were even said to have been allowed the right of dual citizenship, a virtual impossibility elsewhere. The small republic was also something of a Silicon Valley, with one of the Soviet Union's highest densities of scientists and well-funded research institutions. Mutual sympathy characterized Russian-Armenian relations, and the Armenian diaspora in Moscow was perhaps the most successful ethnic minority group in the Soviet capital. An Armenian poet, Avetik Isahakian, epitomized Armenian attitudes when he said, "It is clear that if the Bolsheviks had not overrun Armenia [in 1920], the Turks would have slaughtered the Russian-Armenians also, and that would have met with the approval of Europe and America. For that reason alone, let not a single Bolshevik suffer a nosebleed."

To be sure, what the Armenians call *Hayk Tun,* or the "Armenian cause," did not have to be invented. Quintessential victims of history that they are, compulsive chroniclers of their own national life that they have been since before Christ, the Armenians required no reminder that they deserve a place in the sun. Still, they needed a simple message that would refresh the collective memory. Unwittingly, Buniyatov and Mamedova, the Azeri historians, provided just the occasion for it.

In 1987 an Armenian intellectual, writing in a newspaper still called *Kommunist,* said of the Albanian theory that the Azeri quest for "imaginary ancestors" was more than a "blatant distortion of the history and cultural heritage of the Armenian people." It was, he contended, an attempt to deny half a million Armenians on Azeri soil their identity, as a prelude to assimilation.

The linguist Suren Zolian, however, had much worse fears. Almost ten years after the event, he told me that back in 1987 he had viewed Mamedova's Albanian hypothesis as "the ideological basis for ethnic cleansing. If the Armenians are outsiders, as the proponents of the theory of Caucasian Albania maintain, then they should be driven out. If they are illegitimate occupiers of this land, then repression against them is justified."

Mamedova's logic would have applied to all Armenians south of the Caucasus, since nearly all of them fit the description of either "newcomers" or "Armenianized Albanians." But it was her assault on the antiquity of Armenian Karabakh that earned Mamedova the wrath of the Yerevan intellectuals. Presumably, only her fellow enthusiasts of obscure parchments could have been so moved by what they perceived as the misuse of historical documents.

Zolian, more self-critical than most of his comrades-in-arms, acknowledges that Karabakh was elevated into a cause célèbre by default. The Armenians needed a *current* grievance that would evoke the ultimate *past* grievance, the 1915 genocide. They remembered, Zolian said, that back in 1965, the anniversary of 1915 brought Armenians to the streets in a spontaneous display of national fervor. (Moscow was unhappy but uncharacteristically tolerant.) "Karabakh was initially an abstract notion," Zolian recalled. "People said 'Karabakh,' but what they really meant was 'genocide.'"

Karabakh had the right mix to become a grievance: it was an isolated Armenian community, separated from the rest of the nation, at the mercy of "Turks" (as the Armenians often refer to the Azeris), unarmed, and weak. Was this not the precise situation of many Armenian communities on the eve of the genocide? Did they not count then, as they were counting now, on Russia to come to their rescue? Was it not a false expectation then? Could the nation afford again to rely on others? Had not the time come for empowerment?

Whether the Karabakh Armenians faced a real danger in 1988 is another matter. Zolian could not point to one; nor could many Karabakhis to whom I spoke during my visits to the territory in the 1990s. They had long-standing complaints of neglect at the hands of the Azeri central government, and there was little love lost between the two communities. But Armenians lived in large numbers throughout Azerbaijan, and prior to the events of 1988, no one suggested their lives were in danger. Most of the evidence of mistreatment I gathered was anecdotal and bore the marks of friction between neighbors rather than hostility between mortal enemies.

The gravest story I heard concerned a sexual assault by an Azeri man on an Armenian boy in a Karabakh village, and the commotion that surrounded the assailant's trial. Sexual violence could indeed assume a disproportionate role in an ethnic conflict, but it was a far cry from a genocide in the making.

Everything changed in early 1988. On February 20 the regional assembly, or Supreme Soviet, of Karabakh voted for unification with Armenia. A week later, Azeris murdered about thirty Armenians in the city of Sumgait, far away from Karabakh. Moscow then imposed military rule over Karabakh and accused Armenian nationalists of attempting to derail the entire reform process in the Soviet Union.

Though the Yerevan intellectuals had not made up the Karabakh grievance, they certainly inflated it, and soon it overshadowed all other grievances. Armenians had been complaining for years, however discreetly, about "corruption and gangsterism" in the local Communist government, but their craving for a clean administration would not have sent them into the streets in the thousands, would not have led to a violent confrontation with Soviet troops at Yerevan's airport, and would not have ended in a national revolution.

The outside world realized for the first time the enormity of the events in February 1988, when an amateur photographer videotaped what had probably been the largest opposition rally in Soviet history: about one million chanting Armenians squeezed into Lenin Square to claim justice for Karabakh. A couple of days later, Ter-Petrossian and his colleagues formed the Karabakh Committee, which, from that point on, would be in the forefront of the independence movement. With the benefit of hindsight, one can argue that on that day in Yerevan time was beginning to run out on the USSR.

I heard from a few Armenians that before their enclave emerged as a galvanizing national cause, Karabakhis had been the object of condescension. They were ridiculed for their provincial mannerisms and their funny pronunciation. But in 1988 Karabakh ceased to belong to Karabakhis; it now belonged to the entire Armenian nation. It offered the Armenians an opportunity to reassert control over their destiny and to refight wars long lost. The cry for Karabakh freedom appealed to Armenians worldwide, and volunteers from the diaspora came to fight and die in the mountains. Many of them were buried in a hilly cemetery outside Yerevan: youngsters who had once spent their free time surfing California's Pacific waves or smoking in the seaside cafés of Beirut; some starry-eyed romantics; some professional, violent revolutionaries eager to wreak revenge on "the Turks" (even if the "Turks" in this equation had little to do with those of 1915).

Soon enough a myth—that essential ingredient for any successful national movement—began to emerge. Karabakh was presented as the cradle of Armenian nationhood, where the healthy traits of the nation had been preserved closest to their pristine state; where the language was purest; and where the men were bravest, unspoiled by life under the Ottomans, which had supposedly reduced the Armenians to a class of petty merchants and market vendors. Thus a nation that had lived and thrived for centuries in Anatolia and along the shores of the Mediterranean, a nation of cities and plains, was now redefining itself in terms of the landlocked, misty mountain terrain of Karabakh.

The unlikely role that Nagorno-Karabakh was now assuming was also partly the result of a Soviet folly. What, after all, had been the point of establishing an Armenian autonomous region inside Azerbaijan, just a few miles away from the Armenian-Azeri border? If it deserved autonomy, why separate it from Armenia altogether? Conversely, if it was more rightly included in Azerbaijan, why bother with autonomy? Armenians also blame Turkey for the inclusion of Karabakh in Azerbaijan, in that Turkey would have frowned on a strong, consolidated Armenian republic on its border, and the first Soviet government—friendless and fragile—was eager to win Turkish favor. An Azeri counter-explanation attributes the creation of Nagorno-Karabakh to the undue influence of Armenian individuals in Moscow.

All in all, the creation of Karabakh reflected how little significance the founders of the Soviet state attached to "internal borders." To the creators of that new universe, transferring populations and regions from one ethnic jurisdiction to another was nothing. So enamored were they of their theme of *druzhba narodov* ("friendship of the peoples") that they seemed unwilling to contemplate, or perhaps were intellectually incapable of contemplating, the results of their ethnic engineering.

Within months of the first Armenian claims on Karabakh, the specter of 1915 was raised again: Armenians were massacred in the Azeri city of Sumgait. Shortly thereafter, while the world focused on a devastating earthquake in northern Armenia, the Armenian government helped 200,000 Azeris leave ancestral homes in southern Armenia and enter a life of destitution and hopelessness across the border. In early 1990, a massacre of Armenians in Baku triggered the panicky exodus of 300,000 Armenians. And so within one frightful year, a mutual ethnic cleansing was accomplished, undoing generations of coexistence.

Karabakh was abstract no more. The defense of its 150,000 Armenians against "a second Sumgait" became a supreme national priority, to the detriment of almost everything else.

"Sparta on the Mountains," a Nagorno-Karabakh leader has called his little enclave. The Spartan-Armenian seen here is a fedai, *a word drawn originally from the Arabic, denoting "warrior." I met him in Karabakh in 1992, on the eve of a major battle.*

The Armenians won the Karabakh conflict militarily, but they have paid with a catastrophic reversal of their economic, social, and cultural fortunes. Under a punishing Azeri-Turkish blockade (instantly imposed and still in force), Armenia languished through cold, dark winters. Educated Armenians left en masse for Russia and the United States, and by the time the conflict turned twelve years old, in 2000, Armenia had become a society bitterly divided against itself.

Nagorno-Karabakh evolved into something unintended and unforeseen. Had the Karabakh Committee attained its stated goal, the enclave would have been incorporated into Armenia and reverted to its former sleepiness, an Alamo for diaspora tourists (or better, a triumphant Mussa Dagh, a full reversal of 1915). Instead, Armenia had to forgo annexation and settle for what was universally considered the "sham" of Karabakh's "independence." Few outsiders gave the independence claim any credence, assuming naturally that the little province would be controlled in all but name by the Yerevan government.

Astonishingly, the Karabakh cause became a self-fulfilling prophecy. Its baptism by fire transformed the former icon-on-the-wall into a custodian of Armenian nationalism, a bastion of militancy. In the words of Arkadi Ghukasian, then foreign minister, later president of "the Republic of Mountainous Karabakh," it became a "Sparta on the Mountains."

Through discipline, enormous sacrifice (few Karabakh families did not lose a father or a son in the war), and superior military skills, Karabakh began to set the tone for Armenia rather than the other way around. In 1993 the Karabakh army, reinforced by diaspora volunteers as well as units of the Armenian regular army, soundly defeated Azerbaijan. It was now holding not only Karabakh and two land corridors to Armenia but also a considerable chunk of surrounding Azeri territories. (Hundreds of thousands of Azeris lost their homes in the process, forming one of the largest displaced populations in the world.)

The government in Armenia, though made up of veterans of the Karabakh movement, became increasingly uncomfortable with the rise of a militant Karabakh. Karabakh's refusal to consider any form of compromise, combined with the Azeri-Turkish blockade, left Armenia isolated in its immediate neighborhood, dependent for its day-to-day survival on Iranian food trucks sporting the names of various Tehran merchants in Arabic script, which became a common spectacle in Armenia (and a constant source of Azeri irritation.) Karabakh also helped bring back the ominous specter of intolerance and violence that had plagued Armenian politics in the early years of the twentieth century, one that bred assassinations and civic strife and sowed divisions in the diaspora that have yet to heal.

Time served to significantly moderate the politics of Levon Ter-Petrossian, who was elected president in 1991 and again in 1996. The nationalist agitator of the late 1980s came to recognize that the elation involved in the celebration of icons—important as they may be for the nation's psychology—could not substitute for food and energy. He chose practical needs over excitement.

Ter-Petrossian was as traumatized by history as most Armenians are, but his conclusion was not perpetual defiance of neighbors and perceived enemies. He applied the lessons of the First Armenian Republic (1918–20), when, he believed, Armenia missed a golden opportunity to reach a formula for coexistence with Turkey, Armenia's nemesis. He blamed unrealistic fundamentalism for the failure—the aspiration to establish a Greater Armenia over much of eastern Turkey—and was determined to prevent a similar trend from rising in the Second Republic (as post-Soviet Armenia came to be known among some).

Many might disagree with his interpretation, but it is not difficult to see the profundity of his logic. Ter-Petrossian was trying to provide the Armenians with the scarcest commodity of their long and tortuous history: *normalcy*. Yet normalcy is the declared enemy of all radical nationalisms, those who deride any notion of here-and-now, and treat the present as a mere bridge between a belabored past and an aggrandized future.

To the diaspora opposition, Yerevan's claim to speak for the *Hayk Tun*, the Armenian Cause, was an unacceptable act of impostors. The heart of the Armenian nation is still pounding in Turkish-controlled "West Armenia," even if no Armenians live there any longer. The diaspora, not the Sovietized politicians of "East Armenia," are the true custodians of the *Hayk Tun*, or so believes a considerable section of the diaspora, represented by its most popular party, *Dashnaktsutiun*, Armenian for "federation."*

Ter-Petrossian began to speak openly of compromise almost as soon as Karabakh's defenders had triumphed in the battlefield. In early 1994, while in London, he said that "in terms of reality, the only solution could be one based on compromise." The resistance was so fierce that he first forced the resignation of the Karabakh political leadership, which was identified with *Dashnaktsutiun*; and by the end of 1994 proceeded to banning the party altogether, blaming it for creating a terrorist organization and orchestrating the assassination of leading politicians, including the popular mayor of Yerevan. Extensive trials, denounced by his critics as "show trials," produced death sentences, which—though never carried out—pitted Armenians against each other in a fashion unseen for many decades.

Ter-Petrossian, the hero of yore, was now seen increasingly as a traitor to the Armenian Cause, softened by the perks of office and compromised by the alleged massive corruption in his immediate entourage. Yerevan was now not only poor and desperate but was also haunted by fear and rumors; Ter-Petrossian was increasingly isolated from his people and abandoned by his former friends.

There was even a danger that Karabakh would become a launching pad for insurrection against Ter-Petrossian's government. In late 1994, I

---

* An anecdotal manifestation of diaspora condescension toward East Armenia is the transliteration of Ter-Petrossian's own name in diaspora English-language newspapers. They spell it *Der-Bedrossian*, which is the West Armenian pronunciation of the name. This is no trifle. Transliteration variations help define rival claims to the national mantle elsewhere, as is the case of the conflict between Chinese Communists and Taiwan's Nationalists. Deng Xiaoping and Teng Hsiao Ping are one and the same but denote irreconcilable claims for ascendancy and the right to speak for the national heritage.

spent a couple of hours in the garrison of an elite unit of the Karabakh army, where one member, a diaspora volunteer who introduced himself as "Rafi," a naturalized Canadian who was born in Lebanon, told me of the universal contempt with which he and his comrades-in-arms held the government in Yerevan. "We would love to kick the hell out of them," he said in English. "They are a bunch of thieves and cowards."

A few days later I repeated his words to Ashot Manucharian, a former minister and Karabakh Committee founder, who by that time had broken ranks with Ter-Petrossian. Manucharian nodded, unsurprised. "If we in Armenia tried to reach a compromise with Azerbaijan at Nagorno-Karabakh's expense, their army would march on us, and we would have to surrender Yerevan in two hours." The former high school teacher smiled mischievously and added: "They will come to the center of Yerevan, dislodge all of us from our nice apartments, and move in." That appeared to be a reference to the old image of the Karabakhis as hillbillies. Manucharian may have engaged in a little hyperbole, but having been chief national security adviser to the president, he knew well the strength of the Karabakh army. "Sparta in the Mountains" was indeed capable of matching some of the best fighting forces in the world, and what it lacked in hardware or training, it made up for in spirit and motivation.

In 1996 in an election marred by irregularities and violence, most of Ter-Petrossian's former colleagues in the Karabakh Committee turned against him and mounted a fierce challenge to his presidency. Insofar as I could tell, the streets of Yerevan were decidedly opposed to him and were receptive to the opposition's allegations that he was ready to sell Karabakh down the river. His government was widely despised for its authoritarianism, secretiveness, clannishness, alleged contacts with criminal gangs, and rumored involvement in the assassination of political opponents. The legitimacy of Ter-Petrossian's subsequent victory was believed by few, and international observers came close to proclaiming the election fraudulent.*

A besieged Ter-Petrossian, clearly lacking in a mandate, nonetheless pushed on with a Karabakh compromise that would have restored at least the semblance of Azeri sovereignty. He summoned his nation to a public debate on Karabakh. "Is it possible to maintain the status quo and the unresolved state of the Karabakh question forever or even for an extended period of time?" he asked. "To solve the question of Karabakh, we have only one option, a compromise solution, which does not mean that one side is the victor and the other the loser."

---

* Two years later, Ter-Petrossian's former interior minister, Vano Siradeghian, publicly acknowledged "manipulation" of the results by the government.

Those were highly unpopular words, and the opposition, he complained, rather than engaging him in a serious debate, turned to "profanities, imputations, labeling, and distortions." He went on:

> This is not a debate on losing or not losing Karabakh. Rather, it is on keeping Karabakh Armenian. Karabakh has been inhabited by Armenians for three thousand years, and so it must be for another three thousand years.
>
> The path I have chosen will secure that prospect and the means to preserve it, to reach our desired goal. The path of the adventurers will lead to certain defeat. Already once, "having turned Istanbul into a sea of blood," we lost Western Armenia.

In other words, Armenia had already suffered a devastating loss in 1915 as a result of political blindness and fanaticism—why risk now the little that was left? Unquestionably, they were audacious words, a challenge not merely to Armenian politics of the 1990s but to the way Armenians have perceived themselves since the 1890s: as a nation of victims, with little responsibility for their own predicament.

That the head of the Armenian state would express such heretical views was astounding, an indication of the extent to which Levon Ter-Petrossian had outgrown his contemporaries and lost touch with the Armenian rank-and-file. There he was, the first president of reborn Armenia, exasperated with his own people, full of apocalyptic visions, unable to communicate the gravity of the hour, a tragic figure of historic proportions. With hindsight it is clear that at the time he delivered his remarks, Ter-Petrossian had already been reduced to an impotent figurehead. He seemed to have a good hunch that his days in power were numbered. Perhaps he even expected a bullet, for he drew parallels between his efforts and those of Yitzhak Rabin in Israel. The opposition accused him, he said, of selling out Karabakh so he could cling to power. But that charge, he asserted, was insane, as no one accused of selling out Karabakh could hope to maintain authority.

In reflecting on his own failings as a leader and tribune, he asked himself why he had not done better to curry favor with the masses. His answer was clearly self-serving, but it also constituted a sweeping indictment of the very political culture he had helped shape a decade earlier.

> Is it possible that I do not know the cheap methods of projecting myself as a hero and as the embodiment of all national aspirations, and of pleasing the public at any cost? Couldn't I have cursed the Turks night and day, raised the issue of the recognition of the Geno-

Distant, aloof, guarded by dark silhouettes, Levon Ter-Petrossian is seen here addressing an election rally, September 1996. Soon thereafter the dark silhouettes kicked him out and took over.

cide at the UN, revoked the Treaty of Kars,* demanded from Turkey the territories designated by the Treaty of Sèvres,† presented an ultimatum to Azerbaijan, recognized the independence of Karabakh, declared that we will cede none of the territories, etc.?

I could have used all these ploys cleverly. . . . Was it my education that was inadequate, or my brains that could not cut it? I could have easily earned the reputation of the brave and great patriot, become the idol of the nation, and the symbol of unity of Armenia and the Diaspora.

Toward the end of his presidency, Ter-Petrossian made one last attempt at healing the wounds by turning over Armenia's prime ministership, in 1997, to the president of Nagorno-Karabakh, Robert Kocharyan. Kocharyan was neither an intellectual nor a romantic; nor had he been involved with the original Karabakh movement. (He was a typical young member of the Soviet managerial class, having risen to run a factory in Stepanakert.) But he had proven exceptionally apt in

---

* By which in 1921 Soviet Russia ceded to Turkey two provinces that would have otherwise been included in Armenia.

† Forced on defeated Turkey in 1920 by the victorious powers of World War I. Had it gone into effect, a large Armenian state would have been established over most of eastern Turkey.

marshaling the territory's tiny resources, inspiring confidence amongst its population, and leading it from near-defeat in 1992 to a spectacular victory. He was something Ter-Petrossian could no longer hope to be: a unifying figure, both in Armenia proper and in the diaspora.

Kocharyan's elevation made it increasingly difficult to distinguish between Armenia's domestic politics and those of Karabakh. While Ter-Pertrossian's press secretary was protesting Karabakh's constant "meddling in Armenia's internal affairs," the Karabakhis sneered. "It is time the Armenian politicians were guided by pan-national rather than parochial interests," one proclaimed. Another, a powerful member of the Karabakh parliament, was even more blunt: "The Armenian people," he thundered, "will have to elect a new president who would be able to unite the whole nation."

In February 1998, exactly ten years after the founding of the Karabakh movement, after months of a powerful struggle behind the scenes, Ter-Petrossian's presidency finally collapsed. In announcing his resignation, he said that had he not stepped down, he would have been driven out of office, which is why his end was widely viewed as a virtual military coup mounted by his national security apparatus. The slate of top office holders was swept clean of anyone suspected of supporting him. More than half of his party's parliamentary deputies defected.

Ter-Petrossian bade good-bye to the nation with a measure of self-pity. He was the victim of warmongers, he insisted, and came back to the Rabin analogy. Just as in Israel, he said, the "party of peace and decent accord" was being forced out of power by the party of war. Just over two years earlier Ter-Petrossian had flown to Jerusalem to attend Rabin's funeral service; quite possibly the thought now occurred to him that he should have left the same way Rabin did. This renowned expert on early medieval saints might have enhanced his own cause had he earned a saintly aura in martyrdom. Instead, he was leaving with a whimper, humiliated and scorned. Armenians, both at home and in the diaspora, welcomed his demise with evident relief, so divisive had he become.

Within hours of Ter-Petrossian's resignation, Robert Kocharyan was sworn in as acting president and was soon elected to a full five-year term. In his inauguration speech, he made no reference to his predecessor. Ashot Manucharian's light-hearted prediction had finally come true: the Karabakhis did take over the best apartments in downtown Yerevan. A cause that had been conceived almost as a spiritual exercise, a catharsis of the Armenian national soul, had now consumed the leadership that had created it. Instead of the annexation of Karabakh by Armenia, Karabakh had now annexed Armenia. Ter-Petrossian's party, on the verge of extinction, alleged that Armenia was being run by "the Karabakh clan." The party went on to accuse Kocharyan of rising to power illegally, criminalizing the government, and establishing a police state. In May 1999 the party, out of power and out of favor and no longer under Ter-Petrossian's leadership, won a dismal 1.2 percent of the vote in a parliamentary election, failing to meet the minimum threshold for representation.

Ter-Petrossian, with plenty of time on his hands for reflection and solitude, might well contemplate another defeat: not only had he released the demons of nationalism that he now so abhorred, he also saw the return of the Communist Party to a position of prominence. Having been reduced to electoral ashes in 1990, it was again the best-organized party in the republic. Armenia's former Soviet boss, Karen Demirchian, came close to winning the presidential contest against Kocharyan in 1998. In 1999 he won the parliamentary election hands down at the head of an alliance with Ter-Petrossian's former defense minister, Vazgen Sarkisyan, the non-Karabakh Armenian who is most credited with the remarkable military successes of 1993. Thus, the Communist and the ardent nationalist were to sign Armenia's marching orders into the twenty-first century and possibly back into a union with Russia. A more striking reversal of fortunes is hard to imagine.*

If the ghosts of Albania exacted a heavy price from Armenia, they had devastating results for Azerbaijan. Within a few months of Farida Mamedova's appearance at the Academy of Science in Moscow in 1988, while Armenia was engulfed in its nationalistic uproar, a counteruproar was taking shape in Azerbaijan, prefaced by the pogrom against the Armenians of Sumgait. A few months later, Azerbaijan saw the expulsion of 200,000 ethnic Azeris from Armenia, whose families had lived there for generations.

In January 1990, Baku exploded in rage. Azeris, mostly refugees from Armenia, attacked members of the Armenian community and threatened a massive pogrom. Baku's Armenians, about 300,000 of them, escaped.

Blame for the atrocities was pinned on Azeri nationalists who were organized in a "popular front." The nationalists were candidates to win Azerbaijan's first democratic elections under Soviet rule. Moscow used

---

* In October 1999 a group of hitherto unknown terrorists burst into Armenia's parliament and assassinated both Demirchian and Sarkisyan, an act surpassing the worst Armenian violence against Armenians of previous generations. At the time this book goes to print, lingering suspicions of conspiracy are yet to be proven.

the pretext of restoring order in Baku to help its local Communist allies and undermine the nationalists. Soviet troops imposed martial law in the city.

To sweeten the pill, an Azeri officer was placed at the head of the martial law regime, a virtual military dictator. General Valeri Buniyatov was the son of the Albanian theorist Ziya Buniyatov. The young Buniyatov persecuted nationalist politicians and helped secure an electoral victory for pro-Moscow loyalists. It was not his fault that Moscow itself was faltering. Out of ideas and out of steam, the Soviet government could no longer stem the rising nationalist tide anywhere in the country.

Valeri promised that the military regime would stay in place until "the last Armenian bandit* is disarmed," but that, he hastened to add, was unlikely to happen anytime soon because the Armenians were insatiable in their appetite to acquire more Azeri lands. "As a military man, I think there is only one thing to do," he said at the time. "If they [the Armenians] don't comply, they should be wiped out."

Valeri's father was no longer so sure. Ten months after his son's tirades against the Armenians, he told an Azeri newspaper:

> We drive out the Armenians, and what happens? Construction projects are left hanging, not one roofer is left . . . and enterprise managers cry that there aren't enough specialists. . . . One continues to hear calls to "Beat up the Armenians!" All right, let's assume that we become a monoethnic republic, a sovereign state, and that we secede from the Soviet Union. What happens after that?

Buniyatov's pessimism placed him on a collision course with the new Azeri nationalists. Unlike him, they saw themselves as Turks and derived enormous pride from that. Their leader, Abulfez Elchibey (later president for twelve months), made a point of wearing an Atatürk button on his jacket lapel, clearly implying that he, like the founder of modern Turkey, did not care much for the distant origins of the residents of Azerbaijan so long as they were all willing to become Azeris and give up their historical identities.

The elder Buniyatov found the spectacle of the nationalist rise extremely disagreeable. When nationalist agitators began to campaign against the Soviet Union, he shot back at one of their leaders:

---

* "Bandit" is a favorite Soviet and Russian term for describing nationalist insurgents. This is how Chechen rebels have been described.

I want to ask him: Toward what kind of abyss are you, Vagif Akhmedov, the son of an Azerbaijani mother, pushing your people?! Wasn't last year's tragedy in Sumgait enough for you? I'm not a young man, and I'm a Hero of the Soviet Union: Answer me! . . . Whose side are you on? Are you still one of us?

President-for-one-year Abulfez Elchibey proudly sported an Atatürk button on his lapel, clearly implying his intention to make Azeris of everyone, including those who were not.

An extraordinary exhortation from the son of a Subbotnik Russian woman. Did Buniyatov begin to feel at that time that Azerbaijan was sliding quickly toward disaster? Did he experience any qualms about his own role in awakening a sense of tribalism and xenophobia?

Whether Buniyatov was having second thoughts or not, he made an amazing public statement. A favorite son of the officially atheist Soviet state, he suggested that the time had come for Azerbaijan to return to Islamic spirituality, in order to

first halt and then reverse the process of spiritual and moral impoverishment. . . . A spirituality that consists of perceiving Islam not as a religious dogma but as a bearer of moral and ethical values and the culture of a whole group of peoples of the East, united in terms of harmonious ethnic features and a community of languages, that has made its way through the layers of history.

He seemed to be suggesting the adoption of the Ottoman model, which in its heyday displayed the greatest tolerance toward minorities of any contemporary system. Old Buniyatov was now looking for reconciliation and what Americans might call multiculturalism.

That, alas, was no longer possible. His own son's words about the "Armenian bandits" were now echoed everywhere in Azerbaijan. Ugly cartoons, depicting Armenians the way Nazi cartoons used to depict Jews, were hanging from the front window in Baku's House of Artists. Six months after the collapse of the Soviet Union, the nationalist Elchibey rose to power, vowing to "enter Kakhendi in three months" and then "dip in the water of Gokcha." (Kakhendi was the Azeri name for Stepanakert, Nagorno-Karabakh's provincial capital. Gokcha was

Ugly anti-Armenian cartoons were hanging from the front window in Baku's House of Artists during the height of the war. The one seen here features a hook-nosed Armenian overwhelmed by a muscular Azeri arm bearing the words (in Cyrillicized Azeri) "Nagorno-Karabakh." Well, not quite.

the old name for Lake Sevan, Armenia's main source of water.) A year later, however, not only was Kakhendi still lost, and not only was the entire Nagorno-Karabakh territory under Armenian control, but large chunks of Azerbaijan proper were occupied by the "Defense Forces of Nagorno-Karabakh."

An evidently disgusted Ziya Buniyatov said, after the final defeat, in the summer of 1993, "We are happier opening shops than fighting for our country."

Elchibey himself was driven out of Baku by a pitiful armed rebellion of a few hundred disgruntled opponents, then fled to his native village in the mountains of Nakhichevan, where he remained in hiding for the next three years. (After a failed political comeback, he died in August 2000.) By the fall of 1993, Heydar Aliyev, Buniyatov's former patron and Azerbaijan's Communist chief in the 1970s, was back in power, this time as a born-again democrat and a friend of Western oil interests. Aliyev also made Buniyatov the vice chairman of the ruling party.

On Friday, February 21, 1997, while entering the lobby of his apartment building in Baku, Ziya Buniyatov was shot twice at close range. His assailant then stabbed him four times. The seventy-five-year-old academician died en route to the hospital. Government leaders said it was the essence of a plot to "destabilize" the nation. At this writing, Buniyatov's assassins have not been captured.

In ancient Greek mythology, the Muses had a mother by the name of Mnemosyne, literally "memory," who was omniscient, in possession of every single bit of knowledge. She knew not only the entire past but also the entire future. It was her knowledge that served as the foundation for all life and creativity. The gravest sin against wisdom was forgetfulness. To forget the true sequence of events, to relegate to oblivion the origins of the present, was tantamount to death. Indeed, Lethe, the mythical river of death, destroyed memory.

The struggle to preserve memory in the Caucasus has assumed many forms, and those forms are the centerpiece of this book. In some ways, it is a struggle that deserves the sympathy of any civilized person. But the struggle is often taken beyond the pale of acceptability. At times the quest for one nation's memory turns into an attempt to demolish that of another, as with Buniyatov's Albania hypothesis. Such attempts rarely go unreciprocated.

In the fall of 1996, a group of educated Azeris proposed to launch a newsgroup, or discussion forum on the Internet, devoted to Azeri culture, politics, and history. The Net has more than seventy thousand newsgroups, dealing with an enormous diversity of fields, subjects, personalities, historical periods, and nations. An Azeri newsgroup would certainly have been as legitimate as those that exist concerning amateur radio in Birmingham, Alabama, or the latest developments in Tasmanian culture.

The Net is an anarchic entity, but the establishment of a newsgroup should follow certain voting procedures. Normally these are a mere formality.

But not when the Caucasus is involved. The proposal to start an Azerbaijan newsgroup was heavily defeated. The list of opponents consisted almost exclusively of people with Armenian family names. The Albanian war has now entered virtual reality as well.*

* Eventually an Azeri newsgroup did come into being.

EPILOGUE

THE CAMOUFLAGED MOUNTAIN

As I reach the end of my journey to the Caucasus in quest of memory, I recall the victims of nationalist excesses I have encountered time and again, both groups and individuals. Some cases repeated the predictable pattern of a large, powerful nation bullying a weaker one—the classical injustice that the age of colonial empires generated in abundance. The other pattern, however, was in a way more troubling, because it involved injustice committed by one small, vulnerable, nation with a long record of suffering and abuse, against another small nation, often with the same sorry record. It is a vicious circle, whereby one party's quest for justice gives rise to another party's misfortune. And so injustice is perpetuated, hatreds and vows of vengeance kept alive, future disasters almost assured.

In the fall of 1992, I traveled for the first time to Stepanakert, the capital of Nagorno-Karabakh. Much of the city lay in ruins, the fingerprints of Azeri artillery and short-range missiles. Not one window had glass in it, and that included the offices of the highest-ranking officials. Austerity and sacrifice were the order of the day.

One evening I was invited to dine at the home of a local police official, a young man whose father had been missing for months, in all probability dead at the hands of the Azeris. On the slim chance that the father might still be alive, my host had ventured into Azeri territory and captured a hostage—a custom as old as the peoples occupying this land. "Would you like to take a look at him?" my host inquired of me in the most casual tone. I was stunned and initially declined the offer, but the other guests urged me to go and see, and finally I relented.

His eyes spoke volumes, his terrified eyes that darted about incessantly, seeking desperately a way out but meeting only walls and locked gates. An Azeri hostage in an Armenian basement, Novruz Khudatov, Fall 1992

I was marched into a basement room, which was reasonably furnished and clean, where a twenty-seven-year-old Azeri man with a soft black beard rose to his feet in clear anxiety. We did not have a meaningful conversation—he had no idea who I was and exercised his instincts of self-preservation by volunteering as little information as he could. But words were not necessary. His eyes spoke volumes, his terrified eyes that darted about incessantly, seeking desperately a way out but meeting only walls and locked gates. He was to be released only on one condition: that his own family would conduct a search for the captor's missing father.

Otherwise? I asked.

"Otherwise he will die," my host responded calmly. "This is the law of the mountains."

I do not know what happened to the Azeri hostage. I know only he was the undeserving victim of a small nation seeking the justice it deserved and inflicting injustice at the same time. On my way back from Stepanakert to Yerevan, I asked the driver to stop in a strip of land called Lachin, which the Karabakh Armenians had captured a few months earlier. It had been populated by Muslim Kurds, a tiny minority in Azerbaijan whose misfortune placed them between Nagorno-Karabakh and Armenia proper. The Karabakh Armenians required territorial access to the Armenian republic, and they had turned Lachin into a "humanitarian corridor." So humanitarian was the corridor that the entire Kurdish population was sent fleeing across Azeri lines.

Though my stopover took place roughly six months after Lachin's occupation, the large town looked and felt as though it had been abandoned only a few hours earlier. Doors and windows were wide open, personal belongings were left behind in a hurry. On the roadside, a few steps away from our car, lay a naked doll, armless, half blind, but still a compelling testimony to a human community brutally dispersed. Two years later I stopped again in Lachin. It was now partly repopulated, the cheerful sound of children again filled the streets, and girls were again sporting their dolls—Armenian children, Armenian girls, Armenian dolls.

My journey in quest of memory ends where it began, in a little train station by the Black Sea, in the northwest corner of the Caucasus. For decades, Lazarevskoe had served sun-starved North Russian vacationers. As of late, the resort town had become a point of disembarkation for refugees of various Caucasian conflicts. The most conspicuous were the Georgians, or more precisely the Mingrelians (an ethnic group related to but not identical with the Georgians), who had been displaced by the war in Abkhazia, about a two-hour train ride to the south.

Drawn by the agreeable aroma of freshly baked bread, I soon found myself at a small kiosk on the station platform, craving a warm *khachapuri*, that rich Georgian cheese-based pastry, the omnipresent fast food of the Caucasus. The dim light in the kiosk interior revealed a white-haired woman, perhaps in her early fifties, kneading the dough, wiping her hands with a long apron. She smiled softly when I asked her whether she carried Ajarian *khachapuri*, distinguished from its Georgian counterpart by the egg yolk featured at its center.

I had had my *khachapuri* debut exactly two years earlier, in Batumi, the seaside capital of a tiny Georgian province named Ajaria. Ever since, the Ajarian variety has been associated in my mind with the calm beauty of the Black Sea just before the onset of the rainy season.

The woman shook her head. "No, I have no Ajarian ready, but I'll gladly bake one for you."

I took the liberty to engage her in a little conversation about geography and ethnicity. It turned out she was a Mingrelian from Sukhumi, Abkhazia's capital, and used to teach the Georgian language there to Armenian schoolchildren. Could there be a more delightful Caucasian blend? Could anything come closer to Pliny's observation, some two thousand years ago, about "a hundred languages spoken in a single port city" in the Caucasus?

As the delightful smell of the baking *khachapuri* wafted over to me, I relished the thought of past regional harmony, only to be jarred by the realization that this woman was far from home, probably not by her own choice. Harmony is no longer a Caucasian characteristic, and though multiethnic enclaves still exist, the descent toward monoethnic life has turned into an avalanche. There are few Armenians left in

Sukhumi, and no Georgians or Mingrelians at all. The Abkhazian uprising drove them all out. Some 250,000 refugees huddle in ill-maintained
hotels, while Sukhumi itself, a former gem of the Soviet Black Sea coast,
is run-down and crime-infested.

The *khachapuri* baker had had to leave behind everything she ever
owned. She briefly recalled an abandoned home, lost friends, and a
greatly missed landscape before returning her full attention to my order.
As she bent forward, her back turned to me, I noticed that her upper
body was shaking gently. The unmistakable sound of restrained adult
sobbing filled the narrow space of the kiosk.

"I'm so sorry," I said with a sense of shame. "I did not wish to open old
wounds."

"*Nichevo*," she responded in Russian, *for nothing*. "I should *thank* you for
giving me the chance to speak about these matters." She choked but
quickly recovered her composure. "Sometimes you have to touch your
own pain so as not to turn completely numb," she said as she wiped off
her tears. "Your Ajarian *khachapuri* is ready now."

Pain is taken for granted in this land, which stretches from the green-
sloped hills overlooking the Black Sea to the bare Daghestani shores of
the Caspian, four hundred miles to the east. One can count on almost
any chance meeting to generate a sad tale of betrayal and abandonment.
Almost any interlocutor here is a victim of history. This gentle woman,
who refused to charge me for her pastry, had been dispossessed in the
name of someone else's national liberation.

In 1996 an inconceivable event took place: Russia conceded defeat in a
war with a small North Caucasian nation. The improbable Chechen
victors had little idea what to make of their sudden freedom. Never
known for discipline and moderation, many of them interpreted the victory as a license for utter lawlessness. Hubris and blindness would soon
undo the astonishing 1996 victory. Idle military commanders, bored by
the tasks of day-to-day governing and incapable of adjusting to peaceful
times, fell under the sway of overseas Islamic militants, who urged them
to up the ante in their struggle with Russia.

When the Chechen warlords unleashed an attack against neighboring Daghestan, in the summer of 1999, with the stated aim of overthrowing Russia's yoke in the entire North Caucasus, the Russians had
had enough. Eager to avenge their humiliating defeat, Moscow's generals marched on Grozny. By the time they overran it, they had scored a
spectacular victory over its urban landscape by managing to relevel a
city already leveled once by their predecessors, five years earlier. In the

A common scene in Baku during the Karabakh war: another fallen Azeri laid to rest in the Cemetery of the Martyrs. So common did such funerals become, and so demoralizing was their effect, that the government barred nonresidents from the city's cemeteries.

process they rendered homeless virtually the entire Chechen population, save for some mountainous enclaves. Chechnya finally became the inhabitable land which General Yermolov threatened to make it in the early nineteenth century. Echoing Yermolov, the triumphant Russian leader, Vladimir Putin, hastened to promise the Chechen "terrorists" and "bandits" nothing but blood, sweat, and tears, in a war he is willing to conduct in perpetuity. Sadly, he can count on quite a few Chechens to pick up the gauntlet.

A result of this war is that the names "Chechens" and "Caucasus" need no longer be repeated a few times, and then slowly spelt out, whenever the author of a book wishes to bring the subject up in a social conversation. For the first time in their history, the Chechens enjoy the attention of world leaders and world bankers, all unsure what to do about a wrathful, vindictive Russia.

As for myself, having indulged for long in the relative obscurity of the Caucasus, I am not pleased at all that the specter of an ethnic and religious war is giving this book unexpected topicality—and I cannot help think of my Daghestani acquaintance, the painter Ibragim Supianov.

When Ibragim was a child, he nurtured the dream of finding a cure for cancer. One day he would fill a syringe with all the vitamins that exist, stick its needle into the cancerous tumor, and shoot. So powerful

Ibragim-Khalil Supianov, The Camouflaged Mountain, *1996*
(Reproduced with the painter's permission)

would be the burst of health and vitality that the cancer would simply be blown away.

When Ibragim grew up, he recognized that it was not for artists to cure physical ailments. Yet he did not give up the dream to apply radical treatment, if only metaphorical, to various disfigurements of the human landscape. When the war in Chechnya broke out in late 1994, he thought up the ultimate pacifying device: a huge magnet that would pull in every single piece of metal in Chechnya. Thus, in an instant, the warring armies would be left unarmed and harmless, without tanks or artillery or ammunition.

And then he came up with a more defensive idea: make the mountains disappear from sight. Not vanish into thin air, just become invisible to the holders of binoculars, to gunners struggling to establish mathematical precision before they pull the trigger, to pilots targeting villages and vehicles from a safe altitude.

And how would he pull off the trick? Simply by *painting* the mountains. He would move from one slope to the other, from one summit to the other—and dip them all in oily camouflage.

Inspired, he walked into his little studio, in a main street of Makhachkala, and drew *the camouflaged mountain* on a canvas.

I am still unaware of a better peace formula, and I dedicate my book to Ibragim-Khalil Supianov, the passionate Avar painter from Daghestan, and to his wife, Sheyit Hanum Alisheva, the Kumyk poetess. May the future of the Caucasus be theirs.

Washington, D.C., Summer 2000

BIBLIOGRAPHY AND ESSAY

The literature on the Caucasus in English is vast and of widely varying quality—and much of it is already out of date or irredeemably biased. Such is history in a region where personal and national memory are the coins of the realm. Here I present some of the most important sources and background material for my own work. Please note that the Internet addresses are valid as of late 1999.

GENERAL

As of this writing, the most recent population figures for the North Caucasian nations are from 1989. For a comprehensive analysis, see Paul B. Henze's article in *Central Asian Survey*, 1991 (vol. 10, no. 1–2, pp. 147–70), a scholarly journal published in London by Pergamon Press. Raw population figures can be found in *Report on the USSR* (published by Radio Liberty in Munich, January 1, 1990). Estimates of North Caucasian population during the nineteenth-century Caucasian War are available in Baron August von Haxthausen's *The Tribes of the Caucasus* (London: Chapman & Hall, 1855).

Essential background on the languages of the North Caucasus can be found at:
www.belti.msk.ru/peoples/eng kavkaz.html
Various Web links on the Caucasus are available at:
www.geocities.com/Pentagon/Bunker/4670/
An excellent book about the ethnic diversity of the Black Sea coast is *Black Sea* (New York: Hill & Wang, 1995) by the astute British journalist Neal Ascherson.

Published more than ninety years ago, J. F. Baddeley's *The Russian Conquest of the Caucasus* (1908) was the seminal work on the subject. Much more recent is Moshe Gammer's *Muslim Resistance to the Tsar* (London: Kass, 1995), arguably the most authoritative book on the Russian conquest of the Northeast

Caucasus, whole pages of which could fit easily into today's newspapers. Ever readable and delightful is Lesley Blanche's popularized account of the Caucasian War in *The Sabres of Paradise* (1960; republished in 1995 by Carroll & Graf, New York).

The short-lived Mountainous Republic, which briefly unified the small nations of the North Caucasus at the time of the Russian Civil War (1918–20), is described in two essays by leading figures of the republic, its foreign minister, Haidar Bammate, and its parliamentary speaker, Vassan-Giray Jabagi, reproduced in English in *Central Asian Survey*, 1991 (vol. 10, no. 1–2, pp. 119–32, and no. 4, pp. 1–29, respectively).

Robert Conquest has contributed extensively to Western knowledge of the 1943–44 holocaust of the North Caucasus—the mass deportation of four nations, which cost them at least one-third of their numbers. His books on the subject are *The Soviet Deportation of Nationalities* (New York: St. Martin's Press, 1960) and *The Nation Killers* (New York: Macmillan, 1970). Another informative work on the subject is Aleksandr M. Nekrich's *The Punished Peoples: The Deportation and Fate of Soviet Minorities at the End of the Second World War* (New York: W. W. Norton, c.1978).

Dmitrii Trunov's *A Trip to the North Caucasus* (Moscow: Progress, 1965) is a highly idealized version of *druzhba narodov*, the Soviet notion of boundless "friendship among the peoples." Trunov illustrates how the Soviet system rewrote Caucasian history in an attempt to show that the indigenous populations had sought Russia's benevolent domination for centuries.

An assortment of Caucasian myths and folk tales can be found in George Sava's *Valley of the Forgotten People* (London: Faber & Faber, 1941). It includes some wonderful anecdotes revealing the eclectic nature of religious practices in the Caucasus, such as the story of the pantheistic Khevsurs of the Northwest Caucasus, who have never met a god or goddess they did not like, let alone a religious holiday.

In 1813, as Russian colonization was gathering a pace, Frederika von Freygang wrote her impressions of the region in *Letters from the Caucasus and Georgia*, a charming collection of epistles (London: J. Murray, 1823). One letter, from the spa town of Kislovodsk, begins, "I have bathed—but how can I describe to you the sensation?"

The description of fourteenth-century Abkhazia, where "eternal darkness" prevailed, is reproduced from *The Travels of Sir John Mandeville*, translated by C.W.R.D. Moseley (Harmondsworth, Middlesex, England; New York: Penguin Books, 1983). The book is a magnificent collection of travel tales, plagiarized from various sources, and attributed to a single author who may have never existed. In short, this is what good medieval journalism was all about. Or perhaps not only medieval?

My favorite explorer of the Caucasus is the English alpinist Douglas Freshfield, whose magnificent two-volume *The Exploration of the Caucasus* was published (London and New York: E. Arnold, 1896) on high-quality paper, embellished by the most elaborate illustrations. It attests to tremendously good taste, a love of books, a generous spirit, and an inquisitive mind. An earlier compilation of Freshfield's experiences is *Travels in the Central Caucasus and Bashan* (London: Longmans Green, 1869).

PART I

Biographical background on Admiral Mikhail Lazarev, the conqueror of the Circassian coast, can be found in a Web site devoted to Russian naval history: www.stu.neva.ru

The Nart epic—the North Caucasian myth from which the tale of the last sword is taken—is described in *The Modern Encyclopedia of Russian and Soviet Literatures* (Academic International Press, 1979; vol. 3, pp. 225–34), in an article by John Colarusso, one of the foremost authorities on culture and language in the North Caucasus. Colarusso's article about Circassian languages, in the same encyclopedia, is also worth reading.

The calamitous exodus of the Circassians in 1864 is discussed in *Heroes and Emperors in Circassian History* by Shauket Mufti, a Middle East Circassian (Beirut: Librairie du Liban, 1972). Also important is "Circassian Resistance to Russia," by Paul Henze, one of few American scholars who has devoted considerable attention to the plight of the Circassians; the article appeared in *The North Caucasus Barrier* (New York: St. Martin's Press, 1992).

A wide-ranging essay on Circassian history, from antiquity to the 1930s, by a prominent Circassian émigré, Ramazan Traho, was published in *Central Asian Survey*, 1991 (vol. 10, no. 1–2, pp. 5–63).

Bagrat Shinkuba's *The Last of the Departed* is a literary treatment of the results of the Circassian exodus. Published in the Soviet Union in 1982, it has a flaw common to many contemporary works—its Soviet propagandistic veneer. But beneath the veneer lies a saga of great loss.

Facts about the present North Caucasian diaspora are to be found in a useful article by Egbert Wesselink, on the Web at: www.unhcr.ch/refworld/country/writenet/writur.htm

A highly informative Web site on Circassian life and history, created by a Circassian from Jordan, Amjad Jaimoukha, is: www.geocities.com/Eureka/Enterprises/2493/

An informative Circassian Web site, created by a young Israeli Circassian, is: www.yi.com/home/AbzakhEdris/index.htm

It offers links to related sites. Another site, with details about Khassa, the Circassian national movement, is: www.geocities.com/Heartland/Park/1170/ListE.htm

The following Web site was created by Hasan Jurt in Nalchik, the capital of Kabardino-Balkaria: www.chat.ru/~jurthasan/

A rich, well-designed Web site created by H. Cihat Coskun, a Turkish Circassian, is: members.xoom.com/abrec/

It includes a number of Circassian folk songs.

Circassian folk songs in MP3 format are available at: www.geocities.com/Pentagon/Bunker/4670/Tleprush.htm

Circassian songs are also available at: www.geocities.com/Athens/Oracle/8598/music.htm

An Israeli scholar, Chen Bram, delivered an important paper on the Circassian community in Israel, and its adoption of the "American Jewry" model in its relations with the Caucasian homeland, at the Hebrew University's Truman Institute in 1996.

In the late 1950s, an émigré journal out of Munich called the *Caucasus Review* published a series of informative essays in English on Circassian culture; they are well worth looking up.

Perhaps the earliest comprehensive report on the North Caucasus in English is Julius von Klaproth's *Travels in the Caucasus and Georgia*. A Prussian aristocrat and a member of the Russian Academy of Science in St. Petersburg, von Klaproth traveled to the Caucasus in 1805 and 1807, well before the onset of Russian colonization and a full generation before the beginning of the Caucasian War. His account, translated to English and published in London in 1814, is the source of many Circassian stereotypes that began to appear in Western writings about the Caucasus from then on, generally without attribution. Yet his book is fascinating exactly because of the sweeping nature of his observations, as well as the delightful mixing of hard facts, half-facts, and pure myths. He relates, for example, the tale of the Amazons, the ancient tribe of women warriors visited by the authors of the Greek mythology, and reputed to exist in the Caucasus (pp. 361–68).

In 1838 the British adventurer Edmund Spencer published in London a highly sympathetic report on the Circassians, one of the first ever in English, entitled *Travels in the Western Caucasus*. Two decades later came another sympathetic report, the German traveler Moritz Wagner's *Travels in Persia, Georgia and Koordistan; with sketches of the Cossacks and the Caucasus* (London: Hurst and Blackett, 1856). Considerably less sympathetic is the American George Leighton Ditson's *Circassia—or a Tour of the Caucasus* (New York: Stringer & Townsend, 1850).

A reader interested in European cultural and even aesthetic rationalizations for the extermination of indigenous nations should turn to Peter Gay's *The Bourgeois Experience: Victoria to Freud, Volume 3. The Cultivation of Hatred* (New York: Oxford University Press, 1993), pp. 68–95. It is otherwise a magnificent book from one of the most profound cultural observers of our time.

For a chronology of the Circassian renaissance in the North Caucasus in the 1990s, I relied extensively on the exceptionally useful Foreign Broadcast Information Service (FBIS) *Daily Report—Central Eurasia*, published by the United States government. Its editors and translators are the unsung heroes of the long struggle to make sense of countries whose own media leave much to be desired.

More on Ivan the Terrible's love for the Circassian princess Tamara can be found in Henri Troyat's *Ivan the Terrible* (Dorset Press, 1984).

The notion of Kabarda's "voluntary union" with Russia was rebutted at length by Aytek Namitok in the *Caucasian Review* in 1955 (no. 2, pp. 17–33).

Paul Avrich's *Russian Rebels 1600–1800* (New York and London: W.W. Norton, 1976) gives a good summary of Cossack rebellions against the czarist regime in the seventeenth and eighteenth centuries.

The history of Cossack colonization and militarization of the Caucasus is illuminated in Thomas M. Barrett's *Lines of Uncertainty: The Frontiers of the North Caucasus*, in *The Slavic Review*, 578–601. 54. 1995.

Details of Cossack involvement in massacres of Jews during the Russian Civil War can be found in Richard Pipes's *The Russian Revolution* (New York: Vintage Books, 1991) and Orlando Figes's *A People's Tragedy: A History of the Russian Revolution* (New York: Viking, 1996).

Robert Conquest discusses Cossack persecutions at the hand of Stalin in *The Harvest of Sorrow* (New York: Oxford University Press, 1986).

The *National Geographic* published a good article by Mike Edwards about the revival of Cossack traditions in Russia (November 1998), accompanied by vivid color photographs.

PART II

An excellent article by Karl Horst Schmidt on the languages of Daghestan and the Northeast Caucasus can be found in *The Modern Encyclopedia of Russian and Soviet Literatures* (Academic International Press, 1979; vol. 3, pp. 220–25).

A most inspired book about Daghestan is Robert Chenciner's *Daghestan: Tradition and Survival* (New York: St. Martin's Press, 1997). Chenciner is a British mechanical scientist who fell for the land.

Daghestani Web sites are:
www.caspian.net/daghestan.html
www.geocities.com/CollegePark/Union/6282/index.htm
Both are rich in outside hyperlinks.

An interesting article on the nature of ethnic peace in Daghestan appears in *Center-Periphery Conflict in Post-Soviet Russia*, edited by Mikhail A. Alexseev (New York: St. Martin's Press, 1999).

For a narrative history of the Daghestani nationalities (as well as others), see Mastyugina and Perepelkin's *An Ethnic History of Russia: Pre-Revolutionary Times to the Present*, (Westport, Conn.: Greenwood Press, 1996).

Moshe Gammer's *Muslim Resistance to the Tsar* (London: Kass, 1996) gives a good historical perspective on Islam in Daghestan. Shaykh Muhammad Hisham Kabbani's *The Naqshbandi Sufi Way: History and Guidebook of the Saints of the Golden Chain* (Chicago: Kazi Publications, 1995) gives a Sufi perspective on North Caucasian mysticism. Excerpts are available on the Web at:
http://naqshbandi.net/haqqani/Islam/Shariah/muamalaat/jihad/daghestan.html

On the attempt to establish an independent Daghestan during the Russian Civil War, see W.E.D. Allen and P. Moratov, *Caucasian Battlefields* (Cambridge: Cambridge University Press, 1953), pp. 501 onward.

A helpful guide on the perplexities of languages and ethnicities in the North Caucasus is Ronald Wixman's *Language Aspects of Ethnic Patterns and Processes in the*

North Caucasus (University of Chicago, Department of Geography, 1980). Wixman also published a long article on the subject in *Nationalities Papers*, 1982 (vol. 10, no. 2, pp. 137–56).

For a brief discussion of Lezgin history and the status of the Lezgin language in Daghestan, see Martin Haspelmath, *A Grammar of Lezgian* (Berlin: Mouton de Gruyter, 1993).

The most recent compendium of Khazar theories and myths is Kevin Alan Brook, *The Jews of Khazaria* (Northvale, N.J.: Jason Aronson, 1999). An intriguing Web site devoted to the Jewish-Khazar theory, run by Mr. Brook, is: www.khazaria.com

Arthur Koestler's controversial book *The Thirteenth Tribe* (New York: Random House, 1976) should be read with a sack of salt. My preferred literary choice on the Khazars is the one freed completely from the realm of facts: Milorad Pavić's *Dictionary of the Khazars* (New York: Knopf, 1989). Should a critical reader scold me for sending him to a work of fiction, I might answer, "Precisely!"

Background about the two languages of the Daghestani family (Kryz and Khynalug) can be found in the *Red Book of the Peoples of the Russian Empire* Web site: www.eki.ee/books/redbook/

More about the campaign waged by the Persian monarch, Nadir Shah, to occupy Daghestan in the mid-eighteenth century—a formative experience that later lent credence to the notion of Daghestani unity—can be found in L. Lockhart, *Nadir Shah* (London: Luzac, 1938).

For background on Abkhazia and the Georgian-Abkhaz war, see *The Abkhazians: A Handbook*, edited by George Hewitt (New York: St. Martin's Press, 1998).

For an interesting survey of Imam Shamil's fluctuating standing in Soviet historiography—his ascent to virtual sainthood, his disgrace, and his subsequent rehabilitation—see Paul B. Henze's article in *Caucasian Review*, 1958 (no. 6, pp. 7–29).

The Soviet policy on nationalities (including its manifestations in Daghestan) is discussed in Hélène Carrère d'Encausse, *The Great Challenge: Nationalities and the Bolshevik State 1917–1930*, published in France in 1987 (New York: Holmes & Meier, 1992).

Peter the Great's brief presence in Daghestan, in the early eighteenth century, is described by Robert K. Massie in *Peter the Great* (New York: Wings Books, 1992).

PART III

For the history, meaning, and practices of Sufism, I often consulted *The Oxford Encyclopedia of the Modern Islamic World*, especially the entries for "Sufism," "Sufism and Politics," and "Qadiriya." An extensive bibliography is available at the end of each entry.

Anna Zelkina's exceptionally helpful treatise on Islam in Chechnya was published in *Central Asian Survey* in July 1996 (pp. 240–64). It may be the most detailed treatment in English.

One book I found highly incisive is Alexandre Bennigsen and S. Enders Wimbush, *Mystics and Commissars: Sufism in the Soviet Union* (Berkeley and Los Angeles: University of California Press, 1985). The book has been roundly criticized by scholars, but I think its greater accomplishment is to describe the continuing importance of Islam in the Caucasus and the unique role played by Sufi practices even at the heyday of Soviet rule, which few scholars understand as well as Bennigsen and Wimbush do. Bennigsen's daughter, Marie Bennigsen Broxup, has inherited her father's mantle and written extensively about the Chechens. Three of her essays are included in the anthology *North Caucasus Barrier* (New York: St. Martin's Press, 1992), a book I have found indispensable for recent Caucasian politics and history.

The Boston publisher Brill recently published *Islamic Mysticism: A Short History*, a book on Sufism by the distinguished scholar Alexander Knysh, who has studied Sufism in general but also its manifestations in the Caucasus.

A Sufi guide to *zikr*—and a defense against fundamentalist critics of Sufism—can be found at:
sunnah.org/ibadaat/dhikrtable.htm

A more impartial guide to the intricacies of Sufism, in a wide-ranging presentation by Alan Godlas, is available at the University of Georgia Web site:
www.arches.uga.edu/~godlas/Sufism.html

Web sites devoted to the great Sufi sage Sheikh Abdul Qadir al-Geylani (the name is sometimes transliterated differently) are:
www.al-baz.com/islam/abdalqadirjilani/index.html
www.qadiri-rifai.org/
The latter offers the authentic sounds of a *Qadiri zikr*.

Sufi Web links are available at:
www.unibio.com/spirit/sufiworld.html
www.sufiorder.org/sufilink.html

The *Qadiriya* is employed all the way from the Caucasus to equatorial Africa, as demonstrated on the Web at:
www.rootsworld.com/rw/villagepulse/tabala.html
This site describes the synthesis of Qadiri ritual and Senegalese *tabala wolof*, including audio samples.

The remarkable sounds of *zikr*, performed by adherents of the *Naqshbandi* path, are available on the Web at:
www.naqshbandi.org/dhikr/audio/

Immensely useful in tracing the enmity between Islamic puritans (or "fundamentalists") and Sufis is Frederick de Jong and Brend Radtke's (editors) *Islamic Mysticism Contested: Thirteen Centuries of Controversies* (Leiden, The Netherlands: Brill, 1999). Though the collection does not deal with the Caucasus as such, it helps place Caucasian religious schisms in a broad context. The interested reader may want to take a look at the essays on the Wahhabis, the campaign against Sufism in Egypt (where Sufi survival owes much to modern nationalists, viewing it as a counterweight to reforming puritans), and the struggle pitting Arab and indigenous Islams in Indonesia, the world's largest Muslim country.

Richard Burton's initiation to Sufism is described in Edward Rice, *Captain Sir Richard Francis Burton* (New York: Scribner, 1990), p. 155–61.

Native American dancing in despair is described at great length in James Mooney, *The Ghost Dance* (1896; reproduced by North Dighton, Mass.: J.G. Press, 1996).

The Hasidic tale about the shepherd's whistle on the night of Yom Kippur is one of many collected by the great Yiddish author Y. L. Peretz. It was related about the great Rebbe of Nemirov, in Ukraine, the subject of many a myth.

Citations from Russian authors are reproduced from English translations by Louise and Aylmer Maude, *Great Short Works of Leo Tolstoy* (New York: Perennial Library, 1967); C. E. L'Ami and Alexander Welikotny, *Michael Lermontov: Biography and Translation* (Winnipeg: University of Manitoba Press, 1967); Anatoly Liberman, *Major Poetical Works/Mikhail Lermontov* (Minneapolis: University of Minnesota Press, c. 1983).

An article on the life of Sheikh Mansur, the Chechen leader of the first organized resistance to Russian rule in the North Caucasus, was published in *Central Asian Survey*, 1991 (vol. 10, no. 1–2, pp. 81–92).

For background on the Chechen war, a history of the Russian-Chechen conflict, and a broader analysis of the Russian political context, I recommend two superb books: *Chechnya: Tombstone of Russian Power* by journalist Anatol Lieven (New Haven: Yale University Press, 1998), notable for its analysis and historical insights; and *Chechnya: Calamity in the Caucasus* by a pair of dedicated and courageous journalists, Carlotta Gall and Thomas de Waal (New York: New York University Press, 1998), notable for its excellent reporting. Also commendable is John B. Dunlop, *Russia Confronts Chechnya* (Cambridge and New York: Cambridge University Press, 1998).

The circumstances of the Chechen migration to Turkey, Syria, and Jordan are discussed in an article published in *Central Asian Survey*, 1991 (vol. 10, no. 1–2, pp. 181–87).

The history of Russia's relations with its Caucasian dependencies is discussed at some length in Walter Kolarz, *Russia and Her Colonies* (Hamden, Conn.: Archon Books, 1967).

Russian perceptions of the Caucasus were largely shaped by prose and poetry, which gives a sense of timeliness to Susan Layton's *Russian Literature and Empire: Conquest of the Caucasus from Pushkin to Tolstoy* (New York: Cambridge University Press, 1994). Inspired by Edward Sa'id's famous critique of Orientalism, Ms. Layton does not spare Russia's "reigning mythology about the Caucasian conquest as a civilizing mission." To her, nineteenth-century Russians were "plundering beneficiaries of the empire," apt words which could equally apply nowadays.

For an appreciation of the extraordinary role played by literature in the evolution of Russian attitudes toward the Caucasus, I have also consulted Katya Hokanson's interesting article, "Literary Imperialism, *Narodnost'* and Pushkin's Invention of the Caucasus," in *The Russian Review*, January 1994 (vol. 53, no. 1,

p. 336). "The Caucasus, as Russians know it," Ms. Hokanson writes, "did not really exist until Pushkin created it."

An extraordinary *j'accuse* from Russia's voice of conscience, the human rights activist and former member of parliament Sergei Kovalyov, was printed in English translation in *The New York Review of Books* (February 29, 1996).

Photos and geographic background of Lake Sevan in Armenia, where the Subbotniks settled in the early nineteenth century, can be found at: http://www.cilicia.com/armo5d.html

On the religious circumstances of the rise of the Subbotniks, see Serge Bolshakoff's *Russian Nonconformity* (Philadelphia: Westminster Press, 1950) and Robert O. Crummey, *The Old Believers and the World of Antichrist* (Madison: University of Wisconsin Press, 1970). Crummey's article, "Old Belief as Popular Religion—New Approaches," *Slavic Review*, 1993 (vol. 52, no. 4, pp. 701–12), is helpful as well. James H. Billington's *The Icon and the Axe* (New York: Knopf, 1966) is particularly enlightening; Billington's uniquely incisive interpretations of Russian cultural history never cease to amaze me.

For a view of the Subbotniks by Soviet historiography, see A. I. Klibanov, *History of Religious Sectarianism in Russia, 1860s–1917* (Oxford [Oxfordshire]; New York: Pergamon Press, 1982, pp. 45–46). Klibanov, who headed a study group at the Soviet Academy of Science, and met Subbotniks in Central Russian villages, treated their movement (as might have been expected of an ideologically correct Marxist-Leninist) as a form of social protest aimed at "Orthodox Church feudalism." He viewed their peculiar religious practices as indicating their degeneration into an isolationist "Talmudic" cult. Whereas displeasure with Orthodoxy's monopoly over rural life certainly played a major role in the rise of the Subbotniks, the author's disdain toward and dismissal of spirituality is self-debilitating.

For the long and difficult history of conversions and attempted conversions to Judaism, I suggest Bernard Bamberger's *Proselytism in the Talmudic Period* (New York: Ktav, 1939, 1968) as well as Joseph R. Rosenbloom, *Conversion to Judaism: From the Biblical Period to the Present* (Cincinnati: Hebrew Union College Press, 1978). A fascinating book about "Judaization" in Europe at the time of the Reformation and Counter-Reformation is Daniel Liechty's *Sabbatarianism in the Sixteenth Century* (Berrien Springs, Mich.: Andrews University Press, 1993). Striking are the similarities between the Subbotniks and the European sectaries, which seems to confirm the spontaneity of the shift toward Judaism as well as its Protestant context. Also interesting is David S. Katz's book, *Sabbath and Sectarianism in Seventeenth Century England* (Leiden, N.Y.: E. J. Brill, 1988). I have found particularly helpful Jacob S. Raisin's *Gentile Reactions to Jewish Ideals* (New York: Philosophical Library, 1953), which gives a detailed narrative history of the Subbotniks. The dean of all Jewish historians, Simon Dubnow, discusses the circumstances of the inception of the Subbotnik phenomenon in his *History of the Jews in Russia and Poland* (Philadelphia: Jewish Publications Society of America, 1916), vol. 1, pp. 391–413. Neither work is authoritative; indeed, to the best of my knowledge, no authoritative work on the Subbotniks has ever been written.

PART IV

The extent of collaboration with the Nazis by the Balkars and other North Caucasian nationalities is discussed, probably most authoritatively, in Gerald Reitlinger's *The House Built on Sand: The Conflicts of German Policy in Russia, 1939–1945* (1960; Westport, Conn.: Greenwood Press, 1975). Another helpful work is Jürgen Thorwald, *The Illusion: Soviet Soldiers in Hitler's Armies* (New York: Harcourt Brace Jovanovich, 1975).

The ancient Caucasian Albanians attracted the attention of the first-century Greek geographer Strabo in his monumental *Geography;* see volume 5 (pp. 217–31) of Horace Leonard Jones's English translation (London: William Heinemann, 1917–33). A brief critical discussion of this work is to be found in Ronald Syme, *Anatolica: Studies in Strabo* (Oxford: Clarendon Press, 1995), pp. 67–83.

I have also consulted the entry on "Albania (Caucasian)" in the multivolume *Dictionary of the Middle Ages* (New York: Scribner, 1982–89).

For a good narative history of Azerbaijan, see Audrey L. Altstadt, *The Azerbaijani Turks: Power and Identity under Russian Rule* (Palo Alto, Calif.: Hoover Institution Press, 1992), part of its extremely valuable series on nationalities.

A fascinating treatise on the quest for an imagined past among Turkic nationalities is Victor A. Shnirelman's *Who Gets the Past?: Competition for Ancestors Among Non-Russian Intellectuals in Russia* (Washington, D.C.: Woodrow Wilson Center Press; Baltimore: Johns Hopkins University Press, c. 1996).

If it were not for Mr. Shnirelman's methodical footnoting one might be excused for confusing his narrative for a work of surreal fiction. Some of the characters seem to be so eager to prove uncontested antiquity that they would stop at nothing to preempt any challenge. For example, they claim direct roots to the 330th century B.C. (no typo, three hundred and thirtieth century indeed). Their presumed ethnic ancestors established the first state in the world in the 130th century B.C. The founding great-grandfathers not only infused their modern descendants with extremely healthy genes, but seem to have disseminated their DNA and superior culture all over Central and Eastern Europe, Northern China, and even the Americas, a few thousand years before one Columbus rudely interfered.

Tadeusz Swietochowski and Brian C. Collins compiled the *Historical Dictionary of Azerbaijan* (Lanham, Md.: Scarecrow Press, 1999). Another recent work is Charles van der Leeuw, *Azerbaijan: A Quest for Identity* (New York: St. Martin's Press, 1998). Thomas Goltz, a rogue reporter, is the author of *Azerbaijan Diary: A Rogue Reporter's Adventures in an Oil-Rich, War-Torn, Post-Soviet Republic* (Armonk, N.Y.: M. E. Sharpe, 1998). A lot of fun.

On the roots of the Armenians' alliance with czarist Russia, see Muriel Atkin, *Russia and Iran, 1780–1828* (Minneapolis: University of Minnesota Press, 1980).

The late emergence of an Armenian majority in modern Armenia is discussed in George A. Bournoutian's *The Khanate of Erevan Under Qajar Rule, 1795–1828* (Costa Mesa, Calif.: Mazda Publishers, in association with Bibliotheca Persica, 1992), pp. 58–64.

The reluctance of Armenian nationalists to move from cosmopolitan Tbilisi to tiny and remote Yerevan after Russia's collapse in 1917 is related in Richard G. Hovannisian's *The Republic of Armenia* [in four volumes, covering the period 1918–1921] (Berkeley, University of California Press, 1971–1996). Professor Hovannisian is not only the greatest authority on modern Armenian nationalism but also a brilliant commentator on what one might call "the Armenian condition," both at home and in the diaspora. His son, the California-born-and-bred Rafi Hovannisian, was independent Armenia's first foreign minister (1991–1992).

To the reader who thinks I am too indignant at and exasperated by Armenian-Azeri enmities, I recommend Luigi Villari, *Fire and Sword in the Caucasus* (London: T. F. Unwin, 1906), pp. 144ff. Firuz Kazemzadeh, *The Struggle for Transcaucasia, 1917–1921* (1951; reprinted Westport, Conn.: Hyperion Press, 1981), is a remarkable account of nationalism gone berserk.

EPILOGUE

A catalogue of Ibragim-Khalil Supyanov, the Daghestani artist who would camouflage the mountains, is available in English from the Daghestan Art Fund, 214 Columbia Heights, Brooklyn, NY 11201. I wish to commend the fund's founders, Brian Murray and Andrea Ziegelman, who have been inspired to reach out from their hectic business life in New York City and touch the hearts and minds of Daghestani artists. They can be contacted by e-mail as well, at <Brian.Murray@AIG.com>

As for myself, I can be reached at <ykarny@usa.net>

ACKNOWLEDGMENTS

This book took about eight years to conceive, research, and write, and there are more people who deserve my gratitude than I am able to name here.

I owe an enormous debt of gratitude to my friend Michael Haney, a constant source of inspiration, whose wise comments and striking insights helped this book stay on course and retain its focus;

Special thanks to Dan Gordon, a keen student of history and human behavior, whose advice was always forthcoming and always indispensable;

Heartfelt appreciation to my agent, Deborah Harris, who at times had more faith in this project than I did;

Profound thanks to Jonathan Galassi, editor-in-chief at Farrar, Straus & Giroux, whose patience and generosity of spirit I was most fortunate to have; and Paul Elie, my immediate editor, for his keen observations; as well as Brian Blanchfield of the editorial staff, whose ingenuity has won my admiration.

I am indebted to the elders and members of the Chechen community in Jordan, for so kindly educating me in the spirit of their people.

There are dozens of generous men and women in the Caucasus whose help I am grateful for. I will name but a few:

Ali Kazikhanov, publisher of *Severny Kavkaz*, who showed me unrivaled hospitality, as well as his staff members, Tatyana Gantimurova and Valery Urusmambyekov; the good men and women of the Armenian Assembly, both in Yerevan and in Washington, D.C.; Professor Liliana Edillian of Yerevan State University; Armand Hakopian of the Armenian Foreign Ministry; the ever-loyal and resourceful Igor Ulianovsky and his wife, Maggie, in Yetevan; the staff of the European Union food aid program in Baku, Azerbaijan, particularly Dominique Feldheim, then manager, and Alia Abassova; Daniel Kunin, the (then) able representative of the National Democratic Institute in Tbilisi, Georgia; and Oliver Reisner of Göttingen University, then in Tbilisi. Their generous hospitality and extensive knowledge of Georgia have served me (and many others) well.

There are many in Moscow whom I should thank, among them Konstantin Eggert, once the diplomatic editor of *Izvestia*, whose friendship was indispensable in arranging much of my traveling, and journalist Aleksandr Mnatsakanyan, a faithful and resourceful companion in some of my trips to the Caucasus. And there is another Mnatsakanyan I wish to acknowledge with thanks and admiration: Aleksandr's father, Gari, of Tbilisi, Georgia, a remarkable scientist and humanist.

I offer profuse thanks to the publishers and editors of *Globes*, the Israeli newspaper I call home, who tolerated my never-ending journey to the Caucasus, especially the late publisher Hayyim Bar-On, his successor Ammi Even, editor-in-chief Haggay Golan, and his predecessor Adam Barukh, as well as my immediate editor, Zvika Tsoref.

I also thank my good friend Steve Brodner of New York, the brilliant illustrator, whose advice, artistic and otherwise, I cherished.

End of journey.

INDEX

Ghazi — Ghumuz, p.144
(Kumukh)
146-